URBAN AND REGIONAL PLANNING IN CANADA

URBAN AND REGIONAL PLANNING IN CANADA

J. Barry Cullingworth

Transaction Books
New Brunswick (U.S.A.) and Oxford (U.K.)

Library of Congress Catalog Number: 86-25076
ISBN: 0-88738-135-9
Printed in the United States of America

Library of Congress Cataloging in Publication Data

Cullingworth, J. B.
  Urban and regional planning in Canada.

  Bibliography: p.
  Includes index.
  1. Regional planning—Canada. 2. City planning—
Canada. 3. Canada—Economic policy. I. Title.
HT395.C3C85   1987   307.1′2′0971   86-25076
ISBN 0-88738-135-9

Contents

v

List of Tables

List of Maps

List of Acronyms

ALR	Agricultural Land Reserve (British Columbia)
AMO	Association of Municipalities of Ontario
ARDA	Agricultural Rehabilitation and Development Act (Federal)
BMR	Bureau of Municipal Research (Toronto)
BNA Act	British North America Act 1867 (in 1982 officially renamed the Constitution Act 1867)
CCREM	Canadian Council of Resource and Environment Ministers
CEAC	Canadian Environmental Advisory Council (Federal)
CFMM	Canadian Federation of Mayors and Municipalities
CHBA	Canadian Home Builders Association (formerly HUDAC)
CIP	Canadian Institute of Planners
CLI	Canada Land Inventory
CMHC	Canada (formerly Central) Mortgage and Housing Corporation (Federal)
COLUC	Central Ontario Lakeshore Urban Complex Task Force
COPE	Committee for Original Peoples Entitlement
DIAND	Department of Indian and Northern Development (Federal)
DOE	Department of the Environment (Federal); typically expressed as Environment Canada
DPW	Department of Public Works (Federal)
DREE	Department of Regional Economic Expansion (Federal)

DRIE   Department of Regional Industrial Expansion (Federal)
EARP   Environmental Assessment Review Process (Federal)
ECA   Environment Council of Alberta
EIA   Environmental Impact Assessment
ELUCS   Environment and Land Use Secretariat (British Columbia)
FCM   Federation of Canadian Municipalities
FEARO   Federal Environment Assessment Review Office
FIRA   Foreign Investment Review Act
GDA   General Development Agreement (between the Federal and a Provincial Government)
GRCA   Grand River Conservation Authority (Ontario)
GVRD   Greater Vancouver Regional District
HMSO   Her Majesty's Stationery Office (U.K.)
HUDAC   Housing and Urban Development Association of Canada (now CHBA)
MNR   Ministry of Natural Resources (Ontario)
MSUA   Ministry of State for Urban Affairs (Federal)
MTARTS   Metropolitan Toronto and Region Transportation Study
NCC   National Capital Commission
NRC   Nuclear Regulatory Commission (U.S.A.)
OAPADS   Oshawa Area Planning and Development Study
OECD   Organization for Economic Cooperation and Development (Paris)
OMB   Ontario Municipal Board
OPDQ   Office de planification et de développement du Québec
OWMC   Ontario Waste Management Corporation
PANE   People Against Nuclear Energy (U.S.A.)
PIBC   Planning Institute of British Columbia
PUD   Planned Unit Development
SATRA   Service d'aménagement du territoire de la région aéroportuaire (Quebec)
TCR   Toronto-Centred Region

TDR	Transfer of Development Rights
UDI	Urban Development Institute
UDIRA	Urban Development in Rural Areas (Ontario)

Acknowledgements

Several sections of this book have been previously published. The author makes acknowledgement to the following publishers and publications.

Butterworth and Co (Publishers) Ltd, *Land Use Policy*, "Land Policy Issues in Canada," Vol. 1, No. 4, October 1984.

Butterworth and Co (Publishers) Ltd, *Cities*, "Provincial and Municipal Roles in Canadian Planning," Vol. 2, No. 3, August 1985.

Canadian Institute of Planners, *Plan Canada*, "The Provincial Role in Planning and Development," Vol. 24, No. 2-3, December 1984.

Elsevier Science Publishers B. V. (North Holland), *Urban Law and Policy*, "Expropriation, Eminent Domain and Compulsory Acquisition of Land: A Note on Canadian Complacence," Vol. 7, No. 4-5, December 1985.

Harwood Academic Publishers, *International Property Investment Journal*, "Non-Resident Land Ownership in Canada," Vol. 3, No. 1, 1986.

E. & F. N. Spon Ltd, *Planning Perspectives*, "Groping for a National Urban Policy: the Case of Canada," Vol. 1, No. 2, May 1986.

University of Toronto, Centre for Urban and Community Studies, Land Policy Paper Series, particularly No. 3, S. E. Corke, *Land Use Controls in British Columbia: A Contribution to a Comparative Study of Canadian Planning Systems*, 1983; No. 4, the author's *Canadian Planning and Public*

Participation, 1984; and No. 6, J. M. Wolfe, *Planning in Que-bec,* 1985.

University of Toronto, Department of Urban and Regional Planning, Papers on Planning and Design No.19, *Ontario Planning: Notes on the Comay Report on the Ontario Planning Act,* 1976.

Preface

Canada is a creation of planning

Hans Blumenfeld 1979

This volume is a modest contribution to an immodest ambition: to document and analyze the character of urban and regional planning throughout the constituencies of Canada. It is hoped in a later volume to compare the essentials of this with two more populous countries, Britain and the United States, which exerted considerable influence on the development of Canadian policies and institutions. The area is a fascinating one which neither starts nor stops with that indeterminate field to which the label "urban and regional planning" is applied: indeed, the more keenly one probes, the deeper one becomes immersed in matters of politics, law, economics, social organization and, indeed, the whole gamut of historical and contemporary issues.

The starting point for this study was a personal fascination with the intricate and subtle differences between the formal and the informal planning systems of Ontario (Cullingworth 1978). So much seemed so different from what it was supposed to be; and, though constant reference was made to British and American "influences", it seemed clear (to a recent immigrant) that the planning activities on which these influences were supposedly operating possessed a character of their own, neither British nor American: but distinctive.

But were they distinctively Canadian or, more narrowly, distinctively Ontarian? The question remains open. Though this study presents relevant evidence, it is incomplete and inadequately articulated. This will occasion no surprise to those whose familiarity with the Canadian planning scene is longer and deeper than that of the author. Indeed, as the study progressed, the words of a skeptical (yet friendly) critic began to resound: "a high degree of ignorance is needed before one would attempt a task as complex as this." The critic was correct, though it is hoped that the result will be of value in relation to more modest aims than those originally envisaged by the author.

It is important that the reasons for the gap between initial ambition and final result be set out; not to excuse, but to explain. To attempt to write about *Canadian* urban and regional planning is not dissimilar from an attempt to write about *European* urban and regional planning. The analogy is striking despite the obvious historical, political and other differences. On the one hand, it is apparent (to this writer at least) that there is sufficient similarity between the different countries of Europe to make it credible to talk of European planning. On the other hand, the differences (for example between France and the Netherlands) are of such a degree as to make it arguable whether both could be discussed within the same framework.

There is no need to labor the point: its strengths and weaknesses are sufficiently apparent though certainly not exhausted, or even listed, here.

Another, even more elusive feature presents itself to the traveller in the North American continent. Though there can be no doubt (with a few exceptions such as Quebec) as to which continent our mythical traveller is on, he would undoubtedly be perplexed by the striking differences between Canadian and U.S. cities. Toronto is as different from New York as Ottawa is from Washington; but more striking is the forceful impact of the journey from Detroit to Windsor. This volume hopefully will provide a basis for later discussion of the nature of these differences and the influences which have affected them.

There are many ways in which the subject matter of this book could be structured. An easy way would be to divide the material geographically, producing a chapter for each of the ten provinces, for the federal government and for the territories. This was largely rejected as being inadequate as a framework for a comparative study. It proved difficult to reject it completely, however, since some of the differences between provinces are so large that they require lengthy individual discussion. This is particularly so with Ontario which arguably has the most sophisticated planning system. It certainly has the largest number of planning publications on which one can draw.

The last point is more than a quip. Availability of information on Canadian planning varies between the provinces even more widely than their policies. Though the study involved a considerable amount of travelling, time did not permit this to be as extensive as I would have liked. The uneven coverage is thus largely due to the availability of documentation. Some of the difficulties have been overcome by the commissioning of particular provincial studies. The three which were undertaken by Sue Corke on British Columbia (1983), David Hulchanski on Alberta (1981; 1985) and Jeanne Wolfe on Quebec (1985) show how valuable a more ambitious series of studies in all the provinces would have been. Extensive use has been made of these papers in the writing of this book. Substantial extracts from the Corke and Wolfe studies are incorporated in chapter 9.

A word of explanation is appropriate here of the approach taken by the author to the subject matter of this book. It must be admitted that the volume has no binding thematic thread or even a consistent conceptual framework. This is not accidental, nor is it perverse. It stems from the approach adopted. Essentially this is that the nature of "planning" is an expression of a country's political culture. An adequate understanding of the Canadian planning scene "requires an appreciation of both the shared and different values held in different regions, and of the forces working at each level." These are the words of a reviewer of an earlier draft, who saw my enterprise more clearly than I could. He continued that my approach involved an acceptance of the idea that "a sound observer of the Canadian planning scene does not limit his vision by preconceived notions, but lets the evidence lead him wherever it may. The approach is pragmatic, eclectic, interpretive, and occasionally critical."

The book results from a program of research funded by the Canada Mortgage and Housing Corporation, the Social Science and Humanities Research Council of Canada, the University of Toronto, and the Canadian Embassy in Washington. I am grateful for this financial support and equally to the many colleagues who have contributed directly or indirectly to the program.

Of particular significance have been the contributions of Larry Bourne, Sue Corke, Terry Fenge, David Hulchanski, Judy Kjellberg, Lucia Lo, Stan Makuch, Nigel Richardson, Jim Simmons, Peter Smith, Brahm Wiesman, Jeanne Wolfe and Jim Wilson. I also owe a large debt of gratitude to numerous officials in government agencies throughout Canada who I interviewed between 1981 and 1983. They have provided me with a wealth of material and a depth of insight. I am grateful to Geoff Matthews for the drawing and preparation of the maps, to John Byrne, Ed Ratledge, Pat Grimes and my wife for all their hard work in preparing the text, and to Scott Bramson for guiding it through the Press. Finally, I wish to express my thanks to the anonymous reviewers who made extremely constructive criticisms of earlier drafts. I wish I could feel more confident that the end result fully reflected their wise insights. However, a book which so foolheartedly embraces such a huge and amorphous area cannot hope to satisfy either its readers or its author. I conclude with the formal statement that, of course, errors and omissions are solely my responsibility. The text relates in the main to 1984, but some later references have been added to the bibliography.

J. Barry Cullingworth
Center for Energy and Urban Policy Research
College of Urban Affairs and Public Policy
University of Delaware

Chapter 1
Introduction

Geography holds centerstage in the drama of Canadian politics

Wheball 1983

Despite the validity of the quotation, the focus of this book is not on geography but on government and politics. It attempts to document the responses of the multiplicity of governmental agencies to the problems of population growth, urban development, exploitation of natural resources, regional disparities, and a host of other issues which fall within the scope of "urban and regional planning." Of course, the term has no precise meaning, and its boundaries are unclear. On one interpretation, it encompasses national economic policies (Lithwick 1970), while on another it is basically an extension of municipal law (Makuch 1983). Either approach is legitimate. In the present volume, a generous conception of planning is employed, and an attempt has been made to provide a reasonably comprehensive coverage. However, no claim to completeness is suggested.

The starting point, as befits a book on Canada, is the three levels of government: federal, provincial and municipal. Chapter 2 attempts to summarize the role played by each, but the reader should be warned that the situation is one of constant flux. For anyone wishing to keep up with this shifting scene, there is an endless stream of commentaries.

The federal role is an intriguing one which vacillates between centralization and devolution (Romanow, Ryan and Stanfield 1984), but there are some important land planning

1

functions which it shares with the provinces, and it has a particularly important role in the Yukon and the Northwest Territories. Although "the north" has only 0.3 percent of the Canadian population, it covers almost two-fifths of the land area. Virtually all this land is in federal ownership and is managed by the federal government.

Provincial land ownership varies from 95 percent in Newfoundland to 12 percent in Prince Edward Island (Table 1.1). Much of the provincially owned land is wildland, though rapid and fundamental change is being brought about in many areas by resource development. Environmental issues have become of increasing concern to governments, as have the rights and welfare of native peoples. All provinces have a department responsible for the environment and for resource development (though terminology varies somewhat).

Environmental problems are not, of course, restricted to remote or largely uninhabited areas. Indeed, political and popular interest in "the north" is limited: most Canadians are unconcerned, and there are few votes involved. The center of activity lies in the southernmost parts of the country. Some three-quarters of the twenty-five million inhabitants of Canada live within 500 kilometers of the American border. Three-quarters of the population live in urban areas, and over a half live in the twenty-four census metropolitan areas (CMAs). The latter make up only half of one percent of the land. Indeed, a mere one percent of Canadian land use is urban. Thus there is the paradox that it is only a fraction of the land of Canada which is the concern of urban planning. But this relatively minute area presents major problems, and these have increased with the accelerated urban growth which has taken place since the end of the second world war. In 1941, the proportion of the population classified as urban was 54 percent. (The census definition of urban is an area having a population concentration of 1,000 or more, and a population density of at least 400 per square kilometer.) By 1971 this had increased to 76 percent. Even more striking was the absolute increase: from 6.2 million in 1941 to 16.4 million in 1971. In the following decade, the proportion remained roughly the same, but the number rose to

18.4 million. Much of this growth was natural increase, but a significant amount was the result of large scale immigration (which interacted with economic growth to stimulate further immigration and urban growth).

For Canada as a whole, natural increase between 1941 and 1971 totalled 7.7 million, while net immigration was nearly two million (gross immigration was 3.5 million). The fastest period of growth (in absolute terms) was the 1951-61 decade when natural increase of 3.1 million and net immigration of 1.1 million gave a total population increase of 4.2 million.

The growth of the urban population is now proceeding at a rate very close to that for total population growth (5.8 and 5.9 respectively during 1976-81). There are, however, enormous differences among the twenty-four census metropolitan areas. Over this quinquennium, Calgary grew by a remarkable 25.2 percent while, at the other extreme, Sudbury declined by 4.5 percent (Hooper, Simmons and Bourne 1983). Similar differentials to those between the CMAs are to be seen at the provincial level (Table 1.2). Between 1976 and 1981, net inter-provincial migration from Quebec was 133,375, and from Ontario 74,643. The overall direction of the migratory move was clearly westward, with gains of 98,144 in British Columbia and 152,251 in Alberta. Total population increase varied, in percentage terms, from 0.5 in Manitoba to 21.8 in Alberta. It follows that the pressures being experienced by regional and urban planning authorities vary widely.

At a finer level of analysis, there are indications that urban growth in the traditional sense of the outward spread of cities may be giving way to an emerging new pattern of dispersed living and employment locations. This has been documented in the U.S. where, by the early 1970s, migration to metropolitan areas had been reversed. Between 1970 and 1978 the U.S. metropolitan areas had a net loss of 2.7 million. One-sixth of all metropolitan areas lost population. By contrast, three-quarters of all nonmetropolitan counties gained population (Kasarda 1980: 380). This "nonmetropolitan revival" can be seen as a continuation of the processes of dispersal which have operated since the end of the first world war, though some have argued that it represents "a clean break" with the past (Vining and Strauss 1977). The arguments have been reviewed interestingly (though not exhaustively) by Blumenfeld (1982a: 15) who suggests that much "is really a quarrel about semantics."

Similar forces appear to be operating in Canada, though data limitations have so far precluded the type of locational analysis (of both jobs and homes) that is possible for the U.S. There is, however, an underlying problem of defining the metropolitan orbit. Indeed, it may be questioned whether such a concept is still always relevant. As Blumenfeld has suggested, ultimately the division of settlements into urban and rural is being replaced by an urban-rural continuum, with consequent implications for policy and planning (Blumenfeld 1982b: ii).

Planning for population increase has been a major (but not the only) concern of planning authorities. Chapter 3 deals with the nature of urban plans, while chapter 4 discusses the implementation of plans. In both chapters the objective is to illustrate the great variety of approaches to planning across Canada.

Urban growth in the sixties and seventies gave rise to some acute land problems. The discussion of these is divided between two chapters. Chapter 5 discusses a range of matters such as the escalation of land prices, land speculation and similar problems (together with broader issues including expropriation and nonresident ownership of land). This chapter is thus focused on a range of particular problems. Chapter 6, by contrast, deals with a number of important land uses, such as agriculture, aggregates and forestry.

Of these, agriculture has been perhaps the most pervasive and difficult problem, particularly since many of the urban areas are located near (and in) rich agricultural land. This is a consequence of Canada's settlement history:

> Initially, settlement was oriented towards areas of fertile soils which could supply agricultural products. The success of initial settlement often related to the area's agricultural productivity, which then formed a solid basis for subsequent growth. The result has been a conflict between urban areas and agricultural

resource lands; both urban and agricultural uses are competing
for the same land resource (Neimanis 1979: 3).

Agriculture has been (and remains) important not only in
urban planning but also in regional planning. As is shown in
chapter 7, the need for agricultural rehabilitation and development
provided the starting point for regional planning at the
federal level.

Chapter 8 is devoted entirely to one province: Ontario. It
is, in fact, a detailed case study. This is justified by the fact
that Ontario has attempted more in the field of regional planning
policy than any other province. It has also had at least its
fair share of failures. A fuller account of regional planning in
Ontario is given in a special issue of *Plan Canada* (1984).

That regional planning differs significantly between the
provinces is abundantly clear from chapter 9 where the discussion
relates to the new regional planning system in Alberta,
Quebec's long struggle to introduce regional planning, and British
Columbia's attempts to coordinate regional resource
management with planning.

It would have been interesting to compare metropolitan
planning in these four provinces, taking for example Toronto,
Vancouver, Calgary and Edmonton, Montreal and Quebec.
This, however, clearly warrants a book on its own, and the only
metropolitan area discussed is Toronto.

Currently we are witnessing an unprecedented *Stress on
Land* (Simpson-Lewis et al 1983). Urban growth, pollution,
waste disposal, mining, soil degradation, airport facilities, the
disturbance of forest ecosystems ...; a full list would be surprisingly
lengthy. As governments have become aware of these
environmental problems, and as they have become increasingly
politicized, the realm of environmental protection has expanded.
This is the subject of chapter 10, in which several are selected
for discussion. Initially, the emphasis is on the respective roles
of the federal and provincial governments. This is appropriate
since the major problems in environmental protection are political
and administrative (as well as scientific).

As in other matters, there are marked differences in approach and effectiveness between the provinces, but the main focus is on the federal government and Ontario (partly because of their relative wealth of publications). The importance of the governmental apparatus, however, should not be overemphasized. As is noted in chapter 2, it is not always easy to draw a line between scientific and political judgments. Environmental impact assessments constitute an attempt to do precisely this: to objectively appraise the impacts which a proposed development might have on the environment (now extended to encompass social and cultural as well as physical dimensions). At the same time, however, they increasingly attempt to obtain the maximum amount of public input. How far the public's attitude towards a development can be weighed against "scientific facts" is an open question, and one which experience is showing to be difficult to resolve. The matter is made more complex because typically there is more than one "public": or to use political terminology there are often several constituencies. Resolution of planning problems cannot be "scientific": attempts may be (and are) made to make the process as complete and fair as possible, but inevitably the outcome is based upon a mixture of scientific, social, economic and political issues as perceived by the multiplicity of organizations and individuals involved in the planning process.

This leads us into the subject matter of the last main chapter, which is titled simply "Planning and People." Emphasis here is laid on the essentially political nature of the planning process. A major argument put forward in this chapter is that of a natural bureaucratic response to regard objectors to planning proposals as "people in the way." The phrase is the title of an extraordinary study by J.W. Wilson of the Columbia River Project (Wilson 1973). The extraordinary feature is that Wilson was a turncoat: from being an operational planner he became an independent researcher of operational planners.

In fact, values and subjective judgments are endemic in planning debates. Moreover, to make the issue even more difficult, not only do "the communicating parties use different vocabularies or languages to talk about the same thing, but rather in fact they use differing structures of reasoning. If, as is common, the parties remain unaware that they are using different structures of reasoning, but are aware only of their difficulties, each party tends to perceive the communication difficulties as resulting from the other parties' illogicality, lack of intelligence, or even deceptiveness and insincerity" (Maruyama 1974: 81).

Finally, there is a short epilogue which attempts some reflections on the nature of Canadian planning. In writing this it became very clear that the issues raised would repay much fuller study on the lines indicated at the beginning of the Preface. Preliminary work on this is in progress.

Table 1.1 — Provincial Land Areas by Tenure 1978

	Federal Land %	Provincial Land %	Private Land %	Total km²	Percentage of Total Area
British Columbia	1	93	6	949,000	9.5
Alberta	10	63	28	661,000	6.6
Saskatchewan	2	60	38	652,000	6.5
Manitoba	1	78	21	650,000	6.5
Ontario	1	88	11	1,069,000	10.7
Quebec	*	92	8	1,541,000	15.5
New Brunswick	3	43	54	73,000	0.7
Nova Scotia	3	30	67	56,000	0.6
Prince Edward Island	1	12	87	6,000	0.1
Newfoundland	1	95	4	405,000	4.1
Northwest Territories	100	*	*	3,380,000	34.4
Yukon Territory	100	*	*	536,000	4.8
Canada	40	50	10	9,976,000	100.0

* Less than 0.5 percent

Source: Based on *Canada Year Book 1980-81*, Table 1.8, p. 27

Table 1.2 — Canada and Provinces: Population 1951-81

	1951 (000)	1976 (000)	1981 (000)	Percentage of Total 1981	% Change 1976-81	Net Inter-provincial Migration 1976-81 (#)
British Columbia	1,165	2,467	2,744	11.3	11.3	98,144
Alberta	940	1,838	2,238	9.2	21.8	152,251
Saskatchewan	832	921	968	4.0	5.1	12,718
Manitoba	777	1,022	1,026	4.2	0.5	-45,385
Ontario	4,598	8,264	8,625	35.4	4.4	-74,643
Quebec	4,056	6,234	6,438	26.4	3.3	-133,375
New Brunswick	516	677	696	2.9	2.8	3,752
Nova Scotia	643	829	847	3.5	2.3	-357
Prince Edward Island	98	118	123	0.5	3.6	1,671
Newfoundland	361	558	568	2.3	1.8	-7,990
Northwest Territories	16	43	46	0.2	4.9 ⎞	
Yukon Territory	9	22	23	0.1	4.1 ⎠	-6,786
Canada	14,009	22,993	24,343	100.0	5.9	

Source: Census of Canada, 1981

Table 1.3 — Canada's Urban and Rural Population 1911-81

	Urban		Rural		Total
	'000	%	'000	%	'000
1911	3,273	46	3,934	54	7,207
1941	6,252	54	5,254	46	11,506
1961	12,700	70	5,538	30	18,238
1971	16,411	76	5,158	24	21,569
1976	17,367	75	5,626	25	22,993
1981	18,436	76	5,907	24	24,343

Source: Census of Canada, 1981

Chapter 2
The Agencies of Planning

The Federal Role

Canada is the only country in the world where you can buy a
book on federal-provincial relations at an airport

Anon

Planning, in the narrowest sense of the term, is clearly a
local matter, and thus it is the responsibility of local and provincial governments. In the broadest sense, however, it
embraces a wide range of matters which are far from local in
import. Such matters include environmental controls in relation
to clean air and the sea coast, transcontinental transportation,
regional economic development, and airports. This, however, is
not the limit of federal responsibility: the federal government is
directly responsible for forty percent of the land area of
Canada, including most of the Yukon and the Northwest Territories, and it manages the largest system of national parks in
the world. Additionally, many policies have significant interaction with planning, such as the extensive housing functions of
the Canada Mortgage and Housing Corporation. Then there is
the large number of federal functions which require decisions on
land use, from penitentiaries to post offices. Many of these
functions have important implications which, in turn, are a
major ingredient of urban and regional planning.

Furthermore, there are the federal-provincial financial
arrangements, federally subsidized programs, and more general
tax (and tax relief) provisions; employment policy; energy and

natural   resource policies;   and, of major importance, the income security programs.   These can be more significant for urban and regional planning than any of the more obvious instruments.

But having set the scene in this extremely broad way, there is clearly a difficulty in coping with all the issues which are, or might be, relevant.   For the purposes of this book an arbitrary selection had to be made.   No great loss is thereby incurred: the reader can simply make good any deficiency by referring to other books.   Not so for governments!   Herein lies one of their most intractable problems: that of coordinating a multiplicity of different policies, administered with different objectives, and by different departments.   As Lithwick's *Urban Canada* report (1970) argued, if the disparate policies (which have both intended and unintended impacts on the urban system) could be explicitly administered to achieve common urban objectives, much could be achieved; or, at the least, undesirable side-effects could be avoided or mitigated.   The difficulties with which this seemingly sensible proposal bristles are discussed shortly.

Many of the powers of the federal government are operated in cooperation, or in conjunction, with the provinces.   This may be for political and administrative reasons, or it may be because of shared, or unclear, constitutional responsibility.   Housing is an example of the former;   environmental management of the latter.   On environmental management, Franson and Lucas (1978: 251) comment:

> When the basic division of powers was accomplished in 1867 no one foresaw that environmental management would become a concern. Consequently, the categories of powers that are assigned to the two levels of government bear no relationship to the actual needs of environmental managers. It is usually not possible, therefore, to say that major environmental management tasks fall either to the Dominion or the provinces. The powers that may be used to combat environmental degradation are liberally sprinkled through the heads of power given to each level of government.

Water Resource Management

Much of the water is in the wrong place or is available at inappropriate times

Foster and Sewell 1981

Jurisdiction over water resources is a case where the constitutional position is unclear. The provisions of the BNA Act are capable of variable interpretation and, in any event, there are the residual powers which give the federal government responsibility for any functions which have not been specifically delegated to the provinces. This, of course, is the reverse of the position under the U.S. constitution where residual powers are vested in the States. The precise wording is:

It shall be lawful for the Queen, by and with the Advice and Consent of the Senate and the House of Commons, to make Laws for the Peace, Order and good Government of Canada, in relation to all Matters not coming within the Classes of Subjects by this Act assigned exclusively to the Legislatures of the Provinces ...

It was under this provision that the Canada Water Act of 1970 was passed. The time was one of increasing concern about water resources in general and water pollution in particular (Morley 1972 and 1973). The act provides a framework for federal-provincial study and action by way of joint water quality management agencies. Franson and Lucas note that the act was a milestone in several respects. For example, "it recognized the concept of water management, and reflected the idea that management is a process rather than merely a capacity to react to crises through the imposition of penalties or the mounting of clean-up operations."

This is now conventional wisdom but, in 1970, it represented a major advance in legislative provision. Unfortunately, progress on implementation has been slow, partly because it rests on federal-provincial agreements. This was another of the Franson and Lucas "milestones" though it may appear   more like a rock!: "the act recognized the need for cooperative federal-provincial study and consultation in solving regional water quality management problems."

A 1981 review by Foster and Sewell applauds the attempts at comprehensive cooperative schemes such as the Okanagan, Saskatchewan-Nelson, and St John River studies, but concludes that despite this progress, "water management in Canada still exhibits a fairly limited perspective. Single-purpose schemes predominate. Typically, traditional strategies are emphasized, almost to the exclusion of new ones. This is true not only in the field of flood loss management but also in connection with water quality" (Foster and Sewell 1981: 78).

A major reason for this disappointing progress lies in the fragmentation of authority: "not only is there a division of jurisdiction between the federal and provincial levels of administration, but there are divisions within each level as well ... Inevitably there is a duplication of functions. In many cases too, there is uncertainty as to who is responsible or who should take the lead in initiating action. The slow rate at which action has been taken to deal with such matters as floods, droughts, water quality management, weather modification and acid rain is rooted in large part in this uncertainty" (Ibid). There is further discussion of some of these issues in chapter 6.

The International Joint Commission

The purpose of the Parties is to restore and maintain the chemical, physical and biological integrity of the waters of the Great Lakes Basin Ecosystem

International Joint Commission 1978

The sad story is not restricted to this particular area of federal activity but, in this case, it is complicated further by the fact that a substantial part of Canada's water resource is shared with the U.S., and the organization which has been established to deal with the shared problems has been largely used as an advisory and fact finding body: the International Joint Commission. There was a hopeful time in 1978 when the Great

Lakes Water Quality Agreement was signed: "... the Parties agree to make a maximum effort to develop programs, practices and technology necessary for a better understanding of the Great Lakes Basin Ecosystem and to eliminate or reduce to the maximum extent practicable the discharge of pollutants into the Great Lakes System."

The reports issued under the agreement however show, in appropriately diplomatic language, just how big and difficult the problems are. More discouraging is the failure of the 1980 *Memorandum of Intent* between Canada and the U.S. concerning transboundary air pollution. The problems involved here are not merely political or even administrative (though they are both): they are also scientific. The inadequacy of knowledge is underlined by the disagreement on acid rain. Two years work by U.S. and Canadian scientists produced valuable information and a wide area of agreement; but the U.S. scientists could not accept the Canadian interpretation of the evidence concerning the *generality* of the problem of acid rain fallout. In the Canadian minister's words: "the U.S. scientists have not accepted that the acid rain impacts clearly evident in the hundreds of lakes and rivers studied from Algoma through New England to Nova Scotia apply generally to the thousands of aquatic ecosystems now identified as sensitive to acid rain" (Environment Canada 1983a). In the less tendentious words of the scientific report:

> The U.S. members conclude that reductions in pH, loss of alkalinity, and associated biological changes have occurred in areas receiving acidic deposition, but cause and effects relationships have often not been clearly established. The relative contributions of acidic inputs from the atmosphere, land use changes, and natural terrestrial processes are not known. The key terrestrial processes which provide acidity to the aquatic systems and/or ameliorate atmospheric acidic inputs are neither known nor quantified. The key chemical and biological processes which interact in aquatic ecosystems to determine the chemical environment are not known or quantified. Based on this status of scientific knowledge, the U.S. Work Group concludes that it is not now possible to derive quantitative loading/effects relationships (International Joint Commission 1983).

There is no chance of this winning a Nobel prize for literature, but the thrust of the argument is clear. Unfortunately,
the layman has difficulty in separating scientific facts from political views. He may even suspect that his difficulties are not
unfamiliar to the scientists; or that the scientists are influenced
by the national framework within which they work.

The National Parks System

> ... the parks shall be maintained and made use of so as to leave
> them unimpaired for the enjoyment of future generations ...
>
> Parks Canada 1982

The federal position in relation to national parks is a hap-
pier and less convoluted one, though certainly not trouble free.
The system includes not only national parks but also historic
parks, national historic sites, heritage canals and, more recently,
Canadian landmarks, Canadian heritage rivers and heritage
buildings. The system is essentially a *national* one operating
under federal legislation, mainly the National Parks Act. Provincial agreement is required for the establishment of national
parks or for a change in their boundaries, but once agreement is
reached, policy and control rests with the federal government.
However, an agreement commits the two levels of government
to a common objective: "to protect the park area and to
encourage public understanding and enjoyment of the area at
the time the park is established and in the future."

The parks are intended to protect representative examples
of geographical, geological, biological or historic areas for the
benefit, education and enjoyment of the people of Canada. As
an extension of this, Canada is one of the thirty-eight nations
which have ratified the UNESCO World Heritage Convention to
identify and protect cultural and national properties throughout
the world which are considered to be of outstanding universal
value. In September 1978, Nahanni National Park in the
Northwest Territories and L'Ause aux Meadows in Newfoundland were the first Canadian sites to be named.

The first national park was established in the Rocky Mountains (Banff) in 1885. By the end of the thirties there were sixteen parks, ranging in size from 44,807 square kilometers (Wood Buffalo, established to protect the last remaining herd of wood bison) to four square kilometers (St Lawrence Islands). Of the total twenty-nine national parks, ten were established between 1968 and 1972. This was a response to the major increases in park use and in recreational demand which accompanied the growth in the size and affluence of the population.

Land management within national parks is directed towards maintaining the physical environment in as natural a state as possible. Virtually all the land is publicly owned, though it can be leased to residents and a limited number of businesses. Generally, the overriding objective of protection precludes all forms of extractive resource use. However, in some new national parks certain traditional local resource users are allowed to continue. Unfortunately, as Nelson (1977) has pointed out, there is a dearth of studies on the national parks: their history, the institutional arrangements, the balance between protection and development. Curiously, an unusually wide ranging study is to be found in the *Report of the Special Inquiry on Kouchibouguac National Park* (Parks Canada 1981). This inquiry was ordered by the Minister of the Environment for Canada and the Premier of New Brunswick following the eviction of former residents and a lengthy series of protests and violent outbursts that had marred the operation of the park since expropriation of the lands for the park began in 1969.

It is not feasible for Parks Canada to protect all the areas which would qualify as national parks. Hence emphasis is laid on cooperation, persuasion and publicity with the provinces, territories and other public and voluntary agencies. The same is the case with national historic parks, where the objective is to "protect, for all time, historic resources at places associated with persons, places and events of national historic significance in a system of national historic parks, and to encourage public understanding, appreciation and enjoyment of this historical heritage so as to leave it unimpaired for future generations"

(Parks Canada 1982: 28). Here there is a Historic Sites and Monuments Board of Canada which advises on the establishment of national historic parks.

Examples of national historic parks are Fort Anne (the first, established in 1917), Lower Fort Garry, the Fortress of Louisbourg, Dawson City and the Halifax Citadel. There are also eight heritage canals: Rideau, Trent-Severn, Murray, Carillon, Ste Anne, Chambly, St Ours and St Peters.

National historic sites, of which there are over 600, are places which are commemorated by the erection of a plaque or monument. Financial and technical assistance is given to provincial and municipal governments and also to voluntary organizations to acquire and restore structures of national historic significance which deserve more than a commemorative plaque, but which do not warrant acquisition by Parks Canada as a national historic park.

More broadly, there are provisions for *Agreements for Recreation and Conservation*. These apply to Cooperative Heritage Areas where joint federal-provincial action seems appropriate. The first such agreement, signed in 1975, was the Canada-Ontario Rideau-Trent-Severn (CORTS) agreement. This commits the federal and provincial governments to joint planning in the corridor surrounding the Rideau and Trent-Severn canals.

The Range of Federal Responsibilities

We have now reached a stage where the necessity of intergovernmental coordination and collaboration is not matched with an equivalent capacity for its attainment. We are approaching a condition of federal-provincial paralysis if existing trends continue

Cairns 1979

Water and national parks are merely two illustrations of the federal role in planning. They do demonstrate, however, the positive role which the federal government can play and also the constraints which confederation imposes upon it. In later chapters of this book other fields will be discussed such as regional economic planning, forestry, agriculture, and so forth. However, as already indicated, there are other dimensions of federal involvement in urban and regional planning. These range from the most direct, as with land use planning around airports, to the most indirect, as with taxation policies.

Selection is difficult, but there seems to be sufficient intrinsic interest to include in the present account a short discussion of land use controls around airports (a specific tangible area of federal action), the special case of the National Capital Commission, federal involvement in urban affairs, and the rise and fall of an attempt to devise a national urban policy. First, however, it is necessary to make some reference to the Canadian north.

There is a confusing abundance of legislation for the Yukon (Redpath 1979) and the Northwest Territories (Fenge et al 1979), but there is no gainsaying the primacy of the federal role. The discussion is explicitly of a summary character: though the subject is too important to be omitted, it is far too large to be documented in detail. In any case, there is a wealth of available relevant publications.

The Canadian North

Having no provincial governments and few members of Parliament, the one-third of this country that lies north of the 60th parallel has always struggled to command and sustain the attention of the federal government

Canadian Arctic Resources Committee 1984

Though the Yukon and the Northwest Territories both have elected councils and cabinet style executive councils, formal executive power rests with a federally appointed commissioner in each territory. The commissioners are responsible to the federal Department of Indian and Northern Development (DIAND) but act in consultation with the territorial councils. Moreover, in recent years there has been increased (but still limited) delegation and, in practice, the territories, particularly the Yukon, have moved quite far towards responsible government in their areas of jurisdiction. The Yukon Commissioner was directed by the Clark government to act only on the advice of the Executive Council, so he is now effectively the equivalent of a Lieutenant Governor. The Northwest Territories are moving in the same direction.

One of the most striking marks of the territories' inferior constitutional status is their lack of power to exercise control over "lands, mines, minerals and royalties." While the BNA Act gives the provinces responsibility over these, the Yukon Act and the Northwest Territories Act exclude them. Proprietary and legislative rights rest with the federal government (Beauchamp 1976: 4).

Against this background and, of course, the long and bitter history of native land claims (Canadian Arctic Resources Committee 1978) a continuous battle between exploitation and conservation rages. The COPE claim has been settled (Committee for Original Peoples Entitlement) and the Western Arctic Agreement is in force (DIAND 1984c and 1984d). There has thus been some progress, and more is promised by the active Minister of DIAND, David Crombie. However, the crucial arguments remain both complex and passionate, with a large array of environmental issues, strong pressures for oil and gas development, and a continuing prospect of a huge income for the federal government. Pitted against these are the continuing issues raised by the native land claims, an environmental lobby which seeks to protect long term environmental quality from the impacts of short term exploitation; and, of course, there are the people of the North. Berger's report on the *Mackenzie Valley Pipeline Inquiry* (1977: vii) opens with these words:

> We are now at our last frontier. It is a frontier that all of us have read about, but few of us have seen. Profound issues, touching our deepest concerns as a nation, await us here.

> The north is a frontier, but it is a homeland too, the homeland of the Dene, Inuit and Métis, as it is also the home of the white people who live there. And it is a heritage, a unique

environment that we are called upon to preserve for all Canadians.

The decisions we have to make are not, therefore, simply about northern pipelines. They are decisions about the protection of the northern environment and the future of northern peoples.

The problems of planning in the north are thus highly political. But they are also complicated, in terms of scientific knowledge, political responsibility, administrative coordination, as well as in terms of moral uncertainties.

One example is the fact of Canadian sovereignty over the Arctic Archipelago; but "Canada has given assurances that passage would not be denied to foreign vessels adhering to Canadian safety and pollution control regulations" (DIAND 1982c: 7). Yet the Canadian Arctic Resources Committee (1984a: 7) paints a different picture: one in which "there is uncertainty about almost every aspect of national jurisdiction in the Arctic Ocean. Continuing uncertainty can lead only to serious conflict between coastal neighbors and among the polar nations."

A further complication, not so far mentioned, is that of national defence (Canada Department of Military Plans and Operations 1983); and there are many others...

The federal government's official policy is to secure a balance between the conflicting considerations. The Lancaster Sound green paper (DIAND 1982c) refers to policies which seek "to balance the needs and aspirations of northerners, the maintenance of environmental quality and the development of renewable and non-renewable resources, in a manner that is essentially sound and compatible with both northern and national interests."

These are fine words, but the concept of balanced development has been around for a long time, and it made little progress in the seventies (DIAND 1982). DIAND is subject to conflicting advice. As DIAND's former Director General for the Northern Environment (Yvon Dubé) has written, "many have pointed out that the realities of multiple jurisdictions, land claim negotiations, constitutional development, economic and energy strategies, and so on preclude the realization of any 'grand vision' for conservation in the North. Many say 'think small'. Others say 'don't dream'" (Dubé 1983a: 2).

The latest official position (prior to the change in government in 1984) was set out in *Land Use Planning in Northern Canada* (DIAND 1982a). Issued in draft form but, as we shall see, never revised, this discussed the conflicting pressures in the north, the inadequacy of existing land use planning machinery, and the need for "a more considered and integrated approach ...; an organized process for determining the uses of land and relating resources based on cooperative decision-making by governments, groups and individuals, according to their various needs and desires and to the limitations imposed by the environment."

This reassuring motherhood statement, however, was immediately followed by a series of statements which suggested a pro-industry bias (Rees 1983: 7). Northern land use plans would "provide for orderly development to ensure fulfillment of northern socio-economic goals and national strategies" (assumed to be compatible, or at least reconcilable). Existing policies were apparently to continue unchanged since land use planning was to proceed alongside existing mechanisms with "no freeze ... on resource development." Ongoing projects were to be "integrated smoothly with the land use planning process as they proceed." Though it was to be "an objective of land use planning that all projects in the north be adapted to the land use planning process in an efficient manner," nevertheless "every attempt" was to be made "to ensure that existing schedules are met."

The administrative proposals were in part vague and in part cumbersome. Following the approval of a northern land use plan by the Minister for Indian and Northern Affairs, "all parties will be expected to support the plan and its implementation." Such naivety mirrors that of the Lithwick report on national urban policy over a decade earlier (discussed in a subsequent section of this chapter). It totally ignores the differing perspectives, constituencies and mandates of different agencies and the impossibility of "integrating" conflicts.

The proposed geography of land use planning was not only cumbersome but was so physically based as to result in a separation of land use planning from socio-economic issues. Rees comments that conceivably DIAND was merely naive; but "a more popular assessment is that such biases exist to ensure the continued dominance of *southern* socio-economic interests" (Rees 1983: 9).

Not surprisingly, there was strong objection to the draft paper, and it was quietly buried. A new approach was made in 1983, with negotiated agreements on land use planning between DIAND and the two territories: the Yukon Territorial Government and the Council for Yukon Indians; and the Government of the Northwest Territories and the Native Organizations: the Tungavik Foundation of Nanavut, the Dene Nation, the Métis Association, and the Committee for Original People's Entitlement. The agreements are reproduced, with periodically updated other relevant material, in DIAND's *Northern Land Use Planning Update*.

As with DIAND's *Land Use Planning in Northern Canada,* the agreements are vague on implementation. They are replete with general provisions calling for land use planning to be "related to," or "integrated with other planning processes." As Richardson (1984) notes, they are political documents concerned essentially with the demarcation of political interests and authority. Compromises and the glossing over of problematic issues are only to be expected. For instance, the Yukon agreement provides that "land use planning goals and objectives will be determined by the Government of Canada and the Government of the Yukon, with the involvement of the Council for Yukon Indians." The NWT agreement has a clause which has an essentially similar meaning.

As Richardson comments, "specifically the responsibility is conferred on the Minister for Indian Affairs and Northern Development and the Minister of Renewable Resources on behalf of the respective governments, and the provisions of both agreements   make it clear that, subject to Cabinet/Executive Committee endorsement, ultimate responsibility rests with the two ministers ... In the final reckoning, government policy will prevail. This may be inevitable in practice, and even right in principle. But it compels one to wonder how much substance the land use planning process will have in certain areas" such as mineral exploitation.

Richardson concludes that "the crucial point in evaluating the two land use planning agreements is to recognize what they are, and what they are not. They are political agreements regarding the sharing of authority over land use planning, not detailed blueprints of the system ..." They reflect "an encouraging new recognition by all parties that successful land use planning in the north will demand cooperation, and a willingness at least to give it a try."

There are also grounds for optimism in official reports such as *Environment Canada and the North* (1983) and *Report of the Task Force on Northern Conservation* (DIAND 1984b). Less optimistic analyses have been presented by Hamelin (1984) and Moore and Vanderhaden (1984), while Fenge in his detailed account of the musical chairs of northern policy concludes that "the northern land use planning policy is like a shiny new automobile pointed to the highway with no gas in the tank" (Fenge 1984, 33).

Airports

If an airport is located in a rural municipality please contact the Department of Municipal Affairs for assistance

Nova Scotia 1980b

Airports are unfriendly neighbors, and their siting and operation gives rise to perpetual trouble (Feldman and Milch 1980 and 1983; Radford and Giesen 1984). At one time the Canadian government was held in high esteem by the environmentally concerned of many countries because of its decision to site Montreal's new international airport at Mirabel, over 45 kilometers north of the city. Not only was this location well beyond the outer limits of the built up area; at the same time 88,000 acres of land around the airport were expropriated.

Of this huge area, 71,000 acres were intended to be a buffer zone. (Different sources give different figures; see Canada Lands Company (Mirabel) Ltd (1982) *The Future of Mirabel Peripheral Lands.)* Surrounding this are 340,000 acres of forest and farmlands on which the Quebec government has placed a freeze. Unfortunately, though all this moved noise to an acceptable distance, it also moved the airport to an unacceptable distance. The world's best located airport became a white elephant: indeed with an unusual touch of humor the white elephant was, for a time, officially adopted as the emblem of the airport. The joke turned sour; or at least, it failed to turn the tide, and Dorval airport, which Mirabel was supposed to replace, continues to prosper.

Mirabel is one of 160 airports owned by the federal government. Civil aviation is unequivocally a federal matter. The relevant legislation is the Aeronautics Act and the National Transportation Act. Noise control is dealt with by rules for landing and takeoff angles, night flights, and so on, which are made separately for each airport "seemingly in response to overwhelming complaints from residents" (Estrin and Swaigen 1978: 120).

It is, however, the zoning powers which are of special interest. The Aeronautics Act provides for the making of regulations with respect to "the height, use and location of buildings, structures and objects, including objects of natural growth, situated on lands adjacent to or in the vicinity of airports, for purposes relating to navigation of aircraft and use and operation of airports ..." Zoning around airports is subject to both federal and provincial controls. Federal controls operate on federally owned land and on land subject to a federal airport zoning bylaw. If there is a conflict between federal and provincial land use regulations, the federal regulations prevail, under the constitutional law doctrine of paramountcy (Ince 1977: 117).

Additionally, Transport Canada has established noise contour zones together with recommended land uses suitable to each zone. On the basis of these, CMHC has prepared noise exposure forecast contour maps and a noise exposure land use compatibility table to be used in connection with development in which it participates. Ontario has adopted the same techniques (Ontario Ministry of Housing 1978b).

It is not easy to establish how successful such devices have been. One view is that "all jurisdictions have carried out their responsibilities badly, with the result that much of the housing around Toronto International Airport, and around Regina, Thunder Bay, Windsor and other airports is badly affected by noise" (Estrin and Swaigen 1978: 121). The basic problem, of course, is that an airport is both a major attraction for urban and industrial development and a severe constraint upon surrounding land uses because of noise and aviation safety requirements. It was this conflict which Mirabel airport was hoped to resolve (Quebec Department of Municipal Affairs 1973).

To conclude this short account, mention should be made of one interesting feature of zoning under the Aeronautics Act. This is the specific provision for compensation for injurious affection. Such compensation, payable by the federal government, is given for the amount by which a property is decreased in value by the zoning regulation *minus* "an amount equal to any increase in the value of the property that occurred after the claimant became the owner thereof and is attributable to the airport."

This poses a nice problem of valuation. It also suggests that, though airports may have deleterious effects on nearby neighborhoods, they may also actually increase property values. This has certainly been the case around London's Heathrow airport. Moreover, the evidence is that, despite any growth in air traffic, the problem of airport noise is likely to be reduced by 1990 mainly as a consequence of quieter aircraft coming into service (U.K. 1979: 24).

The National Capital Commission

Until the Queen otherwise directs, the Seat of Government shall
be Ottawa

BNA Act 1867

Canada has had more than its fair share of capital cities. Following the formation in 1841 of the United Province, the capital shifted between Kingston, Toronto, Montreal and Quebec, with continued dispute over the choice of a permanent site. Queen Victoria settled the matter in 1857 by choosing Ottawa.

The reasons given at the time were: the great natural beauty of the site; military security (it was situated 200 kilometers north of the U.S. boundary); the location of the city on the border of the two provinces, and its position midway between Quebec City and Toronto; a population representative of the two linguistic and cultural groups; and, finally, the availability of public property on which government buildings could be erected (vast areas of land had been publicly acquired as early as the 1820s: NCC 1984: 10).

The choice of a backwoods lumber town as the capital was the object of much derision both within Canada and beyond. An American newspaper sarcastically conceded that Ottawa was an excellent choice because it "could not be captured even by the most courageous soldiers: the invaders would inevitably be lost in the woods trying to find it" (NCC: undated).

The government of the province moved to Ottawa in 1866 and, in the following year, the New Dominion of Canada met for the first time. The birth of the federal government gave rise to the issue of federal-provincial relations, though these were relatively simple at the time and were clearly provided for in the BNA Act.

Ottawa had a population of only 18,000, and was variously described as "Westminster in the Wilderness," and "a sub-arctic lumber village converted by royal mandate into a political cockpit" (Mayo Report 1976: 8). The federal role in planning was to acquire Parliament Hill. Indeed, it was not until the end of the century that any special provision was made to protect the beauty of the outstanding site. In 1899 Sir Wilfrid Laurier, who wished to make Ottawa "the Washington of the North," established the Ottawa Improvement Commission.

The commission was essentially concerned with the beautification of the city, but its powers were limited, though it did some significant work, particularly in scenic improvements and the conservation of such areas as parts of Rockcliffe Park and the southern section of what later became Gatineau Park. The Borden government replaced it, in 1913, by the Federal Plan Commission. This quickly got to work and, in 1915, produced the Holt Plan (named after its chairman, Herbert S. Holt, then president of the Royal Bank of Montreal). Nothing came of this, though its major recommendations (including the shifting of the railway tracks, the decentralization of federal government offices to the periphery of the urban area, and the establishment of a green belt around the city) were reflected in later reports such as the Cauchon Report of 1922. More tangibly, the recommendations began to be implemented, particularly after 1927 when the Ottawa Improvement Commission was replaced by the Federal District Commission with wider powers and increased funding.

Progress accelerated after the end of the second world war. A master plan was prepared by Jacques Gréber in conjunction with a National Capital Planning Committee which Gréber insisted should be set up with representatives from across the country. The Gréber Plan of 1950 dealt with a wide range of issues, including those covered in earlier plans, but this time there was much more effective action: an era of unprecedented national growth and prosperity was at hand.

In 1956, a joint parliamentary committee reviewed progress and supported continued implementation of the Gréber Plan, for which further increases in powers and funding were recommended. The recommendations were accepted and the National Capital Act was passed in 1958. This replaced the Federal District Commission with the National Capital Commission, and expanded its area from 2,330 to 4,660 square kilometers. With a population of 741,600, it is the fourth largest urban area in Canada.

The legislation empowers the commission to acquire property; construct and maintain parks, parkways, bridges and other structures; maintain and improve property owned by the federal government; cooperate with local municipalities and others in joint projects; administer, preserve and maintain historic places; and carry out planning related to the development of the region. Additionally, the commission is responsible for coordinating the development and controlling the appearance and location of buildings and all works on all federally owned land (NCC 1984: 32).

The commission has twenty members appointed by the federal government from across Canada. Its terms of reference are "to prepare plans for and assist in the development, conservation and improvement of the National Capital Region in order that the nature and character of the seat of the Government of Canada may be in accordance with its national significance." The commission has translated this "very special mandate" into the goal of attaining "a Capital which stands as a symbol of identity, a model of unity and a source of pride for all Canadians."

The NCC, however, has no jurisdictional authority over any municipal or regional authority or the two provincial governments concerned. Responsibility for planning and all normal local government functions rests with the municipalities. The commission operates by cooperation with these bodies and, not insignificantly, by virtue of its ownership of nearly ten percent of the land area.

The Mayo Commission, which reported in 1976 on the first eight years of the regional municipality of Ottawa-Carleton, noted five features which were unique to the region. First, of course, is the federal-provincial-municipal relationship which is "of a peculiar and intimate sort, and on a daily basis." The complexities of this relationship stem not only from the unusual concern of the federal government for the area but also

administratively   from   the   large   numbers   of   federal   departments, agencies and crown corporations which are involved.

Secondly, the federal government is the chief employer in
the region. This influences "income levels, growth and housing,
the   demographic   composition,   attempts   at   diversifying   the
economic base, etc." Or, in less somber terms, as quoted in the
Mayo Report:

> Ottawa-Carleton, oh luckiest of regions,
> That swarms with civil servants in their legions.
> This is our economic base, which can't go wrong,
> Because - Himself has said - the land is strong.

Thirdly, the federal government is the largest single taxpayer.
To this one might add that the NCC is no mean spender: in
1983-84 it spent over $95 million. (Details are given in the
commission's annual reports.)

Fourthly, the capital "is at the very center of the federal
bilingualism policy, with all that it entails. It affects not only
the question of government employment, but also that of municipal policy, to say nothing of language teaching in the schools,
and the provision of service in both English and French by police, courts, hospitals; and all municipal departments."

Finally, the division of the area between two provinces
raises particular problems of public transit, of bridges and, of
course, wider political relationships not only between Ottawa-
Carleton and Outaouais (and Ontario and Quebec), but also
with the federal government.

In all this, the NCC plays an important role, though it
typically has to operate through advice and negotiation. This
has been complicated by the changes in local government which
have taken place: the establishment of the Regional Municipality of Ottawa-Carleton in 1969 and the Outaouais Regional
Community in the following year. As a consequence "the planning process has increasingly been characterized by a cooperative approach emphasizing joint programmes and projects in

such areas as urban redevelopment, public transit improvements, and capital works programmes" (NCC 1984: 42).

The achievements of the commission, and its predecessor, have been outstanding. One of the most impressive has been a massive relocation of railway lines, one of which is now the twenty-seven kilometer limited access Queensway which crosses the city. A new Ottawa station has been built outside the central area, and the old Union Station is now the Government Conference Center. Many major developments took place on land which was freed, including the construction of Colonel By Drive and the National Arts Center. Other developments were facilitated, for example the Ottawa River Parkway, the LeBreton Flats redevelopment, Rideau Center, and Sussex Drive improvements.

The long established conservation ethic in Ottawa has blossomed into a remarkable network of parks and parkways. With an area of 36,000 hectares, Gatineau Park is the largest and probably best known but, within the city, there is a marvelous range of open spaces and landscaped areas which gives Ottawa a particularly attractive appearance. This has come about by a large scale program of property acquisitions and by direct maintenance, for example of the land around federal government buildings and along the driveways.

Extensive land acquisitions have also taken place in the greenbelt, much of which is managed by the commission. The greenbelt forms a semicircular belt of about 17,600 hectares running in a continuous arc of 45 kilometers on the outer edge of the urban area.

This incomplete list illustrates the range and effectiveness of the work of the commission. Its success has been due to its extensive powers and the way in which these have been carefully used, generous funding, and public support. Perhaps it should also be added that it has a clear focus. In this it could not be more different from the subject of the next section.

Groping for a National Urban Policy

The Ministry of State for Urban Affairs threatened the provinces
and could not deliver to the municipalities

Gertler 1982

Urban policy would appear, at first sight, clearly to be a
provincial rather than a federal responsibility. Municipalities
are, of course, often the agents of implementation while the
federal government may provide financial support by way of
transfer payments. Going one step further, municipalities, particularly in the bigger cities, may be heavily involved in urban
policy-making as well as in implementation, while the federal
government may provide financial support for specific urban
policies in which there is a federal interest, such as railway relocation. Nevertheless, policies in relation to urban areas, to the
extent that such exist or can be articulated, seem to fall unequivocally into the arena of provincial responsibility.

In practice, federal involvement in urban policy is
widespread, both indirectly and directly. The indirect involvement comes from the impact of federal employment, tax systems and transfer payments (Simmons 1981), together with
broader policies relating to economic development, defence,
immigration and so forth. The direct involvement lies in the
multiplicity of federal programs. These change constantly, but
there is a huge range of federal policies which might be "coordinated in some way to achieve urban policy objectives." Moreover, a strong federal presence in certain housing and housing-
related fields was in existence from the early postwar years.
Some sort of urban policy role for the federal government had
been established, if not acclaimed.

Though there is no necessary connection between these,
other strands of federal-provincial relationships conspired to
bring them together: almost. The story peaks with the establishment of a Ministry of State for Urban Affairs with a minister responsible for CMHC. It ends, at least for a time, with the
demise of the same ministry in 1979. It is less easy to say

where it starts: certainly the story does not unfold in a neat progressive way. Instead, true to life, there are many different elements: policy initiatives, political thrusts and, as always, the perpetual inconclusiveness of federal-provincial debate. The underlying force, however, was the rapid rate of urbanization that was putting great strain on existing governmental and financial systems.

Politically, 1964 was an important year: it saw the return of a Liberal government under Lester Pearson and "a new era of constitutional controversy and provincial power thrusts." At the time, CMHC was developing ideas for "the suburban expansion of metropolitan regions (including ... proposals for new communities and transportation corridors), the problems of those regions that do not have much urban growth and economic development, and a general shift of intergovernmental policy so as to direct a larger proportion of public funds towards housing middle and lower income groups" (Carver 1975: 146 and 180).

In December 1967, the first federal-provincial conference on housing and urban development was held. It was "generally regarded as a disaster," and the premiers were unimpressed by Pearson's proposal for an Urban Council, even though it was made to "sound like a respectable counterpart of the Economic Council," whose 1967 annual report contained a much publicized chapter on "the challenge of urban growth" (Carver 1975: 182; Newman 1968: 434).

In the 1968 election which followed shortly after the replacement of Lester Pearson by Pierre Trudeau, urban affairs had a high profile, with the parties putting forward various proposals for policies for cities and urban and regional planning. The Liberal platform was greatly influenced by Paul Hellyer who became Minister of Transport in the new government: a portfolio which also included responsibility for CMHC. One of the proposals was for a task force on urban issues. This was immediately acted upon. Hellyer appointed himself as chairman: a move which, as Cameron has noted, "assured, at the least, that the inquiry would be anything but a dispassionate analysis" (1974: 231).

The Hellyer report warrants its identification with the name of the chairman more than is usually justified. The whole inquiry, widened greatly beyond its original housing remit to embrace urban development, was dominated by him. As Humphrey Carver caustically, though not unfairly, remarks, the report was a strange document in that "the photographic illustrations are not of housing subjects but of members of the task force in various cities with the sun shining on the handsome head of Paul Hellyer" (Carver 1975: 185). Moreover, he "was anxious to protect his task force from contamination by those who had passed along this road before"; as a consequence, the task force purposely "remained outside the mainstream of the policy process save for its direct access to the federal cabinet" (Cameron 1974: 233).

The resulting report was inevitably a personal statement of commitment by Hellyer, and when it was not received with acclaim, he resigned. But he left a legacy which, at the time, could not be ignored. It was, he said, "illogical, if not inconceivable, that the Government of Canada could have ministries dealing with fisheries, forestry, veterans affairs, and other matters which involve a minority of the population, but none to deal on a full-time basis with the urban problems which involve more than seventy percent of the population, not to mention housing which involves virtually everyone" (Hellyer 1969: 73). Thus followed a recommendation for the creation of a Department of Housing and Urban Affairs. The new department, however, was not to be seen as a replacement or competitor to CMHC: its role was to be as "researchers, reviewers and generators of policy."

Curiously, Hellyer's departure from the political scene did not prevent the acceptance of most of his recommendations and, in July 1968, Robert Andras was designated by Trudeau as minister responsible for housing and, in practice, the Cabinet spokesman on urban affairs. Like Hellyer, he argued for terms of reference much broader than housing. The outcome was the commissioning of a report "which would assist the federal government to determine what, if any, role it should play in urban affairs, and the likely consequences of such a role"

(Lithwick 1970). Professor N.H. Lithwick of Carleton University was commissioned to undertake this study.

The Lithwick report was a rapidly produced but powerful document, though Carver commented that, despite its "quite logical conclusions," its "difficult language" reduced its impact: "it was rather as if one was reading a professional validation of the propositions of Jesus Christ" (Carver 1975: 188). The comment symbolizes the rift between CMHC and developments on the wider urban policy front. However, this is to anticipate: it is first necessary to outline the thrust of Lithwick's main argument. Essentially it was focused, as required by his terms of reference, on the legitimacy of a federal role in urban affairs.

Lithwick's argument is cogent and elegant. First, he distinguishes between problems *in* urban areas and problems *of* urban areas. Since most people live in urban areas, most problems will be found there: but this does not make them urban problems. Only if it is possible to identify a range of problems which are truly *of* urban areas does it make sense to talk of urban policy. This Lithwick did; adding the crucial point that urban problems exhibit a unique characteristic in that they are interdependent aspects of urbanization and, since urbanization is basically an aspect of economic development, it follows that urban policy is of legitimate concern to the federal level of government.

To explain in more detail: Lithwick argued that the difference between "in the city" problems and "of the city" problems is basically that the latter are "fundamental aspects of the growing city." In a growing city, problems of housing, transportation, poverty, employment etc are all interrelated. It follows that policies conceived separately for each of the problems are not enough: the problems are merely "symptoms" of urbanization. "Long term solutions require intervention in the urbanization process itself." This necessitates an understanding of what the process is.

In discussing this, Lithwick laid great emphasis on "macroeconomic determinants." Cities are not only affected by economic forces: they constitute the main arena in which modern economic development takes place.

> Cities are what make modern economic systems work. Without them, there may be improvement; but it will necessarily be at a very low level of efficiency, and generally not self sustaining. It is the city that provides a direct link between all the macro variables: capital formation, labour supplies, technological change, incomes, markets. Proximity, the essence of the urban system, permits the joining of these economic processes, and the high level of interaction among them provides the sustained thrust to launch modern economic growth.

Macroeconomic driving forces not only provide the impetus for urban development: in turn they are reinforced by that development. But that is not all: the forces which shape the development of a single urban area also shape all urban areas, and therefore the entire urban network. Thus there is an important link between the course of the national economy and the urbanization process. Indeed, Lithwick argued, "the major forces influencing cities do not lie within their control."

The policy implications were clear: individual cities cannot solve their own problems. The reason why previous policies met with serious failures was that cities were regarded as essentially autonomous elements. The fault had lain "in the simple concept of territoriality that assigns to provinces in whose territories cities happen to be found almost exclusive legislative jurisdiction over them." Under this system, and given projected growth in population, immigration and household formation, the problems of housing, transportation, fiscal ability to cope with urban growth, and urban poverty would increase. The costs would likewise increase and this would affect not only the cities themselves but the nation since the high level costs would be transmitted throughout the national economy.

In summary, Lithwick's diagnosis was:

- that the urban system is a spatial dimension of the national economy, and that economic development will cause and depend upon sound urbanization;

- that, because of this, the urban system is linked nationally in terms of commodity flows, population movements, information links, and so on;

- that these linkages serve to transmit the costs and benefits of urban growth through the nation;

- that managing the growth of the major units can have profound benefits for the nation;

- that all Canadians stand to benefit from managed growth in terms of a greater ability to choose desired life styles ...;

- it is clear that there is room for a federal role in urban policy because of this national dimension to the urban system. The [required policy] requires no new spending or legislative power, but only a direction of present powers to a clearly articulated, commonly accepted, extremely promising end.

In essence, the plea was one for a national urban policy which would be comprehensive and coordinated, and which would be particularly concerned with the management of urban growth. The role of the federal government would be a crucial one: in industrial location, inter-urban transport and communications, inter-urban migration, the channelling of resources to urban areas, and generally in providing a national framework for comprehensive provincial plans for social, economic and physical development.

To give effect to this new conception of a national urban policy, Lithwick proposed a National Urban Council and a large urban research unit. The National Urban Council would "formulate consistent, meaningful, and acceptable urban policy" and would be the forum "where regional and national objectives could be harmonized and integrated." In this it would be assisted by the "understanding of the urban system" provided by the urban research unit.

Whatever the logical basis of Lithwick's analysis, this part of it at least exhibits a high degree of political naivety. Constant reference to rational models of policy making obscured the elementary fact that much of the problem of policy making is the political one of reaching mutually acceptable compromises. This is all the more so in the federal system.

Had Lithwick stopped at this point, his report would have had little impact on the political scene, but he did two other things. First, he demonstrated that an "uncontrolled" future would result in massive urban growth. On his best population projection, Vancouver would grow to 2,482,000 by the year 2001, Montreal to 6,374,000 and Toronto to 6,510,000. Other projections gave even higher figures, e.g. for Toronto of 7,945,000 on one base and of 8,503,000 on another (Goracz, Lithwick and Stone 1971).

The implications of this were briefly spelled out (high land costs, excessive commuting, congested and polluted downtown areas etc), but the figures were as frightening as those which had earlier precipitated a British government into a major increase in its new towns program (Cullingworth 1979). They probably had a greater influence on government reaction to the report than anything else it contained.

Secondly (in this selective summary) Lithwick made much of the lack of what he termed "an urban perspective" or "urban awareness" in the multiplicity of federal programs. They all operated independently, and had no overall framework for urban policy formation. The net effect of this "chaotic approach" was "a general failure to come to grips with the urban reality in which the nation now finds itself." More tangibly, he argued:

> What is needed is a distinct spokesman for the federal government's urban objectives so that [urban] objectives are always clearly articulated and promoted as a guide to the delivery of policy. All federal agencies with an urban impact would need to consider their policies in the light of these objectives, and the development of programs to meet these objectives would permit the authority to draw on various relevant agencies as a matter of priority, not courtesy. Conflicts between objectives of different agencies could be resolved at the Cabinet level, so that urban interests would not be downplayed for lack of an appropriate level of input.

The Lithwick report, as Cameron has neatly commented, "if not convincing in all aspects of its diagnosis and prescription ... nevertheless offered ample ammunition for almost any federal response short of inaction" (1974: 240). The action finally taken reflected external political demands (from within the Liberal Party as well as from the Conservatives and the NDP): this was the establishment of a Ministry of State for Urban Affairs (Bettison 1975: 278). The announcement of this was made by Andras, and was warmly welcomed by all parties in the House of Commons.

However, the announcement was remarkably vague as to precisely what the new ministry would do. Much clearer was what it would not do. It was not to be a traditional Department of Urban Affairs and Housing. Such a department would be trammelled by "policy making and massive program delivery apparatus." Andras explained that in putting forward (to Trudeau) the case for the new ministry, "we argued that because of the interrelatedness and all inclusiveness of urbanization, we preferred the establishment of a research, policy making and coordinative ministry with no delivery system and no direct program responsibility." CMHC was to remain the program delivery organization.

The terms of reference for the new ministry, as set out in the Government Organization Act of 1970, were to:

... formulate and develop policies for implementation through measures within fields of federal jurisdiction in respect of

(a)   the most appropriate means by which the Government of Canada may have a beneficial influence on the evolution of the process of urbanization in Canada;

(b)   the integration of urban policy with other policies and programmes of the Government of Canada;

(c)   the fostering of cooperative relationships in respect of urban affairs with the provinces and, through them, their municipalities, and with the public and with private organizations.

The new ministry was to have the power to make proposals for new policies and programs, to initiate and coordinate research, to consult with all levels of government, and generally to gain "the broadest possible understanding of the process of urbanization and, thereby initiating a consensus in the building of national policies and federal initiatives." The first step would be to put the federal house in order: with 112 federal programs affecting the urban system, 131 relevant research programs, 27 departments and agencies involved with urban areas; "something should come from this alone."

The power to do these laudable things apparently was to rest on persuasion, though how it was to work was unclear. The basic notion was the highly rationalistic idea that research and policy analysis would provide a logical basis for policy making which, by its knowledge base and the strength of its logic, would overcome, not only departmentalism, but also objections emanating from narrow departmental stances.

Politically this fitted in nicely with Trudeau's search for non-traditional mechanisms for coping with complex problems which refused to fit into any departmental mould. It reflected the general embracing of system analysis and similar rationalistic approaches to the problems of government. It implied that complex problems could be managed by new forms of organizations which would be learning mechanisms. In terms of political science, it was an approach which viewed "the political system in cybernetic terms as a goal seeking and error correcting information system that will learn how to learn" (Doern 1971: 67). Trudeau was quite explicit in his enthusiasm for this approach:

> We are aware that the many techniques of cybernetics, by transforming the control function and the manipulation of information, will transform our whole society. With this knowledge we are wide awake, alert, capable of action; no longer are we blind, inert pawns of fate (Ibid: 65).

Yet there must have been doubts. A minister's power rests not only on his knowledge but also on the support he gets in Cabinet, especially from the prime minister. A minister without program responsibilities is at a low level of political visibility, no matter how much knowledge he has. Moreover, he cannot get the required knowledge without the active cooperation of the relevant departments and of those, inside and outside government, who have expertise and experience. His ministry has to mesh in with the complex web of government and the research establishment. It has to understand the problems encountered in service delivery, the attempts made by departments to overcome these, the research capability of the departments and the consultants they have employed, the pressures of the departmental constituents, and so on. The new ministry has to understand the hopes, ambitions and frustrations of the departments; how well they work together; their strengths and weaknesses; and it has to handle its relationships diplomatically.

The departments are likely to regard a newcomer as a threat to their interests and will naturally seek to influence it, either positively in the direction they want to go; or, if they cannot do this, by undermining its position through non-cooperation. Different divisions of departments may take different attitudes; and the new ministry will easily find itself embroiled in inter and intra-departmental conflicts. This is the stuff of administration: no agency can rise above it: unless it is happy to be ignored. It is not surprising that the role of MSUA was left unclear. These difficulties were to be expected.

There is another, bigger doubt about the concept. Even if a new ministry gets all the information it requires, and all the research capability that is available, is the "knowledge is power" hypothesis likely to prove true? (Aucoin and French 1974). Power in government means power to influence. What influence can a minister with no program responsibilities and no budgetary power wield? Could it really be expected that urban policy research could come up with research findings which could make obstacles fall away?

Might there not be an alternative explanation for the MSUA: that the federal government had to demonstrate that it was doing something which seemed impressive yet unthreatening to the provinces? The pressures from Parliament and from bodies   such as the Science Council were strong but, given the difficulties of making the governmental machine more effective while at the same time not upsetting the provinces, the government faced a real dilemma. It had to do something; and it had to respond to the barrage of policy proposals emanating from Lithwick and others. The MSUA was a neat way of appearing "to get ready to get ready" to do something (Ibid: 25).

In retrospect, there must have been further doubts when the minister (Andras) was also given the program responsibilities for CMHC. Now the chances were that there would be severe problems of relationships between the policy body (MSUA) and the program body (CMHC). It was highly likely that it would be the CMHC programs which would command public and political attention, while the nebulous activities of MSUA would sink into the background. This is precisely what happened.

Lithwick was appointed to MSUA, and set about creating "a strongly research based agency ...; a distinctly professional, non-bureaucratic agency, where the necessary cross disciplinary, comprehensive approaches to urban policy could be taken" (Lithwick 1972a: 53).   The approach was rational: research must precede policy. Yet there was also an urgent need for "immediate and extensive intergovernmental liaison" (Aucoin and French 1974: 61). Life would not stop until the research was completed. Yet until more research was done action would be taken in a policy vacuum.

Ironically for an organization committed to the concept of coordination, Lithwick's endeavors were not linked in any sense with other parts of the new ministry's organization. Moreover, no effective machinery existed for carrying out the primary tasks of policy development, evaluation and coordination. The ministry was isolated from the centers of both policy formulation and program delivery that it was supposedly to coordinate.

Lithwick resigned, and what could conceivably have been seen as a period of teething troubles was followed by "a period of chaotic, if predictable, confusion and discontent ... the role of the ministry in its first two years was indeed a tragicomedy"

(Cameron 1974: 246). By 1976 the concept of a comprehensive urban policy "died of a surfeit of irrelevance" and political disillusionment. Downward revisions of population forecasts transformed the demographic scene, and the crisis simply melted away. In its place came the economic problems of the mid-seventies which pushed urban issues into the background. Even the attempts to woo the provinces failed. The tri-level conferences (which are further referred to in a subsequent section) mouthed a lot of words about balanced development, but the feeling was that this was "a peculiar federal fetish which had to be gotten out of the way before it was possible to come to grips with real questions like money and how to bring down the cost of serviced land."

Some specific policy innovations were made, such as the neighborhood improvement program, and federal grants for new community planning, but much of the pace was set by CMHC. There were also measures to decentralize federal offices out of Ottawa, but here the lead was taken by the Department of Regional Economic Expansion.

The root of the difficulty lay in Lithwick's concept of urban policy. He saw this as a policy for urbanization which inevitably leads into economic development and finally into "an all-embracing policy of national development." Cameron's judgement must surely be right: "It is exceedingly unlikely that the incredible diversity of the Canadian reality could sustain a single development policy. It exceeds all bounds of reason to conceive of such a policy's emerging from the isolation and confusion of a Ministry of State" (1974: 249).

What then follows? Certainly there was a need for far more research on urban analysis and urban problems (Simmons 1967); and there remains the need for the two functions which MSUA in its final report (1976-77: 3) declared to be its primary role:

> ... to coordinate efforts in identifying where and how federal programs can be modified to better serve provincial and municipal objectives, and to cooperate with the provinces so that they are

aware of the federal concerns which can be incorporated in provincial and municipal programming.

Yet there are the skeptics. Feldman and Milch, for example, conclude their account of *The Life and Death of the Ministry of State for Urban Affairs* in this way:

> The coordination of state activities in the urban area may be an
> impossible task under the best of circumstances, and it has
> become more difficult with the broad application of rational
> planning techniques that reinforce narrow perspectives in most
> governmental agencies. MSUA has proven unequal to the task;
> so, for that matter, has the Department of Housing and Urban
> Development in the United States. In light of the tendency to
> subdivide the bureaucracy and to establish more specialized
> agencies, it is not obvious that any mechanism could achieve the
> degree of coordination to which the creators of MSUA had
> aspired (Feldman and Milch 1981: 263).

Nevertheless, they continue, coordination "continues to
represent a logical objective opposing incoherence and waste. It
continues, too, as an unrealized dream of government reform."

If such a modest concept of urban policy, for which the
term "urban awareness" seems more apposite, is not viable,
what of the much larger ideas, put forward by Lithwick, for
intervention in the urbanization process? Again, there is a
range of views. Preston argues the need for federal intervention
to promote "growth center strategies," and he warns of the
problems consequent on "the cumulative advantages of the
Windsor-Quebec City axis, of the Georgia Strait Urban Region,
and of the Albertan Development Corridor" (Preston 1980: 137).
Simmons (1975) is iconoclastic, and argues that most traditional
techniques of intervention are inappropriate to Canada, but it is
not clear what might take their place. Martin (1975) is eloquent in his enthusiasm for "a national land use act with a
federal provincial coordinating body to administer it." In striking contrast, Hamilton (1975) argues the case against any direct
federal intervention "in shaping urban regions ... nor should it
adopt any policies which would tend to guide the type or direction of new development." His view is that "maximum

decentralization of land use policy decisions should be the watchword."

Cameron argues that the problems, in so far as they are manageable, should be dealt with at the provincial level. This is not to imply that the provinces are capable of elaborating policies for their cities: it simply means that no one else can.

The Provincial and Municipal Roles

Local government came to Canada slowly and with great difficulty

Siegal 1980

It is clear from the preceding discussion of the federal role in planning that federal and provincial responsibilities and fields of activity cannot be neatly separated. Federal and provincial government coexist. At one and the same time they have an autonomous and interdependent character: they operate in a mutually dependent political relationship. Interdependence, as Simeon has written:

... implies that in many fields, what one government does will have implications for others. Each government's decisions will have spillover effects to which others must adjust. Interdependence also means that many of the fields with which modern governments concern themselves (welfare, economic policy, transportation) cut across formal divisions of responsibility. Governments share functions, and demands from citizens do not necessarily respect constitutional lines of authority. The result is that governments must somehow coordinate their policies, not simply to avoid frustrating each other's policies but also jointly to make overall policies for the nation... The other side of the coin is autonomy. Neither central nor unit governments have hierarchical controls over one another (1972: 3).

Thus cooperation, or liaison, or at the least "accommodation" is an essential feature of federal-provincial relationships.

Provincial-municipal relationships on the other hand are very different. The provinces not only determine what powers municipalities shall have: they are responsible for their actual existence. Reference is frequently made to the fact that municipalities are creations, or even creatures, of the provinces. This does not mean, however, that they are tame pets: they have some political substance. In Crawford's words, "the protection of the municipalities lies, not in their legal or constitutional position, but rather in the needs of the people which must be met and the difficulty, especially in urban communities, of meeting those needs through the medium of any other level of government" (Crawford 1954: 18).

Viewing the intra-provincial scene as a whole, the provincial role in urban and regional planning has three dimensions, one involving federal relationships, one involving municipal relationships, and a third in which it operates independently. Environmental policies discussed earlier fall into the first category. The elaboration of provincial planning policies to be operated by municipalities and the control of this operation falls into the second. Examples of the third are the provincial administration of planning policies either through an ad hoc agency such as the British Columbia Agricultural Land Commission, or directly through a provincial government department as with planning in northern Ontario.

In fact, matters can be more complex than this, with all levels of government, and other bodies such as those responsible for hydro or the railways, having an interest.

In the seventies, tri-level conferences were actively promoted by the federal government but, though welcomed by the municipalities, most provinces were lukewarm at best and antagonistic at worst. To them municipal government was a matter for provincial-municipal relations. To bring the federal government in carried the danger not only of making those relationships more difficult but also of complicating federal-provincial relations, and centralizing political power (Feldman and Graham 1979: chapter 3).

During the debates on the new constitution, the Federation of Canadian Municipalities (1980) argued that municipalities should be recognized as a distinct level of government. Their argument carried little weight and even less support.

It would seem to follow that municipalities are mere agents of the provinces. This, however, is to ignore some more subtle aspects. Municipalities may have only the powers granted them by the provinces, but these are by no means negligible; and, additionally, there is the actual political power they can exercise by virtue of their electoral support and their relationship with provincial governments. Moreover, in some provinces, there is a real attempt to give more, though not too much, power to municipalities. In short, the realities may be somewhat different from the statutory appearances.

Of course, municipalities differ, not just in size and socio-economic character, but also in influence and political clout. One neat illustration of this is Winnipeg which has over fifty percent of the population of Manitoba. This is likely to be at least a partial explanation for Manitoba's untypically positive attitude towards tri-level conferences (Feldman and Graham 1979: 55).

The issue of political relationships between municipal and provincial government is a crucial one. Axworthy's account of the creation of Unicity in Winnipeg succinctly illustrates this (1980). The legislators "overestimated the impact that structural reform can have in altering the decision-making dynamics of a city, and they vastly underestimated the importance of the political process." But, to repeat yet again, there are considerable differences between the provinces.

Municipal reorganization is particularly relevant to this book since, typically, the objective has been to devise an improved apparatus for dealing with the mounting problems of urbanization. Before entering on such a discussion, however, more needs to be said about the character of local government in the different provinces.

The majority of the Canadian population (97 percent) lives in municipalities, though most of the land area (70 percent) is not organized in municipalities (Statistics Canada 1982). In area, the municipalities range widely: from 0.1 square kilometers for the Saskatchewan village of Arelee to 98,165 square kilometers for Alberta Improvement District Number 23. The average size also varies between provinces. On the average, the municipalities of Prince Edward Island are one-sixteenth the size (52.9 square kilometers) of those of Quebec (870.39 square kilometers) and one seventy-fourth those of British Columbia (3,951.65 square kilometers).

There is an extraordinary variety of nomenclature which reflects the differing histories of the provinces: Ontario's townships, Manitoba's rural communities, British Columbia's district municipalities. In Quebec the paroisses, cantons, cantons unis, and municipalités sans désignation are so similar that all the newly created municipalities are called municipalités sans désignation.

The great majority of municipalities are unitary, but there were, in 1983, 168 authorities in a two tier system: fifteen metropolitan and regional municipalities, and 148 counties and regional districts. Of the 4,172 unitary authorities, 3,859 had populations of less than 10,000. Thirty had populations of over 100,000 (Table 2.1).

These bare statistics give a picture of the variety of municipal institutions in Canada. However, the figures are of limited value, except in highlighting the small size of the majority. Municipalities with different names may operate the same functions, while those with the same names may have widely differing functions. Moreover, many local functions are operated by ad hoc bodies. Education is a particular case: in all provinces responsibility lies outside municipal government. Police, public health, parks, and libraries are other functions often performed by ad hoc boards. This proliferation of specialized boards stems in part from U.S. influence.

Table 2.1 — Municipalities in Each Province by Type 1983

	BC	Alta	Sask	Man	Ont	Que	NB	NS	PEI	Nfld	NWT	YT	Canada
Regional municipalities	28	—	—	—	39	96	—	—	—	—	—	—	163
Metropolitan and regional Municipalities[1]	—	—	—	—	12	3	—	—	—	—	—	—	15
Counties and regional districts	28	—	—	—	27	93	—	—	—	—	—	—	148
Unitary municipalities	142	332	805	185	792	1,518	114	66	39	169	7	3	4,172
Cities[2]	35	11	12	5	49	65	6	3	1	2	1	2	192
Towns	10	111	142	35	145	192	23	39	8	167	5	1	878
Villages	55	162	352	40	119	243	85	—	30	—	—	—	1,087
Rural Municipalities[3]	42	48	299	105	479	1,018	—	24	—	—	1	—	2,015
Quasi municipalities[4]	285	19	—	17	7	—	—	—	—	141	26	5	500
Total	455	351	805	202	838	1,614	114	66	39	310	33	8	4,835

[1]Includes urban communities in Quebec; and Metropolitan Toronto, regional municipalities and the district municipality of Muskoka in Ontario

[2]Includes the boroughs of Metropolitan Toronto

[3]Includes municipalities in Nova Scotia; parishes, townships, united townships and municipalities without designation in Quebec; townships in Ontario; rural municipalities in Manitoba and Saskatchewan; municipal districts and counties in Alberta; and districts in British Columbia

[4]Includes local government communities, and the metropolitan area in Newfoundland; improvement districts in Ontario and Alberta; local government districts in Manitoba; local improvement districts in British Columbia and Yukon; and hamlets in Northwest Territories

Source: *Canada Year Book 1985*, Table 19.8, p. 631

> This practice in Canada, more extensive in Ontario and the
> Prairie Provinces than in the rest of the Dominion, was in part
> an imitation of the United States and in part an effort to remove
> from the sometimes penny-pinching control of councils those ser-
> vices which a council might be disposed to sacrifice in preference
> to expenditures which would give more immediate and tangible
> results (Crawford 1954: 131).

As urban and regional planning becomes increasingly concerned with wider social issues (discussed in the following
chapter), this fragmentation can seriously hinder attempts at
coordination and broad community planning. The force of history, however, is strong, and there is still considerable support
for what Plunkett and Betts have called "the apolitical idea"
with the important local functions being put beyond the control
of elected representatives (1978:26). Ontario is extreme, with
over 3,000 ad hoc boards. Though some have been abolished,
such as the planning boards of southern Ontario, new ones continue to be created or proposed. In 1982, for instance, the list
of new bodies included the Guild Inn in Scarborough as a
conference center, Metro's homes for the aged, a future sports
and trade center complex, and the Canadian National Exhibition (Bureau of Municipal Research 1981).

The apolitical philosophy goes deep (Rutherford 1974) and
is used, and misused, in a variety of ways. Thus, in 1983, the
Ontario government declared that it would not introduce legislation to provide for the public election of the chairman of
Metro Toronto, despite recommendations for this from two
royal commissions. This was defended by the province on the
grounds that there had not been "any tidal wave of public opinion that would cause the province to act" and, more startlingly
by a former Metro chairman, Paul Godfrey, who is reported as
saying:

> A publicly elected Metro chairman would become far more polit-
> ical and lose his independence. [Mr Paul Godfrey] said a chair-
> man who also has to worry about facing the electorate might be
> forced into making popular decisions rather than those which
> are in the Metro's long-term best interest *(Globe and Mail,*
> Toronto).

Different provinces, however, have different political traditions. In Newfoundland, though St John's was created a municipality in 1888, it was not until 1938 that any further ones were formed; thus, "the most startling fact about Newfoundland's local government is that apart from the City of St John's, there were no local government bodies in the island until 1938" (Crosbie 1956: 332). There still remains the long standing opposition to the establishment of local governments and the property taxes that go with them. Much preferred is direct provision (and financing) by the province. By contrast Ontario, as Upper Canada, fought fiercely for the right to local self-government and, by the time the Prairie provinces were opened for settlement, "they benefited by the experience of a quarter of a century of municipal government" in the central provinces; "the question at issue was not whether local self-government should be permitted but rather the basis on which it should be established" (Crawford 1954: 19). In British Columbia, geographical isolation necessitated some form of local government.

How far these historical differences continue to bear their mark on the current municipal scene is undocumented and perhaps unclear, except in Newfoundland. What is clear is that the development of local government took place, and continues to do so, in response to population growth and the need for local services, particularly in urban areas.

Local Government and Service Delivery

The preoccupation with government as a provider of services
has remained a central feature of the system to the present day
Tindal and Tindal 1984

Two features of Canadian municipal history heavily reinforced each other: the development of municipal institutions as agencies for service delivery, and their non-political character. Local housekeeping does not provide an arena for the politics of controversy. Numerous commentators have stressed this preoccupation with the administration of services in contrast to the formulation of policy. Thus Plunkett, for example, states: "generally speaking, municipal governments were regarded as being concerned primarily with administration and not policy. From this concept emerged the 'non-partisan' tradition of Canadian municipal councils whose main concerns were to ensure the prudent administration of municipal services without unduly burdening the property taxpayer" (1972: 17). Plunkett uses the past tense because "to this traditional role of municipal government in Canada has now been added a genuinely political dimension."

There are two influences here. First, there is an increase in demand for services which is both quantitative and qualitative. Thus, larger cities require disproportionately larger police forces, and sanitation services have to be bigger and more sophisticated. Secondly, municipal government is now faced with a wide range of decisions on matters which are of economic and social importance. Roads, once considered a purely technical matter, now have to be considered in terms of their environmental and socio-economic impact. Additionally, the cities are now facing, or being presented with, new problems "for which they may have little or no constitutional or fiscal power." Housing is a good example (Ibid: 18).

The problems facing local governments are thus administrative and political; and difficulties with the latter can preclude solutions to the former. The danger is that, without major reorganization, the tendency will be to transfer specific responsibilities to new ad hoc bodies, thus exaggerating the service delivery problem.

Curiously a growing awareness of, and experimentation with, a policy-oriented system of municipal government has come about following reorganizations designed essentially to create better "service delivery authorities." First in the field was Ontario with the establishment of Metropolitan Toronto in 1953. Table 2.2 (based on Tindal and Tindal 1984: 96) summarizes some of the landmarks of reform.

Table 2.2 — Landmarks in Local Government Reform 1953-82

1953	Establishment of Metropolitan Toronto
1959	Establishment of Montreal Metropolitan Corporation
1960	Establishment of Metropolitan Winnipeg
1963	Byrne Commission on New Brunswick
1964	Michener Commission on Manitoba
1965	Goldenberg Commission on Metropolitan Toronto
	Provision for Regional Districts in British Columbia
	Voluntary Amalgamation Act in Quebec
1966	New Brunswick's "Program for Equal Opportunity"
1967	Regional Authority Created for Greater Vancouver
1968	Ontario's Regional Government Policy Statement ("Design for Development Phase 2")
1969	Establishment of Urban Communities in Montreal, Hull and Quebec
1972	Establishment of Winnipeg Unicity
1974	County Restructuring Program in Ontario
	Graham Commission on Nova Scotia
	Whalen Commission on Newfoundland
1977	Robarts Commission on Metropolitan Toronto
1981	Edmonton Annexation Decision
1982	Halifax Commission on City Government

Source: Based on Tindall (1984) p. 96

Local Government Reform

> In the main, and at the risk of oversimplification, local govern-
> ment reorganization in Canada in the post-World War II years
> has proceeded on a piecemeal basis and has rarely been the pro-
> duct of comprehensive provincial policy proposals that contained
> any assumptions about the role of local government or the
> responsibilities it could be expected to discharge and the
> resources it required
>
> Plunkett and Hooson 1975

It is neither feasible nor appropriate in this volume to recount in detail the progress of local government in each of the Canadian provinces. The reader is referred to the excellent text of the Tindalls (1984). The salient features can be noted, how-ever, and the growing importance of planning indicated.

At the outset, it is interesting to note that "reform" has generally proceeded on the basis of mutual agreement between the municipalities concerned. There has been little of the urban rural conflict which has dogged local government reorganization in Britain. On the contrary, though there was strong opposi-tion to the city of Toronto's original proposals for amalgama-tion with the surrounding authorities, there was general support for a two tier system (Rose 1972). The political attractiveness of this was such that all future municipal reorganizations in Ontario (twelve in total, covering over a third of the provincial population) followed the same pattern, even in areas of quite different character.

The crucial element in this was the incapability of the existing municipal structures to cope with urban growth on the scale which emerged in the postwar period. The brute physical planning problems were acute: in Metro's first ten years, the construction program reflected this: "76 percent of spending went for roads, sewers and water mains; 21 percent for schools; and 3 percent for housing and social services" (Baker 1983).

Metro Toronto's two-tier system has worked effectively in the physical provision of services, but new strains may be growing as the need increases for soft services and social planning (Hitchcock and Kjellberg 1980; Toronto City 1983). Its success, in both administrative and political terms, made it a model not only for other reorganizations in Ontario but also in other provinces, though with less happy results. The Montreal Metropolitan Corporation, established in 1959, never solved its internal political problems. The Metropolitan Corporation of Greater Winnipeg, established in 1960, faced similar problems and also a lack of support from the provincial government which had created it (Brownstone and Plunkett 1983). Subsequent reforms created the indirectly elected Montreal Urban Community in 1969, and the single-tier Winnipeg "Unicity" in 1972.

The legislation which created the Montreal Urban Community was paralleled by provisions for the creation of similar bodies for the Quebec and Hull regions (Godin 1974). The Winnipeg solution is unique. These have not operated smoothly, particularly in the field of planning. Part of the difficulty is inherent: planning over a wide area seeks to allocate resources in the interests of the area as a whole. These wider interests can, and do, conflict with local interests. Metropolitan government can also become administratively cumbersome. With a two-tier system, the clash between local and metropolitan interests may lead to the development of machinery which, even if it is effective in achieving reconciliation or compromise, can be slow and inefficient. Such problems can arise even in single-tier government, as is illustrated by the extraordinary, convoluted and lengthy planning process in Winnipeg which the Taraska report documents (1976: 31).

Local government reorganization in Ontario, Quebec and Manitoba was preceded by, and followed by, comprehensive studies. By contrast, British Columbia proceeded stealthily and by what one analysis has termed "the strategy of gentle imposition" (Tennant and Zirnhelt 1973). The story is an interesting one. In essence, the provincial government faced two sets of problems: one relating to five-sixths of the province which was unorganized; the other relating to the remaining area which contained the majority of the population. The latter included Vancouver and the Lower Mainland where various regional authorities had been established over a long period of time, from the Vancouver and Districts Joint Sewerage and Drainage District in 1914, to the Lower Mainland Regional Planning Board in 1948 (Corke 1983: 96). There had thus developed a multiplicity of regional bodies in the urban areas, most of which were the result of municipal initiatives. The result, however, was a mosaic, rather than a system of regional government. Nevertheless, there was no pressure for change or, indeed, any pressing problems requiring action.

Yet there were inadequacies, particularly in the coordination of planning. These were never documented nor made the subject of political debate. Instead, the Department of Municipal Affairs, under an energetic minister, moved in a cautious way "to provide a framework for orderly development of local government in the future ... by June 1964 the basic strategy for regionalization had been decided upon without any participation from outside the department. The strategy rested on what may accurately be termed gentle imposition of departmental policy upon existing municipalities."

The tactics were subtle and effective. A purely enabling act was passed, empowering the province to create regional districts, to determine their boundaries, to name them (a point of some significance, as will be demonstrated), and to decide upon their functions.

In implementing the act, the minister proceeded slowly. The first district was created in August 1965 (several months after the legislation was passed) "in an out of the way part of Vancouver Island." The regional district for Greater Vancouver was not created until June 1967, by which time thirteen other districts had already been created. More Machiavellian, it was given no immediate functions, and it was named the Regional District of Fraser-Burrard. As Tennant and Zirnhelt note, this name "... had no substantive meaning, and since the words Fraser and Burrard referred to bodies of water and had no particular governmental connotation, the name itself gave no hint of its own significance. Quite different would the case have been had the name been 'Corporation of Metropolitan Vancouver'. This tactic proved so successful that difficulty was later encountered when the district began issuing bonds, and so the name was changed in 1968 to Greater Vancouver Regional District (GVRD)." Initially GVRD was simply "tacked on" to the Hospital Board. Gradually new functions were added, e.g. debt management, water, public housing, air pollution control, building regulation, community planning, recreation and transport.

In all, twenty-eight regional districts were established under the act. Much of its political success could be attributed not just to stealth, but to an opting-out provision which, untypically for this piece of legislation, was widely publicized. Though all the municipalities were located in a regional district, they could opt out of any of the functions which had been assigned to the region. This provision was safely repealed following the Broome Report of 1969.

The regional system became well established in British Columbia and, though not without its difficulties, the Regional District Review Committee (1978) recommended its retention in a strengthened form. In 1983, however, the provincial government decided that official regional plans had become an unnecessary level of land use control, and they were abolished. The current situation, in the GVRD is not clear, but an account of emerging trends is given in chapter 9.

The reorganizations of local government so far outlined have been generally criticized by academic writers. Commenting on Ontario, Quebec and British Columbia, Plunkett and Hooson (1975) complain that none of them "can really be described as involving any kind of comprehensive reform and are simply ad hoc adjustments of the existing structure." They exempt Winnipeg and New Brunswick from this criticism. Not so Tindal: he asserts that "none of the varied provincial approaches has constituted a comprehensive philosophy to local government ... the main emphasis of provincial reform appears to be the improved provision of required services. It is difficult to foresee more comprehensive, balanced reforms unless both the government and the public engage in a full examination of what a local government system is supposed to be and then attempt to create such a system" (Tindall 1977: 18 and 45).

Even the New Brunswick reform is inadequate on this approach. Following the report of the Byrne Commission (1963), the province took over direct responsibility for justice, public health and welfare, and also financial responsibility for education; school districts were reduced from 422 to 33; county government was abolished; and municipal taxation reformed, with tax assessment, levy and collection administered by the province (Plunkett 1965; Krueger 1970). This *Program for Equal Opportunity* was, in essence, a transfer of social services and planning (termed "general" services) from local to provincial government, with "local" services (fire, police, streets, sewage etc) remaining at the local level. The distinction was between services of province-wide significance requiring large administrative units and substantial funding, and services of an essentially local nature. A 1965 *White Paper on The Responsibilities of Government* explained that the reallocation of responsibilities between provincial and local government was necessary in order to provide "minimum standards of service and opportunity for all citizens, regardless of the financial resources of the locality in which they live."

A substantial improvement in the social services followed, but local government was inevitably weakened. Indeed, some forty percent of the population were left without any local government. A 1976 task force found that the direct provision of services in rural areas was unsatisfactory and that some of the services, particularly community planning, could not be operated effectively at the provincial level: local input and participation was necessary (New Brunswick 1976). It was recommended that eleven new municipalities be established to take over responsibility from the province.

No action has followed from this report, or from the massive Graham report on Nova Scotia (1974), or the Whalen report on Newfoundland (1974).

The contrast to these large scale reviews of local government systems is the usually relatively minor issue of annexation which can be dealt with, for example in Ontario, by the Ontario Municipal Board (OMB) or in Alberta by the Local Authorities Board (LAB). Thus the Alberta LAB hears some eighty to ninety annexation applications a year: a task which would overwhelm the Cabinet. Delegation to a regulatory agency has obvious administrative attractions. There can also be the bonus of the transfer of politically difficult decisions, or at least (hopefully) the defusing of a delicate political situation. The benefits are not simply for the politicians. As Schindeler notes, "the citizens concerned are less likely to feel that decisions which adversely affect them stem from political bias... this supposed independence from politics may be more apparent than real, but in political life appearances are important" (1969: 70).

The 1979-80 Edmonton annexation was by no means a normal one: indeed it was so large as to warrant classification as a local government reorganization (Plunkett and Lightbody 1982). Previous annexation applications over the period 1947-80 numbered nineteen, and involved a total of some 55,000 acres. The 1979 application, had it been approved in full, would have increased the area of the city from 80,000 to 547,000 acres and its population from 482,000 to 568,000.

This was clearly no conventional application: it involved total amalgamation with adjoining municipalities. This followed the province's rejection of both the Ontario and the British Columbia approaches to the reorganization of local government to cope with the problems of rapid urban growth. Instead, there was an acceptance of the recommendations of the Royal Commission on the Metropolitan Development of Calgary and Edmonton: namely, "the amalgamation of the core cities with their industrial and residential fringe communities." Edmonton followed this line; and the 1979 application was the dramatic climax of its endeavors. In June 1981, the provincial government approved an annexation of only 86,000 acres, thereby excluding the dormitory suburbs (Lightbody 1983: 278; Gordon 1984).

In Saskatchewan, annexation has been the favored method of dealing with the problems of urbanization: "with the exception of the inevitable annexation disputes and some tension between rural and urban municipalities, the system is relatively stable" (Siegel 1980: 286). In Prince Edward Island, the small scale of government (and everything else) has militated against the development of local government. The provincial government takes direct responsibility for many local services: "the system is simple and stable and likely to remain that way" (Ibid: 283).

One other technique for providing adequate machinery to deal with urban growth is to extend the powers of a city beyond its boundaries. This was done in the original 1953 Municipality of Toronto Act. The Metropolitan Toronto Planning Area included not only the 240 square miles within the Metro boundaries, but also an additional 480 square miles in the adjacent rural areas. (In the 1970s these areas became separate regional authorities.) Similarly, the City of Winnipeg Act created an area termed, somewhat uninspiringly, "the additional zone" over which the metropolitan government operates powers for planning, zoning, building controls and property assessment. "This extra-territorial extension of the Metro government's powers was included to prevent suburban sprawl and to control the urbanization of the immediately surrounding region so that the adverse effects of such developments upon the existing urban areas might be kept to a minimum ..." (Taraska Report 1976: 7). (The additional zone was retained when Unicity replaced Metro.)

A variation on this technique is the St John's Metropolitan Area Board which is an ad hoc authority which exercises all local government responsibilities in the unorganized area around St John's and Mount Pearl. Again the purpose was to control urban growth and to "... prevent the countryside from continually being pushed further away by an uncontrolled sprawl outwards from the city and in order to achieve a density suitable for economic servicing" (St John's 1957). The board was established in 1963. Its area of jurisdiction has since been extended, and had a 1976 population of 19,000. The St John's Region as a whole had a population of 140,000.

The St John's board is unique and is, in fact, a politically acceptable alternative to a proper system of regional government which has been strongly recommended by two commissions of inquiry: the Henley Commission (1974-76) and the Whalen Commission (1974).

As already indicated, academic criticism of local government reform is widespread. It is interesting to see this echoed in the Taraska report where, in commenting on the Ontario regional reorganization, it is noted that the still dominant notion is of local government as a provider of municipal services. Some "fundamental issues which lie at the heart of the urban government dilemma" have not been addressed (Taraska Report 1976: 5). The development of a policy-making role has been hindered by the inadequate fiscal basis of local government, and by the prevalence of controls operated by the provinces. These are matters which could be rectified, or at least ameliorated, by provincial action. The following discussion deals with these.

The Fiscal Problem of Local Government

"Puppets on a Shoestring"

CFMM 1976

There is an abundance of writings on the fiscal problems of local government, but the essential points are simple. The heart of the problem is the inadequacy of the property tax to meet the scale of expenditure necessitated by urbanization, the growth of public and social services, and rising demands and expectations. There are several implications, of which two are particularly important. First, policies (in relation to residential and industrial development for instance) can be heavily influenced by their fiscal consequences. Secondly, increasing financial support has been required from the provinces who in turn have exercised the controls which this necessarily involves.

So   great has this become that the Federation of Canadian Municipalities has bitterly complained that local governments have been reduced to the position of "puppets on a shoestring." The anger and frustration is apparent in the following quotation:

> ... the Tri-Level Report shows that government as a whole in Canada has generally operated in the black, on a balanced budget for the past quarter-century. The country is rich. Its public finance system produced enough money to meet public demands.
>
> Municipal government need not be in a crisis, but it is, and it is getting worse.
>
> Why? Because, as the report shows, the Canadian public finance system, which works so effectively when all three government levels are considered as a unit, is a totally inadequate system when municipal government is taken alone.
>
> While balancing handily for the three governments, the system denies municipalities access to tax revenues that would allow them to meet their responsibilities. So they *don't* meet their responsibilities. This leads to a chain of annual new debt, a spiral of dependence and increasing hopelessness. Cynicism and apathy arise in city councils and among municipal voters.

This may be a rather extreme statement, and the financial position has certainly changed since 1976, but the thrust is right. As Nowlan (1976) has pointed out, by the mid-1960s Canadian local government expenditure had come to exceed comparable spending by either the federal or the provincial governments. Of course, this huge increase could not be met by the product of the property tax: indeed, between 1950 and 1974 the proportion of local revenue covered by local sources of finance (predominantly the property tax) declined from 80 percent to 53 percent.

Nowlan rightly warns against viewing this as a fiscal crisis, akin to New York's near bankruptcy. That would be far too simple and deceptive. The basic problem is that of the narrow financial base and its implication that "the right to make municipal decisions is available to the highest bidder, with the result that political responsibility for local matters is drifting upwards." With a neat economy of words, Nowlan goes to the root of the issue. But, as he adds, after a brief but devastating commentary on Forrester-type analysis (Forrester 1969; Rothenberg 1974), "complex systems move complexly," and there is no simple solution.

However, the arena of municipal politics in which a large proportion of the Canadian population resides requires more "home rule for urban policy." This does not mean that municipalities are inherently more capable of making correct decisions than higher levels of government, but it does mean that the alternative is even less preferable:

> With the current upward drift of responsibility for urban matters we lose in two ways. First, senior levels of government are deterred from dealing aggressively with urban matters by the continuing and increasingly noisy existence of local jurisdictions; and second, to the extent that policy making is taking place at senior levels it is hampered by ill defined linkages with local communities (Nowlan 1976: 15).

Nowhere is the inadequacy clearer than in relation to planning. Not only are municipalities compelled to operate solely with the instruments provided by the provincial legislature, they are also constrained by the province's concept of planning. As is demonstrated in chapter 3, the province of Ontario has a much more limited view of this than either the City of Toronto or Metro Toronto. Moreover, the common requirement that municipal plans receive provincial approval is a further constraint, and yet another exists in Ontario with the wide powers of control exercised by the OMB (Makuch 1976: 32).

The Robarts Commission on Metropolitan Toronto argued strongly that municipalities should have "the same kind of flexibility and discretion in policy-making and implementation as the senior levels of government" (1977: 2: 102). Particularly striking (especially from a former premier of Ontario) is the recommendation that: "the legislation governing Metropolitan Toronto and its constituent municipalities be amended to provide general powers to legislate with respect to local affairs, so that within their areas of jurisdiction, councils may pass any

bylaw, so long as it does not conflict with provincial legislation" (Ibid: 103). Despite its authoritative source, there seems
little likelihood that the province would divest itself of so much
power. Nevertheless, there is undoubtedly a movement (in
Ontario at least) to give a greater degree of autonomy to municipalities, while, at the same time, defining more clearly the
proper role for the province.

The Provinces and Planning

"Father Knows Best"

O'Brien 1980a

As with all issues, there are great differences between provinces on the role played by the provincial government. This
applies not only to statutory provisions, but also to "style."
The intimate nature of provincial-municipal relations in New
Brunswick for example is quite different from that of Ontario,
where a formal Provincial-Municipal Liaison Committee has
been established (O'Brien 1980b). Some provinces have a large
operational role, as with Prince Edward Island and its Land Use
Commission. British Columbia has the more specifically focused
Agricultural Land Commission. Both Alberta and Newfoundland have provincial planning boards, but whereas the Alberta
Planning Board really operates (as an appellate review and coordinating body), the Newfoundland Provincial Planning Board
exists only on paper.

The diversity defies summary; and rightly so. The Canadian Institute of Planners' Task Force on the Planning Acts has
been severely criticized for attempting precisely this. Otis (of
the Association of Professional Community Planners of
Saskatchewan) forcefully argued:

> It is doubtful whether one can really draw any definite conclu-
> sions about common trends in recent changes or reviews to
> Canadian planning legislation ... The circumstances and plan-
> ning system in each province is different, amendments being

made in response to perceived needs and issues, and largely reflecting those people who participated in the review process.

For example, some provinces are considering introducing regional planning legislation (e.g. Saskatchewan), others are modifying their regional system (e.g. Ontario, B.C.), and still others are turning away from regional planning (e.g. Nova Scotia, New Brunswick). Similarly, in some provinces, greater centralization is occurring while in others more powers are being delegated to the local level ... Canadian planning legislation is probably as diverse as the Nation as a whole (CIP 1981).

It follows that an adequate analysis would deal separately with each of the ten provinces (plus the Northwest Territories and the Yukon). Since this is impossible within the framework of this book, it is necessary to take an illustrative approach. However, there is one typical feature which emerges from a review of recent official reviews and new planning legislation: this is the desirability of having explicit statements of provincial policy which can serve as a framework for regional and/or municipal planning. The response has not always been positive: politicians do not readily give hostages to fortune. It is far more attractive to make motherhood statements which are of such generality as to be meaningless in practice.

However, several provinces have passed legislation requiring, in spirit if not in the letter of the law, statements of provincial policy. This chapter ends with a description of the new provisions of the 1983 Ontario Planning Act.

In Ontario, a lengthy period of inquiry, consultation, draft proposals, revisions and so on, eventually culminated in the passing of a new planning act in 1983. One of the major issues at debate was the role of the provinces. The Comay committee (1977: 30) argued that while "provincial involvement in municipal planning should not go beyond formally defined provincial interests" this was not the case at the time (the mid-seventies):

The province now acts primarily in a supervisory role. It reviews almost all municipal planning decisions, and most of the important municipal planning actions (official plans, zoning, subdivision approval) are not effective until they have received provincial approval ... It should not be necessary for the province

> to approve municipal planning actions, but simply to make sure that these actions do not violate important provincial interests. We think this is an important distinction. To review in order to approve means that the minister and his staff must make sure that everything is done the way they wish it to be done; to review in order to prevent what the province considers undesirable means that the minister and his staff need only concentrate on matters of direct provincial interest and can leave the rest alone.

This was one aspect of the matter. Another was "the tendency of municipal councils to hide behind provincial coat tails, to pass on to the province the responsibility for making the difficult, nasty decisions, or to settle for easy decisions in the knowledge that the province will have the responsibility for changing those decisions." Finally, and crucially, there was the matter of defining "the provincial interest." Comay proposed four areas:

- implementation of provincial policies and programs, in economic, social and physical development; protection of the natural environment and management of natural resources; and the equitable distribution of social and economic resources;

- maintenance of the provincial financial well being;

- ensuring civil rights and natural justice in the administration of municipal planning;

- ensuring coordination of planning activities of municipalities and other public bodies, and resolving intermunicipal conflicts.

Explicitly omitted from the list was the quality of municipal planning: "the province should not be concerned with whether municipalities engage in 'good planning' but only in whether their planning actions adversely affect the defined provincial interests. Good planning should be considered a matter of local norms and standards, to be left to the municipality and its inhabitants to settle for themselves." It was recommended that official plans should be de-officialized and be made no longer subject to provincial approval.

This was too strong a dose of local autonomy for the province and it was rejected, though it was agreed that more ministerial powers of approval (e.g. of subdivision plans) could be delegated to competent municipalities (Ontario White Paper 1979a). The need for the definition of provincial interests, however, was accepted. Section 2 of the act provides:

> The minister, in carrying out his responsibilities under this Act, will have regard to, among other matters, matters of provincial interest such as
>
> (a)   the protection of the natural environment, including the agricultural resource base of the Province, and the management of natural resources;
>
> (b)   the protection of features of significant natural, architectural, historical or archeological interest;
>
> (c)   the supply, efficient use and conservation of energy;
>
> (d)   the provision of major communications, servicing and transportation facilities;
>
> (e)   the equitable distribution of educational, health and other social facilities;
>
> (f)   the coordination of planning activities of municipalities and other public bodies;
>
> (g)   the resolution of planning conflicts involving municipalities and other public bodies;
>
> (h)   the health and safety of the population; and
>
> (i)   the protection of the financial and economic well being of the province and its municipalities.

The act provides for the publication of policy statements "on matters relating to municipal planning that in the opinion of the minister are of provincial interest." (Interestingly, these policy statements are intended to affect all agencies of government, not only municipalities.) The importance of policy statements is that they provide a framework within which municipalities can plan with a clear appreciation of what the provincial policy is. Often in the past there has been doubt and confusion, not only about policy, but more widely about the provincial decision making-process.

Against the new background there should be effectively more autonomy for local government though, of course, it remains to be seen how successful, and willing, the province will be in articulating its policies. Coupled with the extension of delegated powers to competent municipalities, Ontario seems set on the road of greater autonomy for local government and a clearer and more focused role for the province.

Chapter 3
On the Nature of Urban Plans

At some stage the embarrassing question of why there are plans comes up

Comay Report 1977

As with planning, so it is with plans: the terms are used in an extraordinarily wide variety of ways. The matter is more than one of semantics: there is a spread of (sometimes passionately held) views on what plans are, or should be. The field has been a fertile one for academic writers. An eloquent illustration is Wildavsky's paper "If Planning is Everything, Maybe it's Nothing" (1973), which was followed by Alexander's "If Planning isn't Everything, Maybe it's Something" (1981). This in turn stimulated Reade's "If Planning isn't Everything ...." (1982), and "If Planning is Anything, Maybe it can be Identified" (1983).

The academic library of such works is a large one (Faludi 1973; Burchell and Sternlieb 1981), but it is considerably enlarged by the writings of practitioners, and by the reports of committees established to review particular planning systems. The Ontario review (the Comay report) noted that:

... the persons who are most intimately involved with the operation of municipal planning (municipal and provincial planners, other municipal officials, municipal councillors and planning board members, professional planning consultants and lawyers) are by and large unable to agree on any of the following matters:

- how the planning system actually works;
- how the common planning instruments (official plans, zoning, subdivision approval, consents, development review) are actually used, and how well they are suited for the uses to which they are put;
- the purposes and objectives of municipal planning;
- what should be done to improve the system or its instruments.

Interestingly, the committee found this not surprising, given "the sheer complexity" of the planning system. But the issue goes deeper than that of complexity: there are fundamentally divergent views on what planning should attempt to achieve and how it should operate. There is even disagreement as to whether a plan is a product or a process.

Much of this debate does not need to be dealt with in this volume; this is fortunate since it would otherwise have grown to an inordinate length. Strands which are relevant will be examined in appropriate detail, but firmly within the context of the planning systems which operate in Canada. The discussion in this chapter relates only to urban plans: regional planning in its various guises is dealt with at length in several later chapters.

At the outset it is important to make clear the distinction between some crucial concepts. Unfortunately this presents difficulties, not only because terms are used loosely in common language, but also because their technical meaning can vary from province to province; and they can change over time within a province. Thus, for plans, we have "master plans" (a now virtually defunct term, possibly because of its unacceptably authoritarian overtones), "official plans" (which in fact may have differing degrees of official force depending upon the stage they have reached in the approval process and the statutory provisions which relate to them), "municipal development plans," "general municipal plans," and so forth.

As we shall shortly see, the statutory definition and objectives of these variously named plans differ, but the most important initial distinction to be made is that between a plan and the instrument for the implementation of a plan. Typically this is a zoning bylaw. In principle, a plan is a generalized policy document, while the zoning bylaw provides for its implementation by way of detailed provisions relating to property rights. Thus a general municipal plan in Alberta inter alia describes "the land uses proposed for the municipality," while the former Ontario Planning Act broadly defined an official plan as "a programme and policy ... designed to secure the health, safety, convenience or welfare of the inhabitants of the area."

These plans and any subsequent more detailed plans, usually cannot be implemented until adoption by a zoning bylaw or its equivalent. Thus, conceptually there is an important distinction between planning and zoning (or a plan and a zoning bylaw). One deals with objectives and the other with implementation. Unfortunately, such clarity is seldom found in reality. Plans can be expressed in such general terms as to be virtually meaningless, and then the zoning bylaw becomes the de facto plan. Or the plan can be nothing more than a consolidated patchwork quilt of zoning bylaws. Historically, zoning has typically preceded the introduction of planning or, what amounts to the same thing, was itself considered to be planning. Places where this is still the case are not hard to find.

Part of the current situation is to be accounted for by a combination of history and inertia. (It would be tedious to qualify every statement with a comment about interprovincial differences, but the point has to be continuously borne in mind.) Much of the inertia was rudely shattered by the unprecedented postwar development pressures. Nevertheless, there are other difficulties. One is simply the difficulty of achieving consensus on the tangible objectives of a plan (Jones 1971: 190).

Another is the legal implications of adopting a plan. In most provinces, public works cannot be undertaken except in conformity to a plan. A statutory plan is, by definition, a legal document and has the inevitable inherent restrictions: for instance   "a council that wishes to permit development that conflicts with the policy of the plan is restrained and must first have recourse to the cumbersome machinery for amending the plan and the meticulous scrutiny it entails" *(Re Cadillac Development Corporation and Toronto,* 1 O.R. (2d); 39 D.L.R. (3d) 188). As a result of such factors:

> ... it is not surprising that many municipalities have shown a distinct reluctance to plan if the objective is first, or primarily, to produce and publish a master plan, rather than exercise various controls without reference to a public plan. Some municipalities in fact have back room plans of which they are very proud, but which rarely see the light of day. Sometimes these plans, without legal effect and referred to as ghost plans, are more effective than official documents; for a time at least they are a guiding document for the municipal administration (Milner 1960: 61).

Milner was writing in 1960, and it is probable that the general increase in planning activity, professionalism and public awareness has resulted in fewer ghost plans. This must be conjecture, but there are other routes to the same objective. Well known is Metro Toronto's use of the simple device of accepting, but not formally adopting a plan. Thus, instead of submitting it to the provincial government for approval, it was accepted "as a statement of the policy of the Metropolitan Corporation for the planning of future works and services, and as a guide for future development in the Metropolitan Toronto Planning Area" (Rose 1972: 133).

A paper prepared for the Ontario Planning Act Review Committee (1977b: 14) adds to the list of the inadequacies of plans in relation to the control of development:

> ... some plans concentrate on long term issues without spelling out how the community is going to get there: hence, the plans are not very relevant to current development proposals. Outdated plans naturally can serve no useful purpose at all. A major fault, which applies to the majority of plans, is the absence of any attempt to relate the plan proposals to the available public resources or to test the plans' financial feasibility. Municipal capital budgeting is usually divorced from the

preparation or implementation of the plan. Over the longer term, the notion of establishing and linking a capital improvement program to the official plan is not practiced. Consequently, one of the recognized purposes of having a plan -- to relate policies and plans to forseeable resources -- is not carried out in most municipalities and the local public works program does not necessarily follow the intent or the policies of the plan. The effect of the gap between the plan and development has further consequences. In essence, the outcome of an ineffectual plan is that policy is made, however incrementally, by the development control process.

Statutory Provision for Municipal Plans

Can man plan?

Sir Frederic Osborn 1959

This was the pre-1983 Ontario situation where, among other things, "the overwhelming generality of the Planning Act in defining the scope and function of an official plan has produced ... virtually as many interpretations of the content of such plans as there are municipalities and planning consultants" (Ontario Planning Act Review Committee 1977b: 45). The Comay committee proposed that new legislation should stipulate that plans should:

- specify the particular objectives being sought;

- indicate how the objectives are to be attained (for example, by establishing regulations, programs, or facilities); the standards or specifications to be employed; and the procedures for administering the instrument or program in question;

- establish the procedures for periodic review of the policy or program, and the basis on which a need to change the policy or program will be determined;

- establish the procedure for public information and public consultation in the particular matter.

Conspicuously absent is any reference to the content of plans, though the committee did propose that councils should "have regard for" environmental, social and economic considerations, an issue which is discussed below.

Indeed, the committee was so convinced of the virtues of municipal discretion on plan content (with the legislation simply setting the rules) that it even suggested that municipalities should be free to restrict their planning to specific issues. For this purpose planning statements were proposed. Such a break from the traditional comprehensive approach proved unacceptable to the provincial government. Though it was agreed that plans could, and do, vary according to the size and complexity of different areas, it was felt that planning could not proceed effectively on an incremental policy statement basis. A *White Paper on The Planning Act* (Ontario, 1979a: 72) stated that "the government believes that certain planning elements such as land use, transportation and population density are so interrelated, especially in major urban areas, that policy statements could not really be produced in isolation of each other. It would also be very difficult for citizens to know at any given time exactly what constituted the total plan for their municipality."

The 1983 act, after considerable debate on the extent to which social and economic matters were to be included in the statutory definition, defined an official plan as "a document approved by the minister, containing objectives and policies established primarily to provide guidance for the physical development of a municipality or a part thereof or an area that is without municipal organization, while having regard to the relevant social, economic and environmental matters." In addition, an official plan may contain a description of:

(a) the measures and procedures proposed to attain the objectives of the plan; and

(b) the measures and procedures for informing and securing the views of the public in respect of a proposed amendment to, or of a proposed revision of, the plan, or in respect of a proposed zoning bylaw.

By contrast with Ontario is Nova Scotia, where the Planning Act provides that a municipal planning strategy may include statements of policy with respect to *any or all* of a long list of items ranging from "the goals and objectives of the municipality for its future" to storm water management and any matter "relating to the physical, social or economic environment of the municipality."

The "any or all" provision would appear to provide a great deal of flexibility and to permit the type of planning statements envisaged by Comay. Unfortunately, it has not always been seen as such, and the Nova Scotia Planning Act Review Committee (1981a: 10) recommended that emphasis be laid in revised legislation on permitting municipalities "on their own initiative to prepare and adopt planning documents ranging from simple statements of policy to comprehensive development plans." It is interesting to note the rationale for this:

> If planning is to become a basic on-going function of municipal government, the Planning Act must delegate to the municipalities authority to address local planning problems in the manner they consider effective. The planning process can be incremental, beginning with the identification and resolution of one or two pressing local issues, expanding over time to become a comprehensive plan. For many municipal units this is the only way planning will succeed. The Planning Act must therefore permit municipalities to prepare and adopt plans ranging from simple statements of policy to comprehensive development plans.

> To stress the importance of the planning process and more accurately reflect the ability of the Act to accommodate a wide range of community situations and planning approaches, the name "municipal planning strategy" should be used in preference to "municipal development plan."

This was implemented in the 1983 Provincial and Municipal Planning Act.

Similarly, the Saskatchewan 1983 Planning and Development Act provides for a "basic planning statement" where a development plan is not needed. Such a statement briefly sets out the objectives and policies that will guide the future development of an area. A brochure of Saskatchewan Urban

Affairs (1984) explains that "small urban municipalities and rural municipalities not encouraging large scale development and experiencing only minor changes in land use may find a short form statement of planning policy sufficient to meet the needs of the community."

Essentially, a basic plan is a simplified development plan, the degree of simplification depending upon the local situation. Unlike a development plan, there is no statutory requirement for a capital works plan to be prepared in conjunction with it.

Quite different in approach is the Quebec Land Use Planning and Development Act which, though providing for some "optional content," has a long list of matters of "obligatory content":

(1) the general aims of land development policy for the territory of the regional county municipality;

(2) the general policies on land use for the whole territory of the regional county municipality;

(3) the delimitation of the urbanization perimeters;

(4) the identification of zones where land occupation is subject to special restrictions for reasons of public safety, such as flood zones, erosion zones, landslide zones or zones subject to other severe physical disturbances;

(5) the identification of territories that are of historical, cultural, aesthetic or ecological interest to the regional county municipality;

(6) the identification and the approximate location and, where applicable, the schedule for the setting up of public services and infrastructure which the regional county municipality considers to be intermunicipal in nature;

(7) the identification and the approximate location of the public services and infrastructure to be set up by the government, the government departments and agencies by the public bodies and school corporations;

(8)   the identification and the approximate location of the
      major electricity, gas, telecommunications and cable
      delivery networks.

Cost consciousness varies between the provinces. For
Ontario, Comay argued that financial considerations were
difficult to embrace in a plan: "it is almost impossible to project a municipality's long run financial capability except in the
most general terms, since many of the factors involved cannot
be determined in advance, for example Municipal Board constraints on future borrowing; changes in provincial and federal
grants and funding programs; the tax policies of future councils ..." (Ontario Planning Act Review Committee 1977a: 48).

On the other hand, Nova Scotia includes the finance of
municipal investments as do, for example, Manitoba and Quebec. However, the fact that financial statements may not be
required under planning legislation may simply be a matter of
history or a preference for organizing matters differently. Public investment plans may be required by other legislation. On
the other hand, such "plans" may not warrant the name; they
may merely be forecasts of annual expenditure resulting from
decisions already taken in respect of major capital investments.

There is a wide range of variation here. Less usual is a
thorough-going economic analysis of alternative planning strategies for an area. This requires a degree of sophistication
rarely attained even in the major cities. (Whether such sophistication has any validity is a quite different question!) Metropolitan Toronto's Transportation Plan Review is an exception:
but precisely because it is an exception it does not warrant
detailed exposition here. Indeed, since an excellent analysis of it
has already been made by a participant (Pill 1979) the reader
can be simply referred to this. However, it is interesting to
note in passing that it is only in relation to issues of transportation that such in-depth analyses have been made (or are possible?).

Some Illustrative Plans

Stop Me Before I Plan Again

Hedman 1977

There is an enormous range in the style, coverage and quality of plans. Thus, all that is possible is an illustration of the various types of plan, without any pretence at attempting a typology or classification. What follows is a brief account of a virtually random selection of plans. They are not selected as being representative: there is no immediate way of establishing this. They are purely illustrative of the range of plans which have been prepared across Canada.

Metro Toronto

The official plan for Metropolitan Toronto, approved in September 1981, is explicitly a plan relating to the urban structure. It is a regional plan in the sense that it provides a framework for more detailed local plans though, given the true dimensions of the Toronto Centred Region, it falls short of an adequately conceived regional plan.

The first feature which strikes the reader of this plan is its extreme brevity: it is only sixty-nine pages long, and many of these are blank interleaves. The whole plan could be reproduced on a dozen or so closely typed pages. This is of the nature of a framework plan. It is explicitly focused on the *urban structure* of the metropolitan area "which includes the coordination of the broad distribution of population, households and employment activities, and the coordination and phasing of ... the metropolitan transit system; the metropolitan road system and the rights-of-way of that system; the water supply and sewerage treatment facilities; and the metropolitan open space system."

The basic policy in relation to the urban structure is set out in these terms:

It has been concluded that, as the population and employment grew, the existing urban structure of the Planning Area, especially the concentration of office employment, services and amenities in the central area, will be less adequate to meet the needs of the people of Metropolitan Toronto. The social and environmental impacts inherent in a continued reliance on a centrally oriented urban structure are no longer acceptable. It is necessary, therefore, to commence the long term task of modifying the present structure.

The primary goal of the plan, therefore, is to create an urban structure: that can accommodate and encourage future growth and change while minimizing adverse social and environmental impacts; that broadens and enriches the economic and social base of the suburban communities; and that can be achieved at the least possible cost in terms of investment in physical facilities and the attendant operating expenditures.

These broad policy objectives are fleshed out, though not in any detail, in subsequent pages of the plan. Several interesting aspects can be selected for note. First, despite the limitations of the legislation, there is considerable emphasis on human services, though necessarily constrained: "it is an objective of the council to foster the development of a social environment that will enhance the state of well-being and the quality of life for residents of the municipality and to pursue human services policies that will meet people's changing needs and promote and maintain a healthy community in keeping with the economic resources of the municipality. Such policies shall not, however, form part of the official plan."

From the many other interesting features of the Metropolitan Toronto Plan, one final selection can be made. This relates to low income housing. The fundamental problem here is that of location. (There are many who oppose such housing in principle: there are far more who would oppose a particular development close to where they happen to live.) In a Solomon-type judgment, the metropolitan policy is that "council, in consultation with the area municipalities, shall allocate an assisted housing production target to each area municipality on the basis of the principle of fair share. The fair share principle means that each area municipality should eventually have the same ratio of low income assisted households to its total households."

Charlottetown, Prince Edward Island

Charlottetown is a long way from Toronto, in more than one sense. Its problems are different, though not necessarily less intractable, and *The Charlottetown Plan* (1980) is correspondingly different. It is conceived in these terms:

> In order to further the development of an orderly, economic and attractive urban pattern, a planning area is divided into groups of complementary land uses having related functions which do not ordinarily interface with each other, constitute mutual nuisances or hamper each other's activities.

> One intent of the plan is to guide development into these land use groups, thereby separating activities that have conflicting requirements and functions and distributing recreation, shopping and working areas within a reasonable distance of the major residential sections.

The provisions of the plan, however, go wider than this opening statement might suggest. Of particular importance, however, is the revitalization of the central commercial area, "thereby making this area a dominant feature of the region." It is hoped that this "will induce the improvement of the housing situation in the downtown, and the creation and improvement of commercial outlets." The result will be to increase taxable assessment, encourage a fuller use of the infrastructure (for which "the city has paid"), and to "help create a positive image of the city" to the benefit of both residents and visitors.

A parking authority has been established to assist with the city's difficult parking problems, and the plan proposes an expansion of the existing land assembly program for parking and redevelopment purposes. A number of development opportunities for private and public investment in the downtown area were identified in a commissioned study and a Charlottetown Area Development Corporation was formed to elaborate and where possible to implement the strategy proposed.

Under the subheading "cause for concern," the plan notes the "significant development of new commercial space outside the central commercial area" and the lack of demand to support both peripheral and central developments. Traffic congestion and inadequate parking provision in the central area is identified as a major shortcoming of policy.

Other parts of the plan deal with residential development (including the major objective of encouraging this in the downtown area); parkland ("a beautiful city will attract more tourists and produce beneficial effects upon the city's economy"); industrial development ("there are few potentially suitable industrial sites in the city to accommodate industrial development and thereby assist in providing a more balanced tax base for the city"); the university, the college and the schools; design and amenity; transportation; and so forth.

Fox Creek New Town, Alberta

Toronto is self-assured, Charlottetown is attempting to wrestle with the problems of stagnation if not decline; but our third illustration is of a place unknown outside Alberta (and not so well known inside): Fox Creek is difficult to find in any atlas. Yet its problems are not untypical of frontier towns. Its raison d'etre is described in its general municipal plan as being related to the "harvesting of its timber resources ... in conjunction with coal, oil and gas developments in the region ..."

It is thus a Canadian resource town, of which there are many, with indeterminate future lives (and deaths). Earlier pioneers would have thought more in terms of rape than of a plan, had they thought at all. Modern resource communities (Pressman 1975), however, have at the least a consultant's report, and at best a fully considered plan for their development (and possible demise).

The plan for Fox Creek is a short (twenty-eight pages), crisp, business-like document prepared by the Alberta Department of Municipal Affairs (1980b) as "essentially an action plan." It is intended to provide a framework in which public and private decisions can be made; actions and policies to direct the present and future development of the town; and guidance in the implementation of a land use bylaw. It deals with residential, industrial, and recreation land use; the provision of public buildings, senior citizen housing and the town maintenance yard; transportation and utilities. For each of these there are five columns indicating action. Under a sub-heading of "hospital," for example, the plan states:

Action Now: Provide Lot 9, Block 34, as site for new hospital building

Exploration/Research: Consult with Alberta Hospitals and Medical Care regarding facility design functions, project timing etc before construction start

Future Action: Service site and start construction of hospital by June 30, 1981

Contingency Plans: Maintain existing medical care until the hospital constructed

Related Policies: To reduce servicing costs, residential lots north of 8th Ave and east of 3rd St will be developed at the same time as the hospital

Cambridge, Ontario

It is, of course, easier to give a flavour of a short plan than it is of a long plan. Thus the 185-page official plan for the city of Cambridge (1982) cannot be fully detailed, but it has a number of interesting features which are well worth highlighting. First it has an elaborated series of goals which are collectively termed the "general development concept."

Goal 1   The conservation principle
Goal 2   Housing strategy
Goal 3   Economic development strategy
Goal 4   City center development strategy
Goal 5   Social development strategy

The "conservation principle" includes the development of areas which are already serviced prior to the establishment of new development areas; the preservation of prime foodland;

the protection of natural resources; and so on. It is stressed that this principle of conservation is the dominant theme of the plan, though the full statement appears to aim for the advantages of all worlds: "the principle of conservation, together with the provision of ample lands to provide a choice of areas for new residential and industrial development and accommodate other land uses not foreseen in 1981, is the dominant theme of this plan." This attempt to maximize benefits even at the cost of apparent contradiction is also to be seen in the social development strategy where support is expressed for "the continued development of the city's social unity and cultural diversity." Such paradoxes are not unusual in statements of goals: the crunch comes in the policies which are designed to give effect to them.

This leads to a second interesting feature of the Cambridge plan: its long and detailed set of "general development policies." These deal with housing; social development; energy conservation; community improvement, renewal and revitalization; heritage conservation; environmental protection and safety; underground utilities; pits and quarries; urban development phasing; and major transportation facilities.

Finally there are nine land use policies relating, for example, to residential development, the city center, industrial and commercial uses, open space, and foodlands.

The way in which the plan moves from goals to general development policies and then to land use policies can be illustrated by reference to public transport. Flowing from the conservation principle, a general development policy in relation to public transit is established:

> It is the policy of the council to encourage reductions in the amount of fuel used for intracity travel and in the need for increasing major road capacity by providing a regularly scheduled public transit service within the city limits to facilitate the extensive use of public transit for the journey to work, shopping trips, and trips to major recreational attractions and other centers of activity in the city.

Among the land use policies which stem from this is that of giving density bonuses where these can be expected to encourage the increased use of public transport.

Prince Albert, Saskatchewan

Prince Albert is a city of some 30,000 people in the north of Saskatchewan. Its plan has evolved over a long period of time by way of a succession of studies. These, together with council decisions on particular issues, added up to a set of planning policies. In 1982, against the background of optimism on the benefits to flow from the development of northern resources, it was decided that "good planning is essential to ensure that these benefits are utilized in the most efficient and advantageous manner." The outcome was a municipal plan consisting of four documents: a Background Statement of basic data on the city; a five-year Capital Budget for major capital expenditures; and a Zoning Bylaw to implement policies set out in a Policy Plan.

The policy plan aims "to incorporate all relevant working policies into one document to provide a comprehensive and unified guide to development decisions." The attempt is explicitly made to "strike a balance between being sufficiently general to allow administrative flexibility and being sufficiently specific to prevent misinterpretation and to provide control."

Of the wide range of policies outlined in the plan, four are chosen for inclusion here: housing, shopping centers, industrial beautification and land assembly.

The policy relating to housing states that "where feasible and acceptable, the city shall encourage a mix of housing types and styles in residential areas with a view toward affording all individuals and families of all income levels the opportunity to exercise their housing accommodation preferences." The objective here is to ensure not only a variety of housing types in each residential area, but a distribution of public housing throughout the city. "The policy can be implemented primarily through subdivision design and the subdivision approval process."

Peripheral shopping centers are a worry to many towns, in that they pose a threat to the viability of the traditional central shopping and commercial area. As with Charlottetown, Prince Albert has devised a policy of attempting to steer new development into the center: "no additional peripheral shopping centers shall be permitted except in or near the central business district, unless it can be demonstrated clearly that such development will not have an unfavorable impact upon the viability of the central business district."

The industrial beautification policy is implemented through landscaping provisions in the zoning bylaw and by requiring the dedication of buffer areas for landscaping in subdivisions. The land assembly policy is a positive one which aims at "purchasing and assembling land for all purposes and uses on a regular basis sufficiently in advance of demand so as to meet the needs identified in this policy plan."

It's Our Neighbourhood: A Community's Own Plan

Planning involves professional expertise, but if it is to be politically acceptable, it has to have an adequate degree of public input. In the next section an account is given of a Vancouver area plan in which the local citizenry played a large positive role. Here an outline is given of a more unusual plan: one prepared by a local community in the central area of Regina, the Cathedral Area Community Association.

Unlike a typical plan, this one has no maps and no statistics. It has some telling cartoons and many signatures (from shopkeepers and churchmen as well as from tenants). The plan discusses the many community strengths and the needs "which are not presently being met ... [including those of] senior citizens, adolescents, families and native people."

Though there is an emphasis on social service provision, there are also recommendations concerning the enforcement of municipal bylaws (in relation to land use), the improvement of municipal services (water supplies, sidewalks, curbs, street cleaning, etc), the improvement of the existing housing stock, the control of traffic and parking, the development of recreational facilities, and so forth.

This eloquent plan (of less than thirty pages in length) was submitted to the city of Regina in January 1979 with a request "that it be carefully considered, and that it be adopted by Council as a bylaw to guide the implementation of a neighborhood revitalization plan." It was approved almost unchanged, and was formally adopted as an appendix to the municipal plan. Since then the policy positions espoused in the plan have, by and large, been used as guidelines for development in the neighborhood. The Cathedral Area Community Association remains active and is intimately involved in the planning process.

Similar plans have been produced by other community groups (Regina City 1979b and 1980).

A Vancouver Area Plan: Marpole

Vancouver has "well tried techniques for local planning ... which involve a planner and staff interacting with a Citizen's Advisory Committee, often from a site office" (Vancouver City 1981: 17). One such plan was *The Marpole Plan,* completed in 1979. An appendix to this plan sets out terms of reference and constitution of the Marpole Citizens' Planning Committee. It is worth quoting from this at some length.

> The purposes of the planning program are:
>
> (a)   to prepare a comprehensive plan for Marpole. The contents of the plan are to be determined as part of the planning program; and
>
> (b)   to make recommendations representing local citizens' views on other matters of concern in the area, including zoning and land use, development permits, social and recreational facilities, open space, traffic, parking, housing, changes in social mix and policy development to deal with these and similar issues.

The role of the planning committee is an advisory one, but "City Council should endorse the planning committee as representing the views of Marpole residents on planning matters." The council, however, has the responsibility for the final decisions.

The problem of representativeness is dealt with in three ways. First, membership of the committee is open to anyone living, owning property or working in the area "who shows an interest in the program and is willing to work on the planning committee." (There are rules relating to minimum attendance.) Secondly, all meetings are open to the public and "anyone present shall be entitled to state his or her opinion." Thirdly, the committee is specifically charged "to ascertain the opinions of Marpole residents at an early stage and throughout the planning process through whatever means will best achieve this end and to publicize its decisions and recommendations within the community. It should not be only the majority view which is made known ... The committee should make every effort to ensure that minority viewpoints are presented accurately and effectively."

The planning committee continues in operation until the program is completed. The Marpole program was initiated in October 1977 and the resultant plan was approved, almost in its entirety, in October 1979. The introduction to the plan comments:

> The people of Marpole have responded positively. Attendance of some 350 citizens at an introductory meeting in March 1978 and subsequent interest in the form of a large advisory planning committee and numerous subcommittees has proven that people are excited about being involved in policy-setting for their own community. A satisfying relationship between citizens and staff has led to the development of a comprehensive set of policies covering most things which affect the quality of life in Marpole.

The seventy-page report deals in detail with the problems of the area and its 17,000 inhabitants: parks, recreation and community facilities; housing; traffic and transportation, commercial areas, and industrial areas. In total, fifty-one recommendations are made. These include the provision of parkland adjacent to the river front; increased recreational provision, improvement in the maintenance of rental housing, better design   and quality of new development;   development of a rapid transit line; pedestrianization and beautification of a central commercial area;   and better parking provision.   The list may give the misleading impression of a desire for large scale change.   In fact, "there are no recommendations for major changes of the overall land use pattern in Marpole."

The community input to the Marpole plan was very large, but it also made considerable demands on the time of the city planning staff.   How much can be afforded for such a lengthy task in relation to every community in the city?   There is no easy answer to this, as is illustrated by the city's experience in 1978 when it experimented, in the Shaughnessy Area Program, by providing a planner for only half-time.   "At the end of 1979, the community had become frustrated by not having enough time with the planner, and yet having him press for the completion of the plan.   In turn, the planner was frustrated by not being able to spend the time needed and not being able to meet the target date set for completion" (1980: 7).

This raises some interesting issues which are discussed later in the wider context of public participation.

A Recreation Master Plan

In Alberta, recreation master plans are normally required as a condition for grant aid under the province's Major Cultural Recreational Facilities Development Program.   One example of such a plan is that prepared by the Calgary Regional Planning Commission (1981) for Three Hills and District.   The master plan objectives were:

(1)   to assess the current provision of recreation and cultural facilities and programs to determine future requirements based upon a reasonable projection of perceived community park and recreation needs;

(2)   to ensure coordination of all community and recreation service organizations to best meet the stated requirements of all citizens of Three Hills and District; and

(3)   to assess the current financing of recreation programs and facilities and project future expenditures and revenues based upon anticipated facility and organization requirements, current expenditure patterns, and available funding sources.

The plan includes an inventory of existing recreational provision, an analysis of a social survey undertaken to establish the use of facilities and the likely demand for additional provision, and a comparative statement of "facility development options." The last was an innovative attempt to provide a means of comparing options by using five factors: capital cost, maintenance cost, "questionnaire demand," seasonal/year round use, and age group (measuring what proportion of the population would use each facility). Final weightings to each of the facilities was reserved to the recreational authority, but the preliminary ranking was as follows:

> Improved park facilities
> Additional tennis courts
> Trampolines
> Ball parks
> Upgraded library facilities
> Improvements to existing pool
> Additional playgrounds
> Larger museum
> Outdoor skating rink
> Additional camping facilities

The report is a most interesting one which rises above the all too common platitudes which abound in the field of recreational planning.

Social and Economic Issues in Plans

It is necessary ... that municipalities sort out their social and economic priorities

Comay Report 1977

Social Content of Plans

The degree to which plans contain, or are statutorily permitted to contain, social content varies. Reference has already been made to the Ontario debate and the reference to human services in the Metro Toronto Plan. It is worth examining this further. The Metro Toronto statement concerning its objective "to foster the development of a social environment" (previously quoted) was drafted to meet the objections of the Ministry of Housing to the original version. This read:

> Metropolitan Council recognizes the essential linkage between physical and social planning to ensure that a wide range of human services are provided to the residents of Metropolitan Toronto as an integral component of physical development. Metropolitan Council will ensure that a human services plan is developed through a mechanism which provides for close collaboration between Metropolitan Toronto, the area municipalities, private and voluntary agencies, and the provincial government.

Though Metro considered that it was important to stress "the interrelationship of physical and social planning in the official plan policy and to identify a broad consultative process," the ministry held that this was going beyond the proper limits of an official plan.

The point may appear to be a small one, but it represents the tip of an iceberg. The underlying issue is that of the extent to which municipalities can, and should, be involved in social planning. This in turn raises questions of local autonomy, or at least municipal-provincial relationships; of public participation and neighborhood politics; and a range of politically sensitive matters such as the location of low income housing and group homes. More fundamentally, it touches on difficult problems of social organization, social control and social structure. Supporters of social planning range from those who are concerned to see an improvement in services such as day care to those who hanker after a major reorganization of society.

It is partly because of a fear that social planning could lead into treacherous political areas that it encounters resistance. There is little disagreement that social (and economic) issues are important, and that plans should take them into account: the unresolved issue is one of degree and practicability. "Radical social change" is a long way from "social service delivery."

Canada has not had community development programs similar to those of the U.S. and Britain (which, generally, have been a disappointing failure), and it has lacked the soul-searching debates on the need, or otherwise, for drastic social change, and how this might, or might not, be effected. Yet the increasing relative importance of social services (Lang 1974) and the increasing awareness of the importance of the social impact of planning policies have brought to the forefront of debate the question of the social content of plans.

The Robarts report on Metropolitan Toronto and the Comay report on the Ontario planning act take opposite sides on the issue. Robarts confidently stated that:

In the commission's view, the official plan is an appropriate vehicle for the formal expression of Metro's broad human services objectives ... It must be recognized, however, that many elements of planning regarding the human services are insufficiently sophisticated or generally accepted to permit inclusion of many detailed objectives in the plan.

Where the human services have a physical dimension, such as buildings or open space, objectives and standards for these should be included in the plan. For example, many human services require physical facilities which must be approved through the local zoning process. Should local zoning powers be exercised to discourage the location of an equitable share of such services in any Metro municipality, Metro Council could launch an objection to be heard by the Ontario Municipal Board on the grounds that refusal to provide the zoning contravened a stated policy in the metropolitan plan. This arrangement should go far to solving the problem of distributing more equitably throughout the metropolitan area such needed facilities as day care, assisted family housing, and group homes (Robarts Report 1977: 2: 302).

The Comay report, though largely concerned with the process rather than the substance of planning, argued the contrary case:

The planning tools for securing social or economic objectives are mainly controls on physical development and the provision of public services and facilities. In using these tools, municipalities should be obligated to have regard for the relevant social and economic considerations, and to take account of the likely social and economic consequences of their use ... But if the number of matters to which regard is to be had is not limited in some way, a municipality may well end up immobile, since economic and/or social considerations can be expected to conflict in some degree with each other.

It is necessary, therefore, that municipalities sort out their social and economic priorities. They should be expected to identify those social and economic concerns that are particularly important, and to establish how conflicting concerns will be reconciled. They should also be expected to determine whether there will be conflicting social and economic consequences from the proposed actions. We recommend these considerations as a reasonable constraint on the incorporation of social and economic objectives in the municipal planning process (Comay Report 1977: 47).

There are several points here worth examining. For instance, the statement regarding the conflict which arises with many economic and social considerations is a surprising one: if planning were to be restricted to issues which did not conflict in some degree with each other, there would be little content to it. Indeed, in a real sense, planning is an attempt to achieve a sensible and acceptable compromise to conflicts.

There is, of course, a problem of determining where one kind of planning ends and another begins, but the social and economic content of physical planning is far too crucial to be subject to arbitrary constraints. Unless planning is to be equated narrowly with building codes, there is no escape from the problem. The committee may be right in its contention that social and economic strategies are speculative, but is not all planning?

Curiously, Comay made a particular issue of one aspect of housing policy: as "a matter of provincial policy" municipalities should not, in his view, "be allowed to engage in exclusionary or socially-restricted housing practices." This was considered to be so important that an amendment to the act was proposed to make it illegal. The implication is that municipalities should have a housing policy and, since this is not to be exclusionary, it implies a positive policy. This, however, is more than a matter of zoning or density: the municipalities have to be concerned with the supply of land and services, with housing costs, and a wide range of related matters. An earlier "Comay Report," the *Report of the Advisory Task Force on Housing Policy* (1973) spelled out in detail what was involved. The list is a long one and included, in addition to land matters, the direct provision of public housing; housing assistance; housing for native people, handicapped persons, students and so on; supporting services and facilities; rehabilitation; mobile homes; home purchase protection; rent control; and condominiums. These are all important aspects of housing policy, of which zoning is simply another. The inter-locking web of issues makes the housing problem a complex one. Of course, not all the issues are within the control or responsibility of municipalities, but it is at the municipal level that action, or inaction, takes place. (People live locally not provincially.) Municipal housing policy has to cope with all the issues and articulate them in the local housing context. Zoning cannot be abstracted from the whole: it is merely one of many instruments of policy.

But the matter goes still further. Even if the land is forthcoming through planning policy, and even if housing is affordable by reason of housing policy, there remain issues such as the location of low income housing in relation to the job market and to transport facilities.

The Comay committee did not discuss substantive issues such as these, and it could be that the particular importance attached to restrictive housing policy was not unrelated to the fact that two of the three members of the committee had been involved in the earlier housing task force. One senses that the committee felt that once planning authorities became involved in a broad range of social issues they could easily lose themselves in either rhetoric or incompetence.

The issue of competence is an important one. Many of the issues which are labelled social or economic are not controllable by, or even the nominal responsibility of, municipalities. They cannot control the local job market, still less the economy; they do not administer health services; they have little direct influence on income distribution; and even where they do have some relevant responsibility it is limited, shared with other (typically more powerful) agencies, and subject to different legislation. Nothing would be easier than to concoct a plan embracing all human activity: but this would be for prayer not for operation.

Yet none of this is an argument for not permitting the municipal planning machine to do as much as it can to further social and economic objectives. On the contrary, if it attempts to limit itself to physical factors it will fail. Comay may be right in stressing the limited role of a municipality in a complex society, but it is not powerless: it is one of many actors on the political stage. And once it is admitted that planning is a political process it must also be admitted that it is social and economic as well (Hitchcock and Kjellberg 1980). As the electorate has shown in recent years, social and economic issues can be of greater import than physical or aesthetic ones.

There are, of course, wider issues of the relationship between urban and regional planning and municipal corporate planning. These issues are in the forefront of British debate, with new style policy plans, corporate plans, as well as regional reports, financial plans and structure plans, and they may well be emerging into the Ontario arena (MacDonald and MacLeod 1978). Robarts acknowledged this in proposing that "while the scope of local planning will necessarily be heavily oriented to land use questions, nothing should prevent an area municipality from using its planning process to develop and enunciate broader community goals and policies" (Robarts Report 1977: 2:225). Indeed, within the current framework, planning policy provides the only mechanism for bringing together and attempting to coordinate the whole range of a municipality's activities. It may not be the best way, and eventually it may give way to some other type of planning, but at present it is all that there is to hand.

Economic Content of Plans

In the Ontario debate on the social content of plans, little distinction was made between the social and the economic. Moreover, legislative provisions tend to associate the two together. Thus the Saskatchewan Planning Act provides that a municipal development shall include "the plans and supporting material defining the future physical, social and economic development of the municipality." The Nova Scotia Act provides for the inclusion in a municipal planning strategy of any matter "relating to the physical, social or economic development of the municipality." (The close similarity of the wording of planning provisions in different provinces is not uncommon.) New Brunswick goes slightly further in requiring "studies of the economy, finances, resources, population, land use, transportation facilities, municipal facilities and services, and any other matter related to the present or future economic, social or physical conditions of the municipality."

The actual economic content of municipal plans, however, is typically very limited. So far as industry is concerned, the municipal development plan for Dartmouth expresses the essential points succinctly: "while Dartmouth cannot control the growth or the location of industry within the metro area, it can encourage new firms to locate here. In addition, the city can take steps to insure that new industry is located where it will cause the least disturbance to residential areas" (Dartmouth City 1978: 31). The provision of serviced sites, and access to them, together with environmental controls is the normal limit of municipal action (and, indeed, power).

Thus, the municipal plan for the city of Fredericton sets out the objectives for industrial development as being to attract industries to the area which are compatible with the community's environment and which will keep industrial pollution within acceptable levels; and to provide adequate land at suitable locations and costs for the full development of secondary industry in the city.

Commercial development is usually treated in a similar way, though there may be a special emphasis (as in the Fredericton plan) on maintaining "the traditional position of the central business district as the prime center for specialized and comparison shopping and office accommodation in the Fredericton region." Suburban shopping centers located beyond the city limits and subject to control (if any) by a different planning authority can make such a policy difficult to implement. This is the classic case for a metropolitan or regional planning machinery in large spread-out urban areas.

Aesthetic quality can also be included in the context of commercial development. To quote Fredericton again, there are specific policies in the central business district for "encouragement of Norwich-type schemes for coordinated renovation of storefronts, cleaning and sandblasting public buildings, removal of ugly wires and signs, and incorporation of street furniture such as benches, attractive garbage receptacles and potted trees and flowers; the preservation of the 'human scale' in terms of the relationship of building heights to the spaces around them; and the establishment of sculptures or fountains to enhance public buildings, parks and landmarks ..." (The reference to "Norwich-type" schemes refers to the historic city of Norwich in England, which was a pioneer in beautifying old shopping streets, closing them to traffic and, with cooperation from owners, maintaining a high degree of aesthetic control.)

There are, of course, programs and policies outside the municipal planning system which are addressed to the problems of downtown areas, such as the Ontario Business Improvement Area Program (Ontario Ministry of Housing 1976 and 1979) and the Saskatchewan Main Street Development Program

(Saskatchewan 1978). More broadly, there is the multiplicity of industrial development boards which tend to operate over a regional or subregional level, though some of the larger cities have attempted to incorporate at least some reference to economic development policies in their official plans.

Socio Economic Planning and Land Use Planning

The increased concern for social issues in the 1970s and for economic issues in the 1980s have considerably widened the horizons of those concerned with land use planning. The extent to which this has widened land use planning itself varies greatly across the country. Perhaps the biggest impact has been on the extent to which planning has embraced public participation: a matter which has not been dealt with in this account but is deferred for separate discussion in chapter 11. As we shall see, the result has sometimes been an increased humility in the face of ignorance about the likely consequences of planning policies and about the unknowable aspects of the future. On the other hand, it has sometimes led to exaggerated hopes as to what can be achieved by "good planning": naturally disillusionment has followed.

Nevertheless, planning has generally become more sensitive to social and economic issues, and there can be no denying the importance of attempting to elaborate, to secure broad agreement for, and to operationalize social and economic objectives. Though the task is a difficult (and never-ending) one, and may frequently abort (as did the federal government's attempt to devise an urban policy), it is of the nature of a democratic society that continual attempts be made to promote greater social and economic justice. Yet, by their nature, the outcomes of such debates can be incorporated in a physical planning document only to a limited extent. It may be that more could be done in a corporate plan or a municipal policy plan, or even a social development plan but the operational policies would still need to be devised for the specific plans for education and social services (or for human services), for employment, for income distribution, and so on, as well as for physical development.

Chapter 4
The Instruments of Planning

The Village of Lakefield Ontario, passed noise abatement legislation permitting birds to sing for thirty minutes during the day and fifteen minutes at night

Peter 1984

Canada displays a wealth, if not a confusion, of instruments for the implementation of planning policies or controls. These range from traditional zoning bylaws to flexible development agreements, and from standard subdivision controls to the transfer of air rights. In this chapter the main instruments are examined with selected illustrations from the different provinces.

Zoning

Zoning is the little guy's protection

Munro 1980

As is well known, the first famous (or infamous) use of the technique of zoning was aimed at discriminating against Chinese immigrants to California. Overt methods of discrimination having been held to be unconstitutional, San Francisco devised the simple alternative of excluding laundries from large areas: these were not only an obvious nuisance and fire risk, but they also happened to be Chinese. Similarly the city of Modesto in 1885 ordained that: "it shall be unlawful for any person to establish, maintain, or carry on the business of a public laundry or wash house where articles are washed or cleansed for hire, within the city of Modesto, except that part of the city which lies west of the railroad track and south of G street." As Delafons comments, the "wrong side" of the tracks was thus given statutory definition in the earliest land use controls (1969: 20).

Modern zoning, however, is generally regarded as having started with the 1916 New York ordinance which was the outcome of a land use battle on Fifth Avenue. In Toll's words, this was a double war: "garment manufacturers fighting retail merchants fighting wealthy residents. The entire conflict was much closer in spirit to social Darwinism than to the Geneva Convention. There were no rules and only one objective, survival by any means" (Toll 1969). The outcome was a comprehensive zoning ordinance which included the mapping of zones according to permitted uses. This was in no sense a plan: such planning as there was had an independent, and largely ineffective, existence.

Population growth and urban development were slower in Canada and there was less pressure for zoning controls. Nevertheless, all the provinces eventually passed legislation empowering municipalities to operate zoning controls. The support for these came from the enfranchised property owners who dominated municipal politics. Van Nus (1979: 237) writes that "the principal basis of political support for zoning was the desire to prohibit the intrusion of uses which could reduce neighboring property values. When they set out to sell zoning to the public, planners appealed above all to the determination to maintain property values. They pitched this appeal in particular to real estate interests."

The essential characteristic of zoning is that it is narrowly concerned with the determination and separation of land uses. Initially based on the premise that separation of uses would protect property values, it focuses on the physical use of individual pieces of land rather than on the functions performed by these uses and their inter relationships. It is thus not an appropriate tool for providing for changing conditions (e.g. increases in housing demand from non family households leading to pressures for physical change and increase in density) or for controlling development in the interests of non-local factors, such as traffic flows or the preservation of aesthetic views.

These planning matters have been superimposed on the zoning system with varying degrees of success. This has constituted an attempt to adapt the static concept of zoning to the realities of urban dynamics (Makuch 1973: 297). At the extreme, zoning could be a straitjacket, but its worst effects have been mitigated by two factors. First, zoning ordinances only gradually spread across Canadian cities. Secondly, ways were increasingly found of giving some flexibility to this inherently inflexible instrument.

At the end of the second world war, zoning in Canada existed not as a means of implementing plans but as a legacy of the law of nuisance. Yet statutory planning went much further in words: "to the control of land use in the interests of health, safety, convenience, morals and general well-being." In a 1949 report commissioned by CMHC, Spence-Sales argued that this newer "theory of zoning as an instrument for achieving wide planning purposes" had taken the place of "the theory of zoning as a device for the prevention of nuisance ... A concept of zoning which concentrated mainly upon the fixity of land values by preventing change in the established usages within an area, and regards all such changes as in the nature of nuisances, vitiates the scope and tenor of the purposes of zoning control as a means for attaining a planned use of land as a whole" (1949: 78).

Here Spence-Sales was arguing against the bias in favor of the maintenance of property values which was so widespread in the Canadian provinces and which, indeed, had been hallowed in the Model Zoning Bylaw published by the National Research Council in 1939. His view was that "zoning requires to be looked upon as one of the most important instruments in the implementation of an operative planning scheme, whereby a flexible control is maintained over the constantly changing pattern of urban development."

The notion of flexibility, of course, was foreign to the original concepts of zoning. Indeed, the essence of zoning had been the certainty which it had provided for land owners. This was equally the case in Britain and the United States, though the two countries had attempted to deal in different ways with the consequential difficulties. In Britain, the 1932 planning act had provided for planning schemes which, in effect, were zoning plans. However, "most schemes in fact did little more than accept and ratify existing trends of development, since any attempt at a more radical solution would have involved the planning authority in compensation they could not afford to pay. In most cases the zones were so widely drawn as to place hardly more restriction on the developer than if there had been no scheme at all. Indeed, in the half of the country covered by draft planning schemes in 1937 there was sufficient land zoned for housing to accommodate 300 million people" (Cullingworth 1985: 5).

This was tantamount to resolving the issue by ignoring it. In effect, all that a British scheme did was to ensure that if development did take place in a particular area it would be controlled in certain ways. But the controls were weak and, given the extensive areas of land covered, ineffective. Flexibility was therefore not an issue.

The United States differed from Britain in having a written constitution. A consequence of this was that zoning ordinances had to be elaborated in such a way as to meet constitutional requirements. This involved a degree of particularity and detail which made flexibility most difficult to attain.

However, flexibility could be achieved by a different route, namely by the so-called variance granted by an appeal or adjustment body. The United States 1923 Standard State Zoning Enabling Act, published by the United States Department of Commerce, and widely adopted, described the variance device in these words:

> The board of adjustment shall have the following powers ... to authorize upon appeal in specific cases such variances from the terms of the ordinance as will not be contrary to the public

interest, where, owing to special conditions, a literal enforcement of the provisions of the ordinance will result in unnecessary hardship, and so that the spirit of the ordinance shall be observed and substantial justice done (Babcock 1966: 7).

Given the slow rate of urban development in Canada and the limited use of zoning up to this time, (as well as more subtle matters such as the less litigious nature of Canadians), the variance device seems to have worked more smoothly than was the case in the United States. The particularity issue was very different:

In the case of the technicalities underlying zoning, one of the most critical factors in nullifying the elastic legal basis upon which Canadian planning law is established has, to a very large extent, been frustrated by the particularity of zoning techniques which have been borrowed from American precedents ... The adoption of American zoning techniques in the provinces of Canada raises the important question of their suitability in a country which may have certain similarities in its urban developments, but in which the legal basis for planning is of a different order (Spence-Sales 1949: 83).

Nevertheless, since there was seldom a master plan or any kind of planning policy framework, changes could be made easily simply by amending zoning bylaws. Hulchanski comments that in Edmonton, "the zoning bylaw could be amended from time to time on most any grounds. There was no set of criteria for judging amendments. Either they were approved or they were not. And most applications for amendment were approved. The city did not want to do anything that would discourage development, especially during the depression. Between 1933 and 1945 the zoning bylaw was amended 27 times" (Hulchanski 1981: 42).

There is a burgeoning literature on Canadian urban history, encompassing both zoning and planning (Artibise; Stelter: various dates), but unfortunately most of this stops around the end of the first world war. In fact the period up to the end of the second world war in Canada was not an eventful one for planning (Gerecke 1976). In Humphrey Carver's words (1960: 2):

> In both the U.S. and in Britain the foundations of present plan-
> ning ideas and methods was laid down during the period
> between the two wars. In Canada this did not happen. For us
> the economic Depression of the thirties was a vacuum and a
> complete break with the past. We had no Frederick Osborns,
> Abercrombies and Clarence Steins. We had no public housing
> programs and none of the adventurous social experiments of the
> New Deal ... So in 1946 we almost literally started from
> scratch with no plans or planners and we immediately hit a
> period of tremendous city growth.

There was inevitably a period of improvisation as provinces battled with inadequacies both in staffing and in legislative tools. Most provinces amended their planning acts, though
Ontario, Prince Edward Island and Saskatchewan introduced
new legislation. The staff shortage was met by the import of
planners from Britain and Europe, thus increasing the British
influence on Canadian planning thought (Ibid: 3). The history
of the evolution of the instruments (and the policies) of planning since that time reflects a continuous tug of war between
what might be termed the firm zoning and the discretionary
control philosophies of development control. The general trend
has been from the former to the latter, though there is still considerable adherence, in theory less so than in practice, to the
view that the certainty of zoning is superior to the uncertainty
of any discretionary system. As we shall see, some provinces
have achieved an extraordinary marriage of the two.

The Nature of the Zoning Power

A zoning bylaw typically classifies areas or zones according
to defined restricted uses and also regulates those uses. Thus
the City of St John's zoning bylaw has thirty-five zones including the following:

Residential

Residential-Special	R A
Residential-Low Density	R 1
Residential-Medium Density	R 2
Residential-High Density	R 3
Residential-Downtown	R D

Apartments and Mixed Use

Apartment-Special	A A
Apartment-Low Density	A 1
Apartment-Medium Density	A 2
Apartment-High Density	A 3
Residential-Mixed 1	RM 1
Residential-Mixed 2	RM 2

Commercial

Commercial-Neighborhood	CN
Commercial-Office	CO
Commercial-Highway	CH
Commercial-Industrial	CI
Commercial-Regional	CR
Commercial Central-Retail	CCR
Commercial Central-Office	CCO
Commercial Central-Mixed	CCM

Industrial

Industrial General	IG
Industrial Special	IS

Public

Institutional	I
Open Space	O
Open Space Reserve	OR

Some forty pages of general provisions deal with such matters as control of development (e.g. precluding development which is "premature by reason of the site lacking adequate road access, power, drainage, sanitary facilities, or domestic water supply"); a zoning appeal board; non-conforming uses; and temporary structures. This is followed by detailed off-street parking requirements. The main body of the bylaw then sets out in detail the provisions relating to each zone.

It is obvious from all this that a zoning bylaw is a highly detailed and technical document. This is a consequence of the "certainty principle": the zoning bylaw attempts to set out precisely what uses are permitted; what is not permitted is prohibited.

The certainty, however, can be illusory; and this is generally recognized. For instance Comay (1977: 93) puts the matter thus:

> Two principles are at work. One is the use of zoning to afford the municipality an adequate means of determining the kind of development that should take place. The other is to provide the residents of an area and the owners of individual properties with reasonable certainty as to the kind and intensity of development that will be permitted. These principles are compatible where the municipality is able to establish the future use and characteristics of land development in a conclusive way. They come into conflict, however, in situations where for one reason or another it is not possible for the municipal council to determine in advance precisely how the land in a particular location should be used. Where the use and characteristics of the area are known, conventional zoning bylaws provide the residents with reasonable stability, and give the individual property owner precise knowledge as to what can and cannot be done with his land. Where future uses cannot be precisely determined, no such certainty exists.

In fact, however, this is an oversimplified analysis. As Bourne's study (1967: 173) of private redevelopment in Toronto clearly shows, change is continuous: "defined as a replacement process in the building stock of the city, redevelopment becomes one aspect of a series of structural adaptations to accommodate changing demands for space and location. Most such demands are accommodated within the existing stock by a change in the location or amount of space utilized by a given activity. Replacement occurs only when there is a strong demand for reuse of the site and when the existing building becomes inadequate."

Bourne continues that the location of change shows no simple and predictable pattern: it is selective "both in terms of the areas and types of activities involved." Though public policy decisions are important, economic forces are crucial. Given this widespread, volatile and unpredictable character of urban change, it is necessary for planning policies and controls to work with market forces but harnessing them to socially desirable ends. This is a far cry from traditional zoning. Moreover, it does not allow a simple division of the land into areas of stability and areas of change.

The responses to this dynamism have been varied. They range from simple procedures for allowing minor changes within the framework of the zoning system to a quite different procedure for the ad hoc consideration of specific sites. At the extreme, zoning has been replaced by a discretionary development permit system. This has had a surprisingly widespread use across Canada, as is explained later in this chapter.

Minor Variances

However, detailed zoning provisions may be, cases will arise where some slight variation is desirable or acceptable. It is therefore usual for provincial legislation to provide for some kind of machinery to adjudicate on applications for minor variances or adjustments. In Ontario, provision is made for independent committees of adjustment which are empowered to grant minor variances from a zoning bylaw where they consider that "the general intent and purpose of the bylaw and of the official plan, if any, are maintained" (Ontario Ministry of Housing 1978a and 1980). In Manitoba, variations are dealt with by the local council itself constituted as a variation board. Applications can be made by anyone "who is of the opinion that a zoning bylaw or a planning scheme, as the case may be, injuriously or adversely affects him, his property or his rights." A variation can be granted only when the board "is satisfied that (a) the general environment, amenity and convenience of the community as a whole will not be adversely affected; and (b) the general environment, amenity, convenience, character and value of adjoining properties will not be adversely affected."

Non-Conforming Uses

Another long-standing means for injecting flexibility into zoning is to permit the continuance of uses existing at the date of the passing of a zoning bylaw even if they do not conform to the bylaw. Typically the zoning bylaw, though allowing the use to continue, prohibits any change, expansion or reconstruction. For example, the Nova Scotia act provides that:

If a non-conforming structure or a structure containing a non-conforming use is destroyed or damaged by fire or otherwise

(a)   to an extent of less than seventy-five percent of the market value of the structure, it may be rebuilt, repaired or re-occupied if the structure is substantially the same as it was before the destruction or damage and it is used for the same non-conforming use; or

(b)   to an extent of seventy-five percent or more of the market value of the structure, it shall not be rebuilt, repaired or re-occupied except in conformity with the requirements of the land use bylaw applicable to the property.

A non-conforming use of land or a structure shall not be recommended if it has been discontinued for a continuous period of six months, and in such event the land or structure shall not thereafter be used except in conformity with the requirements of the land use bylaw applicable to the property.

By such devices it is sometimes hoped that non-conforming uses will wither away. In practice, the withering tends to be a very lengthy process. Of course, there may be power to extinguish the use by way of expropriation, but the cost is normally prohibitive. Alternatively, informal powers of persuasion and assistance with relocation may be more effective.

During the review of the Ontario planning act a further alternative was examined in detail, namely amortization. A special study was commissioned of experience in the United States where some zoning bylaws provide for the compulsory termination of non-conforming uses at the end of an amortization period (Ontario White Paper 1979e). The study explains:

> Amortization, like depreciation, rests on the principle of writing off investment over time. Amortization clauses have been included in U.S. zoning bylaws on the theory that property investment depreciates over time, the investment is recouped along with income from the use of the property, and it is therefore reasonable to insist on discontinuation of the use at the end of the amortization period without payment of compensation.

In fact, the study found that the available amortization powers had not been widely used, and had largely been restricted to undesirable open uses which had little or no investment attached to them. The subsequent white paper commented that the technique seemed workable only "for the elimination of such uses as junkyards and other low-investment open uses, over relatively short periods of time, and where no great financial hardship to the owner or operator of the use would result" (Ontario White Paper 1979a: 94).

This limited form of the amortization concept was initially accepted by the provincial government, but it attracted much opposition on the ground that it represented "a strong infringement on private property rights" (Ontario White Paper 1981: 62). The idea was quietly dropped.

Amendment of Zoning Bylaws

Even the most staunch defender of the zoning system would be likely to agree that some mechanism for reviewing and amending zoning bylaws is necessary. The statutory certainty of a zoning bylaw can hardly last for ever. All the provinces therefore provide, whether explicitly or implicitly, powers of amendment. Quebec provides expressly for a quinquennial review. More usually, however, the legislation simply provides for amendment or repeal.

Amendments can be made at the instance of the council or following an application. It is in this connection that a host of techniques has been developed. Apart from a simple amendment (or rezoning) there is spot zoning, site plan control, development agreements and so forth. These involve some discussion, or bargaining, between a planning authority and a developer; and all have the particular feature of discretionary power. The techniques therefore are much more akin to the British development permit system than to the "pure" zoning system.

Before discussing this aspect of zoning amendments, however, it is useful to outline the straightforward use of zoning amendments. A simple illustration is provided by a half-page advertisement in the Toronto *Globe and Mail* of 10 February 1983. This gave notice that the city was applying to the Ontario Municipal Board for approval of two bylaws which, in essence, amended the city's zoning provisions. The first amended certain provisions relating to market gardening and deleted mushroom growing from the definition of the term. The new definition thus read: "market gardening includes vegetable crops and a horticultural nursery, nursery sales station and greenhouse." The second advertisement gave similar notice in respect to amendments "... to permit the replacement or reconstruction of buildings destroyed by termites or wood-destroying insects. The replacement building or portion of the building must be either positioned on the lot in the same way as the old building or positioned so as to have a greater distance between its walls and the lot line than the old building."

Another illustration also shows the great detail included in some zoning bylaws and their highly legal character:

Bylaw No 15675 as amended by Bylaw No 15832 prohibited the use of any land or the erection or use of any building on either side of Yonge Street between Bloor Street and Carlton Street for the purpose of a hand laundry, a junkyard, a junk shop or second hand shop. Those lands are now zoned CR which does not permit a junkyard but does permit second hand shops and a laundry shop which is a defined term restricting the business to a neighborhood operation, located on the ground floor, a laundromat or laundry receiving depot.

This bylaw allows the existing zoning to prevail. Junkyards are not permitted by the zoning in place at this date. The existing zoning permits second hand shops and laundry shops.

A rezoning bylaw with a higher political profile was passed by the "reformed" city council of Toronto which was elected at the end of 1972 (Goldrick 1982: 260). The issue of urban redevelopment had been a major one in the election. The bylaw in question reduced the density of lands owned by Cadillac Development Corporation. An appeal was dismissed on the grounds, inter alia, that there had been no bad faith and that the decision of the council "was one of policy, taken as elected representatives, and if they considered that the bylaw should no longer be supported it was appropriate for them to repeal it ..." (Makuch 1983: 216).

A different line was taken by the board on the much more important 45 foot bylaw (discussed later) and another case in which Toronto tried to prevent the redevelopment of low-rise apartment sites. The problem here was the demolition of older, low-rise, and often rent controlled, apartments and the redevelopment of the site with luxury condominiums. Between 1976 and 1980 only three apartment blocks, containing some ninety rental units, were demolished; but in 1981 proposals totalled twenty blocks with over 750 rental units. The city made various attempts to gain control over this loss of low and medium rented housing, but was constantly frustrated by the OMB or the divisional court (Toronto City 1982a: 10). Thus, a bylaw passed in April 1980 would have limited the depth and height of new developments. It was thought that this would prevent the replacement of low buildings by the more lucrative tall blocks. The OMB, however, considered that the bylaw was patently unjustified. In a decision which criticized the city for not considering the sweeping implications of its actions, the board stated that the city had failed to establish any valid planning reason for forbidding such redevelopment in neighborhoods which already included medium-density and high-density housing.

Spot Zoning

Spot zoning, as the term suggests, is the zoning (or rezoning) of individual plots. This is regarded by some as a dubious practice and, indeed, until a Supreme Court decision in 1959, it was also of doubtful legality *(Bondi v Scarborough* [1959] SCR 444, 18 DLR (2d) 161). There is justification for concern since there is no doubt that the technique has been used on occasion in a discriminatory way. Where bad faith or discrimination can be demonstrated, the courts will uphold an appeal. The same applies even if a municipality disguises a spot zoning by passing a bylaw for a larger area surrounding the "spot." Such a case involving a blatant discrimination arose when the house of the famous author, Mazo de la Roche, was purchased by the Zoroastrian Society of Ontario (Makuch 1983: 213). The land was zoned residential, and confirmation in writing was obtained by the society from the building commissioner that the use of the property as a temple was permitted under the zoning bylaw. There was strong protest from local residents, who were not without influence. As a result, within one week of the purchase agreement being signed, the Borough of North York rezoned the area to exclude church uses. An appeal was lodged and was successful on the ground that the bylaw was aimed solely and exclusively at the society. The court stated that:

> There must be proper planning grounds or standards to warrant discriminatory distinctions between property owners in the same position, classification or zoning category. Here, no planning purpose had been shown to explain, let alone justify, the selection of a single spot in the borough as the subject of this amendatory zoning bylaw. There is no rhyme nor reason, in a planning sense, for it (Ibid).

Holding Bylaws and Interim Controls

Holding bylaws, though formerly of doubtful legality, have grown in popularity in response to the increased tempo of change (Makuch 1983: 228). Specific provision, however, is seldom found in the legislation, though some provinces have power to delay granting building permits for a specified period of time. For example, in British Columbia, the issuance of a building permit can be withheld for up to ninety days "prior to the adoption of a zoning bylaw, an official community plan, an amendment to a zoning bylaw or an alteration, addition or extension to the official community plan." Similar provisions apply in Manitoba (185 days) and Saskatchewan (three months). Manitoba and Ontario also have provision for interim development control, while the 1979 Quebec act introduced provision for a system of interim control. These are all measures designed to control land use while preparation of a permanent provision is in hand.

The 1983 Ontario act empowers municipalities to "hold" a zoning designation. This allows a control over the phasing of development and can be used "to ensure the orderly growth of a neighborhood or to postpone development until conditions required by a municipality, such as the provision of services, have been met" (Ontario White Paper 1979a: 89). This is quite different from the other holding controls in that it is a form of prezoning rather than interim development control. The legislation therefore requires that the official plan contains appropriate justification and explanation. The new Ontario act also provides specifically for interim control bylaws which enable municipalities to place a freeze on land uses for a period of one year (extendable to two years). This again is intended to allow time for the preparation of new or revised land use policies.

The absence of specific legislation in many provinces to enable municipalities to pass holding bylaws or to exercise interim controls does not necessarily mean the absence of some form of holding technique. Development can be effectively frozen by the imposition of an agricultural designation, by continuing obsolete unrealistic zoning, by downzoning to uneconomic densities, or even by a simple formal statement of intention to rezone (Comay Report 1977: 94).

The City of Toronto's 45 Foot Holding Bylaw

Perhaps the most famous case of a holding bylaw is the city of Toronto's 45 Foot Bylaw. (By way of comparison, it may be noted that the downtown height limit of Vancouver is 450 feet.) This was considered, and rejected, by the Ontario Municipal Board in 1974. Apart from its intrinsic interest, the board's judgment raises some significant issues to which further reference is made in other chapters. It is therefore worth while to make more than a passing reference to the case (Ontario Municipal Board 1976).

The bylaw was passed at the instigation of the "reformed" city council in 1973 (the same council whose downzoning of Cadillac Development Corporation's land was upheld by the courts.) It was stimulated by the city's concern about the rate of development particularly in the downtown residential areas. The objective was to put a temporary hold on development in the large area around the city center while studies were undertaken and new planning standards determined. To this end the bylaw, inter alia, imposed a height limitation of 45 feet within the core area of the city and 20 feet within the harbour area. The intention was to force prospective developers to make special application to the city council and be subjected to special controls, which "would be in the absolute discretion of council." The OMB decision was expressed in strong terms:

> The discretion expressed by council would be limitless and subjective ... the effect of the bylaw for all practical purposes has been to freeze downtown development ... In our opinion, council was bent on achieving its objectives in the face of all reasonable opposition and this course represents an act of irresponsibility ... It became apparent in February 1974, just weeks after its enactment, that the holding bylaw was not working. Instead of repealing the bylaw then, the council stubbornly proceeded as if the heart of a great city had not been stilled, and would likely remain dormant for years to come while awaiting studies, reports and final decision; and now the city is audaciously arguing that the holding bylaw is valid in much the same way as such a bylaw in an agricultural area. Such submission is an affront to this board ... Approval should be refused because it is

vague and, in our opinion, is designed to circumvent the provisions of the Planning Act ...

There is much in similar vein.

One point of interest which arose during the lengthy hearing was the question of the position of the city's chief planner vis-a-vis the council. The board was severely critical of its interpretation of) his action in "merely attempting to satisfy the demands of council and political expediency without necessarily the application of proper planning principles." The board added:

> It would be a sad commentary on the profession of an urban planner if he conceived it as his duty to follow only the wishes of council without regard to those standards expected of a professional planner. If a planner believes it to be his function only to act as agent for council, then the board should not place any reliance on his testimony, based on his qualifications as an urban planner. At the very least, such evidence would be suspect.

Another interesting point arose in relation to neighborhood groups, which had been an effective political force for some years. The reformed council, unlike its pro-developer predecessor, had a close relationship with these groups, and more generally there was a growing concern for public participation in the planning process. The board, however, warned of the dangers of paying too much regard to individual neighborhoods and too little to the wider public interest:

> Throughout this hearing ... the position taken by many ratepayers and community associations is one of inflexibility and the preservation of the status quo. While public participation in planning debates is not to be discouraged, it is wrong in our view that decisions finally made be based on narrow interests and not the wider objectives as expressed in an official plan.

The city's appeal to Cabinet included a rebuttal of the board's criticism of the council's attitude to these groups: "it is submitted that such discussions must be left to a popularly elected council to express its mandate as members of council see it after weighing and giving effect to such factors as may commend themselves." In support of its general stance towards development it called in aid a previous OMB decision:

> In the opinion of this board planning for development should be sparked not by the desires of private developers but by decisions of public authorities duly and deliberately arrived at ...

The city complained that the board "erred in using language so extravagant, intemperate and injudicious as for this reason alone to render the decision unsustainable." It also submitted that the board's finding that the enactment of the bylaw was an act of irresponsibility, and its unwarranted and unjustified personal attack on the chief planner amounted to a failure judicially to exercise its proper functions.

There is much in this particular cause celebre which is of interest: indeed it would make an excellent planning text. Some of the issues are referred to elsewhere in this book. To complete the account here it is necessary only to note that Cabinet rejected the 45 foot bylaw but the city was given a deadline for preparing a new plan for the downtown area. In the meantime, holding bylaws could be enacted, for a reduced area, but the council was required to adopt by resolution objective criteria by which exemptions could be considered.

Holding Bylaws in British Columbia

Lest it be thought that Toronto is the only city to attempt a holding bylaw of this character, reference can be made to two cases in British Columbia. The first, in 1969, was made by the Minister of Municipal Affairs and Housing. To prevent development on the Gulf Islands he imposed a blanket ten acre subdivision minimum. Though strictly speaking not a holding bylaw, this was the intent, and it remained in operation until the Islands Trust Act provided adequate machinery for protecting the islands.

The second case is closer to that of Toronto. Facing the same development pressures in the downtown area, and being inadequately equipped to deal with them, the city of Vancouver passed an interim bylaw which reduced the allowable densities to three times coverage. Because Vancouver was operating under powers provided by its own charter no approval of this bylaw was required. Moreover, there was no mechanism of appeal (outside the courts). The contrast with Toronto (subject to OMB and ministerial control) is striking; but as will be shown later, the world of planning in Vancouver is unique.

Bonus Zoning

Zoning is normally restrictive: indeed, until the pre-1983 legislation in Ontario, a zoning bylaw was termed a restricted area bylaw. However, zoning can be used to promote as well as to restrict. Bonus, or incentive, zoning is a means whereby a developer is allowed to increase density if he provides, for example, additional facilities or if he meets certain design requirements. An example of an extensive use of density bonuses is to be found in the city of Cambridge plan (1982: 104), where seven objectives are set out:

(1) encouraging the development or redevelopment of land for residential purposes or mixed residential and commercial purposes in the city center;

(2) encouraging the construction of required assisted housing for families and apartment accommodation for non-family households and elderly persons or couples within the municipality;

(3) encouraging the conservation of the city's heritage resources;

(4) encouraging the conservation and protection of the city's privately owned natural resources which may be subject to development or redevelopment proposals;

(5) encouraging increased public transit ridership;

(6) encouraging the improved design of noise abatement facilities in schemes for the development or redevelopment of lands near major transportation facilities;

(7) encouraging the provision of on site amenities, facilities, services or other matters which, in the opinion of council, are necessary or desirable in, or related to, a development

> or   redevelopment project site or the neighborhood in
> which such a site is located.

Developers who are willing to design a site development scheme
and to enter into an agreement with the city council are allowed
an increase in density.

Bonus zoning is generally considered a useful device,
though Makuch (1983: 229) is critical of it. He submits that the
technique "has the problem of being uniform in application. A
schedule is generally set out and the bonus granted to developers and the benefits received by the municipality are the same
in every case. Therefore, all apartment biuldings built under a
bonus tend to look the same. For example, minimal landscaping with a fountain and open space may be required under the
bonus. Flexibility is therefore really not enhanced and positive
obligations cannot be enforced on subsequent owners in the
absence of legislation."

Mixed Use Zoning

Though the concept of zoning was originally one of total
separation of land uses, there is obviously a limit imposed by
the simple fact that some uses are accessory. A garage is a use
accessory to the main use of a house on the same lot. From
this limited concept of accessory use it is only a short distance
to mixed use zoning. This allows "compatible uses" such as a
neighborhood store in a residential area. Much broader, for
example, is Edmonton's residential mixed use districts and commercial mixed use districts (Edmonton City 1982). The former
appears as part of the city's downtown policy: "to promote the
development of substantial quantities of housing in the downtown, as an essential element in achieving a diverse downtown,
a broader range of housing choices in general, and an efficient
and equitable distribution of medium and high density housing
across the city" (Edmonton City 1980b: 5.4). To achieve this,
new mixed use districts were created in the downtown and provisions made in the bylaw "to promote the development of
housing by making residential development economically more
attractive" (Ibid: 5.5).

Cluster Zoning and Planned Unit Development

Cluster zoning or average density zoning breaks away from the rigid layouts and lot regulations by allowing the developer to concentrate development on one part of a site (i.e. a cluster), leaving the remainder free for community use such as a park (Costonis 1974). The average density for the area is maintained and, since the development is more compact, the provision of services to the site are lower in cost.

Planned unit developments, or PUDs as they are affectionately termed, come in different forms. Typically, they are large comprehensive developments, usually residential but sometimes mixed use, within which there is considerable freedom to vary building types while conforming to regulations relating to the development as a whole. The difference between cluster zoning and PUDs is that the former provides flexibility in relation to lot size and the distribution of density over the area, while the latter additionally relaxes use and building type restrictions. Thus a PUD may have a mixture of detached houses, row houses and apartments without regard for example to the normal standards of height and bulk. There will, however, be standards devised for the PUD.

PUD is an American innovation, and "there are probably as many ways to define the PUD as there are drafters of PUD sections of a zoning ordinance" (So 1979: 435). The former Saskatchewan act made specific provisions for planned unit development but the definition was not very enlightening, and it was dropped from the 1983 act. "Planned unit development means development of land by a method of subdividing land whereby the land is specifically subdivided for uses and purposes specified in the proposed plan of subdivision, as approved." Since a PUD is most likely to involve negotiations and an agreement between a developer and a municipality it is probable that site plan control (discussed later) would be normally used instead.

Transfer of Development Rights

The transfer of development rights (TDR) is another form of incentive zoning. Used initially in relation to the preservation of historic buildings, it involves separating the development rights from one site and transferring them to another. Thus the development rights become marketable and, in the case of an historic building, the owner is enabled to realize the development value of the site by selling the development rights to the owner of another site. It is thus "a means of providing an equitable return on land investment to property owners whose return otherwise might be lessened by regulatory activity" (Schnidman 1978: 532). Though, as illustrated below, use is made of TDR in some of the larger Canadian cities there is no specific authority for it.

The Comay committee (1977: 100) considered TDR to be a useful planning instrument to achieve objectives such as the preservation of privately owned open space; the retention and maintenance of historically or architecturally significant buildings; the retention of axial views or other significant design features; and the promotion of equity between owners of large and small development sites in locations designated for mixed use development. It recommended that "municipalities should be authorized to allow the transfer of development rights between building sites on the basis of planning policy statements which establish the municipality's objectives and the basis on which density will be transferred."

The public reaction to the Comay stance was generally positive, as was that of consultants appointed to examine the whole range of recommendations in relation to development control (Ontario White Paper 1979d: 56). However, the Ontario provincial government was unconvinced:

> ... TDR is a potentially useful device. In theory it can offer, for example, a form of compensation for restricting a landowner's right to change the use of land or demolish buildings. It can also provide a way of preserving historic buildings or private open space, or promoting developer equity within a planning area of multiple ownership. It is evident, however, that the

actual use of TDR has been very limited, and even when used the results have often been less than successful. Literature on the subject is extensive, and different approaches on the use of the power have been proposed, but as yet very few TDR working models exist. It is also evident that to put it into practice a complicated and cumbersome administrative machinery would have to be established (Ontario White Paper 1979a: 56).

The government concluded that "while the concept of TDR has merit in theory, it is too complex a system with too many unknown factors to be authorized at this time." Nevertheless, this was not to "prevent municipalities from experimenting with the technique." Toronto is here in the lead.

The first major case in Toronto was the transfer of the air rights of St Andrew's Presbyterian Church to the Sun Life Assurance Company's commercial development across King Street (Lush 1981). For this, the church received $3.75 million. The church remains, but the TDR meant that office development that could have taken place on the site (if the city had agreed) was added to the Sun Life scheme.

The city's recommended guidelines for TDR (for which the term "sale of air rights" or "density transfers" is used) provide that in any sale, the two sites should be neighbors, within 500 feet of one another, and should not transfer rights between high density and low density zoning districts. Without such a limitation, TDR could seriously jeopardize the Central Area Plan. As a city planning report stressed, "unless the new transfer of density policy is contained in an Official Plan Amendment and is carefully circumscribed, serious difficulties could arise from relaxing the conditions for the transfer of density. The equity and certainty respecting the use and development of land provided by the approved Official Plan could be eroded. Lands adjacent to both the donor and receiving sites in any transfer could be adversely affected, either through the aggregation of excess density or through the creation of 'dead spots' for development through stripping of commercial density. For this reason, the transfer of density, from historic buildings or otherwise, other than in accordance with an Official Plan policy of general   application cannot be recommended" (Toronto City 1982b).

Much more could be written about TDR (Vancouver City 1983), but sufficient has been said to indicate its nature and its ramifications. However, one final point will serve as a relevant lead into the next section.

One of the interesting uses made of TDR by Toronto is in respect of housing provision. Subject to a lengthy and detailed list of requirements, the official plan provides that:

> ... in any high or medium density mixed commercial-residential area, or in the financial district, council may pass bylaws in respect to any two lots located within the same district or area to permit:
>
> (i)   the erection and use, on one lot (hereinafter called the receiving lot) of a building containing conventional housing units not exceeding in number the aggregate of the number permitted by this plan on that lot and on the other lot (hereinafter called the donor lot); and
>
> (ii)   the erection and use on the donor lot of a building containing a commercial gross floor area not exceeding the aggregate of the commercial gross floor area permitted by this plan on that lot and on the receiving lot ...

This is a clever technique to ensure that housing is provided in the downtown area. It was devised in response to the refusal of the OMB to approve a bylaw requiring every commercial development to include a residential component. Approval was given, however, to transfer of rights as set out above. This is also an example of what is termed inclusionary zoning.

Inclusionary Zoning

Inclusionary zoning is a term of the art lacking precision and used in a variety of ways, but its essential feature is the requirement that housing, usually for low, or lower, income households, be provided in a development. Hagman (1982: 169) employs the term in its most common way: "inclusionary zoning (also known as inclusionary housing) is a scheme whereby a developer of market rate housing is permitted to develop only if housing affordable to low and moderate income groups is included."

The Toronto example, included as an example of TDR, untypically has no reference to income groups for which housing was to be provided. Inclusionary zoning can also involve bonusing, and typically requires a planning agreement. Terminology is certainly not consistent: Vancouver uses the term mandatory inclusion zoning. Commenting on the American scene, Callies (1982: 754) has noted:

> Communities concerned with providing low and moderate income housing have tried a variety of techniques over the past twenty years to correct housing imbalances. Many such techniques involve some compulsory quota or percentage. Increasingly, the techniques involve a mandatory level of low income units or money to pay for such units as a precondition for constructing a housing development. Whether the levy is exercised at the rezoning, special permit or building permit stage, it is usually called "inclusionary zoning" as distinguished from "exclusionary zoning," though in fact it is not zoning at all.

To complicate matters further, whatever term is used there is a question as to its legality. The issue has arisen extensively in the United States and, to a limited extent, in both Canada and Britain (Hagman 1980a). Nevertheless, it is clearly alive in a number of the States. For example, "Fairfax County, Virginia requires that development of fifteen multifamily units or more contain not less than six percent low income dwelling units and not less than an additional nine percent of dwelling units for moderate income families. The ordinance provides a density bonus whereby one additional conventional unit will be allowed for every two low or moderate income units, provided that the density increase does not exceed twenty percent" (So 1979: 439).

It is difficult to find Canadian examples, and even more difficult to establish how successful they are. Statements of policy are more common than firm rules. Thus the policy plan of Prince Albert (1982: 10) includes a policy on "mixture of housing" which states that "where feasible and acceptable, the city shall encourage a mix of housing types and styles in residential areas with a view to affording all individuals and families of all income levels the opportunity to exercise their housing accommodation preferences." This has the ring of a typical motherhood statement, but the sting (if indeed there is one) comes in the tail of the section: "the policy can be implemented primarily through subdivision design and the subdivision approval process."

Vancouver has implemented "mandatory inclusion zoning" in the False Creek development plan. The bylaw provides that the household mix over the whole area should be:

Families with children	25 percent
Couples (young and mature)	25 percent
Elderly	15 percent
Singles	35 percent

Moreover, "the population, age and incomes mix as reflected in the Greater Vancouver region" is to be a similar objective (Vancouver City 1974). These guidelines were implemented in that part of the False Creek development which was undertaken on land owned by the city. Development agreements have been made with some private developers, but experience has not been encouraging. Many difficult issues are raised: of equity, of the power of market forces, of the role (and cost) of subsidies, and so forth.

Site Plan Control and Development Agreements

It is very clear from the preceding discussion that zoning is no longer a simple matter of segregating uses according to the provisions of a bylaw. The numerous devices which have been evolved to achieve flexibility and to make zoning a more effective instrument of planning have transformed it.

At some point the changes became so drastic that to use the term zoning at all seems inappropriate. When that point arises we move from zoning to discretionary development controls. The matter is one of degree, as is apparent by the varying amounts of flexibility provided in the numerous zoning instruments. Where the line between the two systems should be drawn is arguable. Here the line is drawn after site plan control. This is included (just) within "zoning" since though the control itself operates with a high degree of discretion, it nevertheless is embedded in a wider framework (in which zoning is an important element), and it is constrained by bylaws, provincial legislation and the OMB. This is the Ontario case, which, in Makuch's words, "does not abandon zoning at all and merely grafts onto the zoning system the ability to impose certain conditions and require agreements with respect to those conditions in areas designated as site plan control areas" (Makuch 1983: 238).

The power is more limited than that provided by, for example, the Nova Scotia act which enables a council to permit development which would not normally be permitted in the zoning bylaw.

Alberta, British Columbia and Newfoundland (it is submitted) have powers which are best considered separately as discretionary development controls.

In Ontario, site plan control (or "development review" as it is sometimes called) is a popular instrument. It is used by three-quarters of the municipalities in Ontario (Reed 1978: 16). It can be applied to any area designated a proposed site plan control area in an official plan. The act lists the specific matters which can be dealt with and, in practice, most bylaws simply reproduce the list. It includes road widenings, access, parking and circulation; site grading, landscaping and floodlighting; site layout, the massing and conceptual design of buildings; and waste storage and removal and snow clearing.

However, despite the reference to "massing and conceptual design," matters of height and density are specifically excluded. These are covered in the zoning bylaw and cannot be reviewed on a site basis.

The Comay committee looked with favor on this instrument of development control. It noted that the powers were significant and "they can yield great benefit to the community in terms of amenity and convenience." However, they "can also sharply reduce the certainty and predictability which are necessary to a fair planning system." Thus the flexibility/certainty dilemma arises yet again.

Discretionary Planning Controls

The key to the [Toronto Central Area] plan is on its last page, which tells developers and others "come and talk to us about amendments"

Sewell 1983

The term "discretionary planning controls" is rather cumbersome, but it avoids the confusion attendant upon the simpler "development permit system." Comay uses the latter to mean the former, but Manitoba uses "development permits" for permission given under a planning scheme or zoning bylaw. The City of Winnipeg Act, on the other hand, provides for "development permission." British Columbia has "development permits" for the implementation of its zoning bylaws, but Vancouver has "development permits" for the implementation of its discretionary control system. To confuse matters even further, Rogers' standard legal text (Section 5.25) refers to "development control" which is defined as "the regulation of land use on a permit basis for each proposed use of land ..." Development control, he submits, "is the control of land use by permission rather than by regulation." It is not difficult to find further confusions.

In essence, the system being referred to is one in which the owner's right to develop is controlled, not by a zoning bylaw, but by a planning authority's discretion. In fact, as is apparent from earlier discussion, it is misleading to think in terms of two totally different systems since, in practice, there is a continuum. At one extreme is a firm zoning provision which provides an

owner with an uncontested right to develop as he wishes subject only to the provisions of the zoning bylaw. At the other
extreme is a totally discretionary scheme which provides no guidance as to what might be allowed but simply gives the planning authority complete power to decide. In between, there are
many possibilities, including discretionary elements in a zoning
system, and a detailed land use plan complete with "guidelines"
or "standards" in a discretionary system.

Ontario

It is paradoxical that, while the Comay report argued
strongly against a comprehensive system of discretionary planning controls, there are two areas in Ontario where such a system already operates: in the unincorporated areas of the northern part of the province, and in the Niagara Escarpment area.
The former is an historical legacy: permits, issued by the Ministry of Natural Resources under the Public Lands Act are
required for building on Crown lands (which constitute most of
the unorganized area).

Development control in the Niagara Escarpment is a very
different matter. This is no legacy: it stems from legislation in
1973: the Niagara Escarpment Planning and Development Act.
The necessity for a discretionary system for control was
accepted on the grounds that traditional zoning instruments
could not provide "the kind of control needed in a large, varied
and environmentally sensitive area such as the Niagara Escarpment" (see chapter 8 below). In a designated "area of development control," all development is subject to approval (or otherwise) and to "such terms and conditions" as are considered
desirable. Contravention of the act is an offence for which a fine
of up to $10,000 can be imposed. Any unapproved development
is subject to an "order to demolish." In short, the provisions
are essentially the same as those provided under the British system of discretionary control. The Niagara Escarpment is, of
course, exceptional and it is unlikely that the development control system operating within the area will be applied elsewhere.

Alberta: The Hybrid

The evolution of land use planning in Alberta is, in significant ways, different from that in other provinces (Alberta Municipal Affairs 1980a). For example, there has been a real attempt to devise an effective framework for regional planning. Even more important has been the "blending" of zoning and discretionary development controls. Laux (1971: 1) commented that the system in that province "combines the best features of zoning and [discretionary] development control while retaining the maximum flexibility for both the planner and the developer." The reference was to the pre-1977 situation, which provided for *both* zoning and discretionary development control. In that year the lengthy discussions on the Alberta planning system, largely focused on *Towards a New Planning Act for Alberta* (Alberta Municipal Affairs 1974) finally culminated in a new planning act. The former dual system (which, as might be assumed, was not without difficulties) was replaced by a true hybrid: the land use bylaw (Macdonald 1984).

This neatly provides both for designated permitted uses of land, as in a zoning bylaw, and for discretionary uses. These broad powers are supplemented by a number of specific provisions. For example, ("without restricting the generality" of the powers), a council can provide in the land use bylaw for a wide range of matters commonly found in zoning bylaws (minimum and maximum area of lots; landscaping, parking provision etc), together with a discretion for a development officer "to decide upon an application for a development permit notwithstanding that the proposed development does not comply with the land use bylaw if, in the opinion of the development officer [sic], (a) the proposed development would not unduly interfere with the amenities of the neighborhood, or materially interfere with or affect the use, enjoyment or value of neighboring properties, and (b) the proposed development does not conflict with the use prescribed for that land or building in the land use bylaw."

In addition to this standard provision, municipalities can also designate "direct control districts" where "the council may regulate and control the use or development of land or buildings ... in such a manner as it considers necessary." The only precondition is that the municipality must have an adopted general municipal plan, presumably setting out the land use objectives and development criteria for the areas designated as direct control districts. Thus "a council may be more responsive to the needs of unique areas, such as inner city neighborhoods experiencing severe pressure for high density development, than would be possible if rigid land use classes were assigned" (Alberta Municipal Affairs 1980a).

Direct control is clearly just a new name for discretionary control; but it is interesting to see, in the other areas, how discretionary control is fused with "permitted uses" (i.e. zoning control). On this, Laux (1979: 37) writes:

> The philosophy behind the distinction between permitted and discretionary uses is simply that, where uses are shown as permitted within a particular district, they are regarded to be of that type as are clearly compatible with one another and, therefore, unlikely to adversely affect neighboring properties in the same district. On the other hand, discretionary uses are classed as such because, by their nature and although generally acceptable in a particular district, they may or may not be reasonably compatible with neighboring properties, depending upon the circumstances. Hence, it is necessary to confer upon the land use administrator a discretion as to whether or not to allow a particular application for such a use.
>
> To take a simple illustration, a day care center is generally regarded as an appropriate use in a neighborhood where one family dwellings are permitted uses. However, whether a particular day care center on a particular lot in such a district is desirable will depend upon such factors as demand for such a facility, the amount of traffic in the neighborhood, the size and design of the structure proposed for the facility, the amount and location of available outdoor play area and the like. Consequently, it is considered appropriate to permit administrators to take into account such factors and either allow or reject the application, depending upon a reasonable assessment of all relevant variables.

Clearly, Alberta can be considered to be more inclined towards discretionary development controls than classic zoning practices. But it is in Vancouver and Newfoundland that the former has, or is becoming, the standard system of land use control. The two areas are different in that Vancouver has steadily increased its use of discretionary controls, whereas Newfoundland simply modelled its system on that of Britain (its far-flung governing country until it entered Confederation in 1949).

Newfoundland's System: A British Import

In planning, as in many other areas, Newfoundland is different from the rest of Canada. The differences stem from its history, its geographic position and its cultural and ethnic character. Even more than the other provinces, a quick perusal can give little of the real flavour of its planning system. Moreover, also unlike most other provinces, little study has been made of its government.

Perhaps the most eloquent illustration of the character of land use controls in Newfoundland is a quotation from the St John's urban region plan (1976: 40):

> The general policies set out in this plan will be refined and amplified to individual local areas, as follows:
>
> (1) It is intended that detailed plans made in accordance with the requirements of the Urban and Regional Planning Act ... shall be required for areas where major development or redevelopment is to take place ...
>
> (2) ... within the local areas covered by detailed plans, such plans shall form the basis of Development Regulations necessary for implementation, while in remaining parts of the region development regulations shall be based directly on the policies contained in this plan.

A set of model regulations (1981) provides for the administration of a development permit system within which there is considerable discretionary power. For example, a municipality "may attach to a permit such conditions as it deems fit in order to ensure that the proposed development will be in accordance with the purposes of the approved plan and these regulations."

Nevertheless, as the earlier quotation from the St John's zoning bylaw illustrates, the development permit system works within the framework of a zoning system. There thus appears to be a similarity with Vancouver, though matters are less formalized in Newfoundland.

Vancouver: The Charter City

British Columbia, as already noted, has two separate planning systems, one in the city of Vancouver, operating under the Vancouver Charter, and the other in the remainder of the province, operating under the Municipal Act. The latter system has a relatively small degree of discretion but it is essentially based on zoning (Thomas 1982). The matter is somewhat confused in that the term "development permits" is used for waivers to a zoning bylaw. The degree of flexibility this provides is real but tightly constrained to matters which are specified in the zoning bylaw, and which are restricted by the provisions of the Municipal Act. Essentially they relate to matters of building structure and servicing. It is interesting to note that this system (which dates only from 1977) replaced a much more discretionary system of "land use contracts" (Corke 1983). The intention has been described by Mackenzie: "the most fundamental objective of this legislation is to return the municipality to a regulatory role as opposed to the present tendency of municipalities to conduct contractual regulations. It is intended that zoning be reinstated as the primary municipal control of land use. Certainty is to become the key word and the major factors of development are to be known at the outset" (Mackenzie 1978: 517).

There could be no greater contrast to Vancouver where its development permits "can deal with virtually any aspect of a development including use and density requirements" (Ince 1984: 122). Though the Vancouver Charter provides for zoning bylaws, the powers are of an enabling nature, and include "designating districts or zones in which there shall be no uniform regulations and in which any person wishing to carry out development must submit such plans and specifications as may be required by the Director of Planning and obtain the approval of council to the form of development." Another section of the Charter provides for bylaws "prohibiting any person from undertaking any development without having obtained a permit therefor."

There are some interesting features here. First, there is a complete integration of zoning and development permit systems. Secondly, the discretionary character is made even more so by a power enabling the delegation to officials of "such powers of discretion relating to zoning matters which to council seem appropriate." These zoning matters include the relaxation of zoning bylaws "in any case where literal enforcement would result in unnecessary hardship."

The Vancouver system would not work if it were not acceptable to the electorate and the development industry. The city has thus evolved an elaborate system for informing, consulting and negotiating.

"The idea of discretionary approvals of projects places a particular responsibility on the process by which development applications are reviewed. In order to ensure fairness and balance with what are at times subtle and subjective questions a new, open and very consultative process was developed" (Vancouver City 1981a). This is contrasted with the earlier rigid system which could not respond to local conditions and which was operated in a secretive way. The process starts with a pre-application discussion with the applicant. The application can be either a preliminary or a complete one depending upon the scale and complexity of the project. It is reviewed for compliance with both the regulations and published guidelines. At this stage there is consultation with other interested departments and a body known as the urban design panel.

The urban design panel, which consists of city appointees, has the duty of advising the council, the director of planning and the Development Permit Board on the urban design of any proposed development (Corke 1983: 83; Vancouver City 1984a: 7).

The public are informed by signs on the site and in some cases by letter, and through the local area planning committees. All plans are freely available for inspection at the city hall.

On the basis of the comments received, negotiations may lead to design changes in the proposed development. "Most projects which go forward are the result of trade-offs among the varying objectives of the different parties." When negotiations have gone as far as either the applicant or the city wants, the project goes to the decision stage. This is given (or otherwise) either by the director of planning himself or, in the case of larger, more controversial projects, to a Development Permit Board. This consists of the director of planning, the director of social planning, and the city engineer. Additionally there is a Development Advisory Board which consists of representatives of the general public, the design profession, and the development industry. Meetings are advertised and public participation in the discussion is encouraged.

The city is proud of its achievements under discretionary zoning. It is not, however, complacent and an ongoing review is expected to improve public understanding and participation, and to lead to more efficient administration (Vancouver City 1984b).

Subdivision

Throughout the history of the planning act an antiphonal relationship has existed between subdividers ... finding new loopholes in the subdivision-control provisions of the act, and the provincial government scurrying about to close the loopholes

Gomme 1984

The term "subdivision" is a perplexing one to European planners who have difficulty in distinguishing between subdivision control and zoning control: why two systems when one would do? The reason lies in history.

Historically, subdivision is the stage which followed the initial division of land, i.e. when it was originally settled, granted or sold (Martin 1973; Cail 1974). In British Columbia, there were three constant factors in successive land acts: "the wish to encourage settlement, the desire to prevent speculation in public lands, and the acute need to provide an adequate revenue with which to administer such a large territory" (Cail 1974: 245). The position has varied, for historical reasons, between the different provinces but one of these three factors has generally been of special significance. There was also, of course, the obvious need for certainty in boundaries and titles, though the sophistication with which this was done varied widely. Newfoundland still has a somewhat rudimentary and incomplete system (Cranmer 1974b).

With urban and suburban subdivisions, a major concern was (and still is) with the street pattern, and the size and shape of lots (Rayner 1976: 3). Much of the earliest legislation, in both Canada and the United States, was in fact concerned solely with these. Thus the Ontario City and Suburbs Plans Act of 1912 provided that:

> Where any person is desirous of surveying and subdividing into lots with a view to the registration of a plan of the survey and sub-division, any tract of land lying within or within five miles of a city, having a population of not less than 50,000, he shall submit a plan of the proposed survey and subdivision to the Ontario Railway and Municipal Board for its approval.

The concern with lot size was explained by Rayner (Ibid) in terms of preventing areas of urban blight, a phrase used to describe land that remained vacant either because it was landlocked or of such a shape or size that no practicable use could be made of it. However, concern with lot size was founded on health and aesthetic reasons as well as economic considerations. Because early sewage disposal systems were based on septic tank systems, the size of lot and density of development limited the amount of waste that could be disposed of in this manner. "The aesthetic consideration was based on changing attitudes with respect to home construction. The slender three story home on a narrow lot gave way to the ranch style bungalow which required greater surface area" (Milner 1965: 50).

Additional support for subdivision control came with the depression which followed the building boom of the 1920s. Both developers and municipalities suffered during this time: the former from foreclosures, the latter from tax arrears. As a result the issue of the timing of subdivision came to the fore, and powers were provided to prevent prematurity of subdivision. The problem is still a live one. In 1965 Milner wrote:

> The tendency to exploit the land beyond the existing market was probably encouraged by the fashion of the day to have municipal services installed by the municipality, but when the owner of a farm could gamble on the market at relatively little risk to himself, he would stand by while roads were graded, pipes laid, sidewalks constructed, all at public cost, hoping that prosperity would continue and he could sell his lots, fully serviced, to a largely unsuspecting taxpayer. Today we speak of land that is "ripe" for subdivision, that is, land for which there is an existing demand, as building lots. And we speak of "premature" subdivision, that is, land put on the market when buyers are withdrawing. Perhaps more than any other condition, it was this economic concern over premature subdivision that inspired the postwar legislative attack on the free market in urbanizing land (Ibid: 51).

This postwar attack had two objectives: the provision of municipal services in newly developing areas, and, "rather more difficult to define ... the creation of a pleasant and convenient environment." The former has had higher political profile as municipalities have battled with the intrinsically conflicting dictates of the planning legislation and the property assessment legislation. Indeed, planning principles have been made subservient on occasion to fiscal considerations: hence the term fiscal zoning. This is determining land use in such a way as to maximize the tax income. The financial problems of municipalities have also led to greater and wider use of levies on developers.

The simplicity of the concept of subdivision is in marked contrast to the complexities of the actual operation. Though subdivision control varies in detail between different provinces, the essential features are similar. The account here is restricted to Ontario (where there is the advantage of the analysis undertaken in connection with the Comay review of the planning acts).

Subdivision control hinges on transfers of title. Before a conveyance can take place a "plan of subdivision" has to be registered. Though historically this was simply a means of ensuring adequate titles, with the growth of land use controls, it has become a major instrument of planning.

A plan of subdivision includes maps and details of the land to be subdivided, the intended uses, adjacent uses, existing and proposed highways, availability of water supplies, municipal services, and so forth. In considering a plan, the views of interested government departments and agencies are taken into account (which can involve a large amount of consultations).

In addition to a general requirement that "regard shall be had, among other matters, to the health, safety, convenience and welfare of the present and future inhabitants of the local municipality," the Ontario act requires consideration of:

(a)   any matters of provincial interest;

(b)   whether the proposed subdivision is premature or in the public interest;

(c)   general conformity to the official plan and any adjacent plans of subdivision;

(d)   the suitability of the land;

(e)   the highway proposals;

(f)   the dimensions and shape of the lots;

(g)   any restrictions on land or buildings;

(h)   conservation of natural resources and flood control;

(i)   adequacy of utilities and municipal services;

(j)   adequacy of school sites;

(k)   any land to be conveyed or dedicated for public purposes;

(l)   energy conservation.

The first and last of these "matters to be regarded" are newcomers introduced by the 1983 act.

One of the most interesting of these matters is the second which deals with prematurity and the public interest. This is an issue which is determined within the discretion of the approving body (i.e. a municipality or the minister) and provides a means for phasing developments or for preventing developments which are uneconomic to the public sector.

The discretionary nature of subdivision control is in sharp contrast to the rights conferred by a zoning bylaw. In fact subdivision control is essentially a form of discretionary development control.

This can be seen again in the provision that approval can be subjected to such conditions as are "reasonable, having regard to the nature of the development ..." The act specifically refers to the conveyance of land for recreational purposes, and for highway construction or widening. It also provides that the landowner "enter into one or more agreements with a municipality" dealing with such matters as may be considered necessary "including the provision of municipal services." Finally, in case these powers are thought to be limiting, they are not to be interpreted "in any way whatsoever" as restricting the general provisions relating to conditions.

The Comay committee took objection to this wide discretion: "an unconstrained ability to impose conditions is wrong in principle, and contains great potential for harsh, inequitable or even improper actions" (1977: 112). It therefore recommended that conditions should be restricted to those which are "reasonably related to the need for facilities generated by the particular subdivision." The province agreed, but the new wording ("reasonable, having regard to the nature of the development proposed for the subdivision") is still very wide. However, it will presumably discourage demands upon developers which are quite unrelated to the development and which simply constitute a contribution to the municipality's finances.

Ontario is perhaps exceptional in the breadth of the power to impose financial conditions but, with one exception, the practice is common to all provinces. As Hamilton has explained (1981: 63):

> Except for Quebec, all provinces require that the developer pay for all on site costs associated with the subdivision and, in addition, make contributions towards all off-site costs created by the subdivision. The municipality takes responsibility, as part of the annual general budget, for all future maintenance and replacement of the services. While these general practices are fairly uniform in broad terms, some considerable variations in the costs occur for three reasons. First, local governments, depending upon their state of development and attitude towards growth, require different services to be installed. Second, the quality or standard of each service varies considerably. Finally, local governments have used a variety of formulas, to determine what off site levies will be charged to the private subdividers and what basis for calculating levies will be used.
>
> Two points are, however, quite clear. Local governments have required more and more services to be installed prior to the approval of any new subdivisions, and the standard or quality of such services has increased as municipalities attempt to capitalize some future maintenance expenses and shift them to the initial developer.

However, conditions change, and the power which municipalities were able to use in the sixties and early seventies was severely curtailed by the tighter market conditions of the later seventies and currently. Increasing numbers of developers have challenged the legality of conditions. "The challenges have, in many cases, proven successful," but a great deal of uncertainty remains (Bucknall 1981).

The Range of Instruments

Any city that starts to sell zoning is doomed to failure
McLaughlin 1984

The multiplicity of the instruments of planning bears witness to the ingenuity of planners. Despite the number discussed in this chapter, the account is not exhaustive, particularly when the twists and turns of individual municipalities are taken into consideration. Moreover, little has been said on implementation. Even a cursory reading of local newspapers is sufficient to indicate that there can be a wide gap between the formal statement of legislative provisions and the reality of the public control of land use.

One particularly striking case makes the point forcibly: the Campeau Corporation's Scotia Plaza development in downtown Toronto. The central area plan provides for a standard density equivalent to eight times the lot size, though in practice a ratio of twelve is not unusual. The Scotia Plaza development, however, is to be sixty-eight storys high with a floor area of sixteen times the lot size. The increase from twelve to sixteen results in an additional profit for the Campeau Corporation of $40 million. For this the corporation not only used a density transfer but also agreed to retain some historic structures, to provide the city with land for 200 non-profit housing units, and to make provision for day-care facilities in the new tower (*Globe and Mail* 20 November 1984).

Not surprisingly, there was widespread criticism of this bargaining procedure, and a citizen's group called "Downtown Action" planned to make a formal objection to the OMB. The hearing would have been an interesting and revealing one, but Campeau bought off the objectors with a $2 million contribution to non-profit housing in the city. Thus both the private and the public sectors benefit. The Campeau Corporation makes a huge profit, the city gets a package of highly desirable benefits, and the non-profit sector gets some sorely needed houses.

Yet the whole matter raises worrisome questions. Will other developers emulate Campeau in seeking higher densities? Of what use is the central area plan? If private interests can now be seen as openly buying off opposition groups, might not future objections to the OMB be designed with this profit in mind?

It is because of these types of difficulties that the planning system was devised. This system is adaptable, but not infinitely so (Makuch 1985). Scotia Plaza is, at the time of writing, an exceptional case. Hopefully it will remain so.

The Bulletin

Chapter 5
Land Policies

Each generation has its own rendez-vous with the land for despite our fee titles and claims of ownership, we are all brief tenants on this planet

Udall 1963

Many of the issues covered in this book could be embraced within a discussion of land policies. Conversely, the issues dealt with in this chapter could be discussed under headings such as land use controls, conservation, land development and the financial aspects of planning. It is, however, convenient to bring together a number of matters which are all concerned with land supply, values and prices. The chapter opens with a discussion of land prices and an analysis of the land price explosion of the early 1970s. This leads into the broader issue of whether planning itself is a factor in land price increases. One element of cost is the servicing of land and the standard at which municipalities require the services to be provided. Of increased importance are the demands made on developers to provide, or to pay cash in lieu of, services beyond the normal infrastructure, such as schools and parks.

Following a discussion of these issues, the focus shifts to the operation of the land market: land speculation, the market power of major developers, land banking and expropriation. The large profits (and losses) incurred in land transactions, sometimes as a direct result of planning policies, have led to a range of measures to recoup betterment and to compensate for worsenment. Various Canadian measures are discussed including levies, capital gains taxes and Ontario's land speculation tax.

The penultimate section deals with nonresident ownership of land. This is an important political issue in a number of provinces. The chapter ends with a short discussion of federal policies in relation to land. The discussion continues in the following chapter where a number of particular land uses are examined.

All aspects of land policy raise intermingled questions of economics and politics. Economic analysis offers some useful analytic tools, but these are typically constrained by the unsustainable limitation of *ceteris paribus*. Unfortunately for the academician, things rarely are equal, and other factors often assume greater significance. Claiming the world as their oyster, economists are inclined to believe that "planning is, to a very large extent, applied economics" (Frankena and Scheffman 1980: vii). Such intellectual arrogance is seldom displayed by other disciplines. Even the aphorism that "it's all politics" is more a popular quip than a serious disciplinary claim. Nevertheless, there are some simple economic precepts which cannot be ignored with impunity; and these certainly apply in the land market. The fact that they are sometimes ignored shows simply that planning is far more than land economics.

These introductory comments are not made as an opening move in an academic interdisciplinary joust: they serve to indicate that the subject matter of this chapter, though often claimed as the territory of economics, is in fact a battleground of conflicting ideologies, academic disciplines and political expediencies.

The point is underlined by the fascinating international comparisons which easily come to mind. Take, for instance, the statement of the British Uthwatt Report (1942: 13) on compensation and betterment:

> It is clear that under a system of well conceived planning the resolution of competing claims and the allocation of land for the

various requirements must proceed on the basis of selecting the most suitable land for the particular purpose, irrespective of the existing values which may attach to the individual parcels of land.

This implies a total subjection of economic to planning considerations. Of course, it does not stem the economic implications of planning decisions: it merely denotes that these are considered to be of little consequence, or at least secondary, though British experience is capable of more than one interpretation (Cullingworth 1980; Denman 1980; Hallett 1977). In Canada, the extent of planning controls is smaller than in Britain, and greater play is allowed for market forces. Nevertheless, as is abundantly clear from earlier discussion, a wide range of controls operate: so much so, in fact, that a campaign is being waged against the "overabundance of government legislation threatening property rights." (In Ontario, the Ontario Real Estate Association declares annually a "private property week.")

Land Prices

Rapidly rising land and housing prices became a widespread urban phenomenon across Canada in the early 1970s

Greenspan Report 1978

Despite the critical comments made above about the inadequacy of a narrow economic approach to land matters, much of the popular debate which took place during (and since) the land and housing price boom of the early 1970s displayed an extreme lack of appreciation of basic economic precepts. Theories of conspiracies abounded: concerning rapacious speculators, villainous property developers, greedy or sluggish municipalities, and manipulating monopolists (Bourne 1977).

A spate of studies, reports and governmental actions followed. Before discussing a number of these it is useful to consider some basic issues of residential land price determination (Nowlan 1978). Land has some distinguishing features which have a special effect on the determination of its price. First, each piece of land is uniquely located and derives its value from its locational attributes. Prices will thus vary enormously from area to area. Moreover, increases in demand for a particular location will inevitably increase prices. There is no way that the supply in a specific location can be increased, though intensification of use is, of course, possible and alternative locations can be developed. Furthermore, transport improvements can increase the range of alternatives.

The term "location," however, is ambiguous and herein lies another interesting feature of land. In Nowlan's words:

> This question of the importance of geographical uniqueness is critical in the consideration of land markets. A market is defined by the buying and selling of more or less alike products. If each piece of land is unique, then each parcel constitutes a separate market. If, however, other characteristics of land units strongly dominate over location, then a single market for residential land might range over the whole of an urban area, with a lot on one side of a city being a ready substitute for a lot twenty miles away on the other side of town.
>
> The question comes down to this matter of substitutability, with each separate market consisting of a set of ready substitutes. The reason the question of uniqueness is so important is that the extent to which individual land owners have control over prices in the market depends heavily on the breadth of the market in which they are operating.

This, it should be noted, is an empirical matter, and thus sweeping statements about monopolistic ownership are likely to be ill-conceived.

A second distinguishing feature of land is that its stream of benefits last for a very long time. Though in some particular cases, such as open cast mining, it can be said that the land has been "used up," more typically it continues to provide benefits for as long as its locational advantages remain. Moreover, since the locational attributes can change (as a result of changes in surrounding land uses, pressure of demand etc), its value can also change. These changes can be of an extreme nature: certainly fluctuations in the value of pieces of land are much greater than is the case with most other goods. The significance of this point cannot be overemphasized. As we shall see, it formed a fundamental element in the thinking of the Greenspan report.

A further point of importance is the significance of the existing stock and its relationship to new supply. Surges, or falls, in the demand for or the supply of new housing units are cushioned by the large existing stock. A major problem here is to delineate the boundaries of particular housing markets. Again this is an empirical issue, not a conceptual one: and it can change with changing conditions. Increases in the costs of commuting will make downtown locations more attractive, but the increased cost of the latter might be so great as to force house buyers out to distant suburbs. After a somewhat breath-taking review of the evidence, the Greenspan report concluded that the evidence "appears to warrant our considering each urban area as one housing market rather than a series of sub-markets."

The Greenspan report was only one of many analyses which were produced at the end of the 1970s on the huge increases in residential land prices in the earlier part of the decade; but it is distinctive in that it is not confined to one province, but encompasses most of Canada.

The Greenspan Report

"The Federal/Provincial Task Force on the Supply and Price of Serviced Residential Land: A Report for the Ministers Responsible for Housing of the Governments of Canada, British Columbia, Manitoba, Newfoundland, New Brunswick, Northwest Territories, Nova Scotia, Ontario, Prince Edward Island, Saskatchewan, 1978 ..."

The full title of the Greenspan report makes apparent the value of the short personalized title. It also indicates that the list of governments has two major omissions: Quebec and Alberta. These two provinces refused to cooperate; but there

were   other doubters and, in fact, the report itself was an
unbefriended waif. Nobody was prepared to accept responsibility for its publication. The first volume (lavishly produced)
bears the name of no publisher but, for a time, could be
obtained from CMHC. The second volume was eventually
"made available" in xerox form to persistent inquirers at the
offices of David Greenspan. A promised third volume never sur-
faced.

This curious history of publication, if that is the right
word, is not unique in the annals of Canadian policy reports,
but it is strange that such an innocuous document (which
absolved all defendants from blame) should have experienced
such difficulty in acquiring a minimum degree of legitimacy.

Be that as it may, the report presents an impressive array
of analysis and incisive comment on a subject which is often
clouded in rhetoric and prejudice. (The inquiry was not asked
to make recommendations: this would have involved the
identification of an addressee!)

The focal point, and the raison d'etre for the establishment, of the Greenspan inquiry was the real estate boom of
1972-75. There was no doubt about the reality of this: in
twenty-five urban areas across the country, lot prices increased
during this period at a rate over forty percent greater than the
general rate of inflation.

This was a remarkable increase and, not surprisingly, there
was a spate of popular theories which purported to explain it.
Greenspan spent a lot of effort in debunking these. He concluded that the 1972-75 boom could not be explained by any of
the popular conspiracy theories: "we find that the land and
house price explosion of the boom of 1972-75 was not caused by:
provincial and municipal red tape; high municipal lot levies;
goldplated municipal services or municipalities protecting their
property base; citizen resistance to new development; or
government tax policies." But, and it was a big but, "each of
these factors has contributed and will contribute to high price
levels."

Nasty developers were also exonerated from blame, along with planners, municipalities, citizen groups and all other popular targets, though there was no doubt about the "very impressive" windfall profits made by land owners. What in fact happened was a coming together of an extraordinary number of disparate happenings: "inflation escalated; real income exploded; the stock market dropped sharply; the baby boom of the 40s and 50s created a young families boom in the early 70s; the only major way for most people to beat the new federal gains tax of 1971 was to buy, occupy and sell a house; through changes in federal law, downpayments became very low, and so the largest mortgages ever became possible ..." More fundamentally, there was an asset revaluation. In Greenspan's words

> An explosion in real income, high general inflation, the sharp decline of returns to alternative assets on the stock market, more mortgage money than ever before and at cheaper real rates, all combined *at once* powerfully to stimulate the demand for housing and land on top of stimulation already provided by smaller downpayment requirements, exemption from capital gains tax and larger numbers of young households. These factors caused homeowners and potential buyers to believe that *future* prices would continue to increase at then *current* rates. Buyers projected past price increases into expected future price increases. Since expectations of future price increases raised the expected return from owning land and housing, the demand for both increased. When the price of butter goes up demand goes down, but when the price of oil company shares goes up demand for those shares often goes up in expectation of future increases. In this way, strong initial increases in demand led to changing expectations which led to a revaluation of the housing stock.

Greenspan's arguments seem persuasive in relation to the short run price increase of the 1972-75 period, but what of the longer period? Though the popular villains of the short run increase appear to be absolved from blame (particularly in the jazzy first volume, written by the chairman himself), the long run increase in price levels (the "long term price creep" to use Greenspan's phrase) is more problematic.

The issues here are, naturally, of long term importance, and thus worth some detailed examination. In the account which follows, material is drawn from other inquiries, particularly the Bellan report on Winnipeg land prices (1977), and studies such as those undertaken by Spurr (1976), Markusen and Scheffman (1977), and Frankena and Scheffman (1980).

The contention that planning raises prices is part of the credo of the development industry. In fact there is considerable evidence that the statement is true, particularly when planning reduces the supply of land, or prevents the development on, say, cheap sites of scenic beauty. The real issue is not whether planning raises prices, but whether it does so with socially beneficial effects. Greenspan has this to say on the matter:

> Governments plan land use because they know what will happen if they don't. They know from bitter and expensive experience in past periods of high growth that unregulated private development can leave behind severe problems such as inadequately treated sewage and the need for expensive transportation systems which create hidden or delayed costs and environmental damage. If not compelled by the planning process, developers and their customers would neither pay for these public costs nor avoid causing this damage. Government regulation is indispensable to encourage patterns of development that minimize such costs and damage.

There are several different issues here, of which three are of particular importance: the efficiency of planning administration; the validity of planning policies; and the adequacy of municipal finance.

The efficiency of planning administration is not an easy matter to assess. What a developer sees as an Alice in Wonderland maze of red tape may on examination turn out to be a series of well organized consultations with public utility providers and a process of public consultation.

On the other hand, there may be delays occasioned by the need to prepare an adequate plan. Thus in 1973 the Ontario Task Force on Housing Policy complained that in the Toronto-Centred Region, the process of formulating regional development proposals had the effect of freezing housing development in critical areas, and no alternative provision had been made. Similarly local government reorganization can lead to extensive delays: this has happened with the establishment of regional governments in Ontario and of Unicity in Winnipeg (where the reorganization gave rise to such acute difficulties that virtually no development proposals were approved for over a year).

There is also the inefficiency which flows from inadequate legal and policy frameworks, from lack of coordination, and from sheer ineptitude. On the first two, the Ontario Planning Act Review noted in a study of *The Operation of Municipal Planning in Ontario* (1977: 40) that the provincial policy framework for municipal planning was deficient and that the administrative and technical organization was inadequate. Further:

> It appears that presently the planning system is mainly concerned with and regulates *where* development occurs far more than with *how* and *when* it occurs. This is because the system is dominated by proposals and reactions to them at a limited number of locations ...

> The planning conflicts between regions and within regions, between municipalities and within municipalities, which remain unsolved, are partly a reflection of the system to cope with coordination.

Of a quite different nature is the contention that the planners' preoccupation with orderly development is a major cause of high land prices. Derkowski has argued this on many occasions. For instance, in the paper he prepared for submission by the Manitoba UDI and HUDAC to the Bellan Commission, he states:

> One of the most prevalent planning principles is orderly, contiguous, sequential development. Planners' insistence on this principle not only severely restricts the total amount of land potentially available for development but also automatically increases the market power of all those who happen to own land within the narrowly defined areas available for immediate development. This policy restricts competition in the land

market   as effectively as any supposed oligopolistic conspiracy (Derkowski 1977: 34).

Of course, an efficient planning system would ensure that land supply as a whole met demand as a whole.

A notable example of the policy of contiguous development was the Winnipeg case. Four guidelines for this policy were formulated in 1973:

(i)   the city will regulate development in directions contiguous to existing urban development in order to obtain the most effective use of existing municipal services and will optimize the capital invesment in new services;

(ii)   the city will prescribe the location and density of urban growth and development that will optimize the use of public services which will accommodate its primary objective of orderly and contiguous development;

(iii)   the city will encourage the development of new integrated residential areas that will allow a variety of accommodation, reasonable cost and choice of location;

(iv)   the city, in consultation with the additional zone municipalities, will prescribe the location and density of rural residential development in the fringe areas and preserve the open rural character of the remaining additional zone.

Strengthening this policy was a prohibition on leap-frogging to the suburban areas, now incorporated in Unicity, where experience had shown that the cost of servicing was very much higher than in the case of contiguously located development.

Bellan comments: "this policy decision in effect restricted new urban development each year to the belt of land that was immediately adjacent to the built up area, and thereby stringently limited the area of land eligible for such development in any year." It thus became one of the factors in the dizzy increase in residential lot prices over the years 1972 to 1976. Nevertheless, Bellan had no hesitation in concluding that the policy was sound and should be maintained. It was effective in minimizing the city's capital outlays on trunk facilities for

Table 5.1 — Index of House and Lot Prices, Winnipeg and Regina 1971-75

	Winnipeg		Regina	
	MLS Transactions	Fully Serviced Lots	MLS Transactions	Fully Serviced Lots
1971	100.0	100.0	100.0	100.0
1972	106.1	112.3	103.9	103.8
1973	116.9	139.2	122.5	116.4
1974	149.7	224.0	160.0	129.5
1975	181.6	286.2	206.9	187.6

The original data for MLS transactions are from Canadian Real Estate Association *Multiple Listing Service Annual Report 1976*. The data for fully serviced lots are from CMHC. These indexes refer to the average cost per frontage foot of fully paid, serviced lots for new housing financed under the National Housing Act.

Source: *Greenspan Report,* Vol. 2, p. 127

new subdivisions as well as the subsequent cost of servicing them. Moreover, "its desirability is strongly reinforced by the looming prospect of much higher energy costs which will substantially increase the cost of moving people, goods and services, and emphasize the advantage of compact urban development." But, he continued, it was necessary for the basic services (streets, trunk water mains and sewers) to be provided in good time.

This is easier said than done, but that it can be done is nicely illustrated by Greenspan's comparison of the situation in Winnipeg (with its tight planning policies and the stresses of reorganization) and in Regina (where the city was able to respond to the increased demand of the early seventies by approving more land for development). The relative effect on price was very marked. As can be seen from Table 5.1, the Winnipeg lot price index moved above the house price indexes in 1972 and remained there. By contrast, the quick response of Regina to the increased demand had the effect of moderating price rises, and the rate of price increase for lots remained below that for the house price index.

This, of course, was a short run situation. In the long run, a continued increase in demand obviously can be met only by a permanent increase in supply. The problem here is the cost of servicing lots. This has commonly been viewed as a major factor in the increase in land and housing costs.

Servicing of Residential Land

The rate at which services are provided, the manner in which they are financed, and the quality of these services will each contribute to the cost for an improved lot

Martin 1975

In examining the issue of the servicing of residential land, it is important to distinguish between the general inflationary price increase in servicing and the cost of municipally imposed higher standards of servicing. There is also the question of who should bear these costs and how they should be paid.

In fact, the conversion of raw land to fully serviced land ready for building can be a complex process. Certainly, practices and standards vary. Moreover, standards and costs of servicing are intertwined with the workings of the property tax and, what may not be the same thing, perceptions of these workings. The Greenspan inquiry devoted considerable attention to this field.

To look quickly at the question of differences in standards nothing can be more eloquent than Greenspan's comparison of Brampton and Scarborough: the former on the west of Metropolitan Toronto, the latter on the east. Both have similar climate, soil, topography, and labor and material costs. There the similarities end: Scarborough's servicing standards are much more costly than Brampton's. but they are far less cost effective. In 1976, the cost in Scarborough was about $4,600 more per lot than in Brampton; but this did not prevent serious and repeated flooding in many Scarborough basements.

Whatever qualifications may be necessary on this, there is no doubt that standards, costs and cost effectiveness vary greatly; and this follows from the fact that servicing standards are the responsibility of individual municipalities which range from the progressive to the antediluvian.

The matter might not have been of such practical and political importance if the costs of servicing, at whatever standard were met by the municipalities. This, in fact, used to be the case; it is no longer universally so. In Greenspan's words:

> Because of compelling financial weakness, municipalities have delegated to developers the responsibility for local servicing. This delegation of responsibility has had an unintended effect. Since they no longer pay for local services, municipalities have had no incentive to adopt the most value/effective servicing standards. The excessive and/or obsolete standards we observe in many municipalities are a predictable result.

There has been considerable criticism by spokesmen for the development industry of the unnecessarily high goldplated standards imposed by some municipalities (Derkowski 1976). However, there is another side to the argument which has been neatly put by Goldberg (1980). Applying cost benefit analysis he concludes that it does pay to goldplate under certain circumstances:

(i)   it always pays if the inflation rate of capital projects is greater than the cost of capital (the discount rate);

(ii)   it also pays if upgrading will eventually be done in any case, and if there are moderate rates of inflation, say five percent.

A major point here, of course, is that of the life of services. Goldberg notes that, in Vancouver, sidewalks and curbs have been lasting for some fifty years; sewer pipes installed at the turn of the century are still in use, eighty or more years later; and watermains put in place over sixty years ago are continuing to function adequately. "In addition to these lengthy service lives, high quality services have considerably lower maintenance costs." Some even more striking figures for the life of services could no doubt be quoted for the Victorian cities of Britain. The problem in Canada is much less severe but, nevertheless, it is growing (FCM 1985).

Problems seem to have arisen in Ontario more than elsewhere: and they are of long standing. The two basic questions arising relate to the standards themselves and the incidence of their cost. On the former, successive Ontario reports have recommended that the provincial government should establish standards and ensure that these are adopted by municipalities (Ontario Advisory Task Force on Housing 1973b and 1973c; Ontario Planning Act Review Committee 1977a). On the latter, concern has been with the unjustifiable and inequitable variations in standards and in the imposition of levies or imposts.

Variations in standards stem from differing conditions (topography, climate etc) and differing municipal attitudes towards new development (exacerbated by political fragmentation of metropolitan regions) while variations in the size and extent of imposts additionally reflect a more general desire to protect the existing inhabitants of a community from financial burdens. Some municipalities have gone further and required the provision of community facilities while others have imposed conditions so as to exclude low income housing, group homes or roomers.   At worst, the requirements are morally indefensible stratagems to safeguard (or even improve) the situation of existing residents: at best they are an attempt to assist financially poor municipalities to provide essential services.

The subject is a much bigger one than may appear at first sight. It involves not only a range of matters relating to the whole development process, but also taxation, the impact of new development on the finances of a municipality, and social and political concerns.

A preliminary point to make is that certain servicing costs are a legitimate charge which can defensibly be included in the price of a house. Though there may be disagreement as to what servicing charges should be included, there can be no disagreement that the absence of a charge constitutes a payment by the municipality, whether this be an unintended gift or an intended subsidy. It is interesting to note that while, in Ontario, argument has raged about the level and incidence of imposts, in Winnipeg the argument has been on precisely the opposite grounds. The 1977 Bellan report argued that the effect of large capital outlays by the city on servicing, in the absence of any impost, resulted in large financial gains to landowners. The relevant figures for the years 1972 through 1976 are given in Table 5.2. Bellan argued thus:

> A very large proportion of the cost of new capital facilities required by growth is paid by the community at large ... It is popularly assumed that these payments by the city at large constitute subsidization of new homeowners by the total community. This has not in fact been the case. The prime beneficiaries of the city's outlays on capital projects to service new subdivisions have not been homebuyers, but the owners of the land out of which the subdivisions were created. The city's outlays on the streets, trunk water mains and sewers that linked tracts of land to the existing street, water and sewer system, made those lands more valuable. The owners sold for prices which incorporated the value conferred on their lands by the services which the city provided. House purchasers paid the market value of these lands, the full value which they possessed thanks to installations which were paid for not by the owners, but by the citizens of Winnipeg at large.

Table 5.2 — Estimated Gains Achieved in Converting Agricultural Land to Winnipeg Residential Building Lots 1972-76

(1) Year	(2) No. of acres built on	(3) Value as farm land, per acre ($)	(4) Servicing and other costs per acre ($)	(5) Value of serviced land per acre ($)	(6) Gain in value per acre (5)−[(3)×(4)] ($)	(7) Aggregate gain for all acres built on (6) × (2) ($)
1972	850	150	21,100	23,800	2,550	2,167,500
1973	800	200	21,100	29,200	7,900	6,320,000
1974	700	300	26,700	45,500	18,500	12,950,000
1975	650	400	37,000	59,900	22,500	14,625,000
1976	700	500	39,500	74,000	34,000	23,800,000

Source: *Bellan Report*, p. 47

It has been the owners of the land, whether farmers, speculators
or developers, who have been the main beneficiaries of the capital outlays made by the city to enable the development of new
land.

The degree to which the gain is shared between the original owners, land purchasers, and developers depended on "such
factors as knowledgeability, astuteness, willingness to take risks
and pure luck." Some of the gain, of course, would be taxed by
federal and provincial governments, while further reductions
would be made by carrying costs, legal fees and so forth. But
the net gain remained large and, in Bellan's view, unjustifiable.
He therefore recommended that a charge be levied on building
lots to cover "the costs of all capital expenditures on streets,
sewers, water mains and the like, which are made to enable
those lands to be serviced; the monies so raised to be paid into
a fund used exclusively to finance such capital installations."

It was the large size of the gain (however much it was
shared between different purchasers or taxed away) that, in
Ontario, allowed municipalities to increase their demands on
developers, particularly when land had been bought some years
earlier at relatively low prices. Tracing the incidence of costs
and benefits in a matter such as this is complex. In
Greenspan's words: "during the boom ... developers probably
absorbed these costs and reduced their windfall profits." This,
however, was the short run. The long run is much more uncertain:

> We cannot be certain about how these costs affect prices in the
> long run. Most likely they are passed around in a complex way:
> a portion is passed back to the farmers in lower prices for raw
> land; a higher proportion is passed forward to house buyers in
> higher prices for lots. To the extent that lot levies may in some
> municipalities exceed actual municipal costs for the lots, some
> wealth may be passed sideways from developers, farmers and
> home buyers to existing residents as those municipalities cash in
> on their planning control by "selling" subdivision approvals. But
> no matter how they may be passed around, in the long run each
> of these costs should increase prices to home buyers.

At the crux of all this is the nature of the property tax. Again we are quickly involved in a complex issue, though Greenspan expressed it succinctly: "why the municipalities resist cheaper land: money, not principle." The research volume of the Greenspan report is appropriately cautious in discussing the measurement of financial impact, but there seems little doubt that, given the structure of the Ontario property tax, most residential development costs a municipality more in providing services than it obtains from the tax. This is simply because residential properties are undertaxed in relation to their demands on municipal services, whereas industrial and commercial properties are overtaxed.

Change is difficult, not only because of a host of complexities ignored here, but because of an elementary political fact. New housing could be made profitable to the municipalities if they increased the residential property tax; but this would hit both newcomers and existing residents.

There is obviously no local incentive for change and so (Greenspan again) "until senior governments do what they can, the municipalities will do what they must." Less enigmatically, changes in the tax framework within which municipalities operate have to be made at a higher level of government.

The demands made by municipalities on developers increased during the boom of the seventies. There was, and still is, earnest debate on what services developers ought to provide (or to pay cash in lieu). For Ontario, there is lengthy discussion of the relevant issues in the numerous reports produced by, for, and following the 1977 Comay report. More generally, however, dedication of land for public purposes is provided for in the legislation of all the provinces.

A common issue is that of the voluntary nature of agreements between developers and municipalities. In the growth situation of the seventies, developers frequently agreed to hard bargains in order to get development moving. With the turn in the economy, the situation is likely to be very different.

For some reason which is not self-evident, the dedication of parkland seems to assume a particular importance. (Perhaps it appears a most reasonable facility to ask a developer to provide?) In Quebec, municipalities can require a dedication of up to ten percent of the land for parks or playgrounds, or cash in lieu. In Ontario, a five percent parkland dedication is a well-established feature of the planning system. In Manitoba, the amount of land to be dedicated as public reserve land is determined by the expected population of the subdivision.

The Comay report opined that even larger dedications were justified in high density developments. Unfortunately, there was no discussion of the principles involved. Why, it may be asked, should this indirect form of betterment be imposed? The Canadian planning scene abounds with such questions.

Not all developments are physically capable of producing a five percent parkland dedication and, hence, there is provision for cash in lieu. This is a treacherous area which is why, in Ontario, ministerial approval is required for each case. The funds can be used for other public purposes, again with ministerial consent.

It should be noted that the growth of these various imposts on developers is related in part to the enormous change in the scale of housing developments in the postwar years. In addition to the traditional small subdivision developed by a small builder, there came the federally encouraged large developer building on the scale of Don Mills (Rudin 1978; Sewell 1977).

This section has focused on Ontario. It is interesting to contrast the British Columbia resolution of the problem. Amendments to the Municipal Act in 1977, and subsequently, "squarely confronted the troublesome issue of development cost charges. The intent ... is to have all development charges and impost fees levied via a development cost charge bylaw" (Ince 1984: 189). The legislation provides that charges can be imposed only "for the sole purpose of providing funds to assist the municipality in paying the capital cost of providing, altering or expanding sewage, water, drainage and highway facilities and public   open space ... in order to serve, directly or indirectly, the development for which the charges are imposed."

Development cost charge bylaws are subject to scrutiny by the Inspector of Municipalities whose approval to them is required. He can refuse approval if "in his opinion the bylaw does not comply with the spirit and intent" of the legislation.

Land Speculation

> You order your agent to hold it until the property rises, then sell out and buy more further out of town .... I do not quite see how this helps the town ... but it is the essence of speculation
>
> Rudyard Kipling 1889

The popular image of the land speculator dies hard. So strong is the image that, on occasion, governments have been forced to take specific action against him. The speculator is, however, an elusive character and, when pinned down, it may transpire that he is a small farmer or a home owner.

It is useful to introduce the subject with some elementary economic commentary (Baxter and Hamilton 1975). The role of the speculator is considered by economists to be a useful one in that his profit seeking activity tends to lead to a more even allocation of resources over space and time. He buys, not for use, but for future price increases:

> To the extent that speculators can accurately forecast the future scarcity of a commodity, their action can result in stabilization of forseeable price fluctuations over a given time period. By buying commodities in one period for release in a future period, speculators cause (1) a withdrawal of present supply, (2) a temporary increase in present price, (3) an increase in amount stored, (4) an increase in future supply, and (5) a reduction in future price: the end result being a relative stabilization of price and consumption over time. Thus, in the commodity market, speculators perform a socially beneficial function.

This is the case in relation to the commodity market, but land has some unique characteristics. In particular it is durable and immobile; and new lots form only a small proportion of the overall supply. (New housing typically adds two to five percent annually to the existing stock.) Land markets, unlike commodity markets, adjust slowly. Thus speculation does not perform its normal economic function. It is simply a holding of land with the expected prospect of a price increase on a scale in excess of the cost of holding the land.

Two important points now arise. First, to identify real speculators one has to ascertain motives. Except at an individual level this is impracticable: in terms of a total market it is impossible. Baxter and Hamilton instance classes of speculators to include a long time resident farmer whose land borders the urban fringe; a development company operating a land bank; an opportunist moving into the path of urban development; the owner of a single-family house in a predominantly apartment area; the owner occupier of a house in an area where property values are rising. In all these cases, the owners can benefit from land value increases: but whether they have the motive or not is generally both unknown and irrelevant. Thus, the speculator is difficult to identify. The image of the powerful owner holding on to land in the hope of a speculative profit becomes obscured. This is not to say that such individuals do not exist: merely that they are not easy to distinguish from the mass of owners, all of whom would welcome a profit.

This leads into the second and more important point: the power of the speculator to affect prices. A speculator may, or may not, make a substantial profit, but it is rarely that he can influence prices. Land prices are residual: what is left over after account is taken of the costs of servicing and building. The determinant of prices is the level of final demand, not the holdings of individual speculators or landowners. Only if the land market is cornered can speculators affect price. This rarely happens, though the issue is empirical, not conceptual.

There have been several studies of the land holdings of developers. Spurr's report (undertaken within but rejected by

CMHC) concluded that "metropolitan land development has been taken over by the giants, who are now consolidating their position by buying up their competition, and the suppliers and materials in the production processes. The small builder, revered in the mythology of housing is an anachronism" (Spurr 1976: 243). This is an extreme view, and the figures used are misinterpreted (or at least misleading). For example, one table shows that twenty-three firms held 41,188 acres on the fringes of Toronto. Four firms held 58.65 percent, and seven firms held 81.75 percent. He concluded: "it seems that most development now planned on the fringe is in the form of integrated projects on large single owner holdings." This, however, is to ignore two factors. First, there is the land not included in his source tables, estimated by the Canadian Institute of Public Real Estate Companies at 564,800 acres, compared with Spurr's 41,188 acres (Gluskin 1976: 208).

Secondly, major developers have to hold more land than they can hope to develop. "The risks in any one place are so great that good business sense requires greater holdings for compensation." A brief to the Royal Commission on Corporate Concentration listed ten factors which inhibited development: conflicts with Toronto Centred Region Plan; within Parkway Belt; municipal restrictions: no growth policy; future highway use; provincial and federal government restrictions; Ministry of Environment requirements; Hydro alignment; regional government restrictions; conservation lands; sanitary, store and water servicing problems.

From the host of other studies (most of which involve painstaking, if not tedious, sifting of inadequate data) the conclusions of the Greenspan inquiry can be quoted:

> The conclusion from these data is almost embarrassingly simple given the tremendous amount of work that went into compiling it. Nowhere among the thirteen metropolitan areas researched is private ownership of undeveloped land concentrated enough to imply market power and resource misallocation. In all cases where ownership is concentrated (Halifax, Ottawa, Regina, Saskatoon), public sector owners dominate. In other areas, the highest percentage owned by the top four firms is 49.5 in

Winnipeg (also with a high degree of public ownership), followed by 46.1 in Calgary. Neither statistic is high by the traditional standards of industrial organization economics, and we know of no mitigating circumstances to not bring in a judgment that significant market power does not exist in these areas.

In the more succinct words of Muller, "land ownership is far less concentrated than popular belief has it, but it is equally far from being unconcentrated, particularly in subregional markets" (Muller 1978: 59).

None of this affects the fact that the development industry made very large profits when the value of their land holdings increased. Nor does it imply that there is no need to be concerned about future concentration. Indeed, Greenspan warned that both the increasing expense (imposed by municipalities) and the increasing risk (due to slower economic and population growth, and tighter planning controls) would tend to favor the large, integrated companies. This would be particularly so in territorially distinct and specialized housing markets. Thus monopoly power could become a significant problem in the future.

The Development Industry

The government, public agencies and private lenders now have a new type of developer to deal with, one who is in part their own creation

Rudin 1978

Whether or not the large developers have had, on occasion, the market power to influence prices, there is no question of their importance on the Canadian urban scene. This importance is not a quantitative one: the ten largest builders produced less than ten percent of total production in 1976 (Gluskin 1976: 133). What is important is the scale of the developments they have been able to undertake and (a highly related point) the way in which their growth was stimulated by government.

The story starts at the end of the war when a major, and increasing, housing shortage was envisaged (Lorimer 1978: 16; Rose 1980: 27). There was, of course, a huge backlog from the Depression years and some urgent needs were met during the war by Wartime Housing Limited, a crown corporation established by C.D. Howe (the minister in charge of war production) to provide houses for workers in wartime industries. This built 19,000 rental houses between 1941 and 1945. In the two immediate postwar years it produced a further 13,000. But rental housing was not envisaged as a long term policy, particularly when provided by public enterprise. The political aim was to foster private enterprise and, as a restraint on potential radicalism, home ownership. Wartime Housing had demonstrated the efficiency of large scale enterprise in one housing sphere and the Central Mortgage and Housing Corporation was established to support the development of a private house building industry. Wartime Housing was abolished and its houses sold to the occupants.

There was a widely held view at this time that a large scale private house building industry was necessary (Carver 1948: 63). Following this line of thought, the federal government introduced a wide range of programs "to support, encourage, finance and subsidize the building industry." The details are now only of historical interest, but there is no question about their effectiveness. Moreover, there were several forces working in the same direction: the result was the rise of the development industry. Aided by very strong government support, the development industry prospered (Spurr 1976: 193). Curiously, further prosperity came with the increasingly widespread practice on the part of municipalities (at least in Ontario) to pass on to developers the responsibility for servicing sites. "The greater cash requirements ... and the advantages that came from dealing with large parcels of vacant land gave a substantial edge to the large developers, and froze many of the small time speculators and developers out of the market" (Lorimer 1978: 97).

The transfer of servicing responsibilities to developers, according to Spurr, became an explicit policy objective of CMHC in the early seventies. This went under the title of the Comprehensive Land Use Management Program, and was directed towards three objectives: (i) to stabilize and where possible reduce serviced land prices by increasing supply; (2) to change the basic nature of the land development process by making it less financially onerous to the municipalities; and (3) to develop more efficient land use and servicing concepts for residential development.

There is little additional reference to this (other than in Spurr's book) as an explicit policy, but Spurr carries on to maintain that "in consequence, the larger firms attained progressively greater shares of the market, and were able to secure further capital by going public as developer shares sold actively on the stock market."

A definitive assessment of this period, if such be possible awaits a painstaking analyst; but by the early nineteen-eighties it had already become a matter of history. The indefatigable James Lorimer was first on the new scene with a collection of essays unambiguously entitled *After The Developers* (Lorimer and MacGregor 1981). The essays are a curiously mixed bunch, but Lorimer himself puts forward a clear, if inconclusive, statement:

Canada's cities have entered a new period in their history. The era of the developers, of rapid urban growth, high rise towers springing up everywhere, suburbs gobbling thousands of acres of farmland, shopping centers and expressways spreading over the countryside, is over. Only in Calgary and Edmonton does the developers era survive. Those two cities are the last bastion of the corporate city where old formulas still work and the old battles rage. The rest of the country has moved on. Moved on to what? No one knows yet ...

Land Banking and Assembly

Ultimately, land ownership is the most effective form of land use
control

                Prince Albert City Policy Plan 1982

"Public land banking, as the term is presently used in
Canada, refers to the process of public acquisition of land with
development potential in advance of the anticipated needs of a
community, for immediate and future use, for residential and
other purposes" (Hamilton 1974: 1). The Ontario Advisory
Task Force on Housing Policy laid less emphasis on scale, and
more on principle:

> Land banking means the public assembly of large and small par-
> cels, for short and long term use, for residential and other
> development purposes ... The land acquired by government may
> be held in reserve for future use (hence the term land banking)
> or it may be used immediately. The government may develop
> the land wholly itself or in partnership with private developers
> or, again, all the land may be developed privately ... Land
> banking constitutes a whole range of programs and should not
> be regarded as merely a single activity for one specific purpose.

Some writers have gone further and argued that "since
land that is anywhere must be somewhere and held by someone,
there has always been in existence a land bank in the sense of a
stock. It has always been possible to obtain releases from the
bank on payment of the market price" (Pennance 1967: 74).

The term land banking is thus used in different ways, but
these differences are small in comparison with the differing political (and academic) stances taken towards it. Typical of the
proponents are the working group which produced the Toronto
report *Living Room* (Toronto City 1973) and the Hellyer report
(1969), both of which recommended extensive programs of land
assembly and banking. Provisions for federal involvement in
such go back to 1949 when Section 40 of the National Housing
Act permitted CMHC to jointly undertake with a province the

acquisition and development of land for housing purposes (with the federal government contributing 75 percent). According to Dennis and Fish (1972: 316), little use was made of this legislation. However, the judgment can be questioned. It could certainly be argued, if one accepts the case for land banking, that the powers could be used much more extensively. The fact remains, however, that between 1950 and 1972 (i.e. before the major extension of the program) a total of $118 million of federal funds were used to finance "the acquisition of 159 separate projects, and their subsequent planning, development and marketing -- and 102 of these projects were large relative to the local housing market" (Spurr 1976: 271).

A very different stance was taken by the Hellyer Task Force who submitted that "to achieve both cost efficiency and planning effectiveness, municipalities ... should acquire and service all or a substantial proportion of the land required for urban growth within their boundaries." For this purpose federal loans should be made. The immediate result was an amendment of the National Housing Act which provided federal assistance towards land acquisition.

It was in 1973, however, that the minister (now Basford) announced a massive increase in this program. The federal government offered to make available $500 million in loans to provinces over the following five years for the acquisition of land that would eventually be serviced and sold as building lots. Legislative provision was made in 1973 by way of amendment to the National Housing Act. It was clearly indicated that the objective was the reduction in land prices, but as Greenspan has noted, "the exact mechanism by which this objective was to be achieved was never really spelled out."

Dennis and Fish, however (who were widely quoted by supporters of government involvement), asserted that there six ways in which the public assembly and development of land resulted in cheaper land prices:

(1)   There is no speculative profit on raw land prices. Land can be acquired well in advance of need, and sold for

acquisition   cost, plus carrying charges, plus servicing
costs plus perhaps a small profit. Over the same period of
time   between acquisition and sale, privately developed
land may turn over a dozen times and raw land prices be
multiplied ten, twenty or more times, under the pressure
of market forces;

(2)   Government can buy more cheaply with the power of
expropriation at fair market value, without paying hold-
out prices;

(3)   Because of its planning powers, government can ensure
that all of its land is marketed. It will always be in the
right place. Private developers must charge enough on
one parcel to cover losses on others;

(4)   Public holding costs are lower, because it can borrow
money more cheaply;

(5)   Public servicing costs may be lower because of economies
of scale. They may also be lower because municipalities
will no longer set the highest possible standards, requiring
goldplated services, when they must pay for them themselves;

(6)   Not only is publicly developed land cheaper than that
developed privately, but large scale public land development activity has a moderating effect on private prices.
The knowledge that a large inventory of public land can
flood the market at any time that price increases get out
of hand discourages excessive profit taking (Dennis and
Fish 1972: 325).

There has been considerable criticism of these points (Carr
and Smith 1975). The Bellan report showed that land acquisition programs in Manitoba actually contributed to the rise in
land prices. Greenspan comments that the first of the Dennis
and Fish arguments "relies heavily for its validity on a government corporation having excellent business sense and good timing." Without this the result can be to exacerbate the situation.

More generally, on the basis of several case studies, Greenspan concludes that they had "mixed evidence" as to whether or
not government corporations can purchase land as cheaply as
private companies are able to do. There was no evidence that

government purchases had resulted in any decrease in speculation or in raw land prices. Indeed, "the record of government corporations on the timing of purchases is poor." In the more arresting words of Greenspan himself:

> Governments are not inherently inefficient or clumsy. In land banking, however, they may be inherently late. The reason is that they face an inherent circular contradiction. Under the pressures caused by the boom, senior governments intensified their commitment to land banking in 1973, increasing funding on joint land banks that year from about 75 million dollars to about 185 million dollars, with Ottawa promising to spend half a billion dollars over the next several years. Governments cannot launch programs of this magnitude until the pressures have developed; but once the pressures exist, inevitably the programs are too late.

On the other hand, there are cases which demonstrate that, given the appropriate circumstances, land banking can be highly successful. Saskatoon and Red Deer are frequently cited examples.

In Saskatoon, about four-fifths of land development in the urban region since 1920 has taken place on public land (Ravis 1973). "This experience is often cited in the opinionated literature of land banking as a model: in fact it is an interesting, unique, parochial, success story" (Spurr 1976: 316). The city of Saskatoon was forced into the land business by the vast number of tax forfeits which occurred during the Depression. By 1945 the city held 8,500 building sites: virtually all the developable land. Experience in selling and developing this land made it apparent that there was considerable benefit to be obtained from this adventitious municipal operation, including orderly planning, assistance to social programs, and large revenues. Of particular, and rare, importance was the fact that the program became accepted by both buyers and sellers. Much credit for this, especially when the city positively extended its land program in the early fifties, must go to the enlightened way in which it was administered.

Judgments on the Saskatoon experience vary, but two points are of particular interest. First, as just noted, there was an enlightened administration which built successfully on the attitudes fashioned by the local history. Spurr comments:

> ... the cooperative relationship between Saskatoon's private and public sectors obviously contributes to the success of the city's land program; while this is atypical today it could become the norm if more municipalities involved themselves in local land markets.

The advantage to the builder is that his carrying costs and risks are reduced. Secondly, the planning powers provided by the Planning and Development Act are remarkably strong, though they have rarely been used on a large scale. They allow a replotting of existing subdivisions, if consent is forthcoming from the owners of at least two thirds of the relevant area. Following replotting, land is returned to the original owners by prorating the new, marketable area.

Red Deer (Alberta), like Saskatoon, slipped into the land development business as a result of tax forfeits, but its history has been markedly different. In the mid-fifties a long term plan was prepared for a large region around Red Deer. In accordance with this plan, the municipality began purchasing land for the phased expansion of trunk services. The actual purchases (or options) were made prior to the finalization of plans for the route of these services. In Watson's words: "this was a trump card. As long as the possibility of servicing one area rather than another was open, negotiations for land purchase could go forward in a reasonable manner. It was pointed out to potential sellers that development would go where land and servicing costs were least" (Watson 1974: 95).

Though the city had powers of expropriation, it did not need to use them: purchases were by agreement. Sales were at prices which included the marginal cost of all the extensions of service required. This prepayment program was financially advantageous both to the city (since it obviated the need for borrowing) and to builders (who were assured adequately serviced lots).

Prince Albert also deals directly in the land market. In the words of its policy plan, "land ownership is the most effective form of land use control." Ownership and release of land are "undertaken in a logical pattern of direction consistent with the city's ability to service these lands and with the promotion of continuous growth and development as outlined in this development plan." The city is the largest owner and developer of land within its boundaries. Since 1960 virtually all new residential areas as well as several industrial areas have been developed by the city. Nearly all areas likely to be developed are in the city's ownership.

As with other Saskatchewan towns, the original municipal ownership came about through tax default. Necessity has turned into a virtue and an extensive and positive land policy is in operation. In this, again as with other Saskatchewan towns, there has been considerable assistance from the province through the Saskatchewan Housing Corporation. The corporation's land assembly program is designed "to assist municipalities with their residential land needs through the provision of capital funding for the acquisition and servicing of lots." The corporation provides 95 percent ($29 million in 1981), while the municipalities contribute the remainder.

It is interesting to examine the work of the corporation further. According to its 1981 annual report:

> The policy of the corporation is to attempt to develop a two to three year supply of serviced lots, supported by a 15 year supply of banked land ready for development. With an adequate supply of lots available for sale, price increases may be better controlled. Excess revenue from lot sales, over and above development costs for land assembly projects undertaken by the corporation, is provided to the community for use in the development of recreational and social facilities. This arrangement resulted in the start of construction during the year of a multi purpose recreation complex in the north west part of the city of Regina. The corporation has committed $2 million toward this project. The funds were generated from revenues resulting from lot sales in that part of Regina.

Other provinces operate land banking, land acquisition and servicing programs, though none appear to make it as profitable a venture as Saskatchewan. However, profits are not the only issue. As Blumenfeld (1980: 18) has repeatedly pointed out, there is another view on this:

> ... the main benefits of public land ownership are greater comprehensiveness and flexibility of planning. The financial gains anticipated from "the elimination of speculation" may be less than expected. Moreover, this "unearned increment" logically should benefit the community which creates it rather than the home buyers, for three reasons. First, buyers of new houses are, by definition, more affluent than the majority of taxpayers; second, allocation is possible only by arbitrary methods, either "first come, first served," or a lottery, or administrative decision; and third, low lot prices encourage excessive land absorption, costly in terms of services, travel time, energy, and environmental damage.

Thus, as is so often the case with urban and regional planning, the definition of the question at issue becomes questionable.

Expropriation

Canada has the most arbitrary system of expropriation of land in the whole of the civilized world

Mr Justice Thorson

The powers of municipalities to purchase land vary greatly not only between provinces, but also within, since several large cities have their own charters or special powers. The federal and provincial governments, on the other hand, have virtually unlimited powers (in a statutory sense: there are, of course, always political limitations).

The law of expropriation in Canada is highly complex. There is nothing unusual in this: the issues are inherently complicated and considerably affected by the accidents of history. What is unusual about the Canadian situation is how late it was before an out-dated and arbitrary system was reformed.

Mr Justice Thorson's statement in *Grayson v The Queen* (1956-60 Ex. C.R. 336) is well known:

> I have frequently called attention to these provisions of the law and stated that Canada has the most arbitrary system of expropriation in the whole of the civilized world. I am not aware of any other country in the civilized world that exercises its right of eminent domain in the arbitrary manner that Canada does. And, unfortunately, the example set by Canada has infected several of the Canadian provinces in which a similar system of expropriation has been adopted.

The specific point at issue here was that title to land could be taken by the mere filing of a plan in the Registry Office. Indeed, most of the older acts, generally pre-1960, authorized expropriation without any prior notice to the owner and without any statutory right of appeal.

The history of reform, which is by no means complete either in scope or geographically, is set out in the standard texts of Todd (1970 and 1976). The position has developed differently in different provinces. Ontario led the way with the Expropriations Act of 1968-69. The Federal Expropriation Act followed in 1970, and these two statutes provided a model for revised legislation in Manitoba (proclaimed 1971), Nova Scotia (1973), New Brunswick (1973) and Alberta (1974). Newfoundland's 1970 act was heavily influenced by the British expropriation code. Elsewhere, (Prince Edward Island, Quebec, Saskatchewan and British Columbia) much of the old law is still applicable.

Before outlining the statutory provisions, it is interesting to take note of the curious, and sometimes perverse, terminology which abounds in this area. As Todd has pointed out (1976: 19), the term *expropriate* means "to dispossess of ownership; to deprive of property." According to *Black's Law Dictionary*, "expropriation primarily denotes a voluntary surrender of rights or claims; the act of divesting oneself of that which was previously claimed as one's own, or renouncing it. In this case it is the opposite of appropriation." Thus the Canadian term "expropriation" does not really convey the element of force which is expressed in the British term "compulsory purchase." Neither terminology indicates that, "historically, the taking was by the Crown or State exercising one of its prerogative powers of sovereignty. This aspect of expropriation is reflected in the American expression eminent domain."

Without going too far into the legal niceties, this reference to legal history is worth a further comment. In common law, and thus in Canada, ownership of land is usually "the estate in fee simple." This provides the maximum rights (or interest) in land. Basically, this is the same "as the interest granted by the King to his Lords in feudal times: the private citizenry may hold land subject to certain restrictions and the right of the Crown to reclaim the land. This right to reclaim is presently embodied in the laws governing expropriation: at the present time the Crown has the right, in common law, to expropriate any privately owned land *without compensation*. Compensation is paid only by choice of the governments through their own statutory provisions, just as the limitations placed on expropriation are created by statute" (Hamilton and Baxter 1977: 82).

Those limitations are hardly exacting: the 1970 federal expropriation act simply provides that "any interest in land ... that, in the opinion of the minister, is required by the Crown for a public work or other public purpose may be expropriated by the Crown ..." No definition is given of "public work or other public purpose."

Similarly, the provinces are subject to no constitutional limitations in regard to expropriation: they can legally pass legislation conferring the power of expropriation on any person or body as they see fit.

There is nothing in Canada equivalent to the U.S. Constitution which provides the safeguard that no person shall "be deprived of life, liberty or property, without due process of law; nor shall private property be taken for public use, without just compensation." Both political realities and the courts have filled this vacuum, though not always satisfactorily.

There is one further point here that contrasts Canada and the United States (Todd 1976: 24). The American courts have expended much energy on "the taking issue." Given the constitutional guarantee of just compensation for the taking of private property for public use, there has been an innumerable succession of cases where the courts have had to distinguish between the taking of property and the exercise of police power over property. "If the particular regulatory measure falls within the classification of police power, an affected property owner does not have the constitutional right to compensation which exists if the power is classified as a taking persuant to the power of eminent domain." Todd adds that "in the absence of constitutional guarantees of 'just compensation' in Canada, the distinction between police power and the power of expropriation would seem to have no practical significance. Classification of powers is unnecessary. The only questions which can arise are matters of statutory interpretation, namely, is the particular power authorized by a statute ... and, if so, does the statute, expressly or implicitly, contemplate the payment of compensation and, if so, on what terms and conditions?"

Most expropriation acts set out general provisions relating to expropriation authorized under other legislation. The number of acts involved can be large. The McRuer report on Ontario noted that, in 1968, there were thirty-five provincial statutes which conferred powers of expropriation. Ontario may be exceptional. (McRuer commented that the power to expropriate land had been conferred "with reckless and unnecessary liberality.") However, the 1964 Clyne report on expropriation in British Columbia listed thirty statutes containing expropriation provisions, while the Alberta Institute of Law Research and Reform listed forty three in that province in 1973. However, such numbers pale into insignificance when one learns from a report by the Law Reform Commission of Canada (1976: 1) that the federal 1970 act "left untouched more than twelve hundred expropriation powers."

Many of these statutes are concerned with matters which have no bearing on urban and regional planning. However, even on a narrow approach, the list contains significant numbers of planning and planning-related acts for most provinces. No comprehensive survey can be attempted here. Rather, a miscellany of significant or interesting examples can be given.

Under the provisions of the New Brunswick Community Planning Act, land can be purchased compulsorily "for the purpose of carrying out any proposal contained in a municipal plan ..." The Ontario Planning Act appears somewhat more restrictive:

> If there is an official plan in effect in a municipality that includes provisions relating to the acquisition of land, which provisions have been approved by the minister ... the council may in accordance with such provisions, acquire and hold land within the municipality for the purpose of developing any feature of the official plan ...

The extent to which such powers are used is not documented, though Blumenfeld commented in 1966 that the Ontario power had never been used, "primarily because the municipalities lack the financial means for large scale investment in land." The powers may also be limited by the more stringent provisions of the governing Expropriation Act. A 1979 study on *Land Value Capture* compared Montreal and Toronto:

> Much of the land for the Montreal Metro was originally acquired for street widening purposes, and the city was then left with many remnant parcels some of which were used for Metro stations or city parking lots. In some older areas, the city was permitted by its charter to assemble land for urban renewal purposes in conjunction with expropriation for the Metro, in order to assemble small lots into developable parcels.

> In contrast, the 1970 revised Ontario Expropriations Act is quite specific about limiting public land purchases to the actual area required for the stated purpose. Excess or remnant lands (as when the right of way "nicks" a lot) can only be taken if the costs of acquisition are thereby minimized (by acquiring the entire parcel rather than paying damages). At present, the expropriated land must be offered back to the original owner if

not needed for the stated purpose. However, in the
Yonge/Lawrence case [a development on a Toronto Transit
Commission station location], for example, properties were
acquired (not expropriated) at above market rates, and therefore
did not have to be offered back to the previous owner" (Planning
Collaborative and Read, Vorhees and Associates 1979: 74).

Expropriation for the purposes of urban renewal or commercial development has been a very contentious issue. Most of
the documentation on this has been highly critical and, indeed,
the general issue of "prodeveloper city government" was responsible for major political changes in 1972 in Toronto and Vancouver. Quite apart from the question as to whether municipalities should expropriate for private development, there were two
other major factors to which much study was given at federal
and provincial level, namely, the basis of compensation, and the
statutory procedures.

Compensation for Expropriation

Many complaints have concerned the amount of compensation
offered by a government authority for the complainant's property

                           Ombudsman of British Columbia 1983

Determining the compensation to be paid upon compulsory
acquisition poses a surprising number of ticklish questions.
Should the basis be market value or, because of the compulsion,
something more than that? Alternatively, since the acquisition
is for the public benefit (and the value of the property may well
be enhanced by public action, e.g. in servicing an adjacent area)
should not a lower price be offered? If, however, market price is
to be the basis, is any account to be taken of the increase in
value which may result from the use to which the acquiring
authority is to put the land? (This would be high in the case of
a shopping center, low in the case of a park.) What if the
owner of a property (e.g. a home owner) cannot obtain an
equivalent property for the amount he is compensated? Should
he get reinstatement value? If so, has he not profited at public

expense?   If the development to be carried out on the compulsorily acquired land makes an adjoining piece of land in the same ownership more valuable, should there be some "set off"? And, on the same line of argument, should there be additional compensation if the adjoining land is depreciated in value?

These are just some of the questions which have to be dealt with in the law of compulsory purchase.   The Canadian federal legislation was modelled on the British, as was that of many of the provinces.   At the extreme was British Columbia which adopted the 1845 Land Clauses Act almost verbatim.

Curiously, these acts provided no definition or criteria for the determination of compensation.   They merely provided a procedure by which it was to be determined.   Hence, the substantive law of compensation became judge made.   It followed that differences would emerge between provinces, and these were widened by the development of statutory provisions, either in place of, or in addition to, the case law.   British Columbia again occupies a special place in that it is the only province in which the central expropriation statute is substantially the same as the English act of 1845.   New legislation was proposed in a 1982 green paper and a bill was introduced in 1984 but lapsed in that year's election.

The main principle to emerge from judicial decisions was that the term value (referred to in the legislation but not defined) meant value to the owner.   Though this was abandoned in England in 1919 (being replaced by market value) it persisted in Canada.   Major changes, however, took place during the late nineteen-sixties and early seventies.   Table 5.3 gives a broad picture of the main features of change.   The table necessarily greatly oversimplifies the position and, though the complexities need not concern us, it is necessary to discuss the meanings of value to the owner, market value and a number of important related matters.

A neat definition of market value which has become widely accepted is that of the Ontario Bureau of Municipal Research: "market value may be simply stated as the price at which a

Table 5.3 — Compensation for Compulsory Acquisition

	Review	Legislation	Main Basis of Compensation
Federal	Law Reform Commission 1975 and 1976	1970	Market value
British Columbia	Clyne Report 1964; Law Reform Commission of B.C. 1971; Green Paper on a new Expropriation Act 1982; Draft Bill 1984	None	Value to owner
Alberta	Institute of Law Research and Reform 1973	1974	Market value
Saskatchewan	(Future review envisaged)	1968	Value to owner
Manitoba	Canadian Bar Association (1960s)	1970	Market value
Ontario	Select Committee 1962	(1962/63)	Market value
	Ontario Law Reform Commission 1967	1968	
	McRuer Report 1968		
	Robinson Report 1974		
Quebec	Study on Exproporation 1968	1973	Value to owner
New Brunswick	Internal study	1973	Market value
Nova Scotia	Internal study	1973	Market value
Prince Edward Island	None	1949	Value to owner
Newfoundland	Based on British 1919 Code	1957	Market value

prudent   owner, under no compulsion to sell, would sell a property to a prudent buyer under no compulsion to buy. Most property has a readily appraisable market value relating to its use and valuation" (Ontario Law Reform Commission 1967: 18). The Ontario Expropriations Act more pithily states that "the market value of land expropriated is the amount that the land might be expected to realize if sold in the open market by a willing seller to a willing buyer." The federal act is very similar.

Of course, this is a legal fiction since, by definition, expropriation involves an unwilling seller. The value of the property being expropriated may be higher to him than he could obtain for it in the market. This higher value (value to the owner) formed the basis of judge made policy on compensation in England in the nineteenth century and, until the new legislation around 1970, was common throughout Canada.

Quebec seemingly takes pride in its explicit statutory omission of provisions specifying the criteria for compensation. The Bar of Quebec is reported to have expressed pleasure "that the legislation has remained within the tradition of French law without adding certain English traditions such as are found in the federal law of expropriation where criteria for compensation are established depriving the expropriation tribunal of the judicial discretion necessary to render justice in special cases" (Todd 1976: 12).

The rationale for the Quebec approach lies in the special circumstances which can apply to particular ownerships. A site may have particular advantages to a specific owner which are not reflected in the market value (for example, for business purposes), or there may be "unmarketable improvements" (such as the installation of a ramp system for a paraplegic or the construction of a bomb shelter), or there may be no market for the purpose for which the land is used (as with a church or hospital).

The alternative way of dealing with these troublesome issues is to make additional separate provision for them as is done, for example, in the federal act where reference is made to "the value to the owner of any element of special economic advantage to him arising out of or incidental to his occupation of the land." The Alberta act provides:

> Where land is expropriated, the compensation payable to the owner shall be based upon
>
> (a)   the market value of the land,
>
> (b)   the damages attributable to disturbance,
>
> (c)   the value to the owner of any element of special economic advantage to him arising out of or incidental to his occupation of the land to the extent that no other provision is made for its inclusion, and
>
> (d)   damages for injurious affection.

It should be noted that in assessing market value no account is normally taken of the effect of planned development.

Other points arise in these provisions. Disturbance damages formed part of the original English value to the owner. It became a separate head of compensation in 1919 and this has been copied by Canadian jurisdictions which have adopted market value as the main basis for compensation. Disturbance can include the cost of moving, depreciation in the value of the machinery caused by the necessary removal or sale, disturbance or loss of business, and loss of goodwill.

Injurious affection means simply consequential damage, though it has acquired a mass of technical overtones. It again stems from the English Land Clauses Consolidation Act of 1845 where specific reference is made to damage sustained by reason of the severing of lands. The most obvious example would be the compulsory acquisition of a strip of land for a railway or a road.

These various provisions can significantly increase the compensation payable upon expropriation above the mere market value of the land. In practice they could be said to constitute a formalization of the value to the owner approach. There is, however, yet another common provision which can go far beyond this, namely the reinstatement principle.

This is applicable in two types of case. First, of ancient and obscure origin, there is the case where there is no market for the land being acquired. Examples are a church, a school, and a cemetery. In such cases the compensation can be based on the cost of equivalent reinstatement.

Secondly, special provision is made in every province except Quebec for the dispossessed home owner who is unable to purchase a new home with the compensation normally payable. This is known, with a charming lapse from typical legalese, as "the home for a home" principle. The problem with which it deals arose with the introduction of urban renewal, when many home owners were inadequately served by the existing legislation.

The home for a home principle was apparently first employed in Newfoundland in connection with a major redevelopment scheme in St John's. Several hundred families were displaced and were unable to obtain alternative houses at the normal compensation rates. To meet the problem, the Newfoundland Legislature passed The Family Homes Expropriation Act which provided that: "the principle of assessment shall be that the owner of the family home shall receive such compensation as will, at current costs and prices, put him in a position to acquire by purchase or construction a home reasonably priced equivalent to that which is being expropriated." The result was an increase in compensation from an estimated $2 million to an actual $3.7 million. It was "no doubt because of this" that the Newfoundland Act was amended in 1967 to provide that "family homes in urban renewal schemes which are either substandard or unfit for human habitation are now compensated solely on the basis of their market value" (Todd 1970: 56). Such owners have to be offered rental accommodation in the renewal scheme.

Newfoundland is rich in unusual statutory provisions. Of particular interest are the extraordinary provisions of the St John Housing Corporation (Lands Act) 1944. Newfoundland was then governed by Britain, and this may partly explain why the British Uthwatt report on compensation and betterment had such a direct influence.. Uthwatt proposed that "all land is valued; a sum is put up equal to the current value, not on all sites but as much as appears likely to be used in (say) twenty years; and it is discounted to allow for the time which will elapse before some of it is used; and the resulting sum is then divided among all the land owners in proportion to their valuations."

Mark Shrimpton, Research Director of the St John's City Planning Department, has written (1981 and 1984):

> Thus owners were to be paid not what they would expect to receive should their land be sold for housing at the time of expropriation, but part of that sum in proportion to the likelihood of such development actually occurring, and discounted to reflect the fact that such development would be spread over a long period of time. This was a complex and radical proposal, and indeed was never implemented in Britain. But with the approval of Westminster ... the powers used to undertake this expropriation were introduced.

Using these powers, some 700 acres of land were purchased. The area, appropriately, was called Churchill Park.

Expropriation Procedures

> Many people admittedly expect the pre-expropriation hearing to be more than it can ever be ... yet the present hearing process achieves less than it should
>
> Law Reform Commission of Canada 1976

Mr Justice Thorson's criticism of the former extraordinary appropriation procedures, or rather lack of them, has already been quoted. Foremost among the deficiencies of the old law was the general absence of provision for "any system of inquiry giving persons who will be affected by an expropriation an opportunity to be heard." Moreover, a decision by the Supreme Court of Canada (1959) held that "the requirements of natural justice do not afford the person affected by an expropriation a right to be heard before permission to expropriate is granted by the minister." A further glaring deficiency of the old law was the frequent absence of machinery for political control over expropriating bodies. Thus in Ontario, exercise of powers of expropriation by conservation authorities, hospitals and universities was subject to authorization by a county or district court judge. This, of course, was quite inappropriate since the issues at stake were essentially matters of policy and its application.

The Ontario McRuer Report (1968: 991) proposed that both these deficiencies, and many more, should be rectified. Except in unusual circumstances those who were to be affected by a proposed expropriation should be given the right to a hearing at a formal inquiry: and "the basic principle which should dictate the selection of the approving authority is that the approving authority should be in a position to accept clear political responsibility for the expropriation decision finally made." These recommendations were enacted in Ontario in 1968 and were reflected in later statutes of other provinces and the federal act of 1970.

What is of interest, as always, is all the differences between the various acts and also the contemporary adequacy of the principles involved.

The first interesting point of comparison is that the federal act does not require that objectors at an inquiry must have a proprietary interest in the property concerned. Thus, historical, archeological, conservation and amenity societies can be heard. This wide, non-legal but popular, concept of the term interest is rejected in the provincial legislation where objectors are generally restricted to "any owner of lands."

On the other hand, the federal act is restrictive in the scope allowed to the public inquiry. The function of the hearing officer is to report to the minister "on the nature and grounds of the objections made." No guidance is given on the scope of the inquiry and there is no requirement that any evidence be presented by the expropriating authority. "Consequently, and also because of the lack of any previous opportunity for the public to question the environmental or ecological aspects of proposed schemes, the few hearings which have been held under the federal act have produced more heat than light" (Todd 1976: 44).

The scope of inquiries at the provincial level is wider, though still restrictive (McRuer 1968: 1007). The Ontario Robinson report of 1974 stated:

> There have been six years of experience as to the issues which are in fact being raised at inquiry hearings. In spite of the clear intention that the authority's objectives are not relevant, they are challenged in almost every hearing, and much time is wasted in minutely defining what the objectives are in the individual case. The question of alternative routes and sites is raised frequently. Strangely, the "main issue" as to the necessity of taking all or part of the particular parcel for purposes of the project is seldom raised; yet paradoxically, this was the principal reason for adopting the inquiry procedure. Fairly frequently the question of compensation is sought to be raised; it is clearly irrelevant at the inquiry stage since no expropriation has taken place (Robinson 1974: 4).

Robinson adds that, in spite of these difficulties, the new procedures have had success (as foreseen by McRuer) in encouraging "the planning of projects at an earlier time and with greater care." But for the individual landowner, the achievements, and the objectives, are more limited: the inquiry "provides him with an opportunity to be heard and to release his feelings against the expropriation." The Law Reform Commission of Canada (1976: 2) echoed the same point in relation to federal inquiries: "it is unrealistic to view it as more than a conduit for complaints to the Minister of Public Works."

Both the Robinson report and the Law Reform Commission report agreed that the solution lay in earlier public participation in the planning process. This is a major subject for discussion in a later chapter.

One final point remains to be made here. The delays occasioned by pre-expropriation public inquiries plus the very high costs which are allowed to owners under the Ontario legislation (increased by the extended length of inquiries) have led to

the   unhealthy philosophy: "buy at any price rather than
expropriate" (Robinson 1974: 16). The problems are therefore
more acute than they appear.

Betterment and Worsenment

Except as provided in this Act and in Section 24 of the Historical Resources Act, nothing in this Act or the regulations or in
any regional plan, ministerial regional plan, replotting scheme or
land use bylaw gives a person a right to compensation

                                                  Alberta Planning Act

In a free market, land values rise and fall according to
demand. Public action may increase the value of particular
lands. New sewerage, water or road facilities will raise land
values, whereas a conservation designation or a down zoning
will do the opposite. These financial implications are of such
importance that an enormous body of analysis, publications and
policies has emerged to deal with them.

Effective planning necessarily controls, limits, or even completely destroys the market value of particular pieces of land.
Is the owner to be compensated for the loss in value? If so, how
is the compensation for this worsenment to be calculated? And
is any balancing payment to be extracted from owners whose
land appreciates in value as a result of planning measures?

In Canada, the main focus of debate has been on worsenment (or depreciation). Generally speaking, public authorities
have succeeded in imposing a wide range of restrictions, and
consequent worsenment, without the payment of compensation.

Defined loosely, betterment is the increase in land value
created by community action. Arguably this increase should
accrue to the public purse, not to private benefit. The argument, however, is not self evident, and even those who might
support the principle may take exception to its application in
their particular case. What homeowner would gladly give up his
right (sic) to the increase in the value of his house?

As with many issues, once one leaves the highly generalized principle, difficulties abound. In England, the principle had been first established in an act of 1662 which authorized the levying of a capital sum or an annual rent in respect of the "melioration" of properties following street widenings in London. There were similar provisions in acts providing for the rebuilding of London after the Great Fire. The principle was revived and extended in the planning acts of 1909 and 1932. These allowed a local authority to claim, first 50 percent, and then (in the later act) 75 percent, of the amount by which any property increased in value as the result of the operation of a planning scheme. In fact, these provisions were largely ineffective since it proved extremely difficult to determine with any certainty which properties had increased in value as a result of the scheme or, where there was a reasonable degree of certainty, how much of the increase in value was directly attributable to the scheme and how much to other factors. The Uthwatt committee noted that there were only three cases in which betterment had actually been paid under the planning acts, and all these were before the 1932 act introduced a provision for the deferment of payment until the increased value had actually been realized either by sale or lease or by change of use. In short, it had not proved possible to devise an equitable and workable system.

The Uthwatt committee concluded that the solution to these problems lay in changing the system of land ownership under which land had a development value dependent upon the prospects of its profitable use. They maintained that no new code for the assessment of compensation or the collection of betterment would be adequate if this individualistic system remained. The system itself has inherent "contradictions provoking a conflict between private and public interest and hindering the proper operation of the planning machinery." A new system was needed which would avoid these contradictions and which so unified existing rights in land as to "enable shifts of value to operate within the same ownership." They concluded that the solution to the problem lay in the nationalization of all development rights in undeveloped land.

Such a dramatic step was possible in Britain at the end of the war, but conditions and attitudes in Canada were very different. The transatlantic difference was a matter of history, attitudes and perceptions of the future. Nevertheless, as is shown in chapter 4, there are some subtle, yet striking, features of the Canadian scene which, on occasion, achieve as much if not more than the seemingly different world of British planning.

The British system was a thorough reform. There was no pressure for an equivalent in Canada. The Depression had greatly reduced development pressures, unlike the situation in Britain where a housing boom developed. The goal in postwar Canada was to facilitate development. A degree of order was considered necessary (hence the 1946 Ontario Planning Act), but this was seen as assisting the entrepreneurs of development rather than controlling them.

Zoning, of course, does restrict the use of land: indeed, until 1983, the Ontario Planning Act referred to "restricted use bylaws." It does not follow, however, that land values are thereby restricted. On the contrary, zoning was conceived as a means of protecting areas from incompatible uses: it can therefore positively protect land values. Whether it does so or not depends upon the nature of the zoning restriction.

There is no provision for recouping any betterment due to planning policies (or to anything else for that matter), though of course increased values would be reflected in assessments for property tax. So far as worsenment is concerned, the position is not so clear (Rogers 1973: section 5.14; Makuch 1983: 220). When the city of Regina down-zoned a piece of land from residential to park use it considerably reduced the price it would have to pay when the site was expropriated for a park. Nevertheless it was held that, though the action was "to some extent confiscatory," this did not affect the validity of the bylaw (Saskatchewan QB 1958). Yet, other decisions have quashed zoning bylaws on the ground that they are confiscatory. For example, North Vancouver was held to be using its power improperly when it rezoned an area for a park in order to acquire the property at an advantageous price (British

Columbia SC 1973). Rogers adds: "moreover, a bylaw that declares private land to be a public park does not merely regulate the use of the land but, because it prohibits any use by the owner apart from the public, constitutes a disguised appropriation."

A recent exposition of the law has been given by the British Columbia Court of Appeal in a case of down-zoning by the city of Vancouver. The intention was clearly to reduce the cost of future acquisition of the land. In summary:

> The city passed a zoning bylaw which reduced the maximum potential development of certain lots by reducing the area to be taken into account for the purpose of calculating permissible building floor space by up to sixty percent. One of the intended purposes, if not the only purpose, of each alderman voting for the bylaw was to restrict or limit the values of the properties in question so that the municipality could more easily acquire the properties in the future for park purposes. An application was granted to quash the bylaw. The city of Vancouver appealed.

The appeal was dismissed on the grounds that "the city ought not to be able, by the exercise of its powers immediately prior to expropriation, to reduce the value of the property that it intends to acquire" (British Columbia CA 1981).

Hamilton (1981: 67) in his study of the regulation of private property has commented that some of the provinces have passed legislation to protect owners from abuses of down-zoning. "Alberta restricts quasi-expropriation by limiting public use zoning (park, school, etc) to lands intended for such use, owned by the municipality, or to be acquired within six months of such zoning." In British Columbia, compensation is permitted when land is zoned exclusively for public use. In Newfoundland, an owner whose property is zoned for public use may require the local municipality to purchase the lands rendered "incapable of reasonably beneficial use in its existing state."

One particularly interesting provision for compensation is to be found in the federal Aeronautics Act which permits the federal government to zone around airports:

> Every person whose property is injuriously affected by the operation of a zoning regulation is entitled to recover from Her Majesty, as compensation, the amount, if any, by which the property was decreased in value by the enactment of the regulation, minus an amount equal to any increase in the value of the property that occurred after the claimant became the owner thereof and is attributable to the airport.

A successful claim for compensation under this provision was made by an owner who submitted that a height regulation resulted in a diminution of the value of his property. The court determined that the property had decreased in value from $57,500 to $40,000 (Supreme Court of Canada 1957).

Similarly, the British Columbia Conservation Act (1977) provides for compensation where a municipal heritage designation decreases the economic value of a property. The provision appears to be discretionary:

> Where designation ... decreases the economic value of the building, structure, or land, the council may, by bylaw, provide a grant, loan, tax relief, or other compensation to the owner. Compensation provided ... shall be deemed to be full and fair compensation for loss or damage suffered by the owner through the designation.

No cases have been reported of any such compensation being paid. There is, however, no general provision akin to these two.

Two provinces have, or have had, unique provisions for betterment. In Newfoundland, the Housing Act provides that where:

> ... land is developed ... for housing ... and any land in or adjacent to the area ... is by reason of this development increased in value ... the minister may make an assessment of the land so increased in value ...

One case of the use of these powers is recorded (Hagman and Misczynski 1978: 647, note 43).

The other striking case is that of the Alberta Unearned Increment Tax. This has the remarkable record of having been in active operation over its whole life, from 1913 to 1956. It was introduced mainly because of the young province's need for revenue (Alberta entered confederation in 1905) and "a desire to reduce land speculation which was a problem during the 'booms' of settlement and railroad expansion." It originally provided for a tax of five percent (increased to ten percent in 1938) on the "increased value of the said land over and above the value thereof according to the last value for the purposes of this Act, excluding in all cases the cost of improvements or of development work actually made or done upon or in connection with the said land" (Ibid: 441).

Unlike the English increment land duty, introduced by Lloyd George in 1909-10, the Alberta act was simple to administer and enforce (which may well have been significant to its longevity). It applied to only one taxable event, namely on sale. Registration of land and the obtaining of a clear title was dependent on the tax being paid by the purchaser. In its last year the tax produced $1.4 million. Reasons for its repeal are a matter for conjecture. Hagman suggests that "perhaps the tax was repealed not because it was ineffective, but because it was finally beginning to bite" (Ibid: 442).

The line between a betterment levy and a capital gains tax on land can be a fine one. Indeed the two terms are often used interchangeably; and there is in fact no difference in principle between a general levy on a realized betterment value and a tax on a realized gain. The differences arise in the details of particular schemes. At the extreme, there is clearly a difference between a charge aimed at recouping betterment value created by specific public action, and a tax levied generally on all increases in land value however caused. In this sense the Alberta Unearned Increment Tax was a capital gain.

The importance of the particular provisions is illustrated by the complex situation in Britain in 1967 following the introduction of both a capital gains tax and a betterment levy. Broadly, the distinguishing principle was that capital gains tax was charged on increases in the current use value of land only, while betterment levy was charged on increases in development value (Cullingworth 1980: 311).

In Canada, there is a general capital gains tax levied by the federal government.   This is not restricted to land;   it extends to shares and works of art. A major exception is the gain made on the sale of an owner occupied house. (This applies to the principal residence only.) One half of a capital gain is taxable at the appropriate corporate or personal rate. Capital losses can be offset.

Apart from this federal tax, there are no other capital gains taxes in Canada, though there was a Land Speculation Tax in Ontario from 1974 to 1978. This is of particular interest, and is worth describing in more detail.

The background, of course, was that of the escalating house and land prices which formed the subject of the Greenspan report, discussed earlier in this chapter.   The widely accepted assumption was that a major factor was speculation in land: buying and selling for profit and without adding anything real to its value (e.g. services). It has already been shown that speculation, even if identifiable, does not have any effect on the final price of land (except in the unlikely event that such a large proportion of land is held that the speculators can wield market power).   Nevertheless, the political pressure to take strong action against the profiteers could not be resisted. But how were the offenders to be identified and separated from the virtuous builder who was following a legitimate role? The Minister of Revenue explained the problem as follows:

> Our problem is twofold: firstly how to focus the taxing effect on speculation without prejudice to normal transfers to property ownership; and secondly how to ensure that the tax would be broad enough to capture speculation in whatever form it might be camouflaged.
>
> I would emphasize that the whole basis of the legislation is to be fair and reasonable and to focus the taxing effect on transactions where increases in sales prices are realized without any real contribution of added value. I would, in fact, say that this element

of added value between transactions is the keystone of the legislation since it is this factor which distinguishes conventional
transfers of property ownership from speculative activity.

I am proposing a new tax to discourage speculative activity.
This tax has two objectives:

(1)   to reduce the escalation of land and housing prices;

(2)   to recover for the public a major share of windfall gains
      from land speculation (Baxter and Hamilton 1975: 6).

These two objectives clash: the more that prices are
reduced the less will be the benefits to the community purse.
Contrariwise, the more that windfall gains accrue to the community, the less will be the restraint on prices. Such a point
was too academic to figure significantly in the debates, and it is
nothing new to find politicians promising the best of all worlds
to their electorate.

There was, however, a great deal of serious discussion on
the Land Speculation Tax Bill and its complexities. In outline,
the legislation provided for a tax of twenty percent (in addition
to the federal gains tax of fifty percent) on all realized gains on
the disposition of real property, subject to specified exemptions.
These exemptions were numerous and complicated, but they
included owner occupied housing (and vacation properties), farm
property which had been owned by the vendor for at least ten
years, property which had previously been the principal
residence of a senior citizen, and land which was included in a
registered plan of subdivision and had been serviced to an
extent that building could commence.

This, of course, is a gross oversimplification of a complex
piece of legislation, but it does indicate the type of exemption
which was made. Moreover, the last example underlines the
government's concern not to penalize legitimate operations in
the land market.

Nonresident Ownership

Alberta Canada: Own your own 3 to 6 acres of farm woodland
60 miles from Edmonton, Alberta. Near town of mostly Ger-
man and Dutch descent. Average price US $20,000.

Advertisement in *The Economist* 7 November 1980

On few land issues is so little known and so much written
as on nonresident ownership. The extent and character of the
problem varies markedly between the provinces, and within
them. An immediate distinction must be made, however,
between nonresident and foreign ownership. The latter is a
more contentious and emotional issue than the former, though
there is a similar paucity of reliable information. It is neatly
characterized by the title of an Ontario committee of inquiry:
The Select Committee on Economic and Cultural Nationalism
(Ontario Legislative Assembly 1973). This, of course, is part of
a wider and long standing concern about foreign ownership,
control and influence in Canadian affairs.

The response of the Trudeau government to this was the
Foreign Investment Review Act (FIRA). Until 1985, this constituted the major federal, as distinct from provincial, control over
foreign acquisition of real estate. At the time of writing, FIRA
is being replaced by the Investment Canada Bill which is
designed to encourage the establishment of new businesses in
Canada. It is, as yet, unclear what (if any) effect this will have
on foreign investment in Canadian real estate. It seems likely
to be negligible.

The FIRA legislation attempted to prevent acquisition by
non-Canadians where there was no significant benefit to
Canada, for example in increasing economic activity, productivity or efficiency. McFadyen's studies conclude that using
these criteria, "certain acquisitions of real property for the purpose of development or redevelopment may be demonstrated to
be of significant benefit to Canada" (McFadyen 1976:70). All
other large real estate transactions are thought likely to be
disallowed. Such is the opinion of the Canadian Real Estate

Association and the Urban Development Institute, but as McFadyen points out, "since few disallowances have been reported to date, and since the identification of significant benefit provides scope for discretion, it is difficult to be certain on this point include foreign purchases of farms valued in excess of $250,000 (except certain purchases for the purpose of development and redevelopment), foreign purchases of rental property (or any other property) in excess of $10 million in value, and foreign take overs of Canadian real estate businesses."

A wide general review of the problems arising from foreign and nonresident ownership was undertaken by the Federal-Provincial Committee on Foreign Ownership of Land (1975). This concluded that the data were insufficient, that some provinces saw no significant problem, and that some of the problems "where they exist" were:

(i) restriction on public access for resident citizens to prime recreational areas such as beach and shoreline areas;

(2) limit on the amount of land that is available for public recreational use by resident citizens;

(3) acceleration of the subdivision of agricultural land and the removal of productive farmland production;

(4) rising property values which in turn may lead to higher tax assessments for local residents;

(5) changes in the character of communities, in that areas become depopulated by summer or occasional residents;

(6) an increased demand for land which results in higher prices thereby making it more difficult for resident citizens to purchase land;

(7) in the case of Prince Edward Island, the real possibility that a majority of the total land mass of the province may shift to nonresident and/or alien ownership;

(8) creation of potential for conflict between the priorities of foreign investors and Canadian economic goals.

This is little more than a catalog of possible impacts.
Unfortunately, except for Prince Edward Island, which clearly
has a special problem, there seem to be few real problems on
which data is adequate for an informed judgment to be made.
However, lack of facts rarely affects a political matter. The
Ontario report nicely illustrates this. After decrying the lack of
suitable data, the committee concluded that its review of a
variety of evidence showed that "the level of foreign ownership
of various categories of land in Ontario is significant." The
report, however, lacks conviction and, in fact, amounts to little
more than a lengthy and sloppy political statement. For
instance:

> ... it cannot be overemphasized that land is a constrained supply
> commodity, and the more so when the different types of land
> and land use, and distance, are taken into account. Many
> citizens and residents of the province feel that they have some
> claim to the benefits and enjoyment of the physical resources of
> Ontario, in the form of reasonable access to private ownership,
> reasonable costs of land as a component of shelter cost, and
> access to outdoor recreational facilities, to name the most com-
> mon. In particular, they feel that their needs and claims prop-
> erly override freedom of access to land ownership on the part of
> non Canadians, or that land ownership, its use or its benefits as
> an investment are not appropriate commodities for export.
> Specifically, many feel all these factors are imperative grounds
> for modifying the rights of private owners of land in Ontario.

The several uses of the word "feel" is noteworthy: the
matter is one in which feelings run high (Cutler 1975). The evidence, however, is decidedly thin, and there are contrary arguments. For instance, a 1980 report of the Prince Edward Island
Land Use Commission notes that, though "fears are expressed
about farmers coming into the province and inflating the price
of land," nevertheless "in the commission's view farmers from
away should be welcomed, since they bring in capital, labor and
in some cases new management ideas. The tobacco industry is
an example of an agricultural sector which probably would not
exist without nonresidential farmers coming to the province."
In short, there are benefits of nonresident ownership.

Yet there are also real problems. Demand for land from foreign sources must tend to increase prices, particularly in areas where there is already heavy pressure. Thus, a Nova Scotia report shows "purchases of rural property by non-residents of Nova Scotia has had a significant impact on land values, particularly on the value of shoreline property" (Antoft et al 1971: 1). It is often argued that, for foreigners, long term capital appreciation is more important than the short term returns on equity favored by Canadian investors. To the extent that this is true, foreigners may outbid Canadians, or at least force up prices. Nonresident ownership can lead also to changes in land use which are economically, or at least politically unacceptable. Some of the problems are more matters of land use control than of ownership, as New Brunswick, Quebec and Nova Scotia have noted.

There were indications in the seventies that the general demand from nonresidents was increasing. Antoft et al noted:

> Our study suggests that Nova Scotia is experiencing the results of a "back to the land" movement, which has its origins in frustrations and apprehensions about urban life in the great metropolitan centers of North America. Modern transportation and communication methods have removed in large measure the province's former remoteness from these centers. As available land has become scarce in such traditional recreational areas as Maine, Vermont, New Hampshire and Northern New York State, the land hunger pressures are seeking new frontiers. There are signs that Nova Scotia is just beginning to feel this phenomenon as the swell that precedes a tidal wave.

This is a somewhat melodramatic statement, but the essential point (about increased demand) is echoed in several reports of the mid seventies (Jones 1976; Spencer 1973; Young 1975).

Whether this will continue through the eighties seems doubtful but, in the meantime, increasing numbers of measures have been taken by the provinces to regulate nonresident ownership.

Controls range from restrictions on the acquisition or leasing of crown land to taxes on land transfers. Until 1975 it was unclear how much, if any, power provinces had to operate general controls on nonresident ownership. In that year the Supreme Court of Canada upheld the validity of a statute of Prince Edward Island. "The court found that absentee ownership of land is a matter of legitimate provincial concern and that it was entirely within provincial jurisdiction to pass laws dealing with land. Furthermore, it was found that the case represented not an attempt to regulate or control alien residents per se but rather a limitation on land holdings by nonresidents" (Environment Canada 1978: 7). Subsequent to this decision, the Canadian Citizenship Act was amended (in 1976) to explicitly delegate to the provinces the power to control ownership of real property by aliens. Prince Edward Island is of particular interest and warrants further discussion.

Canada's smallest province has always had special problems of land ownership (Bolger 1973; Clark 1959). These have stemmed from such factors as its tiny size (less than 850 square kilometers), the significance of its agricultural and recreational land resources and, since the 1960s, a marked increase in the rate of land acquisition by nonresidents. On the latter, a Royal Commission calculated that at the rate of acquisition experienced in the early seventies, the proportion of the island held by nonresidents would increase from five percent to fifty percent by the end of the century (Prince Edward Island 1973: 15).

A 1964 amendment to the Real Property Act reduced the acreage that could be acquired by non-Canadians, without the consent of the Lieutenant Governor in Council from 200 acres to 10 acres. At the same time, a limit on shorefrontage was introduced: without consent, a maximum of five chains (330 feet or 100 meters). However, in the absence of enforcement machinery this limit was ignored. Legislation of the early seventies rectified this (by the simple device of using the land registry system) and extended the limitation to all nonresidents of PEI. Administration is undertaken by the Land Use Commission. In fact, most applications (petitions) are approved:

Cases involving family reasons (gifts, bequests or sales to persons with family connections with Prince Edward Island) have been nearly always approved. They presented almost 36 percent of all approvals between 1972 and 1976. Also it is government policy to approve transactions, even those involving lands of interest to the province for agricultural, forestry, recreation or wildlife purposes, when the stated price exceeds that which can be offered by the Land Development Corporation on behalf of the province. High land prices accounted for 24.5 percent of all cases approved during the five year period [1972-76] ... About 25 percent of petitions approved [during this period] have included lands where the stated intent of use was considered acceptable and the lands were of only marginal interest tothe province and generally of a slightly higher per acre cost than the province could contemplate ... (Environment Canada 1978: 28).

It must be remembered that the PEI controls operate over all nonresidents, Canadian as well as others (predominantly American). Of the 1,083 petitions made between 1972 and 1976, 649 (60 percent) were from Canadians. However, it seems likely that the publicity given to the PEI legislation choked off some incipient demand.

Land which is the subject of petition can be purchased by the Land Development Corporation. The prices are apparently lower than those which nonresidents are prepared to pay, and this gives rise to considerable debate on the island. (Between 1972 and 1973, the land of 41 percent of all denied petitions was acquired by the corporation.)

Another interesting aspect of the PEI policy had been the development of an information system. "A continuous, informative and organized record is maintained on each and every transaction covered by the legislation ..." There is thus more information for PEI on the nonresident land purchase issue than for anywhere else in Canada.

This was increased with the publication of a 1980 report of the Land Use Commission to the Executive Council. This indicates that there is a two way process: land is not only sold by residents to nonresidents, it is also sold by nonresidents to residents. The commission warned against any "alarmist conclusion" on nonresident acquisitions: "a more sober analysis indicates that a large proportion of the land approved for nonresident acquisition will eventually return to Island hands." It continues:

> The conclusion which the commission draws is that, given the current level of nonresident transactions, there is not much long term likelihood that Islanders will again become tenants in their own land as a result of nonresident transactions that are occurring at the present time. The fact that the great majority of petitions are approved, sometimes cited as evidence that the program has no teeth, seems rather to us to indicate that most petitions are of the type that should be approved, unless the province wishes to isolate itself from the rest of Canadian or North American society (Prince Edward Island 1980).

Corporate land ownership, however, was regarded as "a distinctly different matter from nonresidential transactions." The commission explained:

> Nonresident petitions involve small parcels of land and a large number of buyers and sellers. At the present time these transactions are routine, and pose no significant threat to provincial interests. Present legislation is adequate. For corporate transactions this does not appear to be the case ... The government has done little more than monitor the market ... There are glaring loopholes in the existing legislation ... There are fears that a substantial degree of market control could be exercised by a few large processors, and that a form of tenancy would be reintroduced if corporate ownership became widespread.

Matters came to a head in 1981 when a firm already owning some 3,000 acres of land applied to purchase an additional 6,000 acres. This created a public outcry, and forced the government to take action. A Select Standing Committee was established and, following its report (1982), a comprehensive Lands Protection Act was passed.

Interestingly, the issue is now no longer nonresident ownership, but corporate ownership and preserving the family farm (though the act provides that "a person who is not a resident person shall not acquire an aggregate land holding in excess of ten acres or having a shore frontage in excess of five chains unless he first receives permission to do so from the Lieutenant Governor in Council.") The act precludes a personal aggregate land holding in excess of 1,000 acres, and a corporate land holding in excess of 3,000 acres. However, "where it is in the public interest" a permit can be issued for acquisition in excess of this amount, but the administrative procedures have been tightened and a report on each permit has to be made to the Legislative Assembly identifying the applicant, the land concerned, and the reasons for the issue of the permit.

To conclude this account of nonresident ownership, reference needs to be made to a study by Environment Canada which attempted to provide, for the first time, some very general statistics on the dollar values involved in foreign investment in Canadian land (Ward 1984). The study is a benchmark one, to be repeated in a few years' time, which has to wrestle with difficult technical and data problems. It proved impossible "to conclude whether or not foreign land ownership is a significant problem either in terms of land use, land ownership or economics." Though the report stressed that the major factor was that "there is just not enough evidence," it also noted that this was no deterrent to extensive legislation. However, "it appears that much of the existing legislation on agricultural land reacts more to local perceptions of a problem than to facts regarding the existence, significance, or the effects of foreign land ownership."

It is not easy to generalize about nonresident land ownership in Canada. Some provinces seem to have no problem, while in others previous alarms have quietened down (as in Ontario). On the other hand, Manitoba and Prince Edward Island have passed new legislation during the eighties, and both for the same reason: a concern about corporate ownership. What validity this has is conjectural; and the changed economic climate makes it even more so. Even Prince Edward Island is experiencing "a marked reduction in the number of applications" from nonresidents (PEI 1983). The same is the case in Ontario where the number of acres acquired by nonresidents fell from 39,822 acres in 1981 to 7,059 acres in 1984

(Ontario Ministry of Agriculture and Food 1985). More generally, it seems that land planning issues are more important than land ownership. There is a widespread concern for the safeguarding of agricultural land from urban encroachment and for the concentration of development in selected rural areas where infrastructure investments and public services can be economically provided.

Federal Policies

The goal: to ensure that federal policies and programs and the management of federal lands contribute to the wise use of Canada's land resources

Environment Canada 1982b

Environmental impact studies now constitute a veritable growth industry but *land use* impact studies are much less common, partly because there is no statutory requirement for them as is the case with environmental impact studies. The Lands Directorate, however, has a program of studies which though modest has demonstrated the highly significant impact which federal programs can have on land use in a specific region. A pilot study in the Windermere Valley, British Columbia, documents a surprising number of federal programs which have had a land use impact in this small area (initially chosen as a pilot study because it was assumed that the area was one of minimal federal involvement). Many of these impacts are small, but the cumulative effect is significant. A short report lists the individual programs of fourteen (sic) federal government agencies, and details the land use effects of each (McCuaig and Manning 1980).

The federal influences derive "from the ownership of land, from the various financial and regulatory programs that directly affect the economy of the valley, and from a continuing involvement in the planning process through a variety of programs." For instance, the federal government owns large areas of land including the Kootenay national park, two Indian reserves, a national wildlife area, and a national historic site. "All of these tracts of land are removed from the normal economic activity of the valley and placed in a reserved or preserved category." By contrast there are the many small areas of land owned by the federal government for the provision of such key services as police, post office, small harbors, radio, and television. Of course, these are activities of essentially local significance, but the report comments that "the services provided by them affect many of the activities in the valley," and so far as the post office and police facilities are concerned, their central urban location may encourage "the concentration of urban development in existing centers." The concluding section of the report comments briefly on the "federal role in planning and coordination":

> Through its involvement in many industrial sectors, the federal government is included in the planning for many parts of the valley. There is not, however, a direct federal involvement in any form of comprehensive regional planning other than in a sector by sector basis or through specific lands such as the coordinated rangeland units, the Indian reserves, and the parks. In these latter cases, planning occurs primarily within the boundaries of the particular land unit. At present, there is evidence of a lack of day to day communication between the federal government and other levels of government within the valley, all of whom share the means to influence land use within the region. While there may be some coordination at higher managerial levels, the day to day planning at each level of government appears to take place independently. The researchers of this project were often able to carry information from one agency or sector to another and identify for them areas of potential conflict or joint concern.

Coordination is, however, more easily recommended than implemented. This chapter concludes with a discussion of recent attempts in this area.

A concern for federal coordination has commonly been expressed. It reached its zenith with the establishment of the Ministry of State for Urban Affairs. The unhappy history of this institution is described in chapter 2. Here note can be taken of a lower key endeavour, the Interdepartmental Task

Force on Land Use Policy. Some sixteen federal agencies were initially involved in this: the number decreased by one with the demise of Urban Affairs.

The report of the task force, *Land Use in Canada,* was published in 1980, five years after its establishment, as a "glossy". The preface notes that the reason for publication is "to enhance public awareness of the national perspectives of land use issues and federal government perceptions on land use matters." The report deals, in a highly summary fashion, with the facts of land use: agriculture, settlement, outdoor recreation, forestry, wildlife, minerals and energy production. The conclusion is that:

> ... most of Canada's good quality resource lands are limited to only a small proportion of the area of the country. These same rich areas support the bulk of Canadian economic activity, contain most of Canada's population, and satisfy the demands for housing, recreation and transportation. Thus, competition for access to and use of this land is inevitable. The belief that Canada has an inexhaustible supply of good land is not based on the country's proven resources; on the contrary ... the amount of land available for most activities is limited.

An equally brief account of trends in land use, provincial incentives, growing public concern, land prices, energy, the value of agricultural land, urbanization, pollution, and so forth leads, in a somewhat breathtaking manner, to the conclusion that "the federal government has a responsibility to establish guidelines for its own activities as they affect the use of land." The task force "therefore proceeded to recommend a course of action in establishing a federal policy on land use."

The recommendations read like a caricature of a political motherhood statement. They warrant reproduction here only because they demonstrate eloquently the practical limitations of any concept of a coordinated federal policy in relation to land:

> If the major land problems that affect Canada now or in the future are to be satisfactorily resolved, concerted effort is required in several areas. The task force recommends that the federal government should:

(1)   adopt a policy that will establish its approach to the wise use and management of Canada's land resources;

(2)   establish an interdepartmental committee to coordinate federal land research and land using activities and to implement federal policy with respect to land;

(3)   establish a set of land use guidelines to direct its departments and agencies in those activities that could influence the land resource and its use;

(4)   recognize the legislative jurisdiction of the provinces with respect to land and endeavour to support the provinces in their land use policies and activities wherever these are compatible with the interests of the federal government;

(5)   continue to provide the Canadian public with basic information on the characteristics, capability, and use of the land resource.

The challenge to the federal government is to take the initiative and accept the federal responsibilities with respect to land and the federal role in land problems. The current and emerging land problems will not disappear and a timely response may avert foreseen problems and conflicts. There is a clear and pressing need for a federal policy on land use at this time.

The need was met in 1981 when Environment Canada published a short statement, *Federal Policy on Land Use.* The policy incorporates guidelines for the assessment of land use factors in all federal activities. It provides a series of policy positions and land use guidelines to be followed by federal departments and agencies in developing and delivering their programs. These positions and guidelines take into account such issues as the preservation of prime farmland and other high quality resource lands, the maintenance of public access to recreational lands, the proper management of land producing important renewable resources, and the appropriate use of hazard prone lands. "Their application will result in federal programs becoming more sensitive to land use issues and contributing more actively to the achievement of good land use in Canada."

The policy also directs increased attention to the provision of coordinated federal support to the provinces in their efforts to promote sound land management. An interdepartmental committee on land use was established under the direction of the Minister of the Environment to achieve the required coordination., and to provide a federal focal point for discussions with the provinces on land use matters. The committee was also intended to assist federal departments and agencies in adhering to the policy's guidelines.

In announcing the policy, environment minister Roberts noted that, "it is not the intention of the federal government to trespass on provincial responsibilities for land, but rather, to provide a more effective federal support to the provinces in mounting and implementing land use policies and plans that reflect both provincial and national interests."

"The adoption of the federal policy on land use," he continued, "confirms the commitment of the government of Canada to the sound management and wise use of a basic resource - Canada's land. It also demonstrated the willingness of the federal government to cooperate with and support the provinces in working towards this end."

The statement has been critically received. Lash judged that while the task force report was basically praiseworthy, the policy statement "lost its juice" (Lash 1981: 65). A lengthier *Brief to the Federal Government* was issued by the Canadian Institute of Planners in April 1983. This is generally supportive, but asks for an expansion of the responsibilities and powers of the Interdepartmental Committee on Land.

It remains to be seen whether this committee becomes an effective mechanism for coordination or whether it gradually fades away. Seldom do all-encompassing land policies achieve much.

Chapter 6
Natural Resources

The mountains are rich in gold and silver, and all descriptions of minerals, and clothed in some of the finest timber, an inexhaustible means of supplying the treeless expanse of prairies in the Northwest

Sir John A Macdonald 1866

It took less than a century for Canada to move from "the doctrine of usefulness" (Brown 1969) to a "conserver society" (Science Council of Canada 1977b). This gradual shift in values, neatly outlined in Burton's classic essay (1972), are transforming the context within which natural resources are exploited. Both the legal and the political frameworks are out of harmony with this newer ethic, though inherent clashes will always remain, for example, between developmental and conservationist considerations. (The Inco stack at Sudbury is an eloquent symbol of this.)

In this chapter several areas are selected for examination: agricultural land, aggregates, forestry, provincial parks, water and, finally, Ontario's attempts to devise "coordinated program strategies."

Agricultural Land

Is land use and development planning in general now being dominated, distorted perhaps, by the new sanctity of the farm? In most rural areas it is, and properly so

Wilson 1980

Agricultural land is the subject of intense, sometimes acrimonious and typically inconclusive debate. Given the importance of agriculture to the Canadian economy, this is perhaps not surprising: a third of Canadian employment is directly or indirectly linked to agriculture (Bentley 1977). However, the similarity with the debates in the United States and in Britain suggests that there is an issue of deeper significance. Perhaps much can be ascribed to the appealing arguments that agricultural land is limited, that self sufficiency in food supplies is desirable, and that the urbanization of agricultural land is irreversible. The truth lies far from these simple ideas. Agricultural land may be limited, but so are many other types of land and, in any case, to refer to land area without reference to productivity is highly misleading. ʻWhether self sufficiency in food supplies is desirable or of any relevance in the nuclear age is debateable. Here the essence of the argument is political, though the economic costs involved should not be ignored. On the irreversibility question some lessons might be learned from the British "Dig for Victory" campaign in the second world war together with the persuasive, though largely ignored, evidence on the high productivity of gardens in medium and low density housing areas.

The arguments often turn to a focus on preserving the "best" agricultural land. As we shall see, this is a favorite policy across Canada. How effective such a policy can be is problematic, and considerable confusion is occasioned by the statistical sources available. "Facts can be plucked from three parallel streams of data, each providing a partial description of the farmland base" (Bureau of Municipal Research 1977a: 1). The first is the quinquennial Census of Agriculture. Similar, though not identical figures are produced provincially, for example, in Ontario, where annual estimates are made of principal field crop and pasture acreages. Thirdly, there is the Canada Land Inventory which is discussed in the following section.

The Canada Land Inventory

A basis for land use planning

McCormack 1971

The Canada Land Inventory is a major federal enterprise which developed from the same pressures that led to the Agricultural Rehabilitation and Development Act (ARDA) of 1961 (discussed in chapter 7). These pressures emanated primarily from the concern for increasing regional economic disparities, but also from "widespread improper land use, and a variety of emerging resource and land use conflicts in all of the provinces" (Rees 1977). More specifically, the Senate Special Committee on Land Use argued in 1957 the need for an inventory of land classified according to its suitability for particular uses. ARDA provided a statutory framework and in 1963 agreement was reached that the Canada Land Inventory (CLI) should be mounted by ARDA on the basis of working agreements with the provinces. (The CLI was transferred to the Lands Directorate of Environment Canada when that Department was established in 1970.)

There are many ways in which land can be classified, for example, by ownership, tenure, cover (vegetation, construction etc), and so on (Gierman 1981). Most classification systems use a mixture of such variables of land use, and therefore cannot provide a fully adequate typology for the individual variables. In Gierman's words, "all variables have different conceptual origins, means of obtaining data, and end uses. An examination of how these variables overlap with one another will indicate why they should be treated separately. Land cover is the vegetational and artificial construction covering the land's surface. One cover, for example trees, can encompass a variety of activities such as tapping of maple trees, producing fruit, logging, etc. This same cover can have a variety of ownership or tenure patterns such as public, private, leased, owner operated etc. Again this same cover can have different major economic activities or industries such as recreation, lumbering and dairying associated with it."

The CLI classification is a mixture of "land cover" and "land activity" (i.e. the active use made of the land). In fact there are several systems of which those for agriculture, forestry, recreation and wildlife were the first. Each of these systems is independent, and attempts to objectively assess the land resource for the particular purpose (and, of course, at the particular point in time).

For agriculture and forestry, the classification ranges from the most to the least productive. For recreation, on the other hand, the classification is one of potential intensity of outdoor recreation that might be generated and sustained. Land capability for wildlife is classified separately for waterfowl and ungulates. The measure is of the extent to which land can meet the needs of the species or group under consideration.

There have been major developments connected with the CLI since it was started: the Biophysical Land Classification System, the Canada Geographic Information System, and the Land Use Monitoring Program. Moreover, an extensive research program utilizing the wealth of data generated by this work has been undertaken by the Lands Directorate.

The CLI covers about a third of the country, and encompasses all significant land areas capable of sustained agricultural activities (Simpson-Lewis et al 1979: 3). The soil classification groups mineral soils into seven classes (and various subclasses which are not detailed here) according to their potential and limitations for agricultural use as determined by climate and soil characteristics. The first three classes are lands capable of sustained production of commonly cultivated crops; the fourth is marginal for arable culture; the fifth is capable of use only for permanent pasture and hay; the sixth is capable of use only for wild pasture; and the seventh class is for soils and land types considered incapable of use for arable culture or permanent pasture.

An account of the position in each province is given in the Lands Directorate Map Folio *Canada's Special Resource Lands* (Simpson-Lewis et al 1979: 5). Over Canada as a whole, eighty-six percent of the land either has no capability for agriculture or has not been classified for agricultural use. (This includes areas within the CLI boundaries which are unclassified, such as urban areas, military reserves, and parks, as well as organic soils, for which there are insufficient data.) A further two percent are marginal for agriculture (class six) and are suitable only for rough grazing. This leaves only about one million square kilometers, or eleven percent, of Canada's total nine million square kilometers of land which can support agricultural production.

Of this one million square kilometers, less than half (459,934 square kilometers) is free from severe physical limitations and capable of supporting crop production. These are the prime lands: classes one to three of the CLI. The Prairie Provinces and Ontario account for eighty-six percent of these lands. Ontario is particularly richly endowed with class one land: that which has no significant limitations for agriculture and has the highest productivity for a wide range of crops. Over a half of Canada's class one agricultural land is in southern Ontario. It is here that "encroachment by rural residential development, recreation facilities, transportation needs, and urban growth is greatest."

Urbanization of Rural Land

As long as there is no strong farm land preservation commitment at all levels of government, academics, practicing professionals and citizen interest groups will have to continue to keep on the alert and be ready to fight another battle another day

Krueger 1982

A major focus of research in the Lands Directorate has been the urbanization of rural land (Gierman 1976 and 1977; Neimanis 1979; etc). A 1981 paper by Warren and Rump reports in detail the results of a study made possible by incorporating   the monitoring of changes in urban centred regions as a component of the Canada Land Use Monitoring Program. Studies under this program are planned to be carried out every five years (coincident with census years) for all urban areas with populations of over 25,000. The value of these findings lies in their detail, but the following summary, dealing with the general contrasts over the two quinquennia 1966-71 and 1971-76 indicated the character of the data:

> In total, 28 percent less rural land was converted to urban use during 1971-76 compared to 1966-71 ... Despite the total decline in rural land converted, the efficiency of urban land uses, measured by relating population change to the area of land converted was lower. For all urban areas during 1966-71, sixty hectares of rural land per 1,000 change in population were converted. During 1971-76, this conversion rate increased to seventy-two hectares per 1,000 population change. The provinces of British Columbia, Newfoundland, Ontario and Quebec had below average conversion rates tied to population adjustment for 1966-76. The Maritime provinces, on the other hand, had land conversion rates well above the average ...

> Urban expansion in Canada continues to occur on those lands with high capability for agriculture, forestry and ungulate production. Sixty-two percent of the land converted between 1966-76 had high capability for agriculture. Corresponding figures for forestry and ungulate wildlife were 41 percent and 51 percent respectively (Warren and Rump 1981: 47).

A subsequent report on the processes and consequences of agricultural land use change by McCuaig and Manning (1982: 61) expands on a wide range of issues revealed in the statistical analysis. It also succinctly lists the pressures which operate on urban fringe farmers as follows:

(1)   Considerably higher land prices and, therefore, higher opportunity costs on their capital investment;

(2)   More direct opportunities to make one time profits from the sale of all or part of their land for non-agricultural pursuits;

(3) Increased management requirements due to such nuisance factors as vandalism, pilferage, trespass, and neighborhood incompatibilities;

(4) A greater degree of local regulation on the activities they may undertake: for example, limits on the use of equipment on the local roads, replacement of waste and manure, spraying, etc;

(5) Increased demand for new services (often not required or desired by the farm population) to be funded by all residents and consequently increased taxes which, because of their larger holdings, often fall more heavily on farmers;

(6) Transformation of basic infrastructure with emphasis on urban rather than rural requirements.

These amount to a formidable force for change but, as McCuaig and Manning point out, " ... an alternative to urban opportunities is intensification of agricultural activities. This may, in fact, be an intermediate stage before final urbanization. Consequently some of the most productive and highly capitalized farms are found on the urban fringe, and it is these farms that are often displaced by expansion of urban areas." Ironically, the same force which enhances urban fringe agricultural land is also the force which "destroys" it. This does not always happen of course: sometimes the land is allowed to deteriorate in the expectation of early development. The fringe is thus "an area both in transition and in anticipation of transition."

Before turning to policy issues, a further report from the Lands Directorate is of interest and relevance: this deals with agricultural land values.

Agricultural Land Values

Farmers farm poor and retire rich
Manning, McCuaig and
Lacoste 1979

A 1979 study by the Lands Directorate concludes that this aphorism is now more true than it has ever been (Manning, McCuaig and Lacoste 1979). Agricultural land values rose by over 400 percent between 1961 and 1976 (compared with a rise in the consumer price index of just under 60 percent). Part of this rise is due to urban and recreational pressures and the resultant values which bear little or no relation to the values for farming. "Good farmland is also good land for housing, industry, recreation, airports and transport corridors." This situation is made all the more acute by the facts of history: "most Canadian cities were originally located in the areas of highest agricultural capability (Toronto, Montreal, Winnipeg, Edmonton, London etc), partly because of their role as service and transport centers for the agricultural regions." (Within eighty kilometers of the 23 largest Canadian cities lies 57 percent class I agricultural land, 29 percent class 2, and 20 percent of class 3.) Not surprisingly, the largest increases in farmland value have occurred in the areas of major population concentration. The highest was around Toronto where there was a fantastic 2,500 percent increase in the fifteen years 1961 to 1976. In general, the largest increases were experienced in southern Ontario, the south coast of British Columbia, and scattered areas of Alberta, Saskatchewan and Nova Scotia (all with an increase exceeding 800 percent over the period). By contrast remote areas and poorer quality lands had relatively small increases or actual decreases. This is the corollary to the intensification of use, and related increase in value, in areas close to major urban centers.

The study also shows that the total acreage of farmland has declined. The overall decline is small, from 173 million to 168 million acres, but the proportions for the eastern and central provinces are high. New Brunswick, Nova Scotia and Newfoundland lost well over two-fifths of their farmland. On the other hand, British Columbia had an increase of a third.

The authors ascribe the major features to location, competition for land, and agricultural economics. There are, however, also agricultural land policies (or absence of them) which may have had some effect. For example, the increase in farmland in British Columbia may have been assisted by the establishment and the operations of the British Columbia Land Commission, whose primary objective was the preservation of agricultural land. The following pages are devoted to a discussion of agricultural land policies.

Agricultural Land in Ontario

"The Challenge of Abundance"

Ontario Special Committee
on Farm Income 1969

Over a half of Canada's class I agricultural land is in southern Ontario, amounting to over 2.1 million hectares in 1976. Prime land, defined by the provincial government as classes I to 4, amounted to nearly ten million hectares. This area has been falling constantly for a long period. Estimates differ according to the data used and also according to differing interpretations (Bryant and Russwurm 1979: 124), which in turn depend upon whether the "loss" of agricultural land is seen as constituting a crisis (Rodd 1976), or as an insignificant economic change (Frankena and Scheffman 1980). Whatever the loss in area, however, this has been accompanied by a major increase in productivity, giving rise to a "challenge of abundance." It is this very increase in productivity which has been a factor in the reduced land under cultivation. Indeed, withdrawal of less economic agricultural land has been more significant than urbanization, which is popularly regarded as the culprit. Gayler sums up the situation in a 1982 paper: "in Ontario, farm acreages decreased by approximately 25 percent between 1951 and 1976, although only 10 percent of the acreage lost to agriculture was actually converted to urban uses. At the same time, there was an increase of just over 100 percent in agricultural production on the remaining farmland, indicating a diminished demand for agricultural land."

Similarly, after a wide ranging review of some fourteen studies, Frankena and Scheffman concluded that "the data on land use conversion indicate clearly that in the aggregate the rate of conversion of land to built up urban use is low in relation to the rate of productivity increase in agriculture, the stock of agricultural land, and the decrease in the acreage of census farms ... These findings do not indicate that public policy should not be concerned with the rate of agricultural land conversion, but they do indicate that there is little basis in fact for the cataclysmic rhetoric which has sometimes characterized recent discussions of the agricultural land issue" (Frankena and Scheffman 1980: 86).

Policy in relation to agricultural land in Ontario has had two major planks: the prevention of non-farm residential development in rural areas and, later, the preservation of good agricultural land.

Postwar growth in the demand for scattered low density housing in rural areas led to increasing intervention by the province of Ontario in subdivision and part lot consents (Punter 1974). This led to the UDIRA policy (Urban Development in Rural Areas) which, inter alia, attempted to concentrate urban development in areas where adequate servicing was available or could be readily made so. Controls have been systematically extended and strengthened, but there is an administrative limit to the extent to which they can be effectively imposed. The sheer number of applications is too great, and the practical scope for monitoring local consents and appealing bad decisions to the OMB is severely restricted. Additionally, the trend towards more delegated authority to municipalities reduces the province's power of direct control.

Ontario Provincial Guidelines on Agricultural Land

"26 Acres Lost Per Hour"

The UDIRA policy stemmed more from concern about servicing costs than about loss of farmland. The preservation of agricultural land has been a political issue in Ontario only since the mid-seventies, except for the special case of the Niagara fruitlands which have had a longer period of political attention (and which is discussed in chapter 8). The ineffective measures taken in relation to control over subdivision were supplemented in 1974 when the Ministry of Agriculture and Food set up a Food Land Development Branch "to work with local government in planning for ongoing agriculture, to monitor the use of foodland, to comment on new plans and projects, and to develop policy recommendations for the preservation of agricultural land." So stated the ministry's *Strategy for Ontario Farmland,* which opened, significantly, with the words: "food and agriculture are currently in the spotlight".

This particular paper, though occasioned by alarm at the loss of foodland, was at pains to correct the alarmist figures which were being bandied about. A particular target was the "26 acres lost per hour." The figures were, of course, misleading, but then agricultural statistics frequently are (Crewson and Reeds 1982). This was a time of heightened public awareness of the use of natural resources, of the quality of the environment, and of new perceptions of the impact of technology on ecosystems. Indeed, a new vocabulary entered the public arena. Typical of the times were two publications of the Science Council of Canada: *Population, Technology and Resources* (1976) and *People and Agricultural Land* (1977a).

It is within this context that political capital was to be made out of the issues of agricultural land, and the province responded, at least in words. The *Strategy for Ontario Farmland* referred to a major concern "with the priceless lands of the Toronto-Niagara Golden Horseshoe and other fine farmlands taken up by urban expansion." Unfortunately for the argu- ment, rises in agricultural productivity as this time far outstripped any loss in land. Nevertheless, the province felt justified in committing itself "to preserve the better agricultural land in all parts of Ontario." There followed a green paper (in 1977) and a policy statement (in 1978) on *Food Land Guide- lines*.

The guidelines were intended to "provide a method to incorporate agricultural considerations into local plans," and the warning was given that no attempt was being made "to address all of the issues related to planning in rural areas ... forestry, sand and gravel deposits, recreational areas, and environmental areas ..." Shorn of the trappings, the guidelines amounted to lit- tle more than an exhortation to preserve the best agricultural land wherever possible. Where there were conflicting demands, the resolution of these would vary "according to the types of use to be accommodated, the amount and nature of the land available, and the future growth pressures expected."

Illustrations were given of the types of conflict which might arise, e.g. "where potential for such resource uses as forestry or sand or gravel extraction overlap with areas having agricultural potential, it is necessary to determine which activity receives higher priority for any given area. In some instances, forestry or sand and gravel extraction must have priority. In other areas, agriculture will have priority." This is to pose the question, not to answer it; and, of course, no predetermined answers are possible. In the nature of the matter, conflict resolution is dependent upon the pressures of time and place. What the guidelines did was to state that food- lands were important and had to be taken into consideration against other uses.

Such straight talking does not come easily to governments, and the quotation limped to an indeterminate end: "the conflict among these uses is not severe, however, because forest areas can revert to agriculture, and extractive areas can be rehabili- tated for agriculture in many instances." *Can* is the operative word: whether they do or not depends upon the policies and programs devised and implemented by the province. It is here that one of the weakest spots in Ontario land use policy is seen: the inadequacy of the legal, institutional and financial machinery for reclamation of land.

In spite of the critical strictures on the guidelines, they did more than attempt to raise the level of awareness of the food-land issue: they gave some clear pointers for restrictive action. Though perhaps minor in any particular case, they could add up to significant dimensions. Two short examples will illustrate:

- estate residential development must not be permitted on high capability agricultural land

- land use activities such as highway commercial development should be directed to urban areas or permitted only on low capability agricultural lands.

There were several clear guidelines such as these, though there was little by way of effective machinery for enforcement. Two points remain for discussion: the psychological (or political) impact of the guidelines, and the basic validity of any approach which attempts to give agricultural land a special place in the firmament of land uses.

The first can be illustrated by reference to the studies and operations of Ontario Hydro. Against the background already described, Ontario Hydro started, in 1975, "to classify and rank Ontario's foodlands in order that Hydro could plan for transmission routes having the least overall impact on farm-land" (Ontario Hydro 1976). This is perhaps the most striking impact of the provincial foodland policy, though the issues raised are too technical for discussion here (which in itself illustrates part of the wider difficulties involved).

Even more difficult is the question of the valuation of agricultural land. This has exercised the minds of many, both in government and in academia but, mixed with a good sprinkling of politics, the resolution seems elusive.

On the one hand is the argument that the best agricultural land represents a priceless asset. The very term is, of course, unacceptable to an economist, and deadlock can arise at this point, as it did in Britain when an abortive attempt was made to arrive at an agreed system for the valuation of agricultural land (Cullingworth 1979: 564). On the other hand, there is the notion of opportunity cost and the necessity for assessing costs as well as the benefits of "safeguarding" agricultural land. Frankena and Scheffman make the point eloquently:

> Fortunately, the guidelines do at least provide that prime agricultural land may still be converted to other uses when the case for doing so can be justified. This provision is important, because it is fundamentally irrational to argue that all the better agricultural land should be preserved for agriculture, just as it would be irrational to argue that all the better hospital land should be preserved for hospitals, or all the better airport land should be preserved for airports, without considering present and future demands for agricultural products, hospital services, or airport facilities, and without considering alternative uses for the land in question for houses, schools, firms, etc.

Given a context of debate such as this, it is not surprising that there is considerable disagreement on the objectives, scope and achievements of provincial policy in relation to agricultural land. There is no agreement on what the questions should be, let alone the answers.

The food land guidelines were amended in February 1983 in conjunction with the new mineral aggregate resource planning policy statement discussed below. The amendment "recognized that some areas with agricultural potential also have a resource potential for mineral aggregate extraction." In a limited number of areas (for example the Niagara region fruit growing areas) a combination of factors (especially soil quality and climate) enable the production of "special horticultural crops." Such areas are designated "speciality crop areas with restrictive aggregate policies." The policy provides that mineral aggregate extraction will not be permitted on these lands "unless documentation is provided to reasonably show that (a) the site can be rehabilitated for agriculture to allow production of the same acreage of the same speciality crops at the same level of productivity, and (b) there will be no effect on climate or microclimate on which the area may be dependent for speciality crop production."

The guidelines were under review in 1985 and, when approved, are to be issued as a provincial policy statement under the Planning Act.

Agricultural Land Policy in British Columbia

The story of British Columbia's Agricultural Land Commission is the story of one province's success in grasping the nettle of farmland preservation in a free enterprise society. It *is* a nettle; it *has* been grasped; and the story is worth telling

Wilson and Pierce 1982

Ontario is content to rely in the main on market forces in determining whether land should be retained in agricultural use. Neither the operation of planning controls nor the dubious influence of political rhetoric on the "safeguarding" of agricultural land alters this basic fact. British Columbia makes a striking contrast, with a major intervention in the market.

The background is partly political but, aside from politics, there are physical differences which have important implications. Some 90 percent of the land of the province is mountainous and non-arable. Agriculture is limited to the narrow steep walled valleys. The proportion of land which is arable is very small: "only 4.1 percent is suitable for tillage and crop production"; less than one tenth of one percent is class I. Moreover, the best agricultural land is also the best land for many competing uses. The most intense pressure, of course, is in the Lower Fraser and Okanagan Valleys. One result has been land prices higher than can be justified simply by agricultural productive potential (Hudson 1977).

The governmental reaction initially was "organizational": the establishment in 1970 of a Land Use Committee of the Cabinet to assist in the resolution of conflicts between different government departments. The Environment and Land Use Act of 1971 formalized the position of this committee, and gave it sweeping powers (Corke 1983: 10ff) which, however, were not used by the Social Credit Party then in power. Indeed, they look very much like "political window dressing." Be that as it may, "the stage was set for action on farmland preservation."

The political pressures continued to mount, and farmland preservation was a major issue in the 1972 election. The NDP, who were elected, had an election proposal for a "land zoning program to set aside areas for agricultural production and to prevent such land being subdivided for industrial and residential purposes ... [and] establish a land bank to purchase existing and rezoned agricultural land for lease to farmers on a long term basis." After their election they lost no time in acting upon this. Using the powers of the Environment and Land Use Act they put a freeze on the development of farmland. This was followed, in 1973, by permanent legislation establishing the Land Commission. The main function of the commission was to preserve agricultural land. (It also initially had powers in relation to the establishment of urban green belts, land banks, and parklands for recreational use.

These powers were never used. They were repealed in 1977, when the Land Commission was renamed the Agricultural Land Commission. The means provided for preserving agricultural land was essentially a zoning mechanism, though one of awesome power. In brief, the commission was empowered to establish agricultural land reserves (ALRs) in all land capable of sustaining agriculture. There were statutory provisions for determining which lands were to become ALRs (Manning and Eddy 1978). However, as Sue Corke has explained, the commission had some discretion in the initial establishment of ALR boundaries. Although the ALRs were intended to be based on "biophysical parameters of the landscape" (Runka 1978: 16), entirely outside market considerations, it was inevitable that compromises had to be made in order that the boundaries would conform to legal and institutional constraints. In addition, the commission had to exclude high capability lands where they were felt to be in the path of an irreversible urban trend.

Judging the precise amount of land equivalent to the five years' development requirements outlined in their guidelines was a highly objective decision. "Failures" in the scientific approach to agricultural zoning coupled with mounting pressures for urbanization, gave rise to a high volume of appeals, from other government agencies as well a as from the private development sector. These appeals constantly kept the Land Commission under pressure and in the public eye. Although a highly controversial structure, operating a highly controversial piece of legislation, it was, however, sufficiently institutionalized by the time of the 1977 provincial election and return of the Social Credit Party to power that its continued existence was guaranteed (Corke 1983: 18).

The Land Commission Act, in Hagman's words, "may have represented the most massive downzoning in Canada to that date" (Hagman and Misczynski 1978: 283). Some of the reaction was violent, particularly among farmers who saw potentially profitable opportunities for sale swept aside: some "were adamant to the point of threatening acts of civil disobedience, that the right to realize the capital appreciation of the land not be taken away." This was not just an issue of profiteering: land sales often formed a farmer's retirement pension. "On the other hand, it was argued that farmers should make a living from farming, not land speculation, and that proceeds from that living should permit them to retire on a decent income" (Bray 1980: 595).

The solution adopted has been described as "in kind" compensation. The most important provision was the Farm Income Assurance Program which provided income protection by way of indemnities when market returns fell below a certain level. All ALR designations were completed by 1975. They covered an area of some 4.7 million hectares. Under the original act, applications for exclusion of land from an ALR were made to the commission, (and, in specified circumstances to the Environment and Land Use Committee). This was changed in 1977, by the Social Credit government, to allow the minister to give leave for an individual to appeal directly to the Environment and Land Use Committee. With the success rates in these appeals, there is increasing fear that the policy of safeguarding farmland is being diluted. One analyst has maintained that total exclusions are equivalent to "an average yearly rate comparable to the loss of agricultural land in the year preceding the Order in Council which prohibited subdivision of farmland" (Pierce 1981: 51). An earlier review by the Lands Directorate of Environment Canada concluded that designation as an ALR did not ensure that land was actually used for agricultural production (Manning and Eddy 1978), while a recent paper by Wilson points to the success not of the land preservation program alone, but also of the accompanying highly profitable activity of several marketing boards (Wilson and Pierce 1982: 17).

Assessment will, no doubt, continue to prove difficult but, to quote Sue Corke, the commission "has undoubtedly created a precedent for the extension of non-compensable land use regulation in a sector hitherto not explicitly regulated. And this has been done in a political environment ideologically hostile to state intervention in private rights over land use and development" (Corke 1983: 25). The commission itself has no doubt that it has a continuing role (B.C. Provincial Agricultural Land Commission 1983), but the wonder is that it has survived.

Agricultural Zoning in Quebec

In addition to urban areas, rural low density housing in both Quebec and Ontario is threatening the unique lands of good soil and climate, which are truly irreplaceable

Simpson-Lewis et al 1979

Quebec's vast area (135 million hectares) has very little good agricultural land. Only 0.01 percent, or 19,533 hectares, are rated as class I soil. "This valuable resource is located in the vicinity of Montreal and Valleyfield, precisely where urban consumption of land is highest. Other prime areas for agriculture include 909,671 hectares of class 2 soils and 1,281,043 hectares of class 3 land. Most of these favored soils are restricted to the St Lawrence Lowlands" (Simpson-Lewis et al 1979: 5). In short, Quebec's small areas of good agricultural land are mostly located in areas of strong development pressures. Until recently, the position was greatly aggravated by the lack of protection of good lands and an inadequate planning system. The relatively new regional planning organization is described in chapter 9; here we discuss the separate measures taken to protect good agricultural land, leaning heavily on Wolfe's account (1985: 136).

The wasteful use of agricultural land and its rapid urbanization have been under discussion in Quebec since the early sixties. An additional factor of concern is the fact that the province provides only sixty percent of its food requirements (Quebec Ministère de l'Agriculture 1978). In December 1978 the Agricultural Zoning Act was passed. This provides for the designation of land for farming: such a designation prohibits any other (non-existing) use.

Administration rests with the *Commission de protection du territoire agricole du Québec*. Prior to designation, however, there is consultation with the appropriate municipality, owners and other interested parties. Widely publicized hearings are held. Wolfe gives one example: Ville Laval (Ile Jésus), the island of 150,000 population just north of the Island of Montreal. "In this case, about 30,000 acres, almost 50 percent of the total area ... were tentatively zoned, including part of the city's own industrial park. Compromise solutions were found, about half way between the Department of Agriculture's proposal and that of Ville Laval" (Ibid: 138).

Wolfe comments that "since zoning is a municipal responsibility, the role of the Department of Municipal Affairs and local planners in the debate on the ultimate limits of permanent zoning in each municipality was critical. It seems to be generally agreed that sufficient peri-urban space was left untouched to provide land for urban growth for the next twenty years, although this is not distributed evenly among municipalities surrounding urban centers."

Large areas of the St Lawrence and Ottawa Lowlands have been affected by designation. No compensation was paid for this large down-zoning, but a neat preferential land tax provision has given a positive incentive to farmers "to make sure that their farm is included in the zoning." Moreover, there is a serious deterrent to dezoning: if a property is dezoned, imputed back taxes must be paid to the municipality for a period of ten years, and tax rebates received must be refunded for the same period (Schwartz 1981).

The Priarie Provinces and the Family Farm

Canadian settlement policies established the owner-operated family farm as the predominant form of agricultural production unit

Bray 1980

Ontario, British Columbia and Quebec are essentially concerned with agricultural land use. Some provinces, on the other hand, are concerned with ownership and tenure. Bray has pointed out that "the owner-operated family farm is a concept traditional to North American agriculture." Technological changes have undermined this and, as a result, have created both economic and political difficulties. In particular, there has been concern about the "survival of family farms, their ability to compete with commercial corporations or communes, and the effect of their decline on the rural community." Compounding the problem has been the purchase of land by nonresident Canadians and foreigners. In Saskatchewan, the 1974 Farm Ownership Act limits the amount of farmland which can be owned or acquired by nonresidents of the province or by corporations not primarily involved in agricultural production. (The maximum limit was reduced from 160 to 10 acres in 1980.) In Manitoba, the 1977 Agricultural Lands Protection Act limited foreign purchases of farm land to twenty acres. In response to continued inflation of land prices, allegedly due to speculation in farm land, restrictions were extended by the 1983 Farm Lands Ownership Act. Nonresidents of Manitoba and non-farm corporations are now restricted to purchases of ten acres or less.

Nonresident ownership also arises as a significant land problem in Prince Edward Island. Apparently this is perceived "as a serious developing problem by the Island's close knit population whose forebears had struggled for nearly a century to wrest title from absentee English landlords" (Environment Canada 1978: 3). A starting point can be identified in the year 1969, when the federal Department of Regional Economic Expansion prepared a *Development Plan for Prince Edward Island,* and the province established a Land Development Corporation (Environment Canada 1979: 5). It was considered that substantial amounts of potentially productive land existed on the Island and that, if these additional acres were brought into use and production methods increased, it would be possible to triple the value added by agriculture from 1969 to 1983. One means to achieve this goal was the Land Development Corporation which was envisaged as "an intermediary between the community and various government departments.

Through the judicious acquisition and release of land, as well as sound land management practices, land consolidation and farm enlargement could be achieved. At the same time, land unsuited to agricultural production could be managed for other uses such as forestry, fish and wildlife habitat, outdoor recreation, or watershed protection. The corporation was thus believed to fulfill, at least partially, the need for an agency responsible for a comprehensive land management programme which would enable optimum development of the Island's land resources." Reports of the Lands Directorate are generally laudatory, though it is difficult to make any statistical assessment. Typical is a 1980 report which concluded that "the most significant impacts upon land use in PEI ... have been (1) to encourage the maintenance of good farmland in production and (2) to make available to the public, land better suited to other uses" (Kienholz 1980: 77). The net result of the totality of governmental and market forces in PEI, however, has been a reduction in farmland acreage;   but, of course, this is not a trend unique to the Island.

Mining, Land Use and the Environment

Mines are usually located in a setting of relatively unspoiled nature ... A generation ago, this isolated outpost of industry was looked on as a symbol of man's ingenuity and as a proud demonstration of progress toward an ever expanding better future. Now it is looked on by some, perhaps by an increasing number ... as a forerunner of the destruction of the environment which supports us and of which we are a part

Roots 1977

The seventies saw a marked change in the statutory context within which mining in Canada operated. This was despite the 1973 energy crisis which highlighted the need to reconcile the problems arising from resource development with conservation and environmental protection requirements. Licensing and permit approval systems, environmental impact assessments, resource and land use planning, and land reclamation became standard controls. All this reflected changes in public attitudes, illustrated by the quotation above.

Mining has two interesting features: location and length of life. Mineral deposits are where they are: there is no possibility of site selection, only of mining or not mining. But the life of a mining operation is limited: its use of land is transient. Unfortunately, the same is not the case with its aftermath, whether in the form of a changed (or even devastated) landscape, polluted land or water, or derelict buildings. Indeed, estimates by Marshall give a Canadian total of 233,968 hectares for the "land area disturbed by mining wastes" (Marshall 1982: 134). This can be compared with the figure of 284,327 hectares for the "land area disturbed, utilized and alienated by mining" (Ibid: 142). This figure, it should be noted, includes wastes of currently active operations. These figures give some idea of the scale of dereliction due to mining operations. Ontario has a major problem, and it is on this that the present discussion focuses.

Aggregates in Ontario

The Canadian mineral industry has expressed concern about the
effects of environmental regulations on its future development
Energy, Mines and Resources Canada 1981

Canada is the world's largest mineral exporter. The
mineral industry has been a major factor in Canadian economic
development "and is still the main force in the northward
advance of Canada's frontiers of population and economic
activity" (Canada Year Book 1980-81: 449). Much mineral
exploitation takes place in remote areas and, though it presents
problems of environmental damage, control and reclamation,
these tend to be different, at least in degree, from the problems
which arise with aggregates. In this section these problems are
examined in so far as they arise in the province of Ontario.
(There is further discussion, in relation to the Niagara Escarpment, in chapter 8.)

If agricultural land arouses passions, the aggregates industry arouses venom. It would require a psychologist to explain
this irrational difference. Perhaps there is something natural
about agriculture which contrasts with the unnatural exploitation of mineral deposits? Or could it be more simply that, in
many cases, mineral extraction has defaced, if not raped, the
landscape, while agriculture has been much more benign?

Be that as it may, Ontario took little action in relation to
mineral aggregate resources until the unprecedented postwar
growth in the economy and, as a result, in road building and
construction, created supply problems for the industry. Its
difficulty was with municipalities who, using such powers as
were available under the Planning Act and the Municipal Act,
waged a veritable battle against the industry. Eventually,
towards the end of the sixties, a looming shortage led the province to promote an inquiry. This was undertaken by a Mineral
Resources Committee made up of representatives of the provincial government and the industry (Yundt and Messerschmidt
1979: 103).

There was no representation on this committee of environmental interests (which were becoming increasingly vocal, especially in relation to the Niagara Escarpment) or of municipalities. The absence of the latter was particularly surprising since aggregate extraction, though requiring planning at a regional or provincial level, has its major impact on local areas. As a result of their non-participation it was less than surprising that the committee recommended a strong role for the province and took a pro-industry stance (Ontario Mineral Resources Committee 1969). The ensuing protest from the municipalities stimulated the committee to produce a further report aimed at assuaging their apprehensions, but since again there was no direct input from the municipalities, this failed in its purpose. The pace now began to quicken. Conferences were held around the province and it was agreed that new legislation was necessary. It was accepted that the municipalities should be involved, and it was also agreed that there was a need for more data and for greater protection of sensitive areas.

The last point was met, at least symbolically, by the passing of a stop-gap Niagara Escarpment Protection Act in 1970. The need for more data was met by an expansion of the mineral resources mapping program in southern Ontario (a specific recommendation of the committee). Additionally a study was mounted of the economic feasibility of transporting aggregates to the Toronto area by rail from rural parts of the province. (This concluded that the costs would be prohibitive.) Finally, in 1971, the Pits and Quarries Control Act was passed.

The Pits and Quarries Control Act 1971

We have in Ontario a confrontation situation between the extractive industry and the residents of the extractive areas. We have no assurance that resources will be available for the future

Ontario Mineral Working Party 1977

The passing of the 1971 act was both a landmark and a disappointment. It was a landmark because it promised a new era in which rehabilitation would be accelerated and the environmental impact of pit and quarry operations would be minimized while, at the same time, the industry would obtain its requirements. It was a disappointment because it did not work. After five years in operation, an Ontario Mineral Aggregate Working Party reported that the situation was little improved, as the quotation above illustrates. In the working party's view, there was one basic reason why the legislation had not fulfilled its promise: both the act and the report on which it was based had their essential priorities reversed. Resources extraction would be feasible only if local and environmental interests were given priority, in contrast to the existing priority for "maximum utilization of available resources." The shortcomings of the Pits and Quarries Control Act were (and, at the time of writing, still are) clearly serious. Under the act, areas designated by Order (namely, most of southern Ontario, plus Sudbury and Sault Ste Marie), are subject to licensing by the Minister of Natural Resources. A licence application has to be accompanied by a site plan which includes "as far as possible, ultimate pit development ... and ultimate rehabilitation and, where possible, intended use and ownership of the land after the extraction operations have ceased."

In considering an application the minister is required to judge whether the operation of a pit or quarry would be against the public interest taking into account:

- the preservation of the character of the environment;
- the availability of natural environment for the enjoyment of the public;
- the need, if any, for restricting excessively large total pit or quarry output in the locality;
- the traffic density on local roads;
- any possible effects on the water table or surface drainage pattern;
- the nature and location of other land uses that could be affected by the pit or quarry operation; and
- the character, location and size of nearby communities.

The minister can approve an application, make it subject to such terms and conditions as he considers advisable, or reject it. There is a right to a hearing by the OMB, but the final decision rests with the minister.

The rehabilitation provisions are interesting: a security deposit of eight cents per tonne (originally two cents) of material removed is payable up to a certain limit per hectare (currently $3,000 where rehabilitation is not being undertaken or a minimum of $1,000 where it is: the objective here is to encourage progress rehabilitation). If no rehabilitation is undertaken the operator loses his security deposit which can be used for paying the costs of rehabilitation in default.

These provisions appear sensible and satisfactory at first sight, but they failed to achieve what was expected. Estrin and Swaigen have pointed to a number of inadequacies: " ... a combination of relatively weak regulations under the act, insufficient detail in the site plans, and lackadaisical enforcement has meant that little or no improvement in this situation has been achieved" (Estrin and Swaigen 1978: 218). The working party report is replete with similar criticisms. Officials of the Ministry of Natural Resources have commented that the increase in the security deposit was made since many producers considered the original rate (of two cents a tonne) as being so small that it could be regarded as a mere tax: "as a result, rehabilitation, if and when undertaken was not always of a standard satisfactory to the ministry. This led to problems of enforcement and eventually the security deposit was increased to reflect a more realistic average of rehabilitation cost" (Yundt and Wood 1982: 6).

There is no doubt of the many inadequacies in the act, though it is well to be reminded that "the past decade has seen the province of Ontario achieve objectives in the regulation of aggregate operations that have taken Britain and Germany over thirty years to obtain" (Ibid). Moreover, though the absolute achievements may be considered inadequate by the standards of the eighties, there has been a marked increase in the relative amount of rehabilitation (Coates and Scott 1979).

The Ministry of Natural Resources has been keen both to promote the cause of rehabilitation and to raise its own profile on the issue. Of relevance here are two "glossies": *From Pits to Playgrounds* (1979a) and *Pit and Quarry Rehabilitation* (1984b). The area is, of course, a highly political one, as can be seen (if anyone doubts the statement) by the checkered history of the Aggregates Bill.

This new legislation was first introduced in the Ontario legislature in June 1979. It had a rough passage, and it died on the order paper when the election was called in 1981. A redrafted bill is, at the time of writing, awaiting introduction into the legislature. The main features of this are expected to include provision for liaison between the ministry and the municipalities, compensation to municipalities for costs falling upon them as a result of aggregate operations and rehabilitation of abandoned pits and quarries. The general effect will be to impose more stringent controls and to achieve improved planning and management of aggregate operations on a site specific basis. However, the ministry stress that there is no intention here of managing mineral aggregate resources on a provincial or even a regional basis. This function is being dealt with separately in the strategic land use plans (discussed in the final section of this chapter).

Ontario Planning Guidelines

Although potential mineral aggregate resources exist in many parts of Ontario, a reduction in the availability of these resources is occurring in certain areas of the province

Yundt and Wood 1982

Though the main issue of the debate so far summarized has been the site specific impact of aggregate operations, there is a broader issue which is becoming of increasing importance. This might be described simply as a problem of regional planning. A ministry source explains that "the reduction of near market supplies is becoming serious and is not wholly connected with the depletion of these mineral aggregate resources.

Incompatible land uses (e.g. housing, institutions, etc) occurring over or adjacent to deposits have effectively eliminated some mineral aggregate resources, while restrictive planning, legislation and other controls have also made the establishment and operation of pits and quarries difficult" (Ibid). In short, there is a need for a positive planning approach to the protection of areas required for future operations. This requires an overall assessment of future needs and, since implementation is a municipal responsibility, the formulation of provincial guides and their incorporation in municipal plans.

At the same time progressive rehabilitation is required both for its own benefit and also because it is "perhaps the single most important factor in gaining public acceptance of the aggregate industry" (Ibid: 18).

The drafting of acceptable policy guidelines proved troublesome. Certain policy statements were used for a time as an interim measure and, in December 1982, Cabinet approved a provincial planning document *Mineral Aggregate Resource Planning Policy* (Ontario MNR 1983a). This was published in February 1983 and is to be followed by a formal set of implementing guidelines in line with the provisions of the new Planning Act. The main provisions of the policy are:

- to formally recognize the importance to the province of mineral aggregate resources;
- to protect existing pits and quarries and mineral aggregate resources through municipal plans and zoning bylaws;
- to require official plans to provide a method and criteria for establishing new pits and quarries;
- to permit wayside pits and quarries without requiring an official plan amendment;
- to require pit and quarry rehabilitation policies in official plans;
- to establish the functions of the province with regard to mineral aggregate planning and management.

In brief, these provide, inter alia, that government departments and agencies, and the OMB should have "due regard" to the policy: and that the Ministry of Municipal Affairs and Housing, in approving planning documents shall (in consultation with the Ministry of Natural Resources) ensure that they "adequately comply with the policy." The indications here are thus towards a firmer policy, though the orientation is pro-aggregate industry. It remains to be seen how effective the "firmer" policy will be.

Forestry

The Canadian settler cordially hated a tree

Simpson-Lewis et al 1979

The role of forests in Canadian history and development has been told many times and there is no need to repeat it here. The crucial feature of it is the change in attitudes (and later in policies) from exploitation to conservation; or, in different words, from viewing forests as a non-renewable resource. In striking contrast to minerals, it is possible by wise management to ensure that forests are what an earlier generation assumed they were: a perpetual resource. Forests have other important features. They are of great variety: for example, Simpson-Lewis et al open their account of Canadian forestry by noting that "forests, the most ubiquitous feature of the Canadian landscape, serve the country's people economically, socially, and ecologically." Forests may be considered as a crop, a natural element in an agricultural setting, or a recreational asset.

This "multi-use" feature is one of the challenges to forest management. Also of relevance is that "unlike water which may have uses along the course of its bed, forests are location stable and, therefore, the forest industry must have a firm allocation of land for relatively long periods of time; thus land tenure becomes [an] important characteristic for the fibre resource." Additionally, susceptibility to management, fire and disease is another important characteristic.

In provinces such as British Columbia, Manitoba and Newfoundland, the majority of forest land is crown land owned by the provincial governments: relatively small areas are in private ownership. In Ontario about a tenth (42,000 square kilometers) is privately owned, either in large tracts devoted to forest production or smaller holdings usually operated as part of a farm enterprise (Ontario MNR 1981b: ix). In the public sector, forest management plans operate for each area (called forest management units). Each plan outlines the objective for the unit and the ways in which these are to be met. The objectives are based on an analysis of the physical characteristics of the area, projected demand, and other uses. Regeneration is a major feature of these plans (in 1980, 600 million cubic feet of wood were harvested from 197,000 hectares of crown lands).

Ontario has five programs for the private sector: the provision of planting stock program; the woodlands improvement program; the advisory services program; the managed forest tax reduction program; and the agreement forests program. These are discussed in detail in the ministry's 1982 paper *Private Land Forests: A Public Resource.*

The division between public and private is not a clear one in forestry. In the first place, private lands are subject to the programs just listed. These involve the provision of planting and management services by the ministry in exchange for an agreement on cutting. Secondly, and more extensive, are the forest management agreements under which crown land is harvested, regenerated and managed by private companies.

This privatization was accelerated in 1982 and 1983 in an attempt to bring more financial and human resources to bear upon the forestry problems of Ontario. In particular there is the difficulty of rejuvenating the aging forests. (Most of Ontario's forests are boreal, with trees aged 120 to 140 years.) The long term aim is to replace the aged slow growing trees, which are susceptible to fire and disease, with younger and more productive forests. "In the trade off, the companies will assume responsibility for management (harvesting, regenerating and tending) while the government's role will be to assess and audit the plans and their execution" (Robinson 1983). Under the terms of the agreements, each company will manage the forests for a period of twenty years. Annual allowable cuts are calculated every five years, and the company's performance is assessed after the first five year period. If satisfactory, a "full" agreement for the twenty years is entered into. Otherwise the company will have to remedy its deficiencies or lose its cutting rights.

The system of "allowable annual cuts" is now widespread across Canada. Its objective is to achieve "normality" in the forests. This is achieved when a forest contains stands ranging in age from one year to rotation age, and yields continuous harvest (Simpson-Lewis et al 1979: 167). To achieve this, however, is not easy.

Policies vary between the provinces as, of course, does the position of forestry in their economies. As already indicated, Ontario has opted for privatization. In New Brunswick, the deteriorating state of the forests led to a major change in policy (Folster 1981). The problem has developed as a result of generations of myopic forestry practice known as "high grading," i.e. harvesting the best trees and leaving the rest. To check the decay and safeguard future stocks, the province "after years of soul searching," cancelled hundreds of privately held leases on crown timber land. It then restructured the crown forest, constituting about a half of the provincial total, into ten large areas which were licensed to the province's biggest wood users. The legislation, the Crown Lands and Forests Act, came into operation in 1982.

In British Columbia, the largest wood producing province, a royal commission reported in 1976. The Pearse report, as it is usually called after the name of its chairman, unravelled the complexities of what were described as "a complicated panoply of legal provisions and practices; considerably more complex, indeed, than is found in other Canadian jurisdictions." These had resulted from continual shifts in policy (in response to changing conditions) since the turn of the century, when the province ceased issuing crown grants and, instead, issued licenses and leases over crown lands to authorize timber extraction. One of the problems identified was the same as in New Brunswick:

> Timber production in British Columbia has hitherto been based almost entirely on the recovery of virgin "old growth" timber, and the implications of the inevitable adjustment to "second growth" timber will be profound. The old growth timber on which our industry has been built was often of exceptionally high quality, capable of manufacture into products that command premium prices in world markets. As this stock is depleted (and it is appropriate to refer to it as a stock, since it is not reproducible within any meaningful planning horizon), much of the special advantage this province's timber has enjoyed will be lost. On the other hand, the old growth stock poses many problems. Vast tracts are overmature, decadent, and so defective that they cannot be recovered except at a loss; yet they often occupy growing sites that are potentially very productive: a potential that can be realized only if present stands are removed.

Following the Pearse report (and a report from a Forest Policy Advisory Committee), the province introduced a new forest and range resource management system, the legislative basis for which was the Ministry of Forests Act, the Forest Act, and the Range Act, all passed in 1978.

The main engine of the new system is a periodic forest and range resource analysis. This provides a long term perspective on the industry's prospects. The first *Forest and Range Resource Analysis Report* was submitted in September 1979, and was subsequently presented to the British Columbia legislature in March 1980. The report was widely discussed both within and outside of government. The major focus of debate, not surprisingly, was the wood supply analysis which stressed the limited supply of timber and the possibility of local wood shortages in certain parts of the province within the following twenty years.

While the resource analysis sets out a general framework of needs, actual programs to meet these are developed in a five year resource program, which is updated annually. The requirements for this program are stated in the Ministry of Forests Act:

(a)   a set of alternatives for restocking forest land, for increasing the productivity of forest and range land and for otherwise improving forest and range resources in the province, identifying for each alternative relative costs and benefits; and

(b)   a recommended program for implementation by the ministry during the next five years including the respective roles to be played by the Crown and the private sector.

The final step in the new management system of the ministry is the public monitoring of performance as required by the Ministry of Forests Act. This is facilitated by the detailed account of the minsitry's performance given in its annual report. This gives the annual report a much more significant role than is usual for its genre.

Canada's Threatened Forests

Industry now harvests about 800,000 hectares annually, of which only some 200,000 hectares are replanted or reseeded ... One-eighth of Canada's productive forest area has deteriorated to the point where huge tracts lie devastated, unable to regenerate a merchantable crop within the next 60 to 80 years. Each year, some 200,000 to 400,000 hectares of valuable forest are being added to this shameful waste

Science Council of Canada 1983a

There are many problems not so far mentioned. The assistant deputy minister of New Brunswick's Department of Natural Resources has estimated that "insects and disease extract an annual harvest of some 88 million cubic meters from Canada's forests, as compared with 136 million cubic meters recovered by man" (Canadian Pulp and Paper Association 1981:

9).   The chairman of the Canadian Committee on Forest Fire Control has estimated "the ten year average annual loss in timber due to fire at 11,000 square kilometers of destroyed forest, sufficient to supply 78 paper mills for one year" (Ibid: 10).   And, of course, there are the numerous reports on acid rain, to which some reference has already been made in chapter 2.

There are perhaps few areas where the prophets of doom are so vocal.   Of particular note is a report from the Science Council of Canada entitled *Canada's Threatened Forests* from which the above quotation is taken.   The passionate character of this may seem somewhat unusual from a scientific body. What the council has done is to adopt the general vocabulary of debate on this subject.   In fact, the available statistical data are inadequate to support such statements (which does not necessarily mean that they are wrong).   A Statistics Canada study has drawn attention to the fact that the lack of standardized definitions makes it impossible to compare provinces or to add figures up.   "Further, data on forestry depletions, accruals, and associated stressors are generally lacking" (Rapport and Friend 1979: 18).

More recently, *The Report of the Nova Scotia Royal Commission on Forestry* (Nova Scotia 1984) has documented "the forest crisis" in that province where, uniquely, three-quarters of the forest land is in private ownership.   Though the pattern of ownership is unique, the problems are not:

> Everyone ought to be concerned about the present condition of Nova Scotia's forests.   This resource has been diminished by highgrading, the ravages of fire, insects, diseases, weeds and wind, and the failure of society to make the best use of the remaining trees and to restore forest losses.   In consequence, many forest related jobs are in jeopardy, and the environment is deteriorating ... Continuation of current forest practices can only lead to an erosion of the resources, because an adequate long term management policy is lacking.

Among the many proposals of the commission is a restructuring of the Department of Lands and Forests to include an office of the deputy minister of forestry "with the responsibility for restoring, conserving and improving the resource, with appropriate professional and technical staff to guide the management of both private and Crown land by meeting the requirements of scheduling, allocation, marketing, silviculture, and protection." The commission hopes that, because of the industry's long term interests there will be voluntary cooperation with this highly centralized system. Should this fail, legislation may be necessary.

At the federal level, a Minister of State for Forestry has been appointed, one of whose first actions was to sign the Canada-Ontario Forest Resource Development Agreement (MNR 1984c).

Yet another problem facing the forests is the clash between production, conservation and recreation. "We all support new parks, farmland extension and the like. But we must appreciate that if the land involved is productive forest land, the benefit obtained is at a cost to future timber supply ... there is no free lunch" (Canadian Pulp and Paper Association 1981: 4). It is to the subject of parks that we now turn.

Provincial Parks: Ontario

Is there an Ontario Parks System?

University of Waterloo 1982

Some account of federal policy in relation to *national* parks has been given in chapter 2. Here the focus is on parks policy at the provincial level. Ontario is taken as a case study (with the usual warning that the provinces differ).

In terms of legislation, Ontario has national parks, provincial parks, historical parks and wilderness areas, as well as the North Georgian Bay Recreation Reserve, the Niagara Escarpment, not to mention conservation areas, public parks (i.e.

municipal parks) and three park commissions (Niagara Parks, St Lawrence Parks, and St Clair Parkway). Nor is this all: the provincial parks are of six types: wilderness parks, nature reserves, historical parks (not to be confused with the historical parks established under specific legislation), natural environment parks, waterway parks, and recreation parks. This confusing array is a product both of history and of the variety of objectives served by different types of parks.

In this section, our concern is with the provincial park system which falls within the responsibility of the Ontario Ministry of Natural Resources. (The Niagara Escarpment is discussed in chapter 8, and a later section of the current chapter deals with conservation areas.)

The 131 provincial parks extend over 4.26 million hectares (of which the massive Polar Bear Park accounts for over a half). The ministry's 1978 *Ontario Provincial Parks Planning and Management Policies* states that the goal of the provincial park system is "to provide a variety of outdoor recreation opportunities, and to protect provincially significant natural, cultural, and recreational environments." This is spelled out in four "objectives":

(1) **Protection Objective:** to protest provincially significant elements of the natural and cultural landscape of Ontario;

(2) **Recreation Objective:** to provide outdoor recreation opportunities ranging from high intensity day use to low intensity wilderness experiences;

(3) **Heritage Appreciation Objective:** to provide opportunities for exploration and appreciation of the outdoor natural and cultural heritage of Ontario;

(4) **Tourism Objective:** to provide Ontario's residents and out of province visitors with opportunities to discover and experience the distinctive regions of the province.

Needless to say these objectives can, and do, clash: hence the need for a classification system and, within that, a zoning system.

The six classes are described as follows:

Wilderness Parks: substantial areas where the forces of nature are permitted to function freely and where visitors travel by non-mechanized means and experience expansive solitude, challenge, and personal integration with nature.

Nature Reserves: areas selected to represent the distinctive natural habitats and landforms of the province, and are protected for educational purposes as gene pools for research to benefit present and future generations.

Historical Parks: areas selected to represent the distinctive historical resources of the province in open space settings, and are protected for interpretive, educational and research purposes.

Natural Environment Parks: incorporate outstanding recreational landscapes with representative natural features and historical resources to provide high quality recreational and educational experiences.

Waterway Parks: incorporate outstanding recreational water routes with representative features and historical resources to provide high quality recreational and educational experiences.

Recreation Parks: areas which support a wide variety of outdoor recreation opportunities for large numbers of people in attractive surroundings.

Within each park, areas can be zoned as, for example, an historic zone or a natural environment zone. At one time, some zones were categorized as multiple zones. The areas in Algonquin and Lake Superior Parks, where commercial timber harvesting and recreation takes place, have been given the special designation of "recreation-utilization zones" (Priddle 1979: 210ff).

A major problem in these and many other parks is the pressure for exploitation, as is also clearly evident in the Niagara Escarpment area. This has always been acute with the pro-development ethic of Ontario. The classification and zoning systems, plus the detailed policies set out in *Planning and*

Management Policies represent a significant attempt to come to grips with the conflicts which arise, but it will be difficult to subordinate the traditional ethic to a more preservationist one. As Estrin and Swaigen (1978: 332) have put it, "unlike the United States, which has always stressed nature and wilderness preservation in its national parks, Ontario has always emphasized tourism, intensive recreational development, and resource exploitation in its parks. This attitude towards parkland is typified by ... all those who 'apparently felt that the place should be maintained solely for the bees and bugs and the beetles'." Fears over the future of the provincial park system have recently been revived by the "suspension" of management plans. (Nearly thirty of the Ontario provincial parks have management plans, formerly termed master plans.) In 1981 it was reported that "conservation groups have interpreted the move as another indication that the lumber industry is getting the upper hand ..." but the official line is that "the individual park plans have been put on the back burner temporarily so that district plans can be completed" (Truman 1981). These regional plans are the product of the ministry's strategic land use planning program which is discussed in a later section.

The draft plans which emerged from this included proposals for some 245 "candidate parks." If all had been accepted, provincial parks would have increased in number from 131 to 376, and in area from 4.3 million hectares to 9.4 million hectares, the latter representing nearly nine percent of the area of the province (Ontario MNR 1981a: 1:41).

Considerable opposition met these proposals. As a result, the ministry set up a task force of officials. It reported in September 1981. The major problem was identified as one in which "strategic planning" and "park system planning" had got out of phase. The report of the task force was released to the public in March 1982. At the same time, there was published *Background Information on Land Use Planning and Parks System .ul Planning in Ontario*. The official date for the release of these documents was 12 March 1982, when the Minister of Natural Resources (Alan Pope) made a statement to the legislature:

We are now entering the final phase of Ontario's major land use planning program. The completion of the studies and plans that I am tabling today represents a milestone in the planning program ... The tabling of the *Report of the Task Force on Park System Planning* marks a significant step forward for our provincial parks. Parks planning is now on stream with Ontario strategic land use planning. This integration guarantees that park options will receive full consideration in the strategic land use planning process, and it ensures that parks system planning will be balanced with other considerations such as forest management (Ontario MNR 1982d).

In June 1983, the minister released *District Land Use Guidelines* wherein 155 areas were recommended as future provincial parks.

Water

The map of Canada is liberally splashed with lakes and streams

Canada Year Book

Some eight percent of the area of Canada is covered by lakes and rivers. Over seven million tonnes of water fall each year as rain or snow. One might therefore assume that, though there may be problems of water quality, there would be few of quantity. However, reports from across the country testify to a water shortage which is growing in severity. As an example, Nova Scotia which, with the exception of the coastline of British Columbia, has the highest precipitation in Canada, notes that "although relatively clean water is generally available ... in certain areas serious problems exist and in others they seem to be developing. Broadly speaking, present attempts to manage and protect water supply areas (usually watershed lands) are inconsistent across the province and often inadequate" (Nova Scotia 1981: 1). The more serious problems, however, are in the Prairie provinces where the balance between supply and demand has always been tenuous, but where consumption has increased over 300 percent in the past three decades (Environment Canada 1984: 23). The major "consumers" are irrigation (over sixty percent) and reservoir evaporation (over thirty percent).

The demand for water is increasing at a rapid rate, particularly for energy related purposes: "one 600,000 kilowatt CANDU nuclear power station, which is generally accepted to be the smallest economically viable nuclear facility available in this country, has a water intake approximately equal to the combined water withdrawals of all municipalities in western Canada" (Protti 1979). Additionally there are the demands of water based recreation and the increasing recognition of the critical importance of water "in maintaining certain ecosystems, particularly those of marshland areas and arid zones (Foster and Sewell 1981: 14).

This is a difficult area in which to make predictions, but currently there is no doubt that the overall demand for water is growing rapidly. Moreover, even if the national situation is satisfactory, it seems likely that there will be "regions of crisis," in the basins of the Okanagan, Milk, North Saskatchewan, South Saskatchewan, Red-Assiniboine, and Southern Ontario.

Moreover, there is growing pressure on Canadian water supplies from the United States. Water consumption in the Great Lakes region of Canada and the United States is expected to increase fivefold during the half century from 1981. "One effect of the increase in water consumption would be lower water levels on the lakes and reduced flows in the St Lawrence River system. Lower levels would be viewed as positive by shore property owners, who blame high lake levels for erosion and flooding ... but it would be viewed as negative by lake carriers, who prefer high levels to give ships more draft, and by hydroelectric power producers on connecting rivers and the St Lawrence River, who need high levels and flows to maximize their output" (Environment Canada 1984: 25).

Another problem is that of acid rain ("the not so gentle rain"), on which there is now a huge library of writings. Canadian American relationships on this have never been cordial; in the mid-eighties they reached an impasse. Foster and Sewell, after outlining the problem, resort to the bathos of the Canadian government's announcement that it would finance studies

into the breeding of acid resistant fish! More recently, however, both Canada and the United States have become increasingly concerned about the problem and some ameliorative
action may emerge.

A further issue discussed by Foster and Sewell is the miscellany of "other threats to the quality of Canadian water
resources besides that of acidic precipitation." The economic
and scientific progress of the postwar years has taken its toll on
the purity of the Canadian water supply. Pollutants have
grown dramatically. There are two types, technically described
as nondegradable and degradable.

The majority fall in to the first category, "and their
uncontrolled discharge is largely responsible for the growing
seriousness of many of Canada's pollution problems." The
statistics relating to this are not easy to assimilate, but it is
clear that, at the least, there is cause for concern. Some highly
technical terms (and concepts) have passed into the vernacular:
from toxins to mercury pollution, to PCBs (polychlorinated
byphenyls) and chlorofluorocarbons. The orchestration of terminology may detract attention from the seriousness of the
(unquantifiable?) human risks involved.

Simple domestic sewage (like fertilizers and detergents) is
degradable and self-purifying in limited quantities, though not
necessarily particularly pleasant! In excess quantities the results
are severe. For example, there can be major harm to aquatic
life and high rates of algal growth and accelerated entrophica-
tion in lakes. "These problems have been especially pronounced
in Ontario and British Columbia." Pollution from the pulp and
paper industry is by far the worst, again with Ontario (and
Quebec) being the most affected. The Great Lakes is a horror
story in its own right, which has been detailed in the publications of the International Joint Commission.

On toxics, Environment Canada (1984: 17) has stressed the
need for "a remedial strategy to influence responsible parties to
lessen the adverse impacts of chemicals in the environment" and
"a preventive strategy to limit the use of chemicals to ways
that will protect human and environmental health over the long

term." Waste effluents present more difficult problems: "as both the long term effects of minute quantities as well as the possible synergistic effects of combinations of toxic pollutants have to be dealt with, it is difficult to assess the risk and hazard of the effluents as well as to establish acceptable effluent limitations" (Ibid: 19).

It is strange that a country so rich in water should face such huge water problems. The visible apparent abundance has much to do with this, but so has "our politically reinforced regionalism management in many countries have not evolved in Canada" (Quinn 1977: 226). What is of particular significance is the fact that despite oratorical proclamation of the importance of "multi use planning," "coordinated river basin planning" and the like, single purpose schemes predominate. It is difficult to operate otherwise. However, significant if unsteady progress is being made in individual provinces, often under agreements made with the federal ministry. The achievements of the numerous conservation authorities also require recognition. Examples of the former are the policies for the Rideau, Trent-Severn Corridor, and the Thames River Basin in Ontario, and flood damage reduction program agreements with Newfoundland, Nova Scotia and New Brunswick. A wide ranging review of water policies is to be found in the annual *Canada Water Year Book* published by Environment Canada.

More detail can be provided at the provincial level: the following section deals with one aspect of water policy in Ontario.

Conservation and Flood Control in Ontario

A conservation authority could only be formed when the desires of the residents reached the point where they were willing to request the government of Ontario to form an authority

Richardson 1974

The term conservation has a particular meaning, or at least ambience, in Ontario. This is a feature of the history and personalities of the province. Smithies (1974) traces that history back into the nineteenth century (Algonquin Park dates from 1893), though in more popular chronicles it was the 1954 Hurricane Hazel which compelled provincial action. However, for reasons which predate Hurricane Hazel by many decades, "conservation" became focused on flood control. In the thirties the deforestation of southern Ontario led to severe flooding and eventually to the passing of the Grand River Valley Conservation Act in 1938. Even today, the Ontario legislation (the Conservation Authorities Act) starts with the matter of watersheds. But, though this may have been a central issue, there were many others interrelated with it both in (what we would now call) environmental terms, and also in political terms: sewage disposal, reforestation, the safeguarding of agricultural land, aggregates and other minerals, pollution, and so on.

The various strands merged in the nineteen-fifties in a concept which must have been familiar to academics but troublesome to politicians: the concept of the multi-use of land. In Smithies' words, "the new concept saw land as having many potential uses. Planning and capable management were essential to maximize the potential economic benefits to be gained." Of course, this new policy did not appear overnight: it emerged gradually and in the face of downright opposition and (equally problematic) unconcern and inertia.

Interestingly, "sound basic thinking and shrewd planning in the formative years" proved to be "fundamentally right," according to G. Ross Lord, a former chairman of the Metropolitan Toronto and Region Conservation Authority (Richardson 1974: ix). He saw three basic ideas: local initiative, cost sharing, and watershed jurisdiction.

The principle of local initiative is the apotheosis of public participation. It involves a commitment not only to a policy, but also to a responsibility to fund the authority that was necessary to implement that policy. "It has meant that an authority can flourish only when the local people have enough enthusiasm and conviction to support it financially." Cost sharing (on a fifty-fifty basis) "has also meant that the authority

does   not exceed the financial resources of its jurisdiction"
(Ibid).

The issue of watershed jurisdiction was of a different character: this was concerned not with feasibility or political acceptability, but with technical matters. Allied to it was the ideal
of a multi purpose programme for the renewal of natural
resources in an area.

The history of all this is a fascinating one, even if it did
not quite take the path of logical progress chronicled by
Richardson. The new opportunities and new thinking occasioned
by the cessation of hostilities in 1944-45 saw and, indeed, fos-
tered, a further advance in thinking. A visit to the Tennessee
Valley Authority (almost required for any aspirant in resource
management) "demonstrated the need that all natural resources
must be treated as a combined resource development."

This broad concept was translated into practice slowly.
One aspect which is now very apparent in the countryside is the
recreational use of land owned by conservation authorities.
Indeed, to the general public, many conservation authorities are
more likely to be regarded as providers of parks than as flood
prevention agencies. A major stimulus to park provision came
as a byproduct of a change in government policy following the
disastrous Hurricane Hazel in 1954. This convinced the government of the need to control encroachment on flood plains.
Thereafter, acquisition of flood plain lands became an integral
part of flood control projects, together with major protective
works such as dams, channels and diversions, all of which were
emphasized over the next decade or so.

The previous year also saw the passing of a federal measure, the Canadian Water Conservation Assistance Act. This
was later superseded by the Canada Water Act (1970). This
empowers the federal government to enter into agreements with
the provinces on comprehensive water resource management
projects in which there is "a significant national interest."

Despite the development of policy in this area, floods still persist, the most recent serious ones being the Grand River flood in 1974 and the Ganaraska flood at Port Hope in 1980. An inquiry into the former resulted in an interesting report (Leach Report 1975).

Flood Plain Management

... caught in a complex dilemma...

Leach Report 1975

The notoriously unpredictable Grand River has been the subject of eleven reports between 1932 and 1971. Three dams have been built during this period, the Shand (1942), the Luther (1954) and the Conestogo (1959). This was generally accepted as being inadequate, particularly since the population of the watershed had doubled, and urbanization, deforestation and other factors had increased the run off and thereby increased the problems of both flood control and water conservation. However, despite ambitious proposals only one additional dam (at Guelph) was under construction. The hold up was caused by the concern of the constituent municipalities for either the costs involved or the loss of attractive land for the benefit of other (downstream) authorities.

The Grand River Conservation Authority (GRCA) was "caught in a complex dilemma." In the words of the report:

> ... the primary purpose of the Shand and Conestogo, namely to provide flood control protection and low flow augmentation, are conflicting. In the spring, these two dams control and trap the runoff from the melting snow. The reservoirs have to be filled at this time in order to provide dilution downstream the rest of the year. If they do not store sufficient water at that time, the residents downstream would have no sewage dilution. Brantford would have no drinking water, and the river could run dry. It would be a catastrophic situation.

> On the other hand, by filling the reservoirs in the spring to meet the low flow augmentation requirements, almost all the flood

protection is removed for a three month period and a flood could ensue should there be unusual precipitation.

Although a flood is tragic, relatively few people are affected, whereas if the river should run dry, it would affect the lives of a large percentage of the people in the watershed.

The GRCA have followed this policy since the Shand and Conestogo have been constructed. It is a difficult policy to live with.

The solution lay in building more dams: "in effect, the GRCA has been trying to operate a seven cylinder vehicle on two cylinders, and without the funds to correct the problem."

Though inadequate capital investment was a major factor in the Grand River situation, it is noteworthy that control of development in the flood plain was also inadequate. At first sight it is therefore somewhat surprising to find the Ministry of Natural Resources suggesting a relaxation of controls generally throughout Ontario. A discussion paper was issued in 1977 in which a summary was given of an unpublished consultant's study of *Flood Plain Criteria and Management Evaluation* (the Dillon-MacLaren Report). In essence, the issue is one of probabilities: what level of risk is it worth insuring against? Hurricane Hazel was well above the highest level of a one in a hundred years storm. Yet it was also well below the maximum conceivable. How can one devise a policy to accommodate such a range of possibilities?

Public policy decisions cannot easily cope with the roulette character of flooding; and as land values have increased (alongside development pressures) the odds have shifted. The Dillon-MacLaren report proposed that there should be a "two zone floodway flood fringe" concept. This provided that development in the "fringe of a flood plain would be permitted if special flood protection measures were adopted." In the floodway, however, no development would be allowed. (The floodway was conceived as "the danger zone of the flood plain where deep and fast flowing waters would cause loss of life and severe damage to property.")

After a considerable amount of consultation and discussion, an official *Policy Statement of the Government of Ontario on Planning for Flood Plain Lands* emerged in 1982. The policy statement contained six policies of which the first was that "the regulatory flood for designation of flood plains in Ontario is defined as the regional flood or the 100 year flood, whichever is the greater." The second encompassed the two zone concept: "conservation authorities in Ontario, or where no authority exists, the Ministry of Natural Resources, in cooperation with the watershed municipalities, have the option of selective application of the two zone floodway flood fringe concept." This left quite a scope for local determination; but there was more. The third policy provided that where strict application of the first and/or the second policies was not feasible, "the concept of special policy areas within flood plains is recognized and controlled development may be permitted, once such areas are designated and approved by the conservation authority and the Ministries of Natural Resources, and Municipal Affairs and Housing. The Ministries of the Environment and Northern Affairs, when appropriate, are to be consulted about the special policy status for such areas." The remaining three policies were concerned with much more mundane matters such as infill and construction regulations; the calculation and mapping of floodway and flood plain lands; and urban stormwater management.

There was a significant degree of compromise in these policies, and debate continued on whether the provincial government had hit the appropriate balance between regulation of floodplain lands and the individual property rights. The balance is an inherently difficult one to make, as subsequent events showed. In September 1983, a Flood Plain Review Committee was appointed to review the policies and hear evidence concerning them. They reported in March 1984, and proposed (1) that all flood plains should be based on the 100 year flood criterion but with option to go to a higher criterion following full public review and input; (2) that the two zone concept should be abolished: in its place, the floodway would be defined on the basis of local conditions and on physical factors such as depth and velocity of flooding; development would be permitted anywhere in the flood plain if floodproofed to the regulatory level; and (3) that responsibility for administering flood plain policies be transferred from conservation authorities to local municipalities, and integrated with the land use planning process (Ontario MNR 1984a).

These proposals were subject to extensive debate and were largely rejected, though key concepts were accepted: increased flexibility, more opportunities for local input, and greater consideration of local conditions. The Minister of Natural Resources announced that the 100 year flood criterion would be the minimum acceptable standard, but there would be a possibility, where higher standards operated, for a reduction to this level. (This is the reverse of the Flood Plain committee's recommendation.) The two zone concept would be retained, but a degree of flexibility would be introduced to deal with local conditions. Finally, responsibilities for floodplain management would remain with conservation authorities (which have appropriate boundaries), but they would be required to be more open and responsive to public opinion. The Ministry of Natural Resources and the Ministry of Municipal Affairs and Housing are to make arrangements for ensuring that flood plain policies are adequately reflected in municipal planning.

New guidelines are to be issued and subjected to public review and comment.

Coordinated Program Strategies: The Ontario Innovation

> The environment is integrated, and its components are linked by dynamic processes. We cannot use or affect any part without affecting some other parts
>
> Roots 1977

The range of issues discussed in the previous sections, though far from complete, illustrates the diversity of land use pressures, the problems of determining priorities, and the importance of machinery for protecting the environment and resolving conflicts. The fulcrum is unquestionably at the provincial level. For most provinces, machinery for overall coordination (or even review) is not yet in place. In some it perhaps never will be. Nevertheless, there is a trend towards more comprehensive thinking and attempts to bring together a wide range of historically separated land use considerations. Ontario is again in the lead here, in thinking if not in policy implementation. This chapter thus ends with a discussion of Ontario's attempts to devise a new system for coordinated land use policies.

Where large tracts of land are in public ownership, as with crown lands, land uses can be decided upon, and plans put into direct effect, by the relevant ministry: in the case of Ontario, by the Ministry of Natural Resources. Thus *The Lake of the Woods Plan* (1977) was prepared with the goal "to provide a place where the highly desirable environmental characteristics are maintained while still providing acceptable levels of development for quality recreation experiences, community life and resources extraction." On a wider basis are the three "strategic land use plans" which cover the whole province. These plans have been in preparation for nearly a decade and are intended to be comprehensive land use strategies which will constitute a background for detailed land use plans for each of the forty-seven districts of the Ministry of Natural Resources. The hallmark of these regional plans is that they attempt to resolve broad land use conflicts. The approved plan for Northeastern Ontario explains:

> This report presents the Strategic Land Use Plan for Northeastern Ontario. It contains a statement of the refined integrated policies including their associated objectives and targets. Land and water requirements are also identified along with a strategy for implementing the policies. The maps contained in this document indicate those land and water areas which will be particularly important in meeting specific program objectives. All of the policies and maps collectively represent the conceptual Ministry of Natural Resources' Strategic Land Use Plan for Northeastern Ontario. A conceptual land use map for the Northeastern Planning Region indicated very broad land use priorities for various land and water areas (Ontario MNR 1982a: 1).

The Northeastern Ontario Planning Region covers an extensive area extending from Manitoulin Island in Lake Huron to the southern coast of Hudson-James Bay. It includes two-fifths of the total land and water area of the province. Its 1976 population of 585,000 is projected to grow to 666,000 by the end of the century, but this "is largely dependent on the maintenance and expansion of job opportunities provided by uses associated with the region's natural resources." Nevertheless, a major planning principle underlying the plan is that "the natural environment has a limited ability to provide long term benefits and to withstand use ... The principle recognizes that there are limits to the inherent productive capacity of land and water. Overuse or abuse will weaken the ability of the resource base to meet the user's long term expectations in terms of quality and quantity. Resource production on a sustained yield basis will be encouraged in all plans."

Specific resource policies are set out for minerals, forest management, agriculture, wild rice, tourism, fisheries management, wildlife management, provincial parks, crown land recreation, and cottaging. The plan attempts to resolve major land related conflicts: "in so doing, trade-offs and compromises were required between some incompatible land uses in order to arrive at an integrated plan which attempts to meet all Ministry of Natural Resources objectives."

At the regional scale, it is inappropriate to identify the location of all ministry land uses, except where regionally significant areas of mutually exclusive or non complementary uses are concerned. Additionally, there are special areas of provincial or national importance. The plan designates two of these. The first is the North Georgian Bay Recreational Reserve, which is a provincially important recreational area which enjoys specific legislative status (under the North Georgian Bay Recreational Reserve Act). The second is the Hudson-James Bay Coastal Area which is of national importance as a wildlife habitat area primarily for waterfowl and polar bears. Most of the region, however, is multiple use. Broad policies are set out in the strategic plan, but the elaboration of these comes in the preparation of district plans.

Southern Ontario contrasts sharply with the north. In addition to all the obvious differences is the crucial point that most of the land in the south is now in private ownership (hence the description of the plan as a "coordinated program strategy" rather than a "strategic land use plan"). In the laconic words befitting an annual report, the different terminology reflects the point that "land use planning in this area must be done under a different set of conditions. Ministry targets for resource use must be achieved primarily on private land in organized municipalities. Consequently, instead of directly managing the land resource, as is done on crown land in northern Ontario, the ministry must emphasize programs, technical assistance and other forms of encouragement to private landowners ... Also MNR's land use plans must be coordinated with local municipal planning ..."

The strategy assigns targets for ministry programs up to the year 2000 (2020 for forestry) and is based on the assumption of an annual growth of between one and two percent in resource needs. Despite the fact that these targets relate to individual resources, stress is laid on multiple use: "target achievement requires that there be program integration with many activities carried out in the same area. Exclusive use of large areas for a single purpose is generally not possible, although in selected instances it may be necessary to achieve specific program objectives. The ministry strategy in southern Ontario places a major emphasis on integrated resource management" (Ontario MNR 1982b: 3). However, the targets have to be achieved primarily on private land, and thus there is an emphasis on "extension programs, technical assistance and other forms of encouragement to private landowners." Moreover, the land of southern Ontario is largely under municipal jurisdiction, though there are thirty-five conservation authorities and three independent agencies (the St Clair, Niagara and St Lawrence Parks Commissions) as well as a host of federal and provincial departments and agencies (such as Ontario Hydro, the Algonquin Forest Authority, and the Niagara Escarpment Commission). Clearly agency coordination is the crucial aspect of this strategy.

MAPS

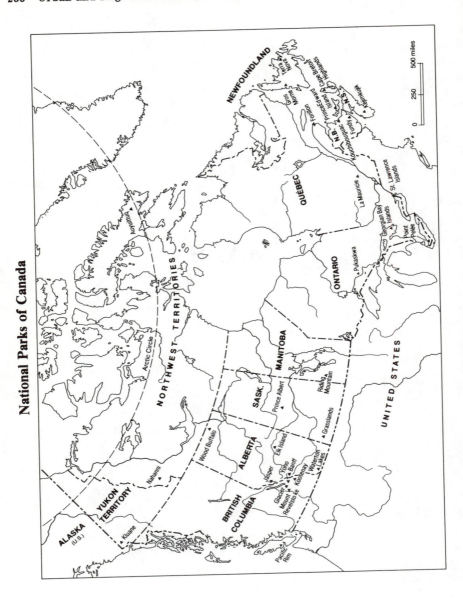

National Parks of Canada

North of 60°

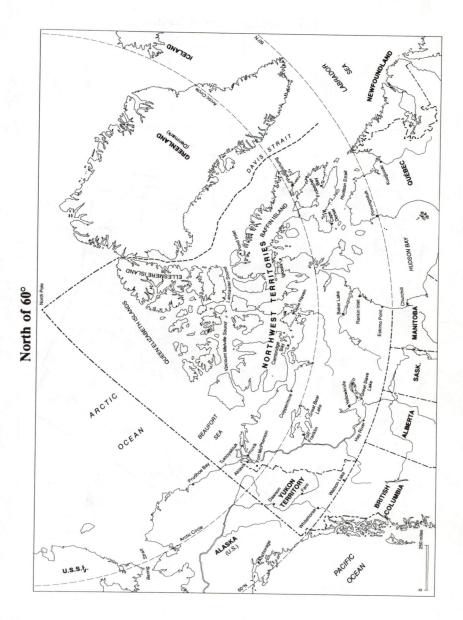

The National Capital Region

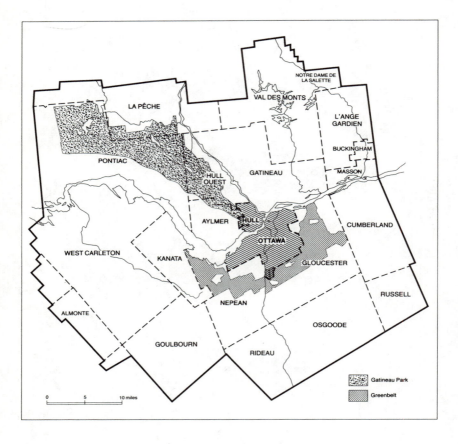

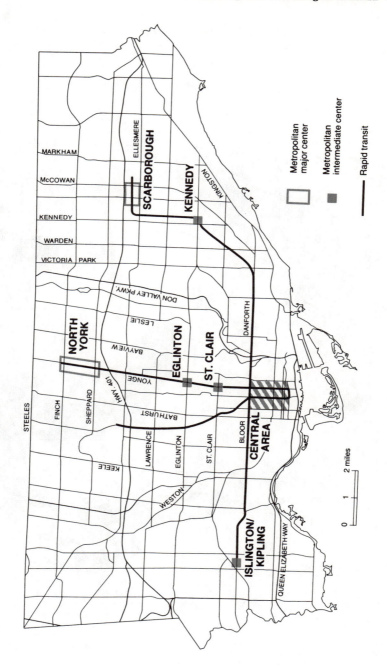

Metropolitan Toronto Urban Structure Plan: Designated Metropolitan Centers

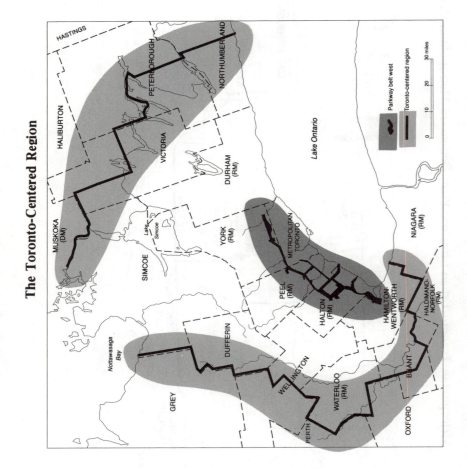

The Toronto-Centered Region

The Niagara Escarpment

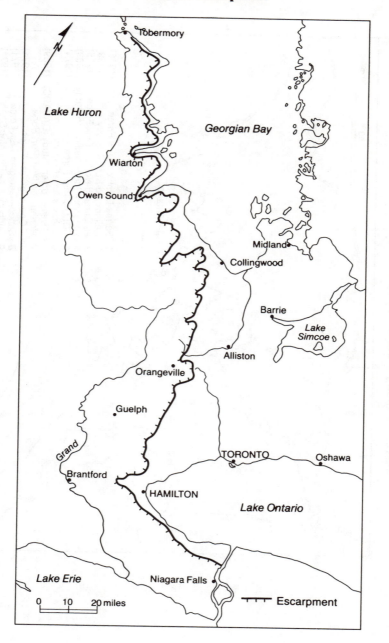

Special Planning Studies and Task Force Areas in Ontario

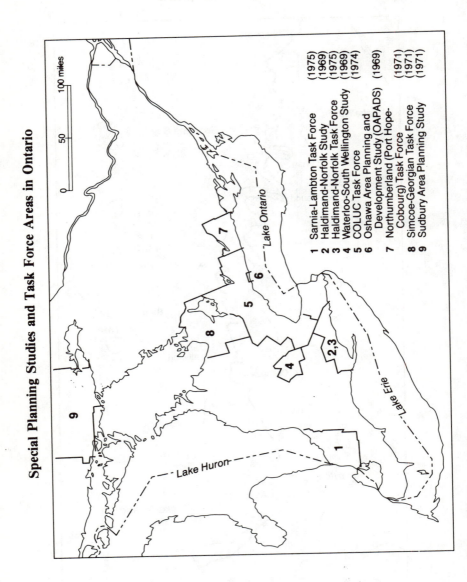

1   Sarnia-Lambton Task Force   (1975)
2   Haldimand-Norfolk Study   (1969)
3   Haldimand-Norfolk Task Force   (1975)
4   Waterloo-South Wellington Study   (1969)
5   COLUC Task Force   (1974)
6   Oshawa Area Planning and
    Development Study (OAPADS)   (1969)
7   Northumberland (Port Hope-
    Cobourg) Task Force   (1971)
8   Simcoe-Georgian Task Force   (1971)
9   Sudbury Area Planning Study   (1971)

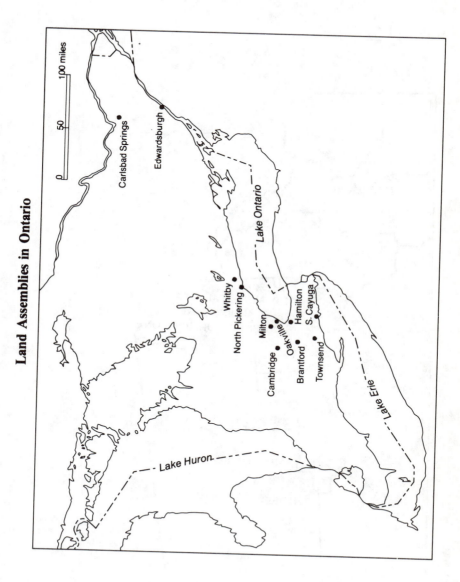

Land Assemblies in Ontario

Alberta Regional Planning Commission Areas 1984

Chapter 7
Regional Planning at the Federal Level

Canadian politics is regional politics; regionalism is one of the pre-eminent facts of Canadian life, whether reflected in the principles of cabinet-building, the acrimony of federal-provincial conferences, or the virtual elimination of class voting on at least a national scale

Simeon and Elkins 1974

Canada has been so preoccupied with issues of unity and nationhood that relatively little attention was paid to regional issues until the late fifties and early sixties. The first initiatives were taken in relation to agriculture (which had an intrinsic regional dimension), but it was Trudeau who philosophically translated these into an element of national unity. In his view, regional disparities, particularly in the Maritimes, constituted a threat to Canadian unity.

This chapter traces the course of events from these beginnings through successive policy changes, none of which have had the desired impact. International comparisons provide little indication that any policy is likely to be as effective as hoped. Unsettled questions abound, even more in the huge federal state of Canada than in the smaller states of Europe.

Major organizational changes were made by the Liberal government in its last months of power in 1984. At the time of writing, it is unclear what new policies will emerge. The chapter ends, as it begins, with a question mark. Such is the essential characteristic of regional planning.

Regional policies present particular difficulties for policy makers in that they inevitably cut across traditional departmental lines. Moreover, while they may start with a particular focus (in the Canadian case on agriculture and rural development), pressures invariably mount for widening them. Similarly, a confined geographical area for the application of policies is difficult to hold. Other areas may have problems of a different nature but, once an attempt is made to reduce regional disparities, claimants refuse to be bound by original program limits or problem definitions. The claims are frequently legitimate, whether in economic, social or political terms. Thus, regional policies have a tendency to develop into a complex miscellany of programs.

These are general problems which are to be seen in the regional development experience of many countries. There are other "intricate conflicts and contradictions in the programs pursued," as Phidd has pointed out (1974: 168):

> First, there is the conflict between growth objectives as represented in the policies pursued under ADA [Area Development Agency] and distributional objectives on an area-basis as well as on a personal income basis, as shown, for example in ARDA [Agricultural Rehabilitation and Development Agency].

> Second, there is the conflict between a centralized as compared to a decentralized response, which is compounded by the fact that the seeming unity of the federal government is unlikely to be reflected in regional development administration because of the strong sectoral pressures working in the opposite direction. Yet there is the general belief that the initiative in regional development must rest in federal hands because that is where the available funds are to be found.

> Third, there are conflicts related to isolating the planning of regional development policies from its implementation, a major dilemma which may undermine the achievement of the objectives sought.

These conflicts are clearly to be seen in the evolution of regional planning in Canada. An increasing number of objectives led quickly to a complex array of programs. At the federal level, one starting point might be set at 1957 with the fiscal equalization scheme. The Federal-Provincial Tax Sharing Arrangements Act of that year provided for unconditional equalization payments to the relatively low-income provinces (Smiley 1980). Such a system had been recommended by the famous Rowell-Sirois Commission in 1940. This was concerned with constitutional issues and stressed the need for a stronger federal role in the field of taxation. (Indeed, it was suggested that the Dominion government should have exclusive powers of direct taxation and that provinces should be given "national adjustment grants" sufficient to enable them to provide services at an agreed national standard.) This was seen as a necessary corollary of Canada's gradual change from an agricultural to an industrial nation in which a stronger central power was needed to equalize costs and benefits over the country as a whole. However, the time had not yet arrived when Canada could take such a large step towards becoming a welfare state. Staunch provincialism, particularly on the part of the richer provinces, meant that the essential political agreement could not be reached even when it was possible to turn attention from the war.

By the year 1957, however, various forces came together to bring about a change: the report of the Royal Commission on Canada's Economic Prospects pointed not only to the size of American investment in Canada but also to the opportunities which lay to hand in the vast resources of the country; Diefenbaker's election brought in a Conservative government, after over twenty years of Liberal rule, committed to improving the position of the disadvantaged regions; and the same year saw the onset of a recession which politically demanded governmental action.

The 1957 scheme has been followed by frequent changes (Canadian Tax Foundation 1966; Romanow, Ryan and Stanfield 1984), and the subject seems unlikely ever to fall from the agenda of federal-provincial negotiations. Mercifully, a book on urban and regional planning need not enter into the intricacies of the various schemes. It must be noted, however, that in the broader scheme of things, federal equalization grants and fiscal policies have a major impact on regional prosperity if not on regional development.

Additionally, to complete this background sketch, reference needs to be made to the role of social security and, more broadly, public sector expenditure in reducing regional disparities.   By the end of the seventies, the federal programs of income security had been transformed into a major instrument of inter-regional redistribution. In Banting's words (1982: 175) "transferring responsibility for welfare to the federal government ... transforms income security into a powerful instrument of redistribution between regions."

Simmons' wider study (1984), which encompasses public sector employment, underlines the same point and, additionally, stresses the significance of government expenditures in stabilizing local economies. He suggests that "the major Canadian regional problem may be not income disparity but income uncertainty. Small centers, particularly in the primary producing periphery, are faced with enormous year-to-year variations in the value of the local economic base." Public expenditure provides a buffer against these erratic fluctuations: "pension checks, family allowances, UIC benefits, and the wages of teachers and mailmen support local economies in hard times."

Agriculture and Regional Planning

Federal countries such as Canada are naturally preoccupied with regional development

Munroe 1978

The first major step in regional policy came with the Agricultural Rehabilitation and Development Act of 1961, together with the work of the 1964 Senate Committee on Land Use in Canada. By this date, Canada was rich enough to afford a new venture, particularly since there were now far fewer farmers. "With the rising prosperity of the forties and fifties went a sharp fall in the absolute number of farm families, and an even sharper fall in their numbers as a proportion of the population. A government can much more easily find a subsidy or build a safety net when the subsidies are few relative to the subsidizers, and when the latter are quickly becoming richer and more numerous" (Bothwell, Drummond and English 1981: 230). The politics were clearer than the programs which the act introduced. In the debates on the bill, the minister "was unable to give a definite account of what it would actually do" or, at the least, he prevaricated on the extent to which the intention was to reduce the number of farms (Brewis 1969). Federal funds were to be made available to those provinces which agreed to enter into a formal agreement (involving a sharing of costs) "to help by various means to improve the income and standard of living of the smaller and more marginal farms, and in that way to help improve the overall position of agriculture."

Part of the difficulty was not merely that this was a new field for government action (hence the provision which was made for research) but also that the issue of uprooting farmers was politically a delicate one. In the words of Buckley and Tihanyi (1967: 19): "an important part of the original ARDA message could be interpreted as saying: we don't know the solution, but we will underwrite research and implement pilot projects in the hope of finding solutions." While some saw a reduction in small farms as being desirable (it was already well under way), others stressed the need for assisting the smaller farmer to become more productive. The initial emphasis was on the latter, and the programs were strongly physical.

Brewis has pointed to another influence here which was of great significance: in the concern expressed in the Senate Land Use Committee on "the physical properties of land and their implications for land use." The consequences of this are important: "as a result of both these influences, and especially of the latter, the emphasis of ARDA programs tended, at the outset, to be on the manner in which land use could be improved, particularly as it affected agriculture, and geographers and soil scientists, who are generally disposed to attach considerable weight to the study of the physical environment as a key to the type of development that should take place, dominated actions initially taken under ARDA ... Their emphasis on the physical

properties of land distracted attention from the more fundamental causes of distress in rural areas" (Brewis 1969: 106).

The same concern gave rise to a massive land capability
survey. A major research program on land use was amounted,
with a comprehensive survey of rural land capability and use.

> The task entails bringing together all existing information on the
> capabilities of uses of land, filling in the gaps in the existing
> information and interpreting the material into suitable
> classification systems ... It is the object of the Canada Land
> Inventory to store, analyze and publish this information in
> forms required for land use planning at the township, provincial,
> regional and national level (Canada: Department of Forestry
> 1965).

The Department of Regional Economic Expansion

> What is there about regional policy that appears to make it a
> no-win enterprise?
>
> Lithwick 1982

ARDA was a forerunner of regional economic development
policy, and the sixties saw a proliferation of programs and agencies culminating in 1969 with the establishment of the Department of Regional Economic Expansion (Lithwick 1978; Smiley
1980). During the sixties, the ARDA intergovernmental agreements were widened to deal with problems of rural poverty; a
fund was established (the Fund for Rural Economic Development: inevitably dubbed FRED) to give grants to rural
development programs in specifically designated areas which
were marked both by poverty and by potential for successful
development; the Atlantic Development Board was set up as an
advisory body concerned with the development of the Atlantic
Region.

The array of institutions was impressive, but it also gave
rise to obvious problems of coordination. To handle these, the
Trudeau government established the Department of Regional
Economic Expansion in 1969 as the central federal agency

concerned   with all activities aimed at promoting regional development.   The political dimension of this move was expressed by Trudeau (1968) in terms of the relevance of regional policy to national unity: "if the under-development of the Atlantic provinces is not corrected ... then the unity of the country is almost as surely destroyed as it would be by the French-English confrontation."   In Phidd's words, this "suggested the extension of the expenditure patterns, initiated in the Atlantic provinces, over the country as a whole. In fact, this strategy was adopted between 1969 and 1972."

Thus, instead of operating only in the worst areas for unemployment and low incomes, the new policy took into account "the relatively prosperous areas within slow growth regions ... [which] often offered the best potential for economic growth" (Brewis 1976: 165). In the words of the minister of the time (Jean Marchand), "there was no use thinking that it would be possible to get new industries to locate in all the most remote areas and in every small town where jobs were scarce and the surrounding rural areas depressed ... Most of the industrial development necessary to achieve high levels of employment in disadvantaged regions would have to be in some of the cities and larger towns."

This constituted a significant shift in emphasis from the manner in which the ARDA programs had operated. Those programs, heavily influenced by local preferences, tended to steer assistance to declining communities, with little attention to their potential for self-sustaining growth. In a careful study of the impact of policy up to the mid-sixties, Buckley and Tihanyi (1967) noted:

> Under the conditions prevailing in most parts of Canada, it is
> likely that a low-income rural area must rely heavily on down-
> ward adjustments in the size of its labor supply before
> significant increases in local productivity and income levels per
> person can be hoped for. The recognition of this necessity has
> been very slow to come and is still far from being generally
> accepted. Out-migration continues to be regarded as a hindrance
> to improving local standards, partly because so little has been
> done by senior governments to alleviate some of its truly

damaging side effects, and partly because population growth has
all too frequently been misused as a measure of political success.

Of course, policy cannot be changed overnight by the passing of an act or the establishment of a department. This is
especially so when legislation has to be operated by the federal
and provincial governments, and even more so when the department is, in many respects not a department, but a governmental organization for coordination (Phidd 1974: 178).

DREE's mandate was a broad one aimed at reducing
regional disparities. The three major planks were, first, to
increase jobs by a program of industrial incentives in areas of
slow growth; secondly, to improve the physical infrastructure
where this would facilitate the realization of economic potential;
and thirdly, to assist in social adjustment and rural development (DREE 1972). The latter embraced a wide range of measures intended to help people in the slow growth regions to take
advantage of the opportunities being provided and to improve
their living conditions. Examples were training programs, coun-
selling, and programs for the development of local economic
potential: in fields such as agriculture, mining and tourism.

There was certainly scope here for a wide range of initiatives in the different regions. Indeed, DREE had quite remarkable powers:

> The minister could decide which regions and firms qualified for
> capital assistance grants. These could range up to $12 million,
> and they could be made anywhere in the Atlantic provinces
> (except Labrador), and in many parts of the other provinces as
> well. DREE quickly became the vehicle for all sorts of federal-
> provincial development plans. In 1974, Ottawa signed general
> development agreements with all the provinces except Prince
> Edward Island, whose needs were provided for under an earlier
> agreement. Thus Newfoundland was sprinkled with "DREE
> schools," New Brunswick acquired "DREE hydro," and so on.
> By 1979, DREE was spending half a billion dollars a year
> (Bothwell, Drummond and English 1981: 410).

Regional policies tend to be characterized by constant reviews and changes in emphasis. So it has been in Canada. The experimental period following the establishment of DREE came to an end with a major policy review in 1972 (OECD 1980b: 25). Drawing on foreign as well as Canadian experience, the review concluded:

(1) Regional disparities were too complex to be dealt with effectively by one government department alone; a comprehensive approach was required whereby the collectivity of government policies was made more cognizant and sensitive to regional development objectives;

(2) Nationally applied programs were not sufficient and should be complemented by selective and flexible measures to take advantage of identified development opportunities and to overcome identified development constraints;

(3) The policy concern should not be regional disparities per se but rather to encourage each region of Canada to realize its potential for economic and social development. This change in perspective was important, indicating a greater emphasis for development rather than on area problems.

The practical implication of this was a major organizational change (the chief characteristic of which was decentralization from Ottawa) and the introduction of "general development agreements" (GDAs) between DREE and the provincial governments for basic strategies for regional development, and cost-shared "subsidiary agreements" for specific projects (DREE 1973a).

DREE was reorganized to enable it to deal more effectively with the provinces, and the Ottawa office was relegated to coordination and support of field activities. The existing ten provincial offices were greatly strengthened, and four regional offices were established: Atlantic, Quebec, Ontario, and Western. Such a decentralization was necessary to cope with the increasing demands of the provinces, but it is also relevant to note that in the election of 1972 much was made of the general ineffectiveness of DREE in reducing regional disparities and the apparent favoritism shown towards Quebec. More eloquent was the Liberal government's humiliating losses in the 1972 election which left it in an almost unworkable position. (The Liberals won 109 seats, the Conservatives 107, the New Democratic Party 31, and the Creditistes 15; there were two independents.)

The decentralization of DREE had some unanticipated results. By virtue of the development of close relationships with provincial officials, programs were developed which were essentially DREE projects (rather than the result of DREE acting as a coordinator of other departments) and which were difficult to challenge politically, despite the essentially political character of the decisions being taken (Savoie 1981; Careless 1977).

Thus not only were "provincial DREE officials in bed with the provinces" (Savoie 1981: 133) but both federal and provincial politicians had difficulty in establishing what was happening and in imposing their political judgments on the administrators' decision-making process.

Much of the difficulty stemmed from the extraordinary nature of the GDA system which, it should be noted, was introduced without any legislative provision. In the laconic words of a DREE annual report, "the GDA does not state specifically what has to be done, nor the means for doing it. Rather it sets out areas of opportunity and concern, and is, in effect, an enabling document designed to permit the signing governments to identify and encourage particular economic projects" (DREE 1982: 1). These projects are the subject of "special development agreements" thrashed out jointly by federal and provincial officials, with DREE putting up most of the finance involved. Though other federal departments might be involved, consultations typically are too late to affect the outcome: "the best they can hope for ... is to be given an opportunity to react to specific proposals. Even then, proposals are often so far advanced that it is too late to influence them" (Savoie 1981: 112). Added to this are the difficulties created by huge geographic distances; the differing priorities, time-frames and budgetary constraints of the different departments; and the fact that agreements are not infrequently designed to take advantage of opportunities as they emerge.

This system operated in such a way as to freeze out the participation of a wide range of concerned parties, not merely the general public and organized interest groups but even ministers. At the federal level, challenges to expenditure estimates for GDA-sponsored projects would typically be difficult given the broad general nature of the documents. At the provincial level there are, of course, differences between the ten provinces, but Savoie's study of New Brunswick clearly revealed the concern, if not alarm, on the part of ministers at the manner in which the GDA system effectively eroded their political control. In the smaller provinces there was additionally a personal style of ministerial behavior that was particularly ill-equipped to deal with the GDA system: their bureaucracies were "nascent"; their research staffs small or non-existent; and "New Brunswick cabinet ministers are reluctant to increase the province's planning capacity in any significant fashion because it would inhibit their ability to dispense political patronage and to base their decisions on purely political partisan considerations" (Ibid: 9).

Size, of course, has a lot to do with this, in terms of civil servants as well as of population. The New Brunswick government as a whole is only slightly bigger than an average federal department.

As pointed out at the beginning of this chapter, regional policies pose particular difficulties, and it is not surprising that they are constantly at the forefront of political attention. Careless, in his study of regional economic development noted that, when DREE was established, the area was one in which "it was simply not known whether funds, education, new industries, mobility or infrastructure were individually or collectively the solution."

The creation of DREE was, in part, a reflection not only of the perceived need for urgent action but also of a dissatisfaction with the rural solution. Instead, "DREE made a hard-headed political decision to focus on jobs," with assistance to private industrial plants and improvement of urban infrastructure "to serve as a lure for new industries and to encourage rural-to-urban migration." The reaction was a strong one against the policies of Alvin Hamilton (the minister responsible for the earlier ARDA program): "he saw farmers running forestry projects, local sawmills, growing worms and blueberries, and making shoes or cider."

Statements of policy, however, did not always accord with what actually happened, partly because of local influences and relationships, partly because of differences of opinion within organizations, and partly because a change of policy from the subsidization of rural poverty to its reduction required major shifts in programming. The arena for disagreement was huge. The large influence of individual civil servants is documented in Careless's study. He also notes that, at one point, there were three factions in the ARDA staff: "one was concerned with the social implications of the development programs; a second believed that spending money gave a program power, and sought to service any provincial project; while a third was concerned with the development of planning." Not surprisingly, "the three often conflicted."

More confusingly, announcements of policy changes, though sometimes dramatic, have been more frequently a change of emphasis or even a simple restatement together with an assurance that a renewed effort was in hand to make things work. (It is striking that the swings in policy between concentrating and spreading investments are to be seen equally on the British economic scene: Cullingworth 1985; Maclennan and Parr 1979). The OECD working party, which visited Canada in 1979, came (cautiously) to the conclusion that regional policy was working relatively well:

> The emphasis appeared to be on viable development, contributing to the sound growth of the Canadian economy and not simply on subsidizing development in the less favored regions without regard to economic justification. If this is true, it could be said that the policy minimizes the potential conflict between the objectives of national economic policy and those of regional policy, perhaps to a greater degree than in some member countries in which regional imbalances are so great as to require a

much   larger diversion of resources to the problems of the weaker regions.

DREE in the Early Eighties

No sizeable lessening of regional disparities has occurred since the formation of DREE

McAllister 1980

The foregoing account summarizes the evolution of policy at the federal level and highlights the major points at issue. The evolution continues, and it is impossible to keep up to date. However, in the next few pages a brief account will be given of the operations of 1980-81 and the (yet again) latest policy review.

The main traditional programs of DREE operate under the provisions of the Department of Regional Economic Expansion Act and the Regional Development Incentives Act (DREE 1973b). Within the framework of federal-provincial GDAs, some 117 subsidiary agreements had been signed between 1974 and 1981. Expenditure in 1981-82 amounted to $342 million: over half DREE's total budget.

DREE's maximum contribution to the cost of implementing a subsidiary agreement varies between the provinces according to the severity of their situation. It is highest in Newfoundland (90 percent) and lowest in Ontario, Alberta and British Columbia (50 percent).

The range of projects is so wide that no short selection could be representative but, to illustrate, two examples are given here: industrial infrastructure in Quebec, and the "Alberta North" agreement (DREE 1982).

Quebec: Industrial Infrastructure

Duration: 26 March 1975 to 31 March 1983

Costs shared by:

	$m
DREE	82.6
Province	55.1
Total estimated cost	137.7
DREE expenditure to date	40.4
DREE expenditure 1980-81	5.9

This agreement consists of a program of financial assistance for municipalities to enable them to set up or improve their infrastructure for industry. This assistance facilitates the creation of industrial parks, the development of industrial space in existing parks, the expansion of industrial parks, and the establishment of well-equipped industrial fishery parks in the Gaspé and on the North Shore. There is extra support for municipalities that do not have the necessary infrastructure for a major industrial project.

Alberta North Agreement

Duration: 1 April 1977 to 31 March 1982

Costs shared by:

	$m
DREE	27.5
DIAND	5.0
Province	22.5
Total estimated cost	55.0
DREE expenditure to date	17.4
DREE expenditure 1980-81	6.7

This agreement, which expands on an earlier interim agreement, is aimed at improving the incomes, employment opportunities, living standards, and community facilities in northern Alberta, so that residents can participate more actively in northern development. Programs are: human development, community services and facilities, community services and facilities on Indian reserves, social adjustment and professional development, and community economic development.

A typical example of the projects initiated under this agreement is the Opportunity Corps. Its overall objective is to reduce the dependency of welfare recipients, by providing practical training to those persons who do not qualify for standard training projects or existing employment opportunities.

DREE spent more than $3.4 million on this project during the 1978-81 period; of this, $1.4 million was spent in 1980-81. Most trainees come from northern centers such as Slave Lake, High Prairie, Fort Vermilion, Fort Chipewyan and Janvier, and from much smaller remote communities. Typical projects range from constructing and renovating day care facilities to building and installing creative playground equipment, using local materials.

Two other projects concern Metis settlement and isolated community housing. The objectives of these projects are to assist in providing affordable and suitable housing to residents of Metis settlements and isolated communities, in order to encourage them to establish a healthy and safe environment to live in.

There are two older programs still in operation: the PFRA and Special ARDA. Both focus assistance to the west. The Prairie Farm Rehabilitation Administration (which started in 1935) was introduced to assist in increased farm productivity (e.g. by irrigation projects). The Special ARDA program consists of agreements under the Agricultural and Rural Development Act. It aims to increase employment and improve living conditions, particularly for people of Native ancestry.

Newer initiatives include a federal grant for the modernization of the pulp and paper industry; the establishment of the Bureau of Business and Economic Development (BBED) which seeks to identify potential growth projects; and the Community Data Base. This has the task of providing "members of Parliament, government organizations and the Canadian public with accurate and timely information on social and economic indicators at the local community level." It is envisaged that such small area information will be "essential for effective policy development or business investment decision making, and will be an important tool for future DREE programming."

There is a growing interest in the role which can be played in regional development by interdepartmental programs. Several of these were developed during 1980-81: the Special Investment Tax Credit Program, the National Energy Program, the Cape Breton Island Development Project, the Local Economic Development Assistance Program, and the Industry and Labor Adjustment Program. Brief details are given in DREE's annual reports. The list strikingly illustrates the blurred boundaries of regional development policy. As Emanuel concluded from his OECD survey: "the distinction between regional and non-regional objectives fades in significance as the scope of the former widens, and as their achievement calls for the increasing adaptation of national policies to take account of regional diversities. National and regional policies which conflict need to be reconciled if they are not mutually to frustrate each other" (Emanuel 1973: 251).

Review and Reorganization 1980-82

The task at hand is to devise a Canada-wide policy that focuses on stimulating "winning" sectors such as resource development and new technology/high productivity industries, while finding ways to restructure industrial "losers": textiles, footwear and farm machinery

Gherson 1982

The turn of the decade saw a further review of regional policy: the *Strategic Regional Development Overview* (DREE 1980). Stress was laid on the need for shaping policies to fit the needs of the individual regions, with a particular focus on areas with development potential. For instance:

> Some past federal programs have had equity, or income mainte-
> nance as objectives. These programs have contributed to an
> easing of regional disparities. But they have also created in
> some places a "dependence effect," inhibiting regional growth,
> corporate entrepreneurship, and individual mobility. The
> current and estimated future federal fiscal position may not per-
> mit large enough cash flows to the regions. The focus of policy,
> therefore, may have to shift more towards the realization of
> economic opportunity. This shift in policy stance will mean that
> new objectives are required. Specific targeting toward regional
> development goals is particularly important in a time of extreme
> federal fiscal restraint (Ibid: 4).

This is a politically treacherous area, and a statement dealing with *Towards a New Policy* was cautious: "traditionally,
the goals of regional economic development have been couched
in terms of increasing incomes and employment, particularly in
lagging regions of the country. Although inequitable regional
circumstances waste manpower resources and are clearly unacceptable, these goals of increasing incomes and employment
opportunities do not fully capture all of the regional concerns
which should be addressed in a regional development strategy.
Such a regional strategy must not only be tailor-made; it must
also include an adequate array of government policies and programs to meet diverse regional objectives" (Ibid: 5).

The emergency requirements for the 1980s were stated as
being to create employment opportunities; to overcome physical and institutional barriers to growth; to ensure the efficient
and effective operation of regional linkages; and to assist the
residents of the region to adjust to new occupations, innovations, and more efficient systems.

A 1981 budget paper set the scene for this reorientation of
regional policy: the emphasis was clearly on national economic
development, with regional dynamics as a consequential issue
(Canada 1981). Happily, there were "genuine prospects for
growth in every region." If this were an unqualified statement,
there would be little scope for regional policy; and, as we shall

see, the policy statements of 1981 and 1982 get close to arguing that regional policy was to become a social relief policy: the emphasis was on the wider economic development opportunities. The paper emphasized that:

> The leading opportunity lies in the development of Canada's rich bounty of natural resources [inclusive of] food products, such as grain and fish, forest products and energy-based industries, such as petrochemicals and further expansion of agriculture, forest-based industries and mining. The massive investment in resource development projects, will generate many billions of dollars worth of opportunities for supplying these projects or developing new resource based products (deFayer 1982).

The emphasis on natural resources raises some long term questions; for example, "when the oil, gas and coal are gone, how will the provinces earn their living, and where can the empire of the St Lawrence turn to for its next generation of staple exports?" (Weaver and Gunton 1982: 31). The political process tends to allow such difficult questions to give way to more immediately demanding, or at least diverting, issues such as those concerned with departmental organization. A lengthy statement on *Reorganization for Economic Development* was issued by the Office of the Prime Minister in January 1982. It would be interesting, but tedious, to subject all this to detailed analysis. It contains a typical range of motherhood statements, incompatibilities, certain and uncertain facts, policies and promises, and a new organizational structure.

The latter took the form of the reorganization of the former Ministry of State for Economic Development into a Ministry of State for Economic and Regional Development; and the merging of most of DREE's program functions with the domestic responsibilities (for industry, tourism and small businesses) of the Department of Industry, Trade and Commerce in a new Department of Regional Industrial Expansion. DREE became DRIE.

Unsettled Questions

... the evaluation of DREE would indicate that the gains may
not have been justified by the costs

Bradfield 1981

A study by McAllister (1982: 196) of regional development
in the European Community, from a Canadian perspective, concluded that:

> In the European Community, as in Canada, the very delineation
> of regional development problems, priorities and options has not
> proven a straightforward task. Neither the Community nor
> Canada can point to accomplishments, on any grand scale, as an
> obvious outcome of their regional development efforts. Even the
> appropriate yardsticks to measure the performance of regional
> policies are still far from agreed upon. In large part, this
> reflects the complexity of many of the issues, as well as the pol-
> itical difficulties inherent in approaching many regional problems
> head on.

It is, indeed, difficult for the academic, untrammeled by
the dictates of politics to decide, and to get to grips with the
subject, since it is not at all clear what the subject is. To
some, it is a question of incomes (Dodge 1975; Ray and Brewis
1976; Reuber 1978). Others see it as a series of questions which
is characterized by a lack of clarity and objectivity. Thus
Courchene writes that, "ideology and value judgment appear to
play a much greater role in analysis of regional issues than is
the case for most other policy areas" (1981: 506). He sees the
crucial issue as being "the failure over time to submit the provinces and regions to the discipline of the market"; governmental policy has thus "exacerbated regional disparities and has
tended to rigidify our industrial structure." Matthews (1981)
strongly disagrees, while Cameron (1981) attempts to clarify the
issues at debate.

The sheer weight of writing in this area is daunting: a
periodic review would be useful. For the present, the reader can
be referred to a special 1982 issue of the *Canadian Journal of*

Regional Science. Of particular interest in this is a paper by Clyde Weaver and Thomas Gunton (which also has a useful bibliography). One of the interesting features of this paper is the way in which it brings together a wide range of writings concerned with the Canadian scene (Britton and Gilmour 1978; Levitt 1970; Marchak 1979; Watkins 1977; etc). The authors are concerned that, in the new structure, "regional development issues will become more diffused within the governmental structure ... [the new policies] represent a major departure from the regional science-based thinking of the last decade ..." A quotation from a ministerial statement supports their argument: "from here on, the national government will invest its capital in areas of prospective growth in the future ..." (Weaver and Gunton 1982: 30). Perhaps the final word can be from McAllister's wide-ranging review: "regional disparities are frequently not just a product of differences in resource and other factor endowments. Often they are a mirror of the long-standing views of national and regional societies about their own priorities" (McAllister 1982: 206).

This seems an appropriately enigmatic note on which to end this discussion.

A Digression: On the Meaning of `Region´

> There is probably about as much certainty that Canada is made
> up of regions as there is confusion over what these regions are
>
> Cameron 1981

It would not be difficult to write at length on the meaning of the term "region." It has been done many times. That, however, is one good reason in itself for not attempting the same task. The reader is referred to some excellent texts (Breton 1982; Brewis 1969; Grigg 1965; Nicholson and Sametz 1961). The intention here is more modest: to point to the ambiguity of the term, to the implications of varying the definition, and finally to the perspectives of different levels of government. This section thus provides a link between the discussion of planning at the federal and provincial levels. Academically, the term can be applied to a wide variety of concepts:

> A region is not an object either self-determined or nature given. It is an intellectual concept, an entity for the purposes of thought, created by the selection of certain features that are relevant to a real interest or problem, and by the disregard of all features that are considered to be irrelevant (Brewis 1969: 45).

This leaves the matter wide open, and the issue becomes one of delineating regions for a given particular purpose. This, however, is where the difficulties arise, since the implications of different purposes may differ significantly. An attempt to draw boundaries around a homogeneous area (however that term is to be defined) will clearly have different results from an attempt to devise an area which is balanced, whether in terms of age, income, occupation or whatever. The effects, of course, will also vary. Averaging social or economic characteristics, for example, will obviously mean very different things. Thus with the provinces of Canada, "averaging at the provincial level conceals the fact that there are a lot of very wealthy people in the Atlantic provinces who need no help from governments and quite a lot of poor ones in Ontario, Alberta and British Columbia who do" (Brewis 1976: 162). The relative size of regions is also of relevance: "the wealthy cities of central Canada contain more people in 'sorry economic circumstances', depending on how that term is defined, than do the poor rural areas of the Atlantic provinces" (Ibid).

This is more than a matter of elementary arithmetic: "whether we are more concerned with proportions than we are with actual numbers will influence the way in which we perceive our regions." The issue is clearly seen in the arguments of the Canada West Foundation:

> Regionalism is a real and legitimate force that must be recognized and accommodated, not ignored nor rejected. In Canada as in other viable federal countries, citizens feel an identity and a loyalty that is connected to a region within the country, as

well as an identity and a loyalty that is connected to the country as a whole. This dual loyalty is a legitimate aspect of any
federal system, and not in any sense "unCanadian."

The practical application of "region" in Canadian politics is in
terms of those regions uniquely contained within provincial
boundaries. Any number of arbitrary quasi-geographical
regional boundaries can be generated that are quite satisfying to
the on-looker or to the analyst, but provinces have a concrete
historical identity and form the practical foundation for the
organized activities of citizens. Multi-province regions, whether
we are speaking about the West, the Prairies, the Maritimes or
the Atlantic provinces, are artificial conglomerates that do not
hold up under closer scrutiny. The fundamental equation region
= province guides our comments on regionalism (McCormick,
Manning and Gibson 1981).

The perspective here is quite different from that which held
sway in Ottawa when DREE was established: "a principal
motivation behind its establishment was the desire to elevate
planning for economic development from the province to the
regional level" (Savoie 1981: 15). And so the ten provinces were
divided into four regions: two were large enough to form their
own regions (Ontario and Quebec) but the four eastern provinces became the Atlantic Region, while the remainder (including the Northwest Territories and the Yukon) became the
Western Region. Nothing could underline the differing perspectives more than the contrast between DREE's "natural" inclusion of Newfoundland in its Atlantic Region and Canada West
Foundation's protest:

Newfoundland is not a Maritime province at all, lying outside
the historical associations and interconnections that generated
this term. Until 1949, Newfoundland stood completely outside
Canada and Canadian politics, its political and commercial
attachments being primarily to the United Kingdom and to the
United States ... Only by neglecting history, logic, and present
political trends can we lump Newfoundland in with the three
Maritime provinces.

There   is   another   aspect   of   "region,"   of   particular
significance to regional planning, which requires mention. To

avoid the confusion attendant upon the Canadian situation it is simpler to illustrate from the British experience (Cullingworth 1985: 293). There is a clear distinction, conceptually if not practically, that can be made between, on the one hand, regional planning which is concerned with the planning of land use, economic investment and such like *within* the region, and on the other hand, regional planning which is concerned with the allocation of resources *between* the regions. The former is, again conceptually, a regional responsibility; the latter is a central government responsibility which is carried out in the light of regional needs and political pressures.

Translated to the Canadian scene, there are obvious difficulties with nomenclature, but an important distinction between the two types of regional planning holds, namely the different perspectives held by the different levels of government. For Britain:

> What central government means by "regional planning" is primarily the correction of economic imbalance between one region and another, and it is only with reluctance that central government is reconciling itself to the fact that this purpose (crucial to its central function in the economic field) necessarily involves the making of investment decisions *within* regions on a territorial as well as a functional basis. What local government means by "regional planning," on the other hand, is primarily the expression of national policies in terms of a comprehensive long term strategy for economic and physical development *within* each provincial-scale region, in the context of which local planning authorities can work out meaningful structure plans for their own areas (Royal Commission on Local Government in England 1969).

These are the issues of regional planning which in Canada arise in very different ways in the different provinces. It is to these that we now turn.

Federal and Provincial Roles in Regional Planning

An unrelenting pursuit of "national efficiency" is not a viable
policy option for Canada

Savoie 1984

As with many of the issues discussed in this book, it is
more difficult to deal with the provincial level than the federal.
This, of course, is as it should be, with ten regions of varied history and character stretching across a whole continent, ranging
in area from less than 5,657 square kilometers (PEI) to
1,540,680 square kilometers (Quebec) and in population (1983)
from 124,000 (PEI) to 8.8 million (Ontario). However, regional
planning presents particular difficulties, not only because of its
ambiguous meaning but also because, in the words of the final
report of the CIP Task Force on Planning Acts (1981), "regional
planning is in a state of flux and no distinct trend emerges."

In the following two chapters, the particular focus of
interest is on the state of flux to which the CIP report refers.
While it may be true to say that no distinct trend emerges,
there is a discernible growth of interest in regional planning in
some provinces which typically involves greater provincial
involvement. However, as we shall see, regional planning is not
progressing in all provinces. By the time this book is published,
it could be that political changes will have resulted in a situation where the trend is towards less rather than more provincially controlled regional planning, but with clearer statements
of provincial policy to which municipalities must pay due
regard.

Chapter 8
Regional Planning
and Development in Ontario

The present scope of regional planning is not clear

Comay Report 1977

This chapter deals with a remarkable planning endeavor which, in the words of a senior civil servant involved in it, was "of a magnitude rarely attempted in a free society" (Macdonald 1984: 92). This was a series of major regional planning efforts by the Ontario provincial government to provide a positive, indeed dramatic, lead into the planning and development of the province: the *Design for Development*. This embraced a wide range of policies including the Toronto-Centred Region concept, the Parkway Belt, the North Pickering new town, nine joint provincial-municipal planning studies, a series of large scale provincial land acquisitions, a policy for controlling urban development in rural areas, and a plan for the Niagara Escarpment. The full story would be a lengthy but fascinating one. It would also be confusing, since it was confused. Fortunately, there is a number of analyses, written largely by planners and civil servants who participated in one or more of these efforts which throw considerable light on their aims, problems and final collapse; for example, Nigel Richardson's "Insubstantial Pageant: The Rise and Fall of Provincial Planning in Ontario" (1981a) and a special issue of *Plan Canada* (1984a).

The chapter was originally drafted before the publication of the latter. It is based on the original published sources, together with Richardson's work, but it has been revised to reflect some of the insights which the *Plan Canada* papers provide.

Following a short introduction and a brief scene setting account of federal and provincial antecedents, the chapter chronicles some of the major elements of Ontario planning which, in the main, lasted for a decade from 1966 to 1975. The story since 1975 is shorter. Only the Niagara Escarpment saga continues (except for the embarrassing aftermath of the provincial land acquisitions), but a newcomer is emerging with coordinated land use plans dealing with natural resources (discussed in chapter 6).

Ontario's attempts at provincial and regional planning are chronicled at length in a library of reports, and the *Plan Canada* (1984) review suggests that there may be an uncomfortable degree of truth in the quip about more words than deeds. It was not intended so: Ontario's intentions were sincere, even if sometimes politically incautious. It could be that Ontario's experience is a lesson in the political hazards which face those planners who attempt to do too much too quickly. Alberta's slower development of regional planning machinery may prove to be longer lasting, although alternatively it may prove to be simply slow.

Ontario is significant also in that, in the postwar years, it has witnessed what one economist has called the economic transformation of the province (Richmond 1974). This transformation is particularly characterized by interrelated surges in employment, production, incomes, population and households, urbanization and a major shift in the character of the economy from manufacturing to service industries.

Ontario, of course, has not been alone in this; indeed, much of western society witnessed such postindustrial development, with corresponding and often severe by-products in subregional decline, social stress, and strains on public services. But Ontario was the first of the Canadian provinces to experience the full force of these postwar forces of change and to adapt its policies to deal with them. Sadly, the province also has the distinction of being the first to effectively back away from provincial planning, mirroring the demise of federal endeavors in shaping a national urban policy. The histories of both these planning efforts provide food for thought on the viability of planning in contemporary volatile times.

There is, however, one immediate point that requires, but defies clarification: the nature of the planning with which we are concerned. Terms abound: regional planning, provincial planning, regional development, and so forth. Unfortunately, except with harder terms such as fiscal and economic planning, it is impossible to get firm meanings affixed to the terms if only because the processes involved are essentially political and politicians are skilled in playing with words. However, since we are here concerned with what was done, and what was promised or claimed to be done, there is no need for an exercise in semantics. It is necessary only to note that Ontario drew a distinction (sometimes) between "regional development," meaning the reduction of regional disparities, and "regional planning," meaning policies and programs related to the particular problems of individual regions (Emanuel 1973). Since at least some of the latter particular problems were matters also of regional disparity, the inherent scope for confusion is obvious.

There is one final point by way of introduction which needs to be constantly borne in mind. Regional planning in Ontario was largely undertaken by the provincial government, not by regional planning authorities: it was what Blumenfeld has termed "top-down" planning. It may be that this was a significant part of its undoing.

The Antecedents

Master plans should be prepared by the appropriate authorities for every town and rural community throughout the Dominion of Canada

Advisory Commission on Reconstruction 1943

Like Britain, Canada emerged from the second world war with haunting memories of the depression of the thirties, and a determination to prevent, or at least mitigate, the effects of a generally anticipated recurrence. A new role for the federal government was forged with national systems of unemployment insurance (1941) and family allowances (1944), and a federal commitment to full employment. The new positive role for Ottawa rested on shaky ground; there was lack of positive support from Ontario and Quebec and, with hindsight, the inappropriateness of Keynesian policies designed to mitigate the effects of an expected recession in unexpected boom conditions (Richmond 1974: 6). What did survive were manpower training programs, regional development and a contemporary version of the National Policy. In Richmond's words: "a new phase of the National Policy was evolving [in the 1950s] consisting of new transportation links across Canada (pipelines, air lines, the Seaway, and conversion of the railways to diesel) and new communication links (the microwave system); the gradual liberalization of trade through the medium of GATT; direct government support and expansion of the aircraft industry and the nationally owned air carrier; and the growing commitment to a nuclear energy program."

This, however, was in the fifties: by the end of the sixties such clarity as had existed in federal policy had crumbled in the face of changing economic and political forces. Certainly, the traditional National Policy was looking decidedly sick, while the provinces were using their newly flexed muscles. On this Ontario was in the lead.

Ontario entered the postwar era with a strong and explicit commitment to industrial expansion. This was reinforced in the fifties when federal government economic policy shifted in line with that of Ontario. Not only was there cooperation in such major projects as the Seaway and the Trans-Canada Highway, but also a myriad of cost-sharing programs developed: for such areas as housing, land assembly, hospitals, highways and welfare.

As this evolved and manifested itself in a concentration of urban development around the western shore of Lake Ontario, aptly nick-named The Golden Horseshoe, increasing concern grew for regional disparities, to use a graphic term which only later became part of the coinage of planning. In December 1954, a "regional development program" (Ontario 1954) for Ontario was announced, but it amounted to little more than a modest encouragement to voluntary regional associations. Much more dramatic was the establishment of the Municipality of Metropolitan Toronto. This not only solved the problems for which it had been designed, particularly the provision of main services such as water and sewerage: it also, by virtue of this very success, "created a powerful counter-pull to industry that had begun to look to other areas of the province" (Richmond 1974: 14).

Against such a powerful magnet, the regional development program could not begin to compete. Between 1956 and 1970, employment in Metro Toronto grew 46 percent from 630,000 to 920,000: the population increase over the same period was 51 percent from 1,358,000 to 2,045,000 (Nader 1976: 2:212). Most of the employment growth in the fifties was in the service sector. Manufacturing employment, on which provincial policies were focused, was virtually stagnant. The recession at the end of the fifties did not halt the dynamic development of this urban region, though new policies, at both provincial and federal levels, began to emerge. These were structural policies, in contrast to the traditional fiscal and monetary policies, concerned with manpower training, the expansion of export markets and such like. At the municipal level, a notable innovation was the creation of the Ontario Water Resources Commission to give assistance in the building of water and sewerage systems. This was of particular importance for areas not located on the shores of the Great Lakes.

There were, however, three persistent problems which remained, and intensified, in boom periods: "the increasing tendency of Ontario's population to concentrate in the large urban areas in the central and southwestern portion of the province, at the expense of rural places and of the north and east; the tendency towards unstructured sprawl [i.e. continuous low density urban development or leapfrogging random development] in the rapidly-growing areas: and the trend towards careless and

unwise   use of the physical setting, e.g. waste of prime farmland, open-pit mining, air and water pollution" (Bureau of Municipal Research 1977b: 2).

Design for Development

Design for Development ... had potential as an administrative tool,
but this was matched by its potential, soon realized, for causing
friction between the province and its municipalities, and within
the provincial bureaucracy

Suichies 1984

It was to deal with these problems that Ontario mounted
its long term *Design for Development,* the primary aim of which
was the stimulation of economic growth in the less favored
regions. The design was essentially an organizational one. No
new programs were announced. Indeed, the crucial feature of
the design was that the resources devoted to existing programs
ranging, for example, from water to education, were of such
magnitude as to be effective as an instrument of regional
development policy, given the necessary coordination. To effect
this, a Cabinet committee and an advisory committee of deputy
ministers were established.

It should be noted that one of the main instruments of the
new regional development policy was to be "the use of government budgetary expenditures directed to regional needs ...
Thus *regional development* will be contained within the broader
spectrum of *provincial development.*" This approach necessitated detailed studies of each of the constituent regions of the
province, a lengthy and arduous task which had to be slimmed
down considerably after reports on four of the ten regions took
five years to produce.

The succession of reports of Phases One, Two and Three,
together with work on the Toronto-Centred Region, the
Niagara Escarpment, and other areas now becomes confusing.
The matter is made even more difficult by the fact that subsequent reports on an area were termed Phase Two Reports (as

with the Northwestern Region); yet Phase Two of *Design for Development* dealt with local government reorganization (Richardson 1981: 565). It was, no doubt, with some relief, that the government could turn to Phase Three which, in the light of experience since 1966, presented proposals for some major changes in the machinery. The Phase Three Statement included "changes in the techniques for implementing regional development in Ontario." The term "techniques" was an odd one, but it was used to mean a reduction of the ten economic regions ("no longer adequate for the purposes of the regional development program") to five planning regions; the local government program (viz Phase Two); and a reorganization of the central planning machinery, the details of which are now purely of historical interest. Comments on local government reorganization and provincial-municipal fiscal relations completed the province's statement. The latter in particular was long in words and short in positive commitment.

With hindsight it is easy to be insouciant in relation to these proposals, but in fact the problems addressed were horribly complex and admitted of no easy solution: indeed some, especially property tax reform, remain to haunt us in the 1980s. The positive fact remains that the province saw (and stated) some important difficult interrelationships, and attempted to come to grips with the problems which they posed. The remarkable thing is that a major attempt to reform was made: it was quite unremarkable that it failed.

The Phase Three Statement was concerned, in part, with local government reorganization, much of it expressed in general terms. More specific were the proposals for a new regional advisory system, with two bodies (one representative of the municipalities, the other of the private sector) for each of the new regions in place of the established ten regional development councils. This was to be accompanied by a parallel change in regional advisory boards of civil servants, and a strengthening of central government coordinating machinery in an Advisory Committee on Urban and Regional Planning, which in fact was the existing deputy ministers committee under a new name.

How far all this, plus proposals for reform in "provincial-municipal fiscal relations," added up to something which could be legitimately termed "the provincial regional development plan" is debateable. Certainly, no provincial plan ever appeared, despite a government statement in October 1974 that one was in preparation (Richardson 1981: 567), and despite the passing, in 1973, of the Ontario Planning and Development Act. This act provided extraordinarily wide powers for the establishment of "development planning areas" and the preparation of plans, but the powers have remained largely unused. The nearest to a plan was *Ontario's Future: Trends and Options*, published in 1976, though this was explicitly denied to be such. In fact, this broad discussion paper represented little advance in thinking or policy. (How far a provincial plan is practicable is another question, but it is perhaps noteworthy that no other province has one apart from Prince Edward Island where the plan is concerned with economic development.)

Not much of significance followed. A draft regional strategy for Northeastern Ontario brought a bitter reaction from the region and was quickly dropped (Weller 1980: 251). The 1978 strategy for the Northwest was a barren document, while the policy statement issued in the following year explicitly rejected the growth area approach which had been central to the earlier strategy.

Of course, the economy of the mid-seventies was very different from that of the mid-sixties: rather than controlling growth and channelling it to needy areas, the problem had become one of stimulating growth. At the same time, the early enthusiasm had evaporated in the face of a perceived widening gap between achievement and effort; of continued, and inherent, clashes of departmental interest; of changing personalities within the civil service, crucially important changes at the ministerial level, and of course, of the more volatile political scene and apparent lack of support for regional policies: at least in some of the rural areas where policies had a tangible impact (and where electoral losses occurred).

The epitaph has now been written, first tentatively by the Bureau of Municipal Research (1977), later more firmly by Richardson (1981) and Suichies (1984). A BMR report of 1977 noted that "a significant swing in provincial policy with respect to regional planning is underway ... The notion of a 'grand plan' for all of Ontario has apparently been abandoned."

Writing in 1981, Richardson described and analyzed "the rise and fall of provincial planning in Ontario." He laid stress on the inadequacy of central government organization, the program's lack of a power base, and the consequent undue reliance on a small group of individuals: in short the program was never "bedded down" in the governmental system. His conclusion was that, "if by the term regional development program we mean a coherent set of undertakings based on thorough and comprehensive analysis and intended to achieve specific objectives at the regional level, it is clear that in ten years this was never fully achieved in Ontario." This, however, is the view of one who was intimately involved in the program, and it might well be considered too black a verdict, though it is echoed by Suichies (1984). Certainly, there were difficulties within the machinery of government, but these beset any planning ministry which seeks to coordinate the programs of line departments: witness the overwhelming difficulties which faced the Ministry of State for Urban Affairs in Ottawa (discussed in chapter 2).

Moreover, there is considerable doubt as to whether a "comprehensive provincial strategy" is a viable concept. "Strategies," say Heclo and Wildavsky, "are simple minded notions with which parties occasionally come into office, and historians sometimes attach as convenient labels for disparate happenings, but which never characterize the actual operations of any government" (1974: 363).

On this more skeptical approach, it would seen appropriate to judge the *Design for Development* program on its specific achievements and not on the large claims made for it on the part of enthusiasts. Yet to do this would be to accept that achievements, and failures, were part of the program and not merely happenings that might (or might not) be included under the *Design for Development* umbrella. For instance, despite quite independent origins, local government reorganizations became a formal part of the *Design for Development* program in the Phase Two statement of 1968. As Richardson points out, its relationship to the original program "was entirely nominal; the only common element was the word 'regional', and that proved to be the source of endless confusion." Going further, would the absence of *Design for Development* have made any difference to the planning of the Niagara Escarpment, or the Parkway Belt, or the Toronto-Centred Region?

It seems preferable to discuss these as independent planning projects, but pointing out interconnections where any can be truly thought to exist. Following this, one can return to Richardson's argument and judge it in a wider context.

In the space available it is impossible to deal with all the major regional planning programs in postwar Ontario. Moreover some cut across a regional planning dimension: agricultural land policy, land banking, or the work of the Ministry of Natural Resources or the Ministry of the Environment for instance. These are discussed in other chapters. Here we select for discussion only those programs which it would be indefensible to omit! These are the Toronto-Centred Region, the Parkway Belt, the Niagara Escarpment, the Joint Provincial-Municipal Planning Studies, and the Provincial Land Acquisitions.

The Toronto-Centred Region

The Toronto-Centred Region Plan was a grand plan based on expectations of high growth that were drastically at odds with the growth being experienced by the time the plan was worked out in detail

Lawson 1984

The Toronto-Centred Region naturally had the lion's share of governmental attention even before *Design for Development* was conceived. Striking testimony to the importance to this region was the establishment of the Municipality of Metropolitan Toronto in 1953 and the planning functions which were allocated to it. The new authority was charged with the responsibility of preparing an official plan, not just for the 240 square miles within the boundaries of Metro, but for a much larger adjacent area which encompassed a further 480 square miles. This was even more extraordinary than the two-tiered federal structure of Metro, since the thirteen municipalities in the wider area had no representation on Metro Council. It was expected that procedures would be worked out between all the authorities concerned and the provincial government to deal with this curious situation. This was never done, and thus a heavy task fell to the provincial government in supervising, controlling and coordinating the planning operations of the authorities involved. The problem was compounded by the fact that, since the outer authorities were not represented on Metro, an official plan was never adopted. However, Metro resorted to the device of a draft plan which was not submitted for provincial approval. Instead it was treated as a statement of Metro policies. It lacked statutory power of course, but it did deal with the political problem of non-representation and had the additional advantage of being flexible. The whole cumbersome process of plan amendments was obviated (Robarts Report 1977: 2:208). The fringe areas were removed from the Metro planning area with the establishment of regional municipalities: York in 1971 and Peel and Durham in 1973.

The initial versions of the draft plan "were used extensively as policy guidelines for metropolitan activities. The 1966 plan formed the basic program for expressway and subway construction, and its land use and services policies formed the basis for Metro's activities in development control and in the installation of sewer and water lines" (Ibid).

Transportation became increasingly important as urbanization proceeded apace and, in 1963, the Metropolitan Toronto and Region Transportation Study (MTARTS) was set up. This had a major input from the provincial government, the other participants being Metro, the Toronto Transit Commission and the railway companies. Transport, of course, is a crucial element in urban development, but just how important the connection is had not been fully appreciated at this time. Nor were the political implications clearly seen: or, to be more precise, transport policies had not yet entered the center of the political stage. It was the Spadina Expressway in Toronto (like the Burrard Peninsula expressway system in Vancouver and the MacKinnon Freeway in Edmonton) which did this (Leo 1977). The saga, as it indeed was, of urban transport planning in various Canadian cities has been often told, and it is not intended to repeat it here.

As its title suggests the MTARTS final report, *Choices for a Growing Region* (1968), sets out a range of choices for the study region, which stretched from Hamilton and Guelph, east to Bowmanville, and north to Lake Simcoe. In the absence of planning controls, it seemed that a continuation of current trends would result, by the end of the century, in a solid mass of development from Port Credit to Brampton; Richmond Hill would be eight miles wide; and many built-up areas would be too far from Lake Ontario for "economical servicing."

As a guide to future development, and to avoid the problems of urban sprawl, MTARTS proposed a set of "goal plans." The preferred choice was for a two-tiered system of urban places along the lakeshore, separated by a parkway belt. This belt, which is discussed more fully below, was needed "to take the pressure off the Queen Elizabeth Way and Highway 401" and, at the same time, to serve a variety of other uses including recreation.

This concept was favored in the province's 1970 statement *Design For Development: The Toronto-Centred Region* (TCR). This area extended over some 8,600 square miles (compared with the MTARTS planning area of about 3,200 square miles). Indeed, looking beyond the immediate planning area, the statement suggested that the "interaction area" was some 15,000 square miles.

The TCR encompassed Kitchener-Waterloo, Brantford, Midland, Peterborough, and recreation districts to the north and northeast. It had a 1966 population of 3.6 million which was expected to increase to around 8 million by the end of the century. "Moreover, increases in family income, mobility and leisure time will make the region more accessible and more extensively used."

These were heady times, and looking at the region in a broader perspective it was confidently stated that it would "continue to grow as part of the Chicago-Detroit-Toronto-Montreal metropolis and as the financial, manufacturing, cultural and communications center of Canada and especially of Ontario."

Fortunately no attempt was made to devise a planning strategy for this section of the globe: the policy was focused on TCR itself within which "growth is increasingly concentrating in the metropolitan core and towards the west and southwest." This growth was of a suburbanizing character and contained "aspects of unstructured sprawl." Land was being "removed prematurely" from agricultural and recreational use "both for low density residential purposes and for speculation." Since the document contained less than seventeen pages of text, it is replete with such striking and unsupported statements. Reference is made, for instance, to "massive urbanization, congestion"; to "inefficiency in the provision of flexible, least-cost, high performance trunk services, such as transportation and water and sewer"; to "insufficient use of districts with good development potential, but beyond easy commuting range of Metropolitan Toronto"; to "misallocation of prime recreation and agricultural areas"; and to "detraction from effective integration of the northern and eastern parts of the province with the Toronto-Centred Region because of the strong thrust to the west and southwest from Metropolitan Toronto."

This embodies the conventional planning wisdom of the time, but there is little doubt that the emerging pattern of urbanization involved inefficiencies and costs which could be avoided if some sensible forethought and control were imposed.

The *Design for Development* statement provided the basic policy:

> The main purpose of the Toronto-Centred Region Development concept are to (i) shape the growth of the region's metropolitan core into a two-tiered urbanized area; (ii) encourage growth in selected communities beyond easy commuting range of Metropolitan Toronto, and thus help to decentralize the region and prevent a swollen growth within and near Metropolitan Toronto; and (iii) set basic guidelines for regional land use. Of the region's expected population of nearly 8 million people, 5.7 million, or 71 percent, are targeted for the lakeshore urbanized area; 300,000 or 4 percent for the adjacent commuting zone; and 2 million, or 25 percent, for the peripheral belt.

In essence, this design for development envisaged a decentralization of people from the lakeshore urbanized area (zone one), beyond the commutershed (zone two) to the peripheral area (zone three).

The language of the first TCR statement was broad (Rose 1972: 148) and, perhaps not surprisingly, it was replete with motherhood statements, particularly evident in the list of twelve goals for the region which began with "the achievements of the region's economic potential, consistent with the overall provincial interest and development," and ended with the development of the region "in a manner that provides flexibility."

Such generalities were probably appropriate at the beginning of a new, and potentially hazardous, attempt at regional planning. The government tentatively tested reactions. They were positive, and a status report was published as early as August 1971. This noted that the concept was undergoing a progressive refinement. In concrete terms, this involved a virtual orgy of consultations. A multiplicity of major planning decisions began to emerge: some were closely related to the TCR plan, such as further planning on the Parkway Belt; others were unconnected but of major long term significance, such as the decision not to allow the extension of the Spadina Expressway.

A major feature of the TCR concept was the "go east" policy. This appeared promising as the second international airport, and associated new town, at Pickering grew in plausibility, but nothing happened, apart from some large scale land acquisitions that gave rise to controversy which rumbled on until the mid-eighties.

There was no doubt, certainly with the absence of the second international airport in the east, that the development pressures to the west of the region were stronger than could be contained (Macdonald 1984: 97) or, at least, "the concept was too general in nature to be translated into programs." In other words, all that existed was a series of broad policy objectives: there was no plan for implementation.

A brave attempt to remedy this was made by the establishment of the Central Ontario Lakeshore Urban Complex Task Force which reported in December 1974. This was an interministerial group of large proportions and wide representation, including members from the relevant municipalities. (In view of the complexity of the representation, and of the issues being addressed, one cannot help but wonder whether the word "complex" was intended to be a noun or an adjective.)

The background to the establishment of this task force, so different in character from the others discussed later in this chapter, is set out in an unpublished paper by Bigenwald and Richardson (1974). Due to the very general nature of the TCR concept, the various ministries of the provincial government which were concerned in one way or another with the implementation of the policy experienced considerable difficulty in applying it to particular situations and translating it into operational plans:

> In 1973, therefore, the decision was made to set up a task force of civil servants from the ministries primarily concerned, to refine the concept to, in effect, a structure plan at a level of detail which would overcome this problem. The decision was not made at the political level, however, but by a committee of deputy ministers: the advisory committee on urban and regional

planning.   This operation was confined to the inner, largely urbanized, part of the region ... The report of the task force released late in 1974 has no formal status and is advisory only ...

COLUC, as it inevitably became termed, produced a very different report from the typical *Design for Development* document: in place of a series of statements there was genuine analysis.   This followed from the fact that the line departments, for the first time, were directly and recognizably associated with a regional planning report.

COLUC took the TCR concept as given: its task was to refine it so that it could be used as "a common framework by the regional municipalities and the various agencies of the provincial government in formulating their policies and programs." This then was no theoretical planning exercise: it was "for real." (As we shall see, this was its undoing.) It would take us too far afield to attempt to summarize the COLUC report, or even to list the issues which it raised. It must suffice, for present purposes, to quote from its final chapter:

> The Toronto-Centred Region concept ... was so general that important issues arising from it tended to be blurred. The further consequence of its imprecision was difficulty in ascertaining the congruence with the concept of later government actions and programs. In fact, since 1970 the provincial government has embarked on a number of undertakings which in retrospect are not supportive of the concept or whose compatibility with it is, to some extent at least, open to question. These include, for example, the Central York Servicing Scheme, the Housing Action Program, the Georgetown GO Service ... At the same time it must be said that in the four years little has been done to give substance to the "go-east" policy, except to the extent that North Pickering, still in the planning stage, does so.

Not content with enumerating the conflicts, COLUC proceeded to stress "the need for a real commitment to the concept because without its present nominal allegiance to TCR policy it is a mere, and increasingly flimsy, preference that in the interests of all concerned would be better dispersed with ..." Such strong words were anathema to those concerned with the arduous task of balancing political forces. For this, generalized statements, lacking specific commitments, are essential. COLUC asked for the opposite and was quietly buried. And so the TCR and *Design for Development* expired.

It might be questioned whether, had there been any political support remaining, a revision of the policy (from "go east" to "go west and north") would have saved the policy (Social Planning Council 1976: 45). The question must be a rhetorical one; but the problems remain, as the following section illustrates.

Toronto in Transition

There appears to be little justification for not believing the population trends of absolute decline in the city and a declining rate of population growth in Metro which were reported in the 1976 Census

Toronto City 1980

No city easily accepts a decline in its status. Civic pride demands that there shall be growth; but, given the strong contemporary migratory trends, this presents difficulties. So far as Toronto is concerned, the city's first reaction to the 1976 Census figures was one of sheer disbelief. An inquiry was mounted into the reported decline in the city's population from 712,786 in 1971 to 633,318 in 1976 (Toronto City 1980a). The unwelcome conclusion is quoted above: the figures appeared to be true. Moreover, it seemed clear that the decline would continue, not only in the city but also for much of the surrounding region. The first report on this (Toronto City 1980b), dealt with demographic issues, particularly the falling average household size: from 3.85 in 1961 to 2.75 in 1976 for the city. There was perhaps some small comfort in the finding that "figures compiled by Metro Toronto planning staff show comparable drops in household size in Canadian cities such as Montreal, Ottawa and Hamilton, and in major U.S. cities including Boston, Chicago, Detroit, Philadelphia, Los Angeles and San Francisco." The implications for regional planning were examined and appeared serious:

Evaluation of emerging trends in the context of housing demand, energy constraints, infrastructure utilization and fiscal costs suggests that all municipalities should carefully re-evaluate their growth expectations in the light of current trends. Clearly there is a need for close collaboration and interaction at the regional level in order to deal effectively with problems related to urban form.

A further study, *Urban Sprawl in the Toronto-Centred Region,* followed in February 1981. This noted that "when expectations of growth are exaggerated, area municipalities designate more land in their official plans for residential development and employment centers than will be required." Coupled with overgenerous provision for infrastructure, the result is the spreading of private development over a wider area than is necessary. This urban sprawl which the TCR was intended to prevent, would be encouraged by existing plans:

> There is double the amount of land already serviced and approved for subdivision than will be required to house the probable population increase to 1986. Of this potential supply of new housing, 82 percent is outside of Metro. With too little growth to go around, the developing municipalities may engage in a fierce competition to attract the population and the industrial and commercial assessment they need to pay for committed services. The city of Toronto and other built-up areas of the region will fight to at least maintain their population and employment levels ...

This transformation of the planning scene, over a period of less than a decade, would have put severe strains on the planning machine for the region, had there been one. The only piece of machinery in fact was the Toronto Area Transit Operating Authority which was created in 1976 to coordinate public transportation. The rest had withered away. The city's report called for a new development concept which would encourage "a more compact urban form." Provincial action was called for in "reaffirming" the curtailment of urban sprawl as a major policy objective for the Toronto Region, and in establishing machinery for reviewing and revising the TCR plan.

The province's reply was to establish the Toronto-Centred Planning and Transportation Coordinating Committee, composed of staff from relevant provincial and regional government, including the Toronto Transit Commission which had earlier produced its own analyses of some of the problems of Metro (1979a and 1979b). Further studies were to be mounted, but what effectiveness such a non-political body will have remains to be seen.

Though TCR may be dead, or at least dormant, some of its constituent parts remain, particularly the Niagara Escarpment plan and remnants of the Parkway Belt.

The Parkway Belt (West)

... the vital and unifying organ of the entire system ...

Design for Development 1970a

It was in these words that the 1970 TCR statement referred to the Parkway Belt. This great swath of land, of high market value, was to be :

A multi-purpose service system which would incorporate many kinds of transportation, pipelines and electric power lines, water and sewer lines, where applicable, with open space added. It would reduce the number of separate swaths cutting through future urban communities. Defined open space would provide trails joining intersecting ravines and the abutting parks, a buffer against traffic noise, room for selected low density public facilities, and respite from the frustrations caused by continuous urbanization. The essentials are that it would include as many parallel transportation facilities, servicing and energy facilities (pipelines as well as electrical) as possible, and at the same time provide the greatest degree of flexibility for the future.

The first specific publication on the Parkway, *Development Planning in Ontario: The Parkway Belt West* (1973), echoed the poetic tone: "as urban sprawl accelerates, urban residents are losing room to breathe, room to move, community space to identify as their own." In essence, the concept was "to help prevent undue pressures on the existing lakeside communities, to provide cities of different size and composition in the two tiers, and to provide physical separation between the cities."

The Parkway Belt was clearly much more than its name suggested. Moreover, on the day that the government policy statement was published, the Parkway Belt Act was introduced. This defined the area and applied special controls to it which were to become effective immediately. In addition: "it should be noted that outright government purchase of lands by the province is a major means of bringing the Parkway Belt into effect. These phased purchases will be for public open space and for the acquisition of present and future transportation and utility rights-of-way."

These appeared to be draconian measures, though a series of public meetings were to be held, and an assurance was given that where land had to be purchased, market value would be paid. It should be noted that all these proposals related only to the western portion of the Parkway Belt: the eastern limit stopped abruptly at Highway 48 in Markham (and was never extended).

The procedures which followed the publication of the Parkway Belt West proposals were extensive, and present a fertile field for a well-focused Ph.D. thesis. Here it is sufficient to make two points. The first is minor, but significant, and it persists to baffle newcomers to the concept of the belt: this is the appropriateness of the term. There was much criticism of the term "belt" and even more of the adjective "parkway," particularly in the Toronto area where the Parkway Belt consists of rather nasty narrow strips with an expressway on one side and a hydro-electric transmission power line on the other. As one of the advisory groups commented, "this is hardly what springs to mind on hearing the word parkway."

The second point is much more serious. In the words of Wronski and Turnbull (1984: 132), "if there were to be any way in which provincial planners would be able to intervene directly in municipal and regional planning, and to ensure that their own ideas would predominate, the western parkway belt program most certainly provided a glorious opportunity." Unfortunately, the opportunity was lost. By the time of the publication of the approved plan in July 1978, its visibility had all but gone. The underlying justification for the parkway (the TCR) had been abandoned; and the other elements of the TCR (even the eastern part of the Parkway Belt) had dropped out of sight. The promise of the 1973 Planning and Development Act, for an energetic positive role for the province in regional planning had largely evaporated. There was no political gain to be made from investing any further time and money in a Parkway Belt which had lost its raison d'etre.

The Niagara Escarpment

... a richly-varied mosaic of forests, farms, scenic views, cliffs, hills, unusual rock formations, streams, rivers, waterfalls, plant and animal life, historic and archeological sites, pits and quarries, hamlets, towns and cities

Niagara Escarpment Commission 1979

The very features which make the Niagara Escarpment a unique part of the heritage of Ontario also makes it a planning nightmare. It is a unique natural landscape stretching some 450 miles from the Queenston Heights on the Niagara River to Tobermory at the northernmost tip of the Bruce Peninsula (Gillard and Tooke 1975). It is at one and the same time a treasure to be preserved and yet a resource to be exploited. Preservation versus exploitation sums up the planning dilemma of the Escarpment. Its wealth takes diverse forms, wherein lies the problems: it has over a hundred sites of geological significance; it is the site of a multi-million dollar extractive industry; it provides natural habitats "for more than 300 species of birds, 53 species of mammals, 36 species of reptiles and amphibians, 90 fish species, and 100 varieties of special interest flora including 37 types of wild orchids. Endangered species such as the West Virginia White Butterfly are also represented ..." The Escarpment stretches through "the highly productive agricultural lands of the Niagara Peninsula, around the intensely-industrialized and populated Golden Horseshoe ..." (Niagara Escarpment Commission 1979: 9).

But that is not all: it has specialized fruit farming on its unique soils; it is the vine-growing center of the Ontario wine industry; and it has recreational delights unsurpassed in central Canada. And it is located, in part, to the west of a dynamically growing urban region. Many of these features, of course, make the area most attractive for residential development, particularly in the south. There is no way of reconciling the varying claims on this land. If ever there was a setting for the politics of compromise this is it. Unfortunately, compromise typically satisfies no one, and so it is with the Niagara Peninsula.

From the viewpoint of the nineteen-eighties it seems incredible that there was little overt controversy over the Escarpment in the nineteen-fifties. Indeed, the first impact on the public stage was made by a small group of enthusiasts who wished to establish a hiking trail similar to the Appalachian Trail in the United States. In those peaceful times the Bruce Trail lobby could establish, by totally voluntary methods, a walkers' way over the whole length of the Escarpment (Horton 1977), an outstanding achievement in our eyes.

These placid times, however, were not to last. Mounting public interest in the Escarpment was accompanied and strengthened by substantial increases in urban and industrial development and in quarrying. The issue grew in political urgency and, in March 1967, Premier John Robarts announced "a wide-ranging study of the Niagara Escarpment with a view to preserving its entire length as a recreation area for the people of Ontario." Professor Leonard Gertler of the University of Waterloo was appointed to coordinate the study which was staffed and administered through the regional development branch of the Department of Treasury and Economics (Gertler 1972). Gertler's proposals dealt with four major issues: land policy; development of a park system; a sub-strategy for pits and quarries; and administration and finance.

So far as land policy was concerned, of the 4,700 square kilometers of the study area, about one-third were selected for varying degrees of control, termed complete (14 percent to be acquired), selective (9 percent to be subject to easement agreements), and regulatory (75 percent to be subject to development control).

The second major element in the strategy was that the Escarpment "should be preserved, planned and developed as a single park network taking into account its special features, the opportunities for diversified recreation, its role as a predominant landscape element and the requirements of circulation within the Escarpment area."

The third element was concerned with "the sharpest and most dramatic, and most difficult to resolve, resource-use conflict: the clash between parks and recreation and pits and quarries." Here the proposals were for a licensing system; compulsory site development plans for extraction and rehabilitation, and embodying provincial performance standards; performance bonds to ensure satisfactory implementation of the plans; and a zoning system which included a prohibition on new openings on the Escarpment edge.

Finally, Gertler dealt with the "classical dilemma of contemporary government, namely the inability to achieve coordination horizontally between the departments and agencies within a single administration." To overcome functional fragmentation, he proposed a special secretariat to be located "in a part of the provincial administration which is not directly involved in the Escarpment area, such as the Treasury Department or the Prime Minister's Office." A committee structure was proposed which "would lock the secretariat into an interdepartmental framework." Additionally an advisory council would act as "a link between the secretariat and the major groups and individuals interested in the future of the Niagara Escarpment." Full financial responsibility was to rest with the Treasury.

The Gertler study was, as Horton has pointed out, "something of a substantial departure from what had been done before in the way of land use and regional planning studies commissioned by the government. Its high visibility and very specificity were major factors in the manner in which it was received by the government" (Horton 1977: 154). True: Gertler had provided what had been requested, but the extensive land acquisition program, the heavy financial implications, and the proposed new and highly restrictive land controls over an unexpectedly wide area (much of which had been subject to very little control) were alarming, to the landowners and developers as well as to the government. Not surprisingly, "it was the province's view that the need for an immediate response to continuing encroachment failed to outweigh political realities and the need for consultation with the electorate in the affected areas" (Ibid). The eventual outcome, in May 1972, was the establishment of an interministerial task force to study the Gertler report, issues of implementation, and public attitudes.

At the same time, some small but significant and positive measures were taken. Land acquisition programs of the province and of conservation authorities were increased (or at least accelerated). Grants to the latter were raised from fifty percent to seventy-five percent for land purchases in the Escarpment. Additionally, under powers provided by the Planning Act, a number of municipalities were directed by the province to incorporate Escarpment preservation measures ("special policy areas") in their official plans. Finally, in relation to the extractive industries, a temporary Niagara Escarpment Protection Act was passed in 1970 to deal with immediate pressures. This was superseded in the following year by the Pits and Quarries Control Act.

The next stage in the story was the establishment of yet another inquiry, the Niagara Escarpment Interministerial Task Force, whose cumbersome bureaucratic-sounding name contrasted sharply with the clarion-call title it gave to its report: *To Save The Escarpment* (1972b). Composed of senior officials from the departments involved with the Escarpment (ironically rather in the style of Gertler's proposed secretariat) its terms of reference were to develop priorities for land acquisition; to establish land use and development standards; to examine methods of land use control and to recommend a system appropriate for the Escarpment; and to advise on all proposals which would result in major changes in existing land use patterns.

Following extensive public meetings and consultations (direct contact was made with over 3,500 people), the task force recommended that "the goal should be to maintain the Niagara Escarpment as a continuous natural environment while seeking to accommodate demands compatible with that environment." This sounds rather like an attempt to get the best of all worlds. However, the task force elaborated the objectives of this goal:

- to protect unique ecologic and historic areas;
- to maintain and enhance the quality and character of natural streams and water supplies;
- to provide adequate opportunities for outdoor recreation, through the public and private sectors;
- to maintain and enhance the open character of the Escarpment by such means as compatible farming or forestry, and by preserving the natural scenery;
- to ensure that all new development is compatible with the goal for the Escarpment;
- to provide adequate access to the Escarpment.

There was much here that showed clearly an appreciation of the political hurdles which lay ahead. Words like "adequate" are capable of many interpretations. Nevertheless, this was a statement of principles which, if accepted by the government, as they were, provided some good guidelines. Additional recommendations included the establishment of a Niagara Escarpment Secretariat; special legislation relating to the area; and a system of development control.

Though not all of the recommendations proved politically acceptable, particularly the form of the new agency for the Escarpment, most were. In June 1973 the government published a statement of its proposals for the Escarpment and, at the same time, the implementing legislation.

The Niagara Escarpment Planning and Development Act 1973

This Act more clearly menaces the rights of property owners than almost any other piece of legislation Queen's Park has passed in the last few years

Oosterhoff and Rayner 1979

The goal and objectives set out by the task force were incorporated in the legislation, but the proposal for a secretariat was replaced by provision for a commission. This, it was submitted, would be more flexible, facilitate direct local participation and be directly accountable to a member of Cabinet, the ultimate policy-making and coordinative body. Left unsaid was the fact that a commission lies a comfortable arm's length away from government. The device is a well-tried one, and it serves a useful political purpose in acting as a defensive shield between a multiplicity of conflicting interests and the central government.

The commission was envisaged as being a temporary body whose functions would be transferred to the regional municipalities, or counties, when it had substantially completed its task of preparing the Niagara Escarpment Plan. The scope of the plan was spelled out in considerable detail and covered a comprehensive range of economic, social and physical matters. Moreover, as the task force recommended, it was to be legally binding on all governments, provincial as well as municipal. (A plan which is binding upon a provincial government is a rare animal in Canada.)

Given the sensibilities and conflicts within the area, it is not surprising that considerable importance was attached to public participation. Provision was also made for a hearing before specially appointed hearing officers.

Perhaps the most striking feature of the act, however, was its acceptance of a system of development control in place of the traditional zoning bylaws. The government accepted the view of the task force that the ordinary zoning bylaws could not provide "the kind of control needed in a large, varied and environmentally sensitive area such as the Niagara Escarpment."

The commission was established in 1973, thus adding yet another body to the crowded arena of public authorities. Local government over much of the Escarpment was reorganized during the same period of policy and institutional review which gave birth to the commission. Four regional municipalities were established in areas affected by the commission: Halton, Hamilton-Wentworth, Niagara and Peel. Moreover, the Ministry of Natural Resources had its own coordinated program strategy (or "strategic land use plans") for the southern region of Ontario (which stretches from Algonquin to Windsor), while the Ministry of the Environment also had extensive responsibilities in the area.

Relationships between all these bodies were not easy, particularly since each was trying to find its rightful place in the wider scheme of things. The Regional Municipality of Niagara produced its draft official plan only to find that it was unacceptable to the provincial government: too much land had been allocated to urban development, and too little protection had been afforded to the fruitlands. The intergovernmental battle raged on this issue for many years, and seems likely to continue, perhaps until many of the unique resources of this southern part of the Niagara Escarpment and its adjacent areas have been completely destroyed (Krueger 1977).

Following the publication of the commission's proposed plan in 1979, there were some two years of public hearings. These were of gargantuan proportions. Over 1,000 applications to attend were made, and there were actually 743 oral submissions. Throughout the twenty-six months of the hearings over 9,300 people were in attendance. The initial stages at least were marked by hostility and disruption. Some of this hostility arose from municipalities who felt that the proposed plan infringed on their local jurisdiction. Some was due to what hearing officers clearly considered to be a high-handed attitude on the part of the commission. To add further spice to the hearings, there was open antagonism by residents (who objected to the plan) to "outsiders" (who came in large numbers to support it).

The hearing officers agreed with much of the proposed plan, but found the size of the area which it embraced to be unacceptable. The arbitrariness of the development control permit process was subject to particular criticism, and the hearing officers recommended that, when finalized, the plan should be implemented at the local level by zoning bylaws. They did, however, support the Bruce Trail. Other recommendations included the designation of high-priority mineral resource protection areas, the easing of restrictions on the creation of new lots in Escarpment natural areas, and permitted expansion of hamlets near to the Escarpment "providing the proper requirements can be met." Unfortunately, the hearing officers never came to grips with the issue of provincial versus municipal interests on the Escarpment. Their report was focused on specific points and provided no guidance on this crucial matter.

The most recent chapters of the Niagara Escarpment story involve a complex of detail, some ambiguities, and a number of uncertainties for the future.

The complexities stem in part from the fact that in 1983 the Provincial Secretary for Resources Development had before him, not only the hearing officers report on the 1979 proposed plan, together with the 1979 plan itself, but also the commission's Final Proposed Plan of 1983. (The latter was particularly important in that it set the tone for the minister's plan.) In 1984, the Provincial Secretary published his three-volume *Niagara Escarpment Plan*. The first of these is concerned with the planning and implementation process; the second with recommended policies of the Provincial Secretary for Resources Development; and the third with responses to the hearing officers report.

Rather than attempt a comparative analysis of all the proposals and counterproposals, the major recommended policies of the Provincial Secretary are summarized, and some of the more important differences from the commission's proposals are highlighted. (With a few exceptions, the minister's plan was substantially in accord with the commission's final proposed plan.)

Perhaps the major issue to emerge from the mammoth series of studies is that of the management of the lands in the Escarpment: what is to be the planning and implementation process? The answer to this is set out in very broad terms in the first volume of the 1984 plan. Not surprisingly it is a compromise between the pressures for a special administrative process for the Escarpment and the pressures for a normal system of development control. In part these reflect the underlying philosophies of conservation versus development.

The implementation strategy proposes that special provisions will apply to the Escarpment. The system will comprise

(1) the Niagara Escarpment Plan (yet to be finally orchestrated). When approved this will stand on its own, but will also be established as a policy statement under the 1983 planning act. Municipalities will be required to bring their official plans into conformity with this;

(2) a special system of land use controls is to be continued but, instead of the development permit system operated by the commission there will be site plan control by local municipalities;

(3) a Niagara Escarpment Parks System will be established on publicly-owned land. This, it is proposed, will be under the control of the Minister of Natural Resources. A new Niagara Escarpment Fund will be established, with a provincial government "contribution" of $2.5 million for ten years; this will be administered by a special Niagara Escarpment Committee (in which the Ontario Heritage

Foundation will play a key role; the chairman of the Niagara Escarpment Commission will be a member);

(4)   the commission will have a reduced role, but its continuing existence "will be a tangible indication of the government's commitment to ensure the consistency of policy implementation along the Escarpment ..." Its main function will be a monitoring one, to be exercised in conjunction with the Ministers of Municipal Affairs and Housing, Natural Resources, and Citizenship and Culture.

These implementation proposals will clearly need some time to work out but, in spite of some vagueness, the general thrust is clear: the maintenance of some special controls over the Escarpment lands, but with a reduced role for the commission and an enhanced role for the municipalities.

The policy recommendations are less easy to summarize; and since further changes can be expected, there is little point in detailing them. However, it appears that a less restrictive policy is to be applied to pits and quarries than the commission had proposed, including wayside pits on which feelings run high. The commission's proposed parks policies have been substantially modified, with powers being transferred from the commission to the ministry and, in particular, a greater emphasis on production as distinct from protection within the parks system.

Despite the brevity of this summary, a large amount of space has been devoted in this chapter to the Niagara Escarpment. This is justified by, first, the intrinsic importance of the area and the complex constellation of planning problems which it exhibits; and, secondly, by the attempts of the province to come to grips with these problems in the face of the cruel fact that progress with one constituency (interest group, lobby or political force) inevitably means the opposite with another.

The problems exhibited on the Niagara Escarpment, and in the Niagara fruitbelt, are not at all atypical of those which arise when serious attempts are made to make regional planning a reality. All that is different in Niagara is that the area has an overabundance of endowments which makes the problem of reconciliation particularly acute. Indeed, there is no solution to the problem, because there is no *one* problem.

Joint Provincial-Municipal Planning Studies

... they were, on the whole, reasonably effective in carrying out their limited assignments

Bigenwald and Richardson 1976

In contrast to the high profile which attended the vicissitudes of planning in the Niagara Escarpment, is the low profile of most of the joint planning studies. The studies were ad hoc provincial-municipal ventures initiated in response to particular situations. In some cases these proved to be the precursors of regional government; in others they were in effect a substitute for the planning program that would have been carried out by a regional government.

The first three of these task forces were started in 1969: the Oshawa Area Planning and Development Study (OAPADS), the Haldimand-Norfolk Study and the Waterloo-South Wellington Study. As Richardson has noted:

That they began in the same year was largely fortuitous; they were connected only to the extent that the Community Planning Branch of the Department of Municipal Affairs ... held some responsibility for each; and in organization and modus operandi they were quite different from each other. But they did have two features in common: each was concerned with the planning of a multi-municipal area; and each involved, though to varying degrees, cooperation between the municipalities and the provincial government (1981: 573).

Over the ensuing five years, six more studies of this nature were undertaken, each designed to meet the particularities of the area concerned, each with its own history and background. Both the OAPADS and the Waterloo-South Wellington Study emerged from transportation study requirements. In Waterloo-South Wellington, the project was confined to land use and transportation planning, and collaboration was mainly at the technical level (professional staff of the Departments of Highways and Municipal Affairs, and the planning boards of the study area) with little political involvement. It was successful in producing an advisory land use and transportation plan. OAPADS, at the instigation of the Department of Municipal Affairs, though mainly at the expense of the Department of Highways, was more ambitious. It extended to a review of municipal government, and acquired an elaborate structure of provincial-municipal political and technical committees. This was perhaps its undoing; it came to a premature end as a result of disagreements by the municipalities with the provincial government and among themselves. Its work did, however, contribute to the creation of the Regional Municipality of Durham and to the preparation of Durham's official plan.

Next came the Simcoe-Georgian and Port Hope-Cobourg (later Northumberland) Area Task Forces. These were established in 1971 as an outcome of the government's planning policy for the Toronto-Centred Region (TCR). An important element of the 1970 TCR concept was the proposal to stimulate growth beyond Toronto's commuting area to the north and east, in Simcoe County and in the Port Hope-Cobourg area, as a means of relieving growth pressures in the inner zone of the Toronto-Centred Region. The purpose of the two area task forces was to provide vehicles for local response to this general policy and to refine it into a more specific plan of action. Each task force comprised a political committee made up of local councillors, and a technical committee composed of appointed municipal officials. The task forces were funded by the government, and they employed consultants to undertake the necessary studies and prepare their reports.

Also formally established in 1971, the Sudbury Area Study was confined to land use planning and had no formal municipal participation, but in fact the staff maintained close liaison with the municipalities of the area and cooperated closely with the planning staff of the city of Sudbury.

Two more formal provincial-municipal task forces were established in 1975. The Haldimand-Norfolk task force will be discussed below. The Sarnia-Lambton task force was created as a result of plans for a large new petrochemical complex (Petrosar) in the Sarnia area. The structure of the task force was similar to that of the Simcoe-Georgian and Northumberland task forces, and its purpose (to prepare a general development strategy to accommodate accelerated growth) was also similar.

These task forces came into existence for a variety of reasons and differed considerably in specific objectives, constitution, and modus operandi. The common theme was that of cooperation between the provincial and municipal governments in developing plans for the areas concerned that would meet the aims of both levels of government. The Haldimand-Norfolk experience has been chosen for detailed examination not because it is typical, since each project is unique in important respects, but because it illustrates the character of these joint planning enterprises.

Haldimand-Norfolk

The Haldimand-Norfolk area has an interesting history. It shared in the late nineteenth-century industrialization of Ontario but, by the end of the century, was being bypassed; by the mid-twentieth century it had relapsed into rural tranquility.

Nevertheless, with its geographical position, with easy access to the midwest markets of the United States, it had great potential. In 1967, this seemed to be recognized by the construction of a thermal generating station by Ontario Hydro. In the same year the Steel Company of Canada (Stelco) announced plans for the construction of a new integrated steel plant. Later, Texaco announced that it would build a large refinery complex adjacent to the Hydro site in the Nanticoke area. The future began to look bright, but also somewhat threatening. Certainly, the municipalities in the area were quite unprepared for major industrial development: their nineteenth-century administrative and political organizations were quite unequal to the challenge posed by the new industrial initiatives.

The solution to the problem was announced by Darcy McKeough (Minister of Municipal Affairs) in March 1969. This was the establishment of a special unit, within his department, to be devoted to the problems of the area. This went under the unexciting title of the Haldimand-Norfolk Study. It was complemented by the formation of a joint committee of the county councils of Haldimand and Norfolk.

Interestingly, and by no means a typical feature of regional planning, the resultant structure of interagency liaison was such that the arrangement proved workable and productive. The experience of provincial and municipal planners working together amounted to an "unconscious learning process." This particular venture, and its wider implications, deserve much wider study than it has so far received, but the details do not concern us here. It is, however, relevant to note that proposals emerged for local government reorganization which, because of the "working together" proved politically acceptable and workable.

Encouraged by the evidence of general support from the local politicians, the government moved rapidly to bring about municipal reorganization, and the regional municipality of Haldimand-Norfolk officially came into existence on April 1, 1974. Meanwhile, the interim planning measures recommended by the study, though never formally adopted by the government, were in practice largely followed by the departments concerned.

In the climate of the mid-seventies, the defined issue was that of accommodating the pressures of growth that were to flow from the large scale industrial developments in the area. Stelco started construction of its mill and, though it substantially scaled down its original employment forecasts, it became apparent that the new regional municipality would face major difficulties. It was understandably preoccupied with the problems of its own creation and, at best, could cope only with short term development control problems. It was essential to have both interim development guidelines pending the completion and approval of the region's official plan, and a detailed long term strategy. This realization led to the creation of the Haldimand-Norfolk task force.

The task force was appointed in January 1975. It was given a budget of about $100,000 and directed to accomplish two specific tasks. The first was to prepare a set of interim guidelines for use by the region until an official plan was approved. The second was to employ consultants to prepare a development strategy for the region.

Like several of its predecessors, the task force was composed of two separate committees: a steering committee of senior provincial officials and elected representatives from the region; and a technical committee of senior technical staff from the region and the province. Their first product was a set of guidelines relating to growth and development within the region, less detailed than a typical zoning bylaw, but more specific than the average official plan. These served as the beginnings of an official plan as well as an interim development control mechanism.

As with the earlier Haldimand-Norfolk study, the interim guidelines were an ad hoc and extra-legal device to deal with a situation not adequately provided for by orthodox procedures. Pending the approval of a regional official plan, the only development control mechanisms available to the region were the hodge-podge of official plans and zoning bylaws from the former twenty-eight municipalities. Hence, the very reason for the creation of the regional municipality, the ability to react to the huge development of Stelco and other enterprises in an organized and regional fashion, was undermined by the inability of the region to act regionally in the crucial area of planning and development.

It was in recognition of this state of affairs that the task force was given its second mandate, to prepare a development strategy. The intention was to provide the region with some basic information and analysis necessary to develop its official plan under the planning act, and also to provide the region with a basic framework for guiding decision-making until the official plan was completed.

To develop a series of alternatives, and ultimately to recommend a strategy and implementation program, a consultant was commissioned by the task force. The strategy project, however, was not carried out without difficulty. The major problem arose in the fall of 1975, revolving around the selection of a regional center for Haldimand-Norfolk. Through its analysis, the consultant began to question whether a new town site (Townsend), which had been purchased by the province, was in fact the best possible choice for a regional center, and indeed whether a new town was needed at all. Needless to say, this conclusion led to a long series of often heated debates and discussions, particularly since both the province and the region had already made commitments to the new town. The final recommendations produced by the consultant were in fact a compromise, less than acceptable to all parties. In essence, alternatives were produced under both assumptions, i.e. with and without the new town as a regional center. The report was accepted but not approved by the task force, and submitted without recommendation to the regional council of Haldimand-Norfolk.

The two particular mandates of the Haldimand-Norfolk task force, and how they were handled, point out the peculiar strengths and weaknesses of the task force approach. For the rapid completion of large volumes of work, such as the formulation of a comprehensive set of interim guidelines, this approach was particularly useful. On the other hand, the preparation of the development strategy pointed up its Achilles heel. Where major controversy arose, the task force, by virtue of its own makeup, was not well equipped to resolve issues or to make a clear decision, so that no real decision was made at all in relation to a regional strategy.

The story of this intervention has been, from the beginning, one of improvisation: the use of unorthodox, extra-legal devices to respond to circumstances with which the normal governmental, legal and administrative machinery could not adequately cope. In a sense, this may have been both the greatest strength of the provincial response, but, at the same time, its greatest weakness. The government's original response to the situation created in Haldimand-Norfolk was firm and, for the most part, quick and decisive. But this was largely due to the forceful character and political strength of one man, Darcy McKeough (then Minister of Municipal Affairs). The decision to set up the original study was his, and he continued to take an active interest in it as long as he remained minister. In practice, if not in theory, the study director reported directly to him. This, with the rather unorthodox position of the study outside the normal bureaucratic structure, gave the study group some measure of freedom from normal administrative constraints, and permitted quick decisions, a high degree of operational flexibility, and a generally expeditious program. Even more important, it gave the study director a degree of independence of the government, with McKeough's support, that helped greatly in securing local confidence and cooperation.

However, such an operation, not clearly grounded in law or precedent, is extremely vulnerable to the technical capability of the individuals involved as well as to the vicissitudes of governmental actions and interpersonal relationships between the actors. Often success or failure can depend as much on chance as on the ability of the particular people involved.

It is unfortunate that there is no adequate chronicle of the operation of the task forces. Any judgment on them must therefore be tentative. Nevertheless, it does seem that they were, on the whole, reasonably effective in carrying out their limited assignments. They allowed a quick response to specific situations that probably could not have been accomplished in any other way short of the virtual surrender of municipal responsibilities. They also provided a necessary bridge between local planning and wider provincial and subprovincial planning. In this respect they helped to fill an obvious and serious gap in the Ontario planning system. Unfortunately, because of their limited role, they necessarily fell far short of filling the gap completely.

Provincial Land Acquisitions

... to have and to hold ...

Whatever success attended the work of the task forces was politically overshadowed by the disastrous series of land acquisitions. The story of these again awaits its chronicler. Given its extraordinary character this is surprising: perhaps it is the difficulty of unravelling the complexities which has been the deterrent. Certainly the complexities cannot be dealt with here. However, some account is necessary partly because the story, which lingers on, is intrinsically important in the history of Ontario planning, and partly because the land acquisitions probably did more to discredit the image of planning than anything else. So far as the Haldimand-Norfolk purchases are concerned they, together with the creation of the regional municipality, cost the Conservative government a seat it had held for thirty years. Planning in practice was shown to be electorally less popular than planning in theory.

The story can be picked up at the point when a private initiative in land assembly was made at Townsend in the Haldimand-Norfolk area. Recognizing that large scale growth in the area appeared inevitable, a private consortium stole a march on the government by quickly undertaking a large scale land assembly. Though it transpired that the site they chose was not the one recommended by the Haldimand-Norfolk study, the consortium approached the government, in 1972, with proposals for a private development in the area. The government rejected the consortium's proposals, but acquired outright its interest in the 4,500 hectare Townsend site. In November of the same year it was announced that the government itself had also quietly assembled, through a private real estate firm, 4,900 hectares at another nearby site, known as South Cayuga, though no decision had yet been made as to the timing or the nature of the development in the area. The Townsend site was selected for early development; a Townsend community development program was established in the Ministry of Housing; and the planning of a new town on this site was entrusted to a firm of consultants.

What is extraordinary is that *two* sites were acquired when, at most, only one was needed. The responsible minister, John White, who had replaced McKeough as Treasurer, defended the purchase on various grounds, including its value as "insurance" in case some of the consortium controlling Townsend refused to sell. However, he also more positively proclaimed that "having two cities of 250,000 people each is better than having one of 400,000 or 600,000." It is not clear where these figures came from.

One month after the purchase, White was moved in a Cabinet shuffle to Minister without Portfolio, "giving rise to wide speculation that his land policies had finally hit an unpopular note within the government." Certainly the policy underlying these two purchases was hardly brilliant: but others could be regarded as being worse. At least Townsend is proceeding, though at a snail's pace. South Cayuga has proved unacceptable for a liquid waste disposal site, or for anything else. Some 4,000 hectares at Edwardsburgh in eastern Ontario (near Prescott), purchased for large scale industrial development, proved unattractive and unsuitable, and the land is now producing hybrid poplar for the Ministry of Natural Resources. The largest acquisition, made when McKeough was minister, was 8,000 hectares for an "airport community" at North Pickering (Budden and Ernst 1973). Since the airport was never built, there was no justification for a related "community"; and it too has been abandoned.

It is, of course, easy to be wise after the event but, to be generous, Ontario has been particularly unfortunate in its land assembly ventures.

Overview

Provincial planning in Ontario flowered in the sixties, flourished
for some ten or fifteen years, and is now utterly dead

Comay 1984

What conclusions can be drawn from this survey of the
role of the province in regional planning and development in
Ontario? Certainly, as dealt with in this chapter, it cannot be
said to be a coherent activity of government. On the other
hand, the extent of its activities is so broad that it permeates a
major part of the provincial government. Coherence is easier
on narrow fronts than on broad inter-related issues.

Writing of the period up to the mid-seventies, Richardson
(1981a) tolls the death-knell of regional planning, and Comay
(in the quotation above) writes the epitaph. So far as the original *Design for Development* concepts were concerned this is
undoubtedly appropriate. The disillusionment of, or perhaps
more accurately, the non-acceptance by, the electorate of the
new regional governments was in striking contrast to the favor-
able disposition towards Metro Toronto (Jacek 1980). Misread-
ing the signs, the provincial government forgot how "outside
Toronto, the provincial government is seen as an aloof institution whose power over the lives of non-Metro residents must be
buffered by responsive local institutions." The government
losses in the 1975 election left it in no doubt that the land
acquisition and regionalization programs should be abandoned.

The regional development policy probably suffered by association, even though its relationship to the regional government
program was loose. Paradoxically, in more recent years, the
existence of regional governments and the statutory requirement
that they produce plans has been used as a rationale for aban-
doning regional planning. The theory is that the aggregation of
regional official plans in the Golden Horseshoe collectively
comprise a development plan for that urban region. Though
the regions do a varyingly good job within their limits, this

double-think represents a retreat from regional planning in the broader sense of the term.

But, apart from political rationalizations, there are some inherently difficult issues with which the government had, and still has, trouble. Much of the provincial economy is heavily influenced, if not buffeted, by wider economic forces, and over these the provincial government has little power. There was also, more subtly, the fact that the growth policies of the provincial government were not necessarily shared by the areas which were intended to benefit. As Jacek argues:

> There is no doubt that people are happy to see the quality of government services increase, but the improvement in quality may not be worth the higher taxes that go along with it, at least in the eyes of the public. This would seem to be true especially in rural areas and indeed is true often for the outer fringe of suburbia. People move to these areas so that they can build a big house on a big lot. They do not expect to have sewers, water mains, sidewalks, or street lighting and the tax costs that go with these services ...
>
> Finally, there are many local opponents to rapid economic growth and development. The deep-seated hostility to the Pickering airport proposal is a prime example. For a large number of local people, economic development means noise, inconvenience, higher taxes, loss of green space and a general unwanted disruption of people's daily lives. Once again, the values of the central administrators clash with the preferred lifestyles of local residents (Ibid: 161).

Two other trends worked towards the same direction. First there were the eloquent failures of policy in relation to land assembly, new towns and the like, together with increasing unease about the Toronto-Centred region. Downward revisions of population projections proved too optimistic. Immigration rose to a peak of 120,000 in 1974 but dropped dramatically in subsequent years. High rates of household formation masked some of the trends (Toronto City 1980) but increasingly the prognosis for the province looked gloomy: much that had been planned   no longer seemed to be wanted (Toronto City 1981). The image of planning became tainted.

The second trend was and is very different: the growth of awareness of ecology, energy and, above all, the environment (Leiss 1979). The vocabulary of political debate changed; minority concerns became popular debating points; the growth ethic became threatened if not overshadowed by the conserver ethic. Things do not change overnight, of course. Indeed, these newer concerns had been growing during the great era of postwar urban and metropolitan growth. Ontario responded quickly and, it is submitted, with some effect. New departments have emerged: for energy, environment and natural resources. By the back door, as it were, new planning systems have emerged; and these have found themselves inevitably forced to operate, or at least to think, in regional terms.

The recent emergence of "coordinated program strategies" and "strategic land use plans" in the Ministry of Natural Resources (discussed in chapter 6) are illustrations of the most advanced of these new endeavors in regional planning. It is too soon to attempt a judgment, though one must question how far they can progress in the absence of regional agencies. This could seriously limit their effectiveness, yet there is little likelihood of another orgy of institutional change. Techniques may have to be developed, perhaps after lengthy and wearying discussions (is there the drive for these?) of working through existing institutions. Here the new planning act provision for statements of provincial interest is of particular relevance.

There are thus some grounds for mild optimism.

Chapter 9
Regional Planning
in Other Provinces

Regional planning processes in Canada are not highly developed
Gertler, Lord and Stewart 1975

The lengthy account of regional planning in Ontario presented in the preceding chapter obviously cannot be replicated for all the provinces, particularly since regional planning operates in very different ways in the ten provinces.

Indeed, rather than attempting to develop regional planning further, some provinces seem set in the opposite direction. In Nova Scotia, for example, the Planning Act Review Committee recommended the deletion of all provisions for preparing and adopting regional plans. In its interim report (1980a: 13) it stated that:

> Rather than attempting to integrate certain features of province-wide planning with inter-municipal considerations under the umbrella of a regional development plan, the committee feels there would be merit in removing regional planning from the act, and in its place substituting firstly a mechanism for the province to state its interests in areas of provincial concern and secondly a means for locally initiated inter-municipal planning to take place.

This was accepted and given effect by the 1983 Provincial and Municipal Act.

Similarly, the parallel review in New Brunswick (1979: 15) unequivocally stated that regional planning was cumbersome and unnecessary. "It appears extremely difficult to specify planning policies for such diverse and large areas as those encompassed within a regional plan area in detail enough to warrant such a special plan. A concise statement of planning policy on a provincial level should be sufficient." Though no positive action has been taken on this recommendation, regional planning in the province is inoperative.

Saskatchewan, after a lengthy debate, rejected a regional level of planning in favor of planning districts to be formed by voluntary affiliation of member authorities (Saskatchewan Urban Law Review Committee 1979 and 1980; Saskatchewan Planning Act Review Committee 1982; Saskatchewan Urban Affairs 1983).

Clearly there is much rethinking taking place on the subject of regional planning, but it has to be stressed that the circumstances and approaches of the different provinces vary widely. In this chapter three approaches are illustrated: the highly formalized system in Alberta devised after lengthy and detailed study; the slow progress towards a limited scale of regional planning experienced in Quebec; and that part of the British Columbia system which has developed in response to the need to deal with inter-agency coordination in the development of natural resources.

Regional planning is in a continuing state of evolution, and it changes both in the light of experience and in order to adapt to changing circumstances. Changes in Alberta are emerging as a result of two factors. First, the 1977 act reduced generally the degree of detailed control and provided for greater municipal autonomy. Secondly, this trend to less government was accelerated by the relatively sudden cessation of rapid economic growth in the province. In British Columbia, the major impetus to change was political, expressed in terms of freeing municipalities from unnecessary and wasteful regional controls. There is no reason to suspect that such changes will not continue.

Regional Planning in Alberta

The success of the system is clearly shown by the total lack of
unplanned development in this region
                    Edmonton Regional Planning Commission 1980

The student of regional planning in Alberta is fortunate in
the wealth of material that is available. Quite apart from the
various regional plans themselves, there is the massive provincial Regional Planning System Study (1979-81), the Revised
Guidelines for Regional Plan Preparation and Review (1982)
and reports such as the history produced by the Edmonton
Metropolitan Regional Planning Commission (1984). A particularly useful succinct statement of the Alberta planning system is
to be found in *Planning in Alberta: A Guide and Directory,*
published by Alberta Municipal Affairs (1980a). In this chapter,
the major features of the regional planning system in Alberta
are discussed. First, however, it is helpful to have a brief overview.

Alberta has had regional planning since 1950, though since
then it has changed markedly in character. The trend has been
to give increased powers and responsibilities to municpalitiess
and to encourage municipal cooperation in regional planning.
Regional planning commissions are comprised entirely of municipal representatives. (Membership of a minority of provincial
representatives was abolished in the seventies.) Regional plans
have also become less detailed and more concerned with essentially regional matters.

There are ten regional planning commissions covering a
large portion of the area of the province. Their main task is to
prepare a regional plan, the fundamental purpose of which is to
provide a policy framework for municipal land use planning.
The plan, in draft form, is submitted to the Alberta Planing
Board (a body of senior civil servants and citizens-at-large)
which is concerned to ensure that provincial policies are adequately considered, that the plan is compatible with the framework, and that the statutory provisions have been carried out.

(See, for instance, its 1980 report on the Edmonton Draft Regional Plan which extends to nearly one hundred pages.)

At this stage, the regional plan may be referred back to the planning commission with suggested changes. When it has been approved by the board, it is subject to ministerial review and ratification. General municipal plans (and all other municipal plans and land use bylaws) must conform to the broad policies of the regional plan. In turn, the more detailed area structure plans are required to conform to the appropriate general municipal plan.

Regional planning commissions are also responsible for processing subdivision applications.

The Background to the New Regional Planning System

The Alberta regional planning system has developed in response to the dramatic changes which have taken place in the province (Woods Gordon 1981). Between 1966 and 1980, the province's population increased by forty-four percent (over twice the national rate of twenty percent) from 1,463,000 to 2,113,000. The basic driving force, of course, was economic development, particularly in industries related to oil, gas, coal and pulp. The gross domestic product, at market prices, rose from $5,000 million in 1966 to over $35,000 million in 1979.

Massive urban growth resulted, especially in Calgary and Edmonton. Growth was also significant elsewhere, for example in Lethbridge and Medicine Hat. Municipal expenditures rose 352 percent from $341 million in 1966 to $1,540 million in 1980 (in constant dollars).

The strains on municipal, regional and provincial government were serious, and large changes took place in policy; new governmental roles emerged in response to increasing pressures and affluence; social and economic considerations grew in importance while traditional land use planning continued. A striking index of change is provided by the figures for the provincial civil service (including crown corporations): the numbers grew from 18,900 in 1966 to 34,500 in 1971, and 68,500 in 1980.

The pressures for suburban and rural residential development involved a major expansion of the work of the regional planning commissions, protracted annexation studies and hearings, and a big increase in the consulting and advisory roles of the commissions. As elsewhere, the rate of growth led to rising expectations. This, of course, was not only directly related to economic progress but was "also bound up with the pattern of metropolitan primacy (e.g. Calgary and Edmonton) which characterizes and dominates the Alberta urban system" (Ibid).

The pressures were prodigious in their consumption of manpower, but they were further increased by the response of the provincial government. Of particular significance in this was "the emergence of new high-growth, active policy agencies" such as Alberta Public Works and Housing, and "the high profile role and widespread influence of the relatively new Department of the Environment." Other factors included " ... some competition between these agencies and the growing complexity of a protracted referral system; the announced decentralization of the provincial government combined with a lack of real decision-making in regional offices; the arrival and turnover in short time periods of a great number of new faces in the field, and a widespread feeling that there was a considerable dearth of experience and sensitivity to local issues and conditions" (Ibid: 27).

The strains on the regional planning system were increased still further by two other provincial initiatives: the establishment of the Alberta Planning Fund in 1970; and the passing of the 1977 planning act.

The introduction of the Alberta Planning Fund had dramatic long term effects on the evolution of the regional planning system. Since it provides for contributions from municipalities it stimulated their participation in, and subsequent demands upon, the commission. The fund, to which the province contributes some two-thirds (originally four-fifths) of the total budget, is used to finance the operation of the regional planning commissions. The fund's income was $5.5 million in 1977-78 but rose steadily to $13.6 million in 1982-83. With the downturn in the provincial economy the trend was reversed, and the 1983-84 figure fell to $11.1 million.

The Woods Gordon report concluded that "the Alberta regional planning system has proven itself competent and robust in a period of considerable growth, uncertainty and turbulence. In the main [it] ... enters the 1980s well poised to fulfill its mandate and consolidate its gains and experience garnered over the last eventful fifteen years" (Ibid: 69). This was echoed in the regional planning system study which is summarized in the following section.

The Regional Planning System Study

Commencing in the summer of 1978 the Inter-Agency Planning Branch of Alberta Municipal Affairs embarked upon a wide ranging review of the regional planning system. Involving a high degree of participation from all the public and private interests concerned, the study had four objectives:

(1)   to develop a clear understanding of the roles and relationships between the departments of the provincial government, the Alberta Planning Board, Alberta Municipal Affairs, regional planning commissions, and the municipalities in the regional planning system;

(2)   to determine the strengths and weaknesses of the system;

(3)   to identify areas for improvement, for both the short and long term;

(4)   to develop a consultative process such that all participants in the regional planning system can become involved in the development as well as the implementation of recommendations.

The study demonstrated that, over the thirty years since 1950, there had been "a gradual handing down of the land use planning function from the provincial government to the local level." But by local level was meant the regional organization which embraced and coordinated municipal planning.

Reviewing the contribution made by the regional planning system over the thirty years 1950-80, the report concluded that, during this tumultuous period, there were three major contributions:

- It has contributed to the development of a sound approach to the planning and development of both public and private lands, and in so doing has prevented many of the abuses of the physical and community environments so common in high growth areas.

- The regional planning commissions have provided, at the local municipal level, a readily available source of advice and expertise on planning and governmental matters which has contributed in important ways to the development of responsible municipal government, in a generally cost effective manner.

- Until the provincial government undertook a more comprehensive and aggressive role in environmental planning and management matters in the 1970s, the regional planning commissions were one of the major watchdogs of the broad "public interest" in these areas.

The story so far is thus one of considerable success. There are, however, some qualifications to this. First, to quote the *Preliminary Findings:* "ironically, the very success of the regional planning commissions in encouraging municipal awareness of planning issues has now become their greatest source of criticism, as many municipalities respond to the requirements of the new planning act only to perceive that the regional planning commissions have effectively limited their abilities to discharge local responsibilities."

As is so often the case, there is a delicate problem (both technically and politically) of balancing local, regional and provincial considerations. The key problems and recommendations for dealing with them include the following.

First and foremost is the question of the level of detail or generality to which a regional plan should aspire. The review showed   that regional plans were generally "seen to be so detailed, regulatory, and inflexible as to pre-empt the municipal prerogatives in land use planning." It was, therefore, recommended that in future a regional plan should be designed as a broad policy document.

Another issue was the inadequacy of consultation between the regional planning commissions and the levels of government above and below them, namely provincial and municipal government. So far as the former was concerned, " ... regional plans have generally failed to take account of provincial policies or activities; many departments are not aware of the potential value of closer coordination with the regional planning commissions; and the commissions, in turn, do not always receive the most helpful input from the departments, especially since departments may no longer sit on the commissions."

This pointed up a weakness in the operation of the Alberta Planning Board. It had been too preoccupied with deciding on appeals and on administering the Alberta Planning Fund. As a result it had neglected its broader policy development and coordination role. This problem is being dealt with by changes in internal procedures and organization. There has also been the publication of regional guidelines. These are discussed below, but here it is relevant to note that they are intended to assist all three levels of government by clarifying the concepts and purposes of regional planning in the province. The survey identified widespread misunderstanding as a major general problem at all levels. Additionally, there was "a lack of an unequivocal agreement about the role of the regional plan vis-a-vis municipal and provincial responsibility for growth management." This had led to policy conflicts and, in particular, the problem of municipalities circumventing regional plan policies. The solution proposed for this is to "put in place certain procedural safeguards so that municipal plans are developed in conformity with the regional plan, through a continuing process of municipal-regional consultation."

`The Regional Plan Is Supreme´

The 1977 planning act clearly establishes the regional plan as the supreme document in a hierarchy of statutory instruments all of which must conform to its provisions, i.e. general municipal plans, area structure and redevelopment plans, and land use bylaws. Curiously, however, the legislation is not only silent as to how this conformity is to be accomplished (a matter which is now being dealt with by administrative reforms): it is also vague as to what a regional plan is supposed to be. The 1977 act initially defines a regional plan as "a plan, as amended from time to time in accordance with this act, adopted by a regional planning commission, approved by the [Alberta Planning] Board and ratified by the minister as a regional plan." A later elaboration merely provides that a regional plan "shall provide for the present and future land use and development of the planning region, and may regulate and control the use and development of land in the planning region." The review strongly recommended that the Alberta Planning Board " ... through its review and approval of regional plans, act to establish the regional plan as a leadership document, designed to bring about a high quality in the regional environment and to enhance the quality of life of the region's inhabitants, through the management of growth and change. The plan should, therefore, be simply written, in non-technical language easily comprehended by the layman, and should be in a format serving the needs of the various plan users."

The regional plan thus emerges as "a policy document for the management of regional growth and change, forming the framework for guiding similar municipal efforts." The original guidelines, issued in February 1980, before the completion of the review, dealt in considerable detail with the preparation, review and approval of regional plans. Following the review, issued in September 1981, a much crisper and concise revision of the guidelines was published, with only eleven pages compared with fifty-five in the earlier version.

Regional Plan Guidelines

The guidelines are of particular interest in that they clearly set out the intended nature and scope of regional plans in Alberta:

> The fundamental purpose of a regional plan is to express the manner in which the municipalities of a region are to be guided in their management of land use planning matters. Since general municipal plans and land use bylaws will implement municipal concerns related to land use planning, within the framework provided by the regional plan, the latter should be a policy rather than a detailed, regulatory tool. A properly-framed policy plan, at the regional level, will permit municipal governments the degree of flexibility they require to meet the requirements of the act and to satisfy local aspirations.

> The process of approving a regional plan provides an opportunity to reflect provincial goals and objectives in a statutory document. The regional plan cannot be a definitive statement of provincial policy and the provincial government is not legally bound by it. Nevertheless, it provides a vehicle for interpreting provincial goals and objectives at a regional level in its areas of legitimate concern, and for coordinating both between municipal and provincial levels of administration.

There are eight plan-approval criteria which translate into specific requirements the general purpose of the legislation to "achieve the orderly, economical and beneficial development and use of land and patterns of human settlement," and to "maintain and improve the quality of the physical environment within which patterns of human settlement are situated in Alberta, without infringing on the rights of individuals except to the extent that is necessary for the greater public interest." The eight criteria are:

(1)   that the regional plan sets out an orientation which clearly indicates how the plan is to meet all formal requirements of the act; that is, that the proposed pattern of development will be orderly and rational, and that the policies do not unduly affect individual rights or municipal autonomy;

(2)   that a clearly articulated plan strategy describe how growth and development is to be accomplished through a

preferred pattern of development that adequately reflects provincial and municipal goals and objectives;

(3) that the regional policies are not in conflict with provincial policy;

(4) that the plan reflects full and continuing coordination between the regional planning commissions, the provincial departments and local municipalities, authorities and boards;

(5) that the plan is internally consistent insofar as inter-related policies are mutually compatible and the policies are consistent with the goals and objectives of the plan;

(6) that the policies are supported by reasoned justification for their adoption, in accompanying documents rather than in the plan itself;

(7) that the plan will be implemented in a manner commensurate with available resources, and that it provides an adequate basis for the preparation of general municipal plans and related statutory documents, e.g. area structure plans, area redevelopment plans and land use bylaws; and

(8) monitoring and review provisions should be outlined in separate documents.

The regional plan is thus a broad statement of policies arrived at after consultation with provincial departments, municipalities and other agencies.

Since the guidelines appeared, all of the regional plans which were in preparation were required to be redone. What was called for were policy-oriented plans which would provide a guiding framework for the more detailed local plans. The mass of detail which characterized the former regional plans had to be shed. This proved difficult for most of the regional planning commissions. Giving up detailed regulatory planning (to the more appropriate municipal level) and embracing a facilitative, policy planning approach involved major changes not only in plan-content but also in basic approach. The Edmonton Regional Planning Commission, in its annual report for 1983, noted that its regional plan had been returned by the Alberta

Planning Board three times for revision. With a note of frustration it commented that "there seems to have been some difficulty in communication and interpretation between the commission and the Alberta Planning Board." The plan was approved in 1984.

Similar difficulties beset the Calgary Regional Plan (Alberta Municipal Affairs 1983a and 1983b). However, five plans were approved between 1982 and 1984: Battle River, Calgary, Edmonton, Palliser and Southeast Alberta. By this time, of course, the economic downturn had transformed Alberta's rapid growth to a precarious stagnation. In the words of a 1984 white paper: "the fact is that Alberta is in transition from a period of super-heated artificially high growth to one of more normal sustainable growth."

The impact on the planning scene has been significant (Hulchanski 1985): planning staffs have been cut; subdivision applications have fallen; funding for regional planning commissions has been reduced; and it is being suggested by the Alberta Municipal Affairs (1984a) that planners should act as "catalysts" rather than as "regulators."

Of course, Alberta is not alone in its difficulties, but its small size and its lack of economic diversity make it very dependent upon wider economic forces, particularly the demand for energy. Moreover, the change from rapid growth (employment grew from 643,000 in 1971 to 1,111,000 in 1984) implies a painful psychological adjustment. More tangibly "as a result of the boom psychology, wage rates in certain sectors have become out of balance with other parts of North America, rendering us, in part, non-competitive in these sectors." The construction and real estate industries are also now disproportionately large and "cannot be sustained during normal economic conditions" (Alberta White Paper 1984: 7). Indeed, Alberta has, at least in some locations, a superabundance of infrastructure investment.

Thus the framework within which regional planning operates has changed markedly: it is likely that its form and content will do likewise. The increasing emphasis on local autonomy could lead the planning commissions to seek new areas of endeavor such as regional economic development, but a more pessimistic view suggests that their powers could be further eroded (Dale and Burton 1984). On the other hand, an upturn in the economy might provide a new lease of life.

Regional Planning in Quebec

It faut que ca change

Liberal slogan,
1960 Quebec Election

At the beginning of her monograph on *Planning in Quebec* (1985), on which this account is largely based, Jeanne Wolfe comments that Quebec is "a province of extreme contrasts." Paradoxically, while some of its planning initiatives are "firsts," others are well behind other provinces. It had "the first comprehensive regional popular consultation program (BAEQ: the bureau d'aménagement de l'est du Québec), the first extensive underground pedestrian system, the first Canadian railroad redevelopment scheme (Place Ville Marie), the first Canadian world exhibition, the first northern new town designed specifically to ameliorate climatic conditions (Fermont), and the first television participatory community development program." Yet, on the other hand, Quebec was the last of the Canadian provinces to have a planning act. It was only in 1979, when "an act respecting land use planning and development" was passed, that Quebec obtained its first general planning legislation.

Nevertheless, as Professor Wolfe's historical chapters show, there had been a series of abortive attempts to get a planning act on the statute book. As with all aspects of government and society in Quebec, planning was affected by "the quiet revolution": the transformation of a traditional conservatism into an aggressive nationalism with major social change being engineered by state action. One planning issue which is of particular relevance to this chapter is that of the degree to which the system was centralized. It was in this context that new,

and   unique,   provisions   for   regional   planning   eventually
emerged. The story can be understood only in the wider framework of the tumultuous twenty or so years of dramatic social
and political change.

The quiet revolution is particularly associated with the
Liberal government of Jean Lesage (1960-66) with its slogan of
"maitres chez nous." It was dedicated to the modernization of
the province, as an end to laisser-faire in economic and physical
development, and a "rattrapage" (catching up) with the rest of
North America. The promises of equality, justice and prosperity for all could never be fully met, but there is no questioning
the dramatic changes which were set in motion. There was no
change in direction when the Liberals were replaced in 1966 by
the Union Nationale under a more conservative Daniel Johnson:
the four years of the government could be seen as a holding
period, with the enthusiastic expectations of the early sixties
dampened by unemployment and severe economic problems.

The re-election of the Liberals in 1970 under the leadership
of Robert Bourassa was "again marked by a burst of interventions: the starting up of the James Bay hydro development, the
implementation of health and social care schemes, reforms in
environmental   and   cultural   properties   law,   and   thwarted
attempts to frame agricultural zoning and planning legislation,"
of which more shortly. René Levesque and the Parti Québecois
came to power in 1976 and the pace of reform accelerated. In
the wider arena of change, planning may not be considered of
great importance but, as we shall see, the emphasis placed by
the Parti Québecois on local autonomy and decentralization of
power had a profound effect on the character of the new planning system.

The dramatic changes brought about by the quiet revolution, not forgetting the impact on the federal government and
on federalism itself, cannot be overstressed. They included a
major reorganization of the educational system, the establishment of health and welfare services (regionally organized but
with local community centers), and widespread intervention in
the provincial economy. Changes took place in all aspects of

Quebec life: intellectual and cultural fervor, trade union militancy, a decline in the social and political influence of the Roman Catholic Church, and so on (Van Loon and Whittington 1976; Postgate and McRoberts 1976; McWhinney 1979).

The First Steps Towards Regional Planning

One of the early acts of the Lesage government was to establish an economic advisory council: the conseil d'orientation économique du Québec (COEQ). This was given the mandate "to prepare a plan for the economic organization of the province with a view to the most complete utilization of its material and human resources," and more generally to advise the government on any economic matter.

Though COEQ published some interesting reports, no plan was forthcoming. Indeed, the council explicitly explained in its 1967 annual report why a plan could not at that stage be drawn up. Important prerequisites were missing:

(1) the existence of adequate information, both in quantity and quality;

(2) the existence of properly qualified personnel, both for preparing and executing plans;

(3) the creation of regional structures, capable of involving the population in the planning process;

(4) the coordination of the diverse activities of the various government departments;

(5) more efficient forms of collaboration between different levels of government;

(6) the creation of a climate, or states of mind more receptive to planning, which presupposes profound modifications in the attitudes of agents of economic development.

Though the council produced no plan, they did have influence on what Professor Wolfe calls "the consciousness-raising of individuals," and on the wide diffusion of ideas. This came about, not only as a result of the publication of the report, but also because the council involved large numbers of civil servants (from almost every department) in its preparation. Thus there was a heightened awareness of the need for change. Highly significant among the institutional changes was the creation of the Quebec Bureau of Statistics. There also followed the establishment of Le comité d'aménagement des resources (CPAR) which consisted of the deputy ministers of the relevant departments; and the bureau d'aménagement de l'est du Québec (BAEQ) which was established in 1963 to take advantage of federal economic development programs.

At the end of the sixties, a fledgling central planning organization was emerging. Foremost, and now taking a leading role, is l'office de planification et de développement du Québec (OPDQ). Also established was an interdepartmental planning committee: the commission interministérielle de planification et de développement (CIPD). This is also still in operation. In addition to this central machinery there were regional councils (conseils économique regionaux) which started off as voluntary initiatives in depressed parts of the province. Later they became institutionalized, and funded by OPDQ; and their areas of operation were modified to fit in with the ten administrative regions adopted by the government in 1966.

In the meantime, a broad review of planning was undertaken by the La Haye Commission. This reported in 1968, and recommended a strongly centralized approach to urban and regional planning. With the strong tradition of autonomous local government in Quebec this could make no progress.

However, in 1969 local government in three regions was reorganized, with the establishment of the Montreal Urban Community, the Quebec Urban Community and the Outaouais (Hull) Regional Community. The last was termed "regional" since it includes a large amount of scattered development in rural areas. These communities are comparable to Metropolitan Toronto (Bernard, Léveillé and Lord 1974 and 1975).

Despite Montreal's prime position in the economy of Quebec (and policies designed to encourage dispersal of some of its prosperity to less fortunate areas in the province), there was increasing concern at the end of the sixties about the soundness of its economic base. The 1970 report by Higgins, Martin and Raynauld "sounded the alarm." Montreal was losing ground not only in comparison with Toronto but also in terms of its own development. It was against this background that, in the words of Professor Wolfe:

> It is small wonder ... that Mayor Jean Drapeau strove to get the Olympics to reassert the glory of the city, that the various governments decided on large investments in downtown office buildings, and that moves were made to capitalize on the introduction of the new airport, to boost the Contrecoeur steel complex, to develop James Bay, to promote the Becancour industrial park, and that the region of Montreal was declared a special area for aid to industries under DREE legislation.

It was at this point in time that a number of separate strands came together to weave into a set of operational programs, e.g. for the new airport, and also a less clear-cut attempt to devise a new planning act. The airport makes a fascinating story (Feldman and Milch 1983); in essence, after much wrangling between the provincial and city governments, which both wanted a location south of Montreal, and the federal government, which wanted a location on the west, a site was chosen on the north!

At the same time, the subregion containing the site was designated a special area under the DREE scheme. Several different agencies now became involved. In addition to DREE there was OPDQ, responsible for the planning and development of the subregion; the Quebec Department of Transport, responsible for the autoroute and rapid transit system to serve the airport; the Department of Industry and Commerce, for the promotion of industrial development; and the Department of Municipal Affairs, for land use planning controls.

The detailed administrative arrangements were in fact much more complex than this suggests, but it is sufficient for present purposes simply to note that a key component was a project office of the Department of Municipal Affairs known as SATRA: service d'aménagement du territoire de la région aéroportuaire (Perry 1974: 55). This had a mandate to prepare a physical plan for the airport subregion; to give technical assistance to the municipalities, to help them in the formulation of their plans, and to encourage their participation in the formulation of strategies for the area; to identify problems related to the establishment of the airport, and to advise the responsible agencies. Bill 60 (Loi concernant les environs du nouvel aéroport international) of 1970 required the preparation of a regional plan by SATRA followed by local master plans to be prepared by the local municipalities, of which fourteen were amalgamated in whole or in part in a new municipality of Ste-Scholastique, later renamed Mirabel. An account of the planning process is to be found in Professor Wolfe's monograph, from which the following section is taken.

Municipal Reform for Planning

While ad hoc agencies were being established for specific regional purposes, efforts were made to reorganize local government. In Professor Wolfe's words, "the period of the late sixties and early seventies can be characterized on the municipal front as one of non-coercive attempts to improve municipal government and management in order to set the stage for the introduction of a land use planning act."

The high degree of autonomy possessed by Quebec municipalities, coupled with the current emphasis on local participation in decision making, meant that the reform of local government had to proceed on a voluntary, and hence slow, basis. The 1965 Voluntary Amalgamation of Municipalities Act (Loi de la fusion voluntaires des municipalités) provided precisely what its title suggests: the powers for municipalities to amalgamate voluntarily.

Despite the persuasion of the Department of Municipal Affairs, progress was minimal. More success attended an act of 1971 (Loi favorisant le regroupement des municipalités) which provided for provincial definition of regroupment units where this was considered to be advantageous to an area. The success was due to the provision of an outright bribe: "the minister may make to any new municipality constituted under this act a grant not exceeding fifteen dollars per capita payable in five annual and consecutive instalments."

This and other measures, however, failed to bring about reorganization on a scale adequate to facilitate urban and regional planning. A parallel effort to create special planning districts was much more successful. The first was the fusion of the fourteen municipalities on the Ile Jésus into the new city of Laval in 1965. Others (some of which have already been mentioned) included the Montreal and Quebec urban communities and the Outaouais regional community in 1969; the new international airport region in 1970; the James Bay development corporation (Société de développement de la Baie James) in 1971; and the regional park areas of Forillon (1970), St Anne (1971) and Mauricie (1972). These and similar measures led to the result that, by the mid-seventies, about a half of the population of the province was covered by compulsory planning legislation, even though there was still no planning act as such.

As indicated earlier, the La Haye proposals for a centralized urban and regional planning system were shelved. Another attempt was made in 1971, when a white paper on local government and a draft planning act were published. The white paper proposed the regrouping of municipalities into coherent urban-centered, planning districts. The draft planning act "proposed the preparation by the OPDQ of regional development plans for each of the province's ten administrative regions, the grouping of the 1,586 municipalities into 131 secteurs d'aménagement (planning districts) for planning purposes as delimited in the white paper, the preparation of a general plan for each district by a mandated municipality and, finally, the preparation of a town plan by each municipality in conformity with the district plan." Additionally there was provision for a range of municipal planning powers.

These proposals made no progress, mainly because of the unacceptability of the concept of a mandated authority, "hinting as it did of territorial domination and possible future annexations."

Yet another draft planning act was produced in 1976 following the Castonguay report on "L'urbanisation au Québec," but this fell with the defeat of the Liberals. The task of devising a system of urban and regional planning in Quebec now passed to the Parti Québecois.

The Parti Québécois and the 1979 Planning Act

The Parti Québécois was returned to power committed to a wide range of reforms including a planning act. It was explicitly recognized that this necessitated a reorganization of local government, a reform of municipal finance, protective agricultural zoning (which essentially sets a perimeter for urban development), and a range of similarly associated changes. At the same time, the Parti Québécois had a long-standing commitment in favor of local autonomy: the rock on which previous attempts to devise a planning system had foundered.

The difficulty was met by a huge program of public consultation and lengthy negotiations with local authority associations. Significantly, the Ministère de l'aménagement was retitled Ministère de l'aménagement et de la décentralisation. In fact decentralization was a major goal of the legislation, in contrast to the earlier abortive proposals. Four main principles formed the basis of the new act:

(1) Planning is a political rather than a technical act and therefore planning decisions should be taken by elected representatives in consultation with their constituents;

(2) Public involvement should be built in throughout the planning process;

(3) The provincial, county and local levels of government each have their own responsibilities in development control;

(4) There should be consultation among the levels of government to ensure that the objectives are consistent. Plans may not conflict with those of the next higher level of government (CIP 1980: 26).

A major feature of the act, which was passed in November 1979, was that it provided a framework for land use planning and development through the establishment of regional county municipalities. These were planning subregions whose boundaries were determined after full consultation and negotiation with the public and existing local governments in each area.

By 1984 there were some ninety regional county municipalities (and the three communities which remain under the new system). They are required to prepare and adopt interim control bylaws and then a development plan establishing explicit development policy guidelines and incorporating provincial proposals. There are detailed, perhaps cumbersome, provisions for consultation, not only with the public but also with provincial bodies.

A regional plan forms the framework for local plan-making. The regional county municipality has to certify that local plans, bylaws and projects are in conformity with its plan.

The act also established a provincial commission nationale de l'aménagement whose main function was to "give assessments respecting the conformity of a planning program or a zoning, subdivision or building bylaw with the objectives of a development plan ... " It was conceived as an administrative agency to referee plan conformity, not as an appellate body like the Ontario Municipal Board. (All land disputes in Quebec are heard in the courts.) This commission was disbanded in 1984 and its duties transferred to the Municipal Commission, for reasons which, at the time of writing, were not clear.

This sketch of the 1979 Quebec planning act omits much: its 269 sections extend over sixty-seven pages. Its particular interest, however, lies not so much in its detailed provisions but in the fact that a form of regional planning has been designed which is politically acceptable in a province which has for so long resisted it. It is fitting that this account should end with a further brief discussion of the importance played by consultation in this.

Une responsabilité politique

As already noted, the planning act was based on the premise that "l'aménagement est d'abord une responsibilité politique et non-uniquement une question technique." This statement of political responsibility was constantly reiterated by the leading politicians who had the task of getting the act to work.

Though the act provides that, before determining the establishment of a regional county municipality, the government must consult, in fact this has been interpreted to mean that the municipalities should make the decision. In the words of Professor Wolfe: " ... the ministries did not delimit the regional county municipalities, but the local municipalities had to decide among themselves upon the appropriate delimitation. This was achieved through a process of consultation, with the backing of both the Quebec Union of Municipalities and the Union of County Councils."

> The process began in March 1980 when the province was divided by the Secrétariat d'Etat pour l'Aménagement into nineteen temporary zones for the purpose of consultation. In each zone a temporary consultation committee was set up consisting of one mayor from an urban municipality, one from a rural municipality, a representative of the milieu (usually someone who had been involved in some municipal work) as president, and a secretary (usually a civil servant from the Secretariat) to take care of minor administrative matters such as notices of meetings, room rentals, minutes and suchlike. These committees then started meeting with the various institutionalized bodies in each district such as the municipal mayors and councils, school boards, regional development boards, chambres de commerce, and service clubs, and in each locality they promoted the formation of provisional committees of mayors of potential county municipalities.

> At the same time, the Department of Municipal Affairs started a three-stage information program with the "monde municipale," that is the mayors, councils and senior civil servants in each municipality. In March and April 1980, twenty qualified ministry planners were engaged in this process. By the summer this was reduced to ten, and it was estimated that by the autumn almost 80 percent of Quebec's municipalities had been directly consulted. An information session consisted of an audio-visual

presentation on the nature of planning, a verbal description of the provisions of the Act, the distribution of numerous explanatory pamphlets, and a question-and-answer or workshop period. Follow-up information sessions were held as requested.

This was a remarkable method of effecting a change which was recognized to be both necessary and difficult. It is not surprising that the result has been criticized, particularly on the grounds that the new regions are too small (CIP 1980: 26). It could hardly be expected that extensive consultation would lead to the establishment of large planning districts.

There is a here a dilemma which continually faces those who seek to reorganize local government to meet the complex needs of the contemporary society. In the words of the wag, "big may be better, but small is beautiful."

The 1979 planning act has had its teething troubles, some of which have led to amending legislation, and some of which arise from lack of harmony between the act and other legislation such as the Cultural Properties Act and the Agricultural Zoning Act (Giroux 1981: 73). Nevertheless, Wolfe ends her study on an optimistic note. In particular, she concludes that it provides "an equitable vehicle for intermunicipal coordination." In practice it seems unlikely that there will be any startling changes. "It is evident from the sense of the act that most regional county municipality plans will ultimately be an amalgamation of plans already made, land use patterns already determined, and controls already imposed by the agricultural zoning and cultural properties act. In this sense the regional plans will become vehicles of accommodation and adjustment, ensuring the filling in of semi-urbanized spaces, the appropriate deployment of *terrains vagues,* and the full use of underused services ... This scenario, in a period of slow urban population growth and energy shortages has great merit. It had been calculated that the agricultural zoning leaves enough fringe area for urban growth for the next fifteen to twenty years at present land consumption rates, if all the holes in the tapestry of semi-urban land uses are filled up." In Wolfe's view, the province faces much more intractable problems of poverty and the control of pollution.

Regional Planning in British Columbia

> All regional plans and official plans ... are cancelled and have no effect
>
> Municipal Amendment Act 1983

Regional planning often emerges as a response to the problems caused by the pressures of large numbers of people on a limited area of land: the complexities of the situation demand a new level of governmental organization. But regional planning can be necessitated by precisely the opposite conditions: a small scattering of population over a large resource-rich region. This is the situation in the Highlands and Islands of Scotland, in northern Scandinavia, over much of the northern part of Canada, and in large parts of British Columbia.

British Columbia has a population approaching three million, the majority of whom live in the southwest corner of the province. This heavily urbanized area has a well-established system of local government. On the other hand, at the time of the introduction of regional districts in 1965, about a quarter of a million people lived in scattered and isolated communities which had not been incorporated as self-governing municipalities. Of the province's 366,000 square miles, only 2,870 were incorporated areas. The major part of the land was unorganized territory, that is an area having no government other than that provided by a distant provincial capital, though a limited range of services might be provided through field offices. The problems could well be met by a system of regional government. Enabling legislation was passed in 1965, and gradually regional districts were established over the whole of the province except for the northwest corner. Some of the history of this has been outlined in chapter 2. Here the focus is on the regional planning function in the unincorporated areas. First, however, it is necessary to outline the provincial role in regional planning.

As Sue Corke has written (1983), British Columbia's history has been one of infinite resources to be exploited and infinite land to be developed. Inevitably, as settlements and population density grew, the real constraints on these resources became clearer and, as elsewhere, land use conflicts erupted with increasing frequency. There were disagreements between local governments and provincial agencies over objectives and priorities; conflicts between settlement programs (urban, industrial, transportation, energy) and natural resource management programs; and conflicts between exploitive resource management, in sectors such as mining, agriculture and forestry and conservation-oriented programs, such as wildlife and environmental protection.

By the late 1960s, such disagreements had escalated to the point where ministers and deputy ministers were increasingly involved in conflict-resolution, and in 1970 a Land Use Committee of Cabinet was formed to mediate these occurrences. In 1971 this committee was formalized through the passage of the Environment and Land Use Act.

The Environment and Land Use Act is very short and potentially very powerful. It establishes the Environment and Land Use Committee, whose members are appointed by Cabinet. The statutory duties of this cabinet committee are to initiate programs to foster public concern for the environment; to ensure all aspects of the preservation and maintenance of the natural environment are fully considered in the administration of land use and resource development in accordance with maximum beneficial land use and to minimize and prevent waste; to make recommendations to the Lieutenant Governor in Council regarding the environment and development and use of land and other natural resources; to study matters relating to the environment and land use; and to prepare reports and make recommendations to Cabinet.

The real muscle of the act lies in Section 6 which gives power to Cabinet to make orders respecting the environment or land use which have paramountcy over any other act or regulation in the province of British Columbia (Ince 1984: 24).

Among the orders which Cabinet has enacted under this legislation was the very important 1972 regulation to freeze farmland development. This regulation, later replaced by specific legislation (the Land Commission Act), illustrates the extraordinary power granted to Cabinet by the Environment and Land Use Act. In effect, it was able to place a freeze on all uses of agricultural land, other than farming, for a temporary period across the entire province, in response to political pressure. (This is discussed at length in chapter 6.)

The Environment and Land Use Act has had other important influences on land use planning and control in British Columbia, besides providing the power to respond quickly to perceived crises. The cabinet committee has been active in establishing other committees and resource groups through which jurisdictional conflicts could be mediated, researched and resolved. The most controversial of these supporting functions was the Environment and Land Use Secretariat (ELUCS), established by the committee in 1973. The secretariat was responsible for developing the technical support for the committee, which it provided through data collection, and the preparation of plans and guidelines. It also had an important coordinating function in the elaborate decision-making process through which all problems referred to the cabinet committee had to pass. For a variety of reasons, not the least of which was the unpopularity of its technical work with its political masters, it was abolished in 1980.

A subcommittee which continued to function until 1983 was the technical committee. This committee was a forum for deputy ministers of the variety of land-related ministries to enable them to discuss and resolve matters of overlapping jurisdictions.

Two years after the cabinet committee's establishment, there was a strong push to formalize the institutional structures which handled the resource conflicts in different parts of the province. In 1975, regional resource management committees were established in seven districts covering the province, replacing the existing informal inter-sectoral coordinating groups which had evolved to mediate the conflicts among the various departments over resource management and development goals. These committees were composed of senior resource agency officials responsible for resource management on crown lands. Ministries represented have included agriculture; environment; forests; industry and small business development; lands, parks and housing; mines, energy and petroleum resources; recreation; transportation and highways; and municipal affairs and housing.

This formal, provincial-level institutional structure coexisted (until 1983 when it was abolished) in a rather uneasy relationship with the system of regional district governments established under the Municipal Act. It is these regional districts which form the main subject of this section.

Regional Districts 1965-83

A sketch of the background to the introduction of regional districts in British Columbia is given in chapter 2. There the focus was on urban areas, and the Lower Mainland in particular. Here we are concerned with the twenty-six districts which Lane (1981) has neatly termed "trading area regions." Each of these regions has boundaries drawn to include a major center in its trading area. In fact this excludes only the two metropolitan regions of Greater Vancouver and the Capital, though these two contain over half of the population of the province.

A regional district is officially defined as "a government unit covering a large area of the province established to provide the means by which existing municipalities within a region, in cooperation with unincorporated areas, can deal effectively with regional problems as well as furnish municipal-type services to small unincorporated communities and rural areas within the regional district."

Regional districts are functional rather than political organizations and are presided over by regional boards. The functions are provided for each individual district by letters patent and they vary greatly. In the words of the Regional District Review Committee (1978: 43), the districts had been:

> ... permitted to take unto themselves whatever jurisdiction
> their constituent parts wished to acquire, subject to obtaining
> supplementary letters patent for the function from the provin-
> cial government. The result of this provision for voluntary
> assumption of functions has been that some regional districts
> have taken on functions responsibly and carefully, and have car-
> ried them out to the satisfaction of their constituents. Some
> have been reluctant to take on any responsibilities. Some have
> taken on too many tasks, spreading their capabilities rather
> thinly, and others have taken on functions without adequately
> researching the need for them or the ongoing costs involved.

The variability stems, at least in part, from the curious
nature of the districts. Their boards consist of appointees from
the constituent municipal councils, and elected members from
the electoral areas of the unorganized territories. This duality
gives rise to stresses, particularly with regards to planning
where, to put the matter bluntly, all wanted the benefits but
few were happy with the costs. The result was a reluctance to
assume planning functions: until this reluctance forced the provincial government to make them mandatory, which it did in
1970. A further legislative change in 1972 required regional districts to appoint a planning director and to establish a technical
planning committee (a permissive provision until this time). As
we shall see, these provisions were drastically altered in 1983.

The technical committees were comprised of the district's
planning director, and representatives from the constituent
localities, from the provincial departments and, on occasion,
from federal agencies. (The past tense is used because the
regional planning function was abolished in 1983.) Their role
was to advise the board on all planning matters, to prepare
regional plans, and to act as a liaison between the various
bodies involved. A report of the Alberta Regional Planning
Study commented that, "interestingly, while the regional district does determine its own official plan, it has little chance of
being implemented without adoption as a policy by provincial
agencies who are not obliged to respect regional statements.
This has had the effect of placing a great amount of indirect
responsibility for regional planning at the provincial level."

This becomes a more troublesome issue once regional planning became mandatory on the regional districts.

Official Regional and Settlement Plans

In the trading areas, which constitute twenty-six of the twenty-eight regional districts, most of the land is crown land. This makes the troublesome issue even more so. Lane (1981) notes that "since more than 90 percent of the province is crown land, and since regional district boards are subordinate legislatures, effective regional planning at the regional district level is confined to property privately held, both within and without the boundaries of member municipalities. By necessity, much of what constitutes true regional planning is carried on by individual provincial ministries through the application of a system of policies, reserves, licenses, land use corridors and the like." Given these various jurisdictions and the wide differences between the districts, it is hardly surprising that the regional planning function of the legislation was applied in differing ways across the province. Lane reinforces this point:

> The Environment and Land Use Act, adopted in 1971, has been used to coordinate the management of resources within the seven resource management regions established by British Columbia Regulation 32/75. In a sense, this constituted a withdrawal of regional planning powers from the regional districts, made necessary by resource conflicts arising in the extensive crown lands of the province. Understandably, in the trading area regional districts, regional planning has been largely concerned with the general allocation of privately held land, outside the municipalities, for urban, rural and recreation use, sometimes including the location of major highways.

The actual provisions of the act are that "the regional board shall prepare regional plans applicable to the regional district and revise them as necessary, and for this purpose a regional plan means a general scheme without detail for the projected uses of land within the regional district, including the location of major highways." Although legally ambiguous (Ince 1984: 48), the Ministry of Municipal Affairs (1979: 3) described its intent as follows:

> An official regional plan is a conceptual or schematic plan estab-
> lishing broad objectives and policies for the development of a
> regional district or a major sub-area thereof including both
> municipal and non-municipal areas. Once adopted by the
> regional board, the official regional plan will be used as a long-
> range policy guide to decisions about the physical development
> of the regional district and will serve as the framework for more
> detailed plans.

Although the making of this plan was mandatory, its adoption as official through the passing of a bylaw requiring an affirmative majority vote, was not. No public hearing was required and, as with other official plans under the Municipal Act, private property rights were not affected unless the neces-sary land use bylaws implementing the plan were subsequently passed. Provincial approval for the regional plan was not required unless the plan involved lands in the Lower Fraser Val-ley Flood Plain (Corke 1983: 103).

In contrast to the official regional plans are settlement plans, which were not affected by the 1983 legislation. These apply to the unorganized territory of a regional district. Perhaps unexpectedly, they are considerably more detailed than the policy-oriented plans, and the legislation sets out in great detail the content of these plans and the method by which they came into force (Ince 1984: 51).

An official settlement plan has been defined by the Minis-try of Municipal Affairs (1979) as "a comprehensive land use plan, more detailed in content than an official regional plan, establishing land use policies for areas of the regional district which are unincorporated." The Municipal Act spells out eleven specific matters which must be addressed in an official settle-ment plan:

(1)   the location, amount and type of major commercial, industrial, institutional, recreational and public utility uses;

(2)   the location, amount, type and density of residential development required to meet the anticipated housing needs over a period of at least five years in the area

covered by the plan;

(3)   the protection of land areas subject to hazardous conditions;

(4)   the preservation, protection, and enhancement of land and water areas of special importance for scenic or recreational value or natural, historical or scientific interest;

(5)   the preservation and continuing use of agricultural land for present and future food production;

(6)   the proposed sequence of urban development and redevelopment, including, where ascertainable, the proposed timing, location and phasing of trunk sewer and water services;

(7)   the need for and provision of public facilities, including schools, parks and solid waste disposal sites;

(8)   the location in schematic form of a major road system for the plan area;

(9)   the location, amount and type of development to be permitted within one kilometer of a controlled access highway designated under Part 6 of the Highway Act;

(10) the distribution of major land use areas and concentration of activity in relation to the provision of existing or potential public transit services; and

(11) a program identifying the actions required by the regional board to implement the official settlement plan.

These policies must be discussed within a broad statement of the social, economic and environmental objectives to be achieved. The minister has the prerogative of directing further matters to be considered (Corke 1983: 107).

During the preparation of the official settlement plan, formal consideration must be given to the probable social, environmental and economic consequences of the proposed policies; the stated objectives, policies and programs of the government; the suitability of land for various uses; land area requirements for uses related to projections of population and economic growth; and the prevention of pollution of air, water and land.

Until the 1983 legislation, an official regional plan had to be in place before an official settlement plan could be adopted. The official settlement plan had to be prepared in consultation with member municipalities of the regional board, elected area representatives, and the Ministry of Municipal Affairs.

Regional district planning functions were not successfully exercised in many cases, not exercised at all in others. Stachelrodt-Crook (1975) noted that many regional districts, although obliged to prepare an official plan, had not complied or adopted them. The reasons for this failure to exercise a statutory function are complex and in 1977 a regional district review committee was established by the provincial government to examine these (and other) issues more closely, and to recommend solutions and future change.

The Regional District Review

The regional district planning function, as provided for in the legislation since 1965, never really "took off," except in the two metropolitan regions. For several years there was frustration with the regional role from all quarters and, through various legislative amendments, the provincial government tried to smooth the way. But there were certain fundamental contradictions in the entire province-wide planning framework which could not be smoothed away.

In 1975 Stachelrodt-Crook listed the many problems with which the regional district planning function was beset:

(1)   the lack of a clear definition of its (the regional district system's) planning role by the provincial government;

(2)   the existence of government agencies with environment and land use jurisdictions which are independent of the regional districts;

(3)   the fact that the regional district boards do not possess autonomous planning jurisdictions, but are, to some

extent, dependent upon the support of member municipalities;

(4) the geographically-inappropriate nature of some of the
areas which have been designated as regional districts;

(5) a failure at all levels of government to pay due consideration to regional district concerns and priorities;

(6) an inability at all levels of government to appreciate the
utility of the regional district approach to planning;

(7) the inadequate funding of the regional district planning
process;

(8) the chronic shortage of planners, particularly those with
rural planning experience;

(9) the tendency of the regional district boards to become
preoccupied with regulatory zoning;

(10) the unsatisfactory nature of some technical planning committee deliberations;

(11) the absence of adequate inventory data and mapping in
many areas.

As Sue Corke has noted, most of these problems were fundamental in that they emerged from the basic structure of planning in the province. They could not be remedied through legislative tinkering.

In line with the experience in other provinces, a basic issue
was the relationship of the region to the provincial government
in all its manifestations. The establishment of the regional district review committee in 1977 offered some hope that the province recognized the extent of the difficulties, and was prepared
to view the whole matter with an open mind. Corke (1983:
111) continues as follows.

The mandate of the review committee was to examine the
jurisdictional role of regional districts, specifically through an
examination of their structural and administrative organization
and their relationship with other levels of government. The
committee held public hearings, received many briefs, and in

October 1978 published its report. Fifty-two recommendations were made, several of which were relevant to the future of the regional district planning function.

The report noted that regional districts were "nowhere alike": they had different kinds of boards, different geographical contexts, and different functional evolutions. Nevertheless, the broad set of problems the report identified were common to most. Largely echoing the problem list discussed above, the committee found six major areas of difficulty: the lack of support from the Ministry of Municipal Affairs; a general lack of commitment to the regional district concept by the provincial government; a lack of cooperation by other ministries and field agencies; a lack of specified responsibilities for regional districts; a lack of understanding by the public; and occasional poor performance by regional districts.

With regard to the jurisdictional role of regional districts, the committee found that the 1965 legislation gave no clear jurisdictional role. Besides specific authority for planning and building regulations, they had acquired whatever other thirty-six functions they wished subject to the province granting the necessary letters patent. Later, additional duties were imposed regarding the administration of politically contentious legislation such as the Agricultural Land Commission Act and the Soil Conservation Act.

The committee stated, critically, that it had "gained the impression that the regional concept had been conceived and launched in some haste and that once implemented, the newly formed regional districts had been literally cast adrift by the provincial authorities with only marginal guidance and support."

During its deliberations the committee requested explicit input regarding the attitudes of other levels of government to their relationship with the regional districts. Municipal representatives expressed a number of causes of conflict which had damaged their relations with the regional board, among them the fear or erosion of local power by the regional district;

conflict over the regional district administration of the Agricultural Land Commission Act; and resistance to cost-sharing.

Provincial ministries and the Agricultural Land Commission expressed the view that regional districts were uncooperative, while the regional districts themselves spoke of their concern over a number of issues including poor relations with the Ministry of Municipal Affairs, (resulting in approvals delays and hostility); the "chaos of non-cooperation" with other provincial agencies especially the crown development agencies; the lack of power vis-a-vis municipalities; concern over the structure of the regional district board, especially the weighting of votes.

Addressing the issues of specific responsibilities, and the relationship of regional planning to provincial planning, the committee recommended that the legislation provide for three categories of responsibility. First, there were mandatory responsibilities. These would consist of:

- land use planning with the authority to adopt bylaws in the region, and in electoral areas, subject to an official plan, provincial power of veto, and a specified time frame;
- regional road system planning;
- economic development planning and coordination;
- participation with the province in resource management and development planning.

Such statutory responsibilities would mean a greatly enlarged regional role in the provincial planning framework. Although a rational response to the problems of regional impotence, the past political climate surrounding the regional role indicated that this direction would be a unlikely one.

Secondly, there were permissive or voluntary responsibilities subject to all board members' approval: these would consist of:

- water supply services;
- sewage disposal services;
- solid waste disposal;

- regional parks;
- grants-in-aid;
- fire protection;
- provision of development services such as building permits and inspection;
- recreation and cultural services;
- contract services to municipalities.

Such voluntary responsibilities would not include responsibility for ambulance services, air pollution, dog control, senior citizen housing, flood control or community health services which would remain provincial responsibilities.

Finally, there was a number of additional powers, including assigned functions by the province, on a negotiated fee for service basis.

In addition, the report made recommendations regarding training of regional planners; crown land subdivision with full regional consultation; the role of the technical planning committee as a policy body; and improving the efficiency of processing land use matters. Further, the committee recognized the wide variety of statutes relating to provincial, regional and municipal planning functions and recommended the introduction of a provincial planning act to consolidate planning provisions currently dispersed among a number of statutes; the introduction of a provincial planning appeals board; special provisions for metropolitan regional districts; and full membership of the regional district in the provincially established regional resource management committees.

Uncertainties of the 1980s

Some of these recommendations were incorporated in the 1980 draft planning act, but this did not survive the political rapids (Corke 1983; Wiesman 1980). Neither did a revised (1981) draft land use act (Wiesman 1982). Sue Corke summarizes the philosophy underlying the provisions relating to regional planning as follows.

The draft planning act attempted a rational, consensual resolution to the difficulties of achieving coordination, and proposed a hierarchical planning system at the pinnacle of which was an open declaration of provincial policies reflected in a provincial planning statement. Large regional planning agencies, akin to the existing regional resource committees, would translate these statements for the sub-areas of the province, and local municipalities would interpret and conform to them at their own level. The Land Use Act, with all due expediency engendered through the political bartering process, lopped off the top of the planning pyramid as earlier conceived and proposed instead regional planning statements on a larger scale, to which local planning would conform. Regional district planning as was currently practiced in British Columbia (in particular the urban variety of intermunicipal or metropolitan planning) would effectively be lost and replaced by much broader scale planning. Thus, the difficulties which beset regional planning from the outset and which were remarked upon by the regional district review committee were ultimately to be resolved by the removal of the planning function from this level of government. With regard to the grand conception of provincial planning and coordinated policy, it was not entirely lost: there was a provision in the Land Use Act for the establishment of resource planning areas by Cabinet where the impacts of proposed resource development were likely to be significant.

But as a general rule declarations of provincial policy as a coordinated guideline were lost. In their place a philosophy of strengthened regionalism was proposed, but not the kind of regionalism to which British Columbia had become accustomed.

With regard to the provincial role in the administration of local authority planning, there was increased involvement anticipated in both pieces of legislation for the Minister of Municipal Affairs and his Inspector of Municipalities (usually the deputy minister). In particular, of course, formal approval from the minister was required to ensure regional plan conformity at the local level. Local autonomy in planning matters was threatened severely by both new legislative drafts, but neither passed into law. Instead, there was passed a very short act, amending the Municipal Act, which eliminated regional plans.

At the time of writing, the situation has not become clear, and it has become even less clear with successive ministerial statements. The 1983 act was heralded (by the government) as a measure which "reinforces the primary role of municipalities in determining land use patterns in local communities." Now that so many comprehensive municipal plans were in place, "the official regional plans have become an unnecessary level of land use." These statements were reported in provincial government news releases. One of the releases makes the different point that the legislation was intended "to support the government's economic recovery plan through the application of deregulation principles to British Columbia's planning and development approvals process."

With developments so current, it is unwise to attempt a judgment, particularly since further legislation is promised specifically relating to the land use section of the Municipal Act. An ominous comment by the minister (Ritchie) points to a different political issue. Between 1972 and 1982, municipal planning expenditure increased by about twenty percent per year (from $4 million to $24 million). Moreover, according to the minister, "money ... is least needed in rural areas. People live in rural areas ... because they want to get away from red tape" (PIBC 1984).

This statement does not deal with the regional problems of urbanized agglomerations. In fact, the Municipal Act provides for municipalities to enter into voluntary cooperative agreements for the establishment of regional development services. This is of particular importance in the highly urbanized areas. At the time of writing, (early 1985) there was no progress in this direction except for the Greater Vancouver Regional District (Cameron 1984: 16).

It is obvious that regional planning in British Columbia is currently in a state of flux. This is nothing new. In the words of a senior civil servant, "British Columbians have a higher than normal ambivalence about planning. This could be engendered by the conflict between the strong attachment we feel with our unique environment and the 'last frontier' attitude of rugged individualism, resource exploitation and general rape and pillage. This conflict is accentuated by the limited base of arable and habitable land upon which it is played out." Additionally, British Columbia in contrast to Alberta, Ontario and Quebec "has never had a county system to establish a basic precedent for two-tiered government. Consequently there is little support at any point on the political spectrum for the concept that a level of policy-making is needed or desirable between the level of the province and that of the locality."

Nevertheless, regional planning is still alive, particularly in the Greater Vancouver region (which is briefly referred to in chapter 2). A review by Dan Campbell (who as Minister of Municipal Affairs introduced the regional district system) concluded that "the Greater Vancouver Regional District is generally a mature and effective organization. It benefits from a strong sense of commitment from its member municipalities and demonstrates an ability to respond to necessary changes" (Campbell Report 1984: 2).

One thing, however, is clear: any province that institutes a system of regional government is likely to find itself involved in continual review of its creation.

Chapter 10
Environmental Protection

What do you do when you see a nearly extinct species of bird eating a nearly extinct species of plant?

Globe and Mail (Toronto)

Environmental protection covers a vast area, from air quality control to motor vehicle emissions, from acid rain to pesticides, and from water to noise. Franson and Lucas helpfully suggest a fourfold classification of environmental laws: "those that regulate potentially harmful conduct; those that encourage the development of alternative technologies; those that are designed to produce the information needed to make sound environmental management decisions; and those that seek to compensate people harmed by environmental degradation" (Franson and Lucas 1978: 205). Writing in the late seventies, they comment that, up to that time, Canadian governments had placed their primary emphasis on the first: the regulation of waste handling (the discharge of solid, liquid and gaseous waste); the regulation of the production of waste (returnable containers; phosphorous content of detergents); and measures aimed at preventing direct damage to the environment (e.g. siltation of streams, the loss of topsoil, and pesticide control).

The situation, as always, varies between the provinces, but certain trends are observable. For instance, there is a growing emphasis on policies which prevent environmental damage, increasing concern for the total functioning of natural systems, and interesting attempts to devise coordinated, integrated plans which deal with ecosystems as a whole.

There is much in this which is promise for the future, and a large part of this chapter deals with the more limited programs and practices which, with varying degrees of success, are operating across Canada. It starts with an overview of the roles of the federal and provincial governments. This sets the scene for a more detailed discussion of environmental provisions in Ontario. Two environmental advisory bodies are then briefly discussed, one in Alberta and the other in Saskatchewan. A major technique, of growing significance, in environmental protection is the assessment of the impact which a proposed development is likely to have. A large part of the chapter is devoted to this. Four sections deal with environmental impact assessment at the federal level, environmental assessment in Ontario, the extension of environmental assessment to include social and cultural issues (especially in the north), and the nature and role of environmental assessment in the larger decision-making process.

This is followed by a short discussion of environmental regulation versus pricing, and the chapter ends with the subject of heritage conservation.

The Federal Role

... to foster harmony between society and the environment for the economic, social and cultural benefit of present and future generations of Canadians

Environment Canada 1982

Such is the federal ministry's mission. The ministry, whose name is generally shortened from Ministry of the Environment to Environment Canada, was created in 1970 at the high tide of public concern for environmental issues. Functions from several departments were transferred. These included fisheries, forests, water, air pollution control, the land inventory program, wildlife and meteorology. In 1979, the terms of reference were broadened to give an emphasis on environmental quality, and to placing the ministry in a leadership role vis-a-vis other parts of the federal government machine. Environment Canada is also required to promote and encourage "the institution of practices and conduct leading to the better preservation and enhancement of environmental quality," and to cooperate with provincial governments and agencies and "any bodies or persons in any programs having similar objects."

1979 also saw the hiving off of fisheries to a new Department of Fisheries and Oceans, and the extension of Environment Canada's responsibilities to encompass Parks Canada. According to the department's 1982 *Environment Canada: Its Evolving Mission,* the department pursues four principal objectives:

(1) ensure that human activities are conducted in a way that will achieve and maintain a state of the environment necessary for the health and well-being of man, the health and diversity of species and of ecosystems, and the sustained use of natural resources for social and economic benefit;

(2) conserve and enhance Canada's renewable resources of water, land, forests and wildlife and their related ecosystems and promote their wise use in a sustainable manner for economic and social benefit;

(3) facilitate the adaptation of human activities to the environment;

(4) protect for all time those places which are significant examples of Canada's natural and cultural heritage and encourage public understanding, appreciation and enjoyment of this heritage in ways which leave it unimpaired for future generations.

These are fine words, and they express sincere and important concepts. Yet they clearly have to be translated into something more tangible. In so doing, Environment Canada distinguishes between products and processes. Products comprise the concrete outputs from departmentally managed

programs. The term process is used to refer to its advisory and
advocacy roles and its many levers of influence.

The legislation for which Environment Canada is responsible covers an extremely wide range of activity:

> Legislation passed by Parliament and currently assigned to the
> Minister of the Environment, includes the Canada Water Act,
> the Canada Wildlife Act, the Clean Air Act, the Environmental
> Contaminants Act, the Forestry Development and Research Act,
> the Game Export Act, the International River Improvements
> Act, the Migratory Birds Convention Act, the National Parks
> Act, the Historic Sites and Monuments Act, the Ocean Dumping
> Control Act, and the Weather Modification Information Act.
> The department is also responsible for administering the pollu-
> tion control provisions of the Fisheries Act and for providing
> specific advice and information under certain sections of federal
> legislation assigned to other federal departments, such as the
> emissions provisions of the Motor Vehicle Safety Act (Ibid: 17).

The department has many ways of influencing what it has
called "the harmonization of human activity to the rhythms of
the interconnected global ecosystems." Apart from direct participation with other federal ministries, it has a major research
function, an expanding public consultation and information
availability policy, a network of wildlife, forestry and nature
interpretation centers, and so forth, together with active participation in a large number of management, advisory and consultative bodies. Additionally, there are three independent but
related bodies which report directly to the minister: the Canadian Environmental Advisory Council, the Canadian Forestry
Advisory Council, and the Federal Environmental Assessment
Review Office.

Because of its particular interest, we select for discussion
here the Central Environmental Advisory Council (CEAC).
(The Federal Environmental Assessment Review Office is discussed in a later section on environmental impact analysis.)

One interesting aspect of the Central Environmental
Advisory Council (CEAC) is that it is a very tangible manifestation of Environment Canada's concern for public interest and

support (discussed further in the following chapter on public participation). Without public support, and the political pressures which flow from this, Environment Canada would have little influence. Moreover, "public appreciation of environmental values increases with opportunities to experience examples of natural and cultural heritage unimpaired by exploitation. Consciousness of those values can foster harmony between society and its natural environment, and preserve options for the future" (Environment Canada 1982e: 6).

The council consists of sixteen members "representing a cross-section of Canadians who are knowledgeable and concerned about the environment including social and economic ramifications" (CEAC 1984). It meets about six times a year, usually with the minister to whom it acts in a confidential advisory capacity. It provides him with an alternative source of advice to that of his civil servant advisors.

> Advice to the minister has varied from formal recommendations for action to simple expressions of concern, and has spanned a broad spectrum of environmental concerns, including: the organization and mandate of the department, funding of citizens' groups, native rights claims, endangered species, air and water quality, the management of estuaries, the impact of open pit mining, spruce budworm spraying, shore zone management, the Migratory Birds Act, ecological reserves, the environmental aspects of foreign aid, a new national park on Ellesmere Island, biotechnology, a pollution-free community concept, control of access to Kluane Park, and land use policies (CEAC 1985: 36).

The council also maintains contact with environmental public interest groups and organizes periodic meetings, the proceedings of which are published (CEAC 1978). It also meets with provincial environmental advisory groups at which resolutions are passed for forwarding to the councils' respective ministers. Finally, mention should be made of its publications which, though small in number, are wide in range: from environmental ethics (1975 and 1977) to pest control (1981), and from ecotoxicity (1979) to water management (1983).

Environment Canada's *Strategic Plan 1985-89,* the third it has produced, lists seven priority issues for the second half of the eighties. The first priority is to deal with the problem of toxic substances. The basic strategy is to prevent toxic substances from entering the environment. To implement this, a reduction in the amount of toxic waste is advocated: "by the adoption of more conserving lifestyles, direct reuse, recycling and detoxification."

The second priority is to reduce acid deposition (acid rain). Negotiations to this end are to be conducted with the provinces and the United States.

Thirdly is the development of the key resource sector of forestry (transferred in 1984 by the new Conservative government to the Department of Agriculture). The forest sector accounts, directly and indirectly, for ten percent of Canadian employment and is by far the country's largest net export earner. The policy is to expand exports and eventually to achieve a self-sustaining and growing forest sector in Canada.

Water management is the fourth priority. It may well rise in the ranking of priorities since "fresh water could be the issue in the 1990s that energy was in the 1970s."

The fifth priority is climate change. The problem here is that increasing atmospheric pollutants, particularly carbon monoxide, present an acute climate problem on a world-wide scale. Carbon dioxide concentration levels are increasing by three percent per decade as a result of the burning of fossil fuels, deforestation and other changes in land use.

> This rate of increase may produce significant warming of the earth's surface within the economic lifetime of projects and structures now being planned and built. A warmer climate would expand growing and maritime transportation seasons in the north but, at the same time, it would increase aridity in the southern Prairies ...

The sixth priority is the protection of national heritage. Poetically, the strategic plan stresses that "a society's wealth comes not solely from its economic prowess, but from its contribution to knowledge, its pursuit of social justice, its cultural endeavors, and its ability to pass on its heritage from generation to generation." In more mundane terms, the policy is to extend the areas of protection, particularly by way of "the acquisition of national parks and wildlife conservation areas in the north."

Concern for the north is central to the seventh priority: "the environmental uniqueness and sensitivity of the area north of 60 ° N, its harsh climate and geography for economic development, and the federal government's broad responsibilities in the territories all make the north DoE priority." Three policy issues are to be emphasized: "northern conservation, environmentally sound technology, and appropriate resource use."

Federal government has a particular liking for elaborate policy statements and strategies such as this; and there is an obvious danger that the shadow of rhetoric may assume more significance than the substance of action. On the other hand, since much of the work of Environment Canada is of a persuasive, exhortatory and collaborative character, declarations of policy have a real utility.

The Provincial Role: Expanding Responsibilities

The general list of powers in the BNA Act makes clear the intention that local matters should be dealt with locally, while national matters are dealt with nationally. However, the net result is the absence of comprehensive jurisdictions at either level of government over all aspects of environmental management

Stein 1971

Stein, in the paper from which this quotation is taken, argues for a clear allocation of environmental management powers to a hierarchy of agencies, with a powerful role for the national level. He continues that "there has not, as yet, been any agreement on the establishment of agencies having environmental management jurisdiction delegated to them from both levels of government. Thus while the creation of an institutional framework for comprehensive environmental management is, through the techniques of delegation, constitutionally feasible, it has not yet become a political reality."

There are no signs that it may become so. Indeed, the increasing concern of the provinces with issues of environmental management is likely to make them wish to hold on to and develop these powers further, and independently. A historical point of relevance here is that environmental management has grown out of local public health concerns. Originally a local matter, except in major epidemics, the provinces became increasingly involved in the finance of public health services, particularly with the rapid rate of postwar urbanization. The scope of public health was at first limited to measures aimed at controlling disease. Thus, while control over water pollution became widespread, there was relatively little control over other types of pollution.

The 1950s, however, saw the beginning of a major change. It then "became apparent that pollution control involved more than ensuring safe domestic water supplies and effective waste disposal systems. Since water also served industry, agriculture, recreation, and wildlife, it was recognized that a public health focus, while important, was too narrow. The outcome was the establishment of specialized provincial agencies responsible for controlling pollution. The creation of the Ontario Water Resources Commission in 1956 set a precedent which was followed by other provinces" (Mitchell 1980: 51).

These agencies had a relatively short life before being reorganized as parts of new provincial ministries. Thus, the functions of the Ontario Water Resources Commission were transferred to a new Ministry of the Environment. In Newfoundland, the Clean Air, Water and Soil Authority had less than three years of operation before being replaced by a Department of Provincial Affairs and Environment in 1973. Similarly, responsibility for pollution control in Quebec was moved in 1972 from the Quebec Water Board to the Ministry of the Environment.

Mitchell comments that "this reorganization of responsibilities stresses an important aspect: the provincial approach to pollution control has steadily been broadened." While this is certainly true, the position varies between the provinces. In the following pages, a general account is given of the Ontario situation. This is followed by a discussion of the Environmental Council of Alberta.

The Ontario Environmental Protection Act

In April 1983, after a shutdown lasting ten months, Inco reopened: with a local unemployment rate of 33 percent there was good reason for reporting that "smoke from the 391 meter chimney is a welcome sight"

Globe and Mail (Toronto)

The Ontario Environmental Protection Act states its objectives in lofty terms: "the purpose of this act is to provide for the protection and conservation of the natural environment." However, this belies its rather modest provisions. Essentially, these are concerned with the protection of the natural environment against pollution, or "contaminants" as they are termed. Its limitations have been illustrated by Estrin and Swaigen (1978):

In general, the act does not protect parkland from overly intensive recreational use or resource exploitation, or prevent the filling of marshes, the flooding of land by dam-builders, changes in topography from soil erosion or road building, the manufacture or sale of toxic chemicals, damaging technological innovations, the squandering of scarce energy resources, and other acts of injury to the natural environment.

A statute which did all these things would be formidable indeed! Moreover, there are other acts, particularly the Environmental Assessment Act, which deal with some of these matters.

The Environmental Protection Act is concerned with contaminants, defined as " ... any solid, liquid, gas, odor heat, sound, vibration, radiation or combination of any of them resulting directly from the activities of man that may (1) impair the quality of the natural environment for any use that can be made of it; (2) cause injury or damage to property or to plant or animal life; (3) cause harm or material discomfort to any person, (4) adversely affect the health or impair the safety of any person; or, (5) render any property or plant or animal life unfit for use by man.

Such contamination is prohibited: "no person shall deposit in, add to, emit, or discharge into the natural environment any contaminants ... in an amount, concentration or level in excess of that prescribed by the regulations." A wide range of regulations have been issued, for example for air pollution, containers for carbonated soft drinks, discharge of sewage from pleasure boats, sulphur content of fuels, and transfers of liquid industrial waste.

The act gives the Minister of the Environment a broad array of powers to investigate, conduct research, and disseminate information on pollution problems, waste management, waste disposal, litter management and litter disposal. For instance, in conjunction with Environment Canada, studies have been undertaken in Toronto of the quality of the fill material entering the Leslie Street Spit (1982). Through the agency of the Ontario Waste Management Advisory Board, studies have been made of litter abatement programs, attitudes to recycling and resource conservation, and waste reduction (Rudolph 1979; Haussman Consulting 1979; Boston Gilbert Henry Associates 1980).

The major part of the act, however, is concerned with waste management. Two important questions arise here. What classes of contaminant, or source contamination, are excluded from control or are dealt with leniently? And how effective are the enforcement provisions?

The first question may not seem self-evidently important, but experience suggests that any regulatory system has to permit exemptions, either for administrative convenience (it is wasteful and possibly counter-productive to attempt to control all activities in a given class since many may be quite insignificant) or for practical reasons (it is impossible to abolish some undesirable things because the cost involves things which are even more undesirable). To illustrate: the Environmental Protection Act provides for certain exemptions in relation to the following sources of air pollution:

- equipment for the preparation of food in a domestic residence;
- fuel burning equipment used solely for the purpose of comfort heating in a dwelling used for the housing of not more than three families;
- equipment for construction or maintenance of a highway while the equipment is being used on the highway.

These examples also illustrate the legal (and legalistic) niceties which necessarily abound in this and similar fields.

Another exemption, of quite different character, relates to de-icing salt. This is, without question, a vicious contaminant: it rots cars, destroys shoes and clothing, causes pavement deterioration, kills trees and other vegetation and can seriously pollute drinking water. Winnipeg tried, in 1976-77, to do without de-icing salt, but the result was reportedly an increase in road accidents of eighty percent. Thus, despite its undesirable character as a contaminant, the Ontario Ministry of the Environment decided that it was necessary to make a specific exclusion:

> Where any substance used on a highway by the Crown as represented by the Minister of Transportation and Communications or any road authority ... for the purpose of keeping the highway safe for traffic under conditions of snow or ice or both is a contaminant, it is classified and is exempt from the provisions of the Act and the regulations (Estrin and Swaigen 1978: 194).

Hopefully, research will eventually discover an alternative to salt which does not have its deleterious effects.

Quite different, but politically more hazardous, is the clash that can arise between environmental protection and employment. A dramatic example of this in the Inco problem at Sudbury, where employment creates pollution, and clean air creates unemployment. Sudbury, however, is only one example, though it may be an extreme one. The basic point in cases such as this is that the benefits of pollution arise in a particular locality, while the costs are widespread. In different words, the costs of pollution control fall on a small area, in terms of unemployment and its multiplier effects, while the benefits are spread across a continent. This presents social and political problems of an acute nature.

So far as enforcement is concerned, the powers are extensive. "The ministry can issue certificates of approval, program approvals, control orders, stop orders, repair orders (informally known as 'clean up' orders) and equipment orders; and it can prosecute. The ministry also has the power to do anything itself that it may order the polluter to do, and do it at the polluter's expense. In addition, the ministry can ask the court for a restraint order" (Ibid: 32). But, how far are these powers used? And how are they used? Curiously, this is an aspect of government which is rarely studied; and annual reports, though useful, are typically limited.

There has been no lack of criticism of the misuse, or nonuse, of the powers, and though subscribers to conspiracy theories of government can find abundant material which they can profitably use, independent assessments are rare. It is, nevertheless, interesting to summarize an official version of the attempt of the Ontario Ministry of the Environment to police environmental controls.

At the beginning of 1981, the ministry established a special investigations unit. Thirteen officers were appointed to actively enforce environmental law "as they stake out illegal dump sites, clean up hazardous spills, and testify in court cases." These thirteen officers are designated "provincial offences officers," and can exercise a wide range of powers. They have the right of entry; they can obtain police assistance; they can examine books, documents and records necessary to their investigation, and remove samples, copies or extracts of documents.

The unit is separate from the ordinary staff of environment officers. Though the latter are also designated provincial offences officers and have the same power as members of the unit, they are more concerned with abatement, for example technical investigation such as the calculation of emissions and the pollutant loading of discharges. In the first year of operation (1981), the special investigations unit made 213 investigations and assisted environmental officers on a further 115.

> In addition they conducted 88 surveillances and investigated the operations of 1029 transporters of liquid industrial waste. The unit was responsible for laying 114 charges and assisted in a further 116, for a total of 230 charges. The courts have made decisions on 88 of these cases, resulting in 71 convictions ...

The Ontario Waste Management Corporation

NIMBY: Not In My Back Yard

Armour 1984

Policing environmental controls can be effective only if adequate facilities exist for waste disposal. Unfortunately, the siting of such facilities presents a range of technical and political problems, not the least of which is the violent reaction of people living near a proposed site. In the 1970s, evidence mounted about the harmful effects of toxic waste at the same time as the production of waste increased. As a result, large volumes of toxic wastes were discharged untreated into sewers or put into municipal landfills which were not properly equipped to dispose of them safely (OWMC 1982b).

In Ontario, an ad hoc body was established in 1981 to assist in dealing with the problems, the Ontario Waste Management Corporation. Its terms of reference are "to design, construct and operate a province-wide system for the treatment and disposal of liquid industrial waste and hazardous waste, and to develop a long term program to assist in the reduction and recycling of such wastes" (OWMC 1982a: 1). The announcement of the creation of the new corporation was made at the same time as the announcement of a site in South Cayuga, in the regional municipality of Haldimand-Norfolk, as the location for an industrial waste treatment and disposal facility.

The Cayuga announcement met with articulate and well-organized opposition, which the government's adroit decision to appoint a leading environmentalist (Donald Chant of Pollution Probe) as chairman of OWMC did not dispel. However, it did not take OWMC long to reject the Cayuga site as unsuitable. (OWMC was too polite to mention that the initial attraction of Cayuga was not unconnected with the fact that the site had been purchased by the provincial government for a new city which never materialized.)

The corporation not only rejected the Cayuga site: it also decided that its task involved far more than the search for an alternative. It took the view that a good waste management program should not be led by the need for finding locations for secure landfill: a landfill site was seen as only part of a comprehensive waste management system (and, indeed, preferably a small part). The other main components of the system were to include the development of waste abatement and recycling procedures and technologies, and collection and treatment facilities. The proposed facilities comprise three major components: a rotary kiln incineration plant, a physical/chemical treatment plant which includes a solidification facility, and an engineered landfill for treated waste (OWMC 1982b).

The first step *(Phase I)* was to identify and measure waste generation and management in the province. Since it was immediately apparent that existing statistical sources were inadequate, some basic studies had to be undertaken. A "waste quantities" study was undertaken to provide a comprehensive and detailed basis for planning. A definition of waste was determined that captured "all the types of waste posing potential danger to human health or the environment." This involved a new concept of *special waste:* "all non-radioactive waste that cannot properly be treated and disposed of by conventional municipal facilities, such as sewage treatment plants, municipal incinerators, and municipal landfills. Such special waste is distinguished from conventional waste by requiring treatment and disposal technologies that are not currently available in the public sector in Ontario" (OWMC 1983a).

This is one of the subjects under study by OWMC. Another, of course, is the selection of sites. This has to be undertaken without regard to administrative boundaries. The *Phase 2 Report* noted that about seventy percent of Ontario's special waste is generated in and around the so-called Golden Horseshoe at the west end of Lake Ontario, stretching from Oshawa to Fort Erie). The initial step in site selection was based on the fact that "because the costs of transporting special waste on public roads are significant and increase in proportion to the distance travelled, there would have to be strong compensating reasons to consider locating outside the Golden Horseshoe area." (There was also a principle involved here: the "social justice" of treating wastes in the region in which they are generated.) However, this was subject to the important qualification that, if satisfactory sites could not be found in the area, the search would be extended over a wider area. This simple sounding statement is the basic rationale for a wide ranging regional approach to an issue such as waste disposal.

Eight "candidate sites" were identified in the *Phase 3 Report* published in 1984. At the time of writing these are being subjected to detailed study. The preferred site, or sites, will be announced in a *Phase 4 Report*. (The first part of this was published in 1985.) This will be followed by a period of further "on-the-land-site-specific testing" before the corporation makes a final siting recommendation to a hearing panel on industrial waste management (1984b).

In the meantime (June 1983) the Ontario Ministry of the Environment issued a *Blueprint for Waste Management in Ontario* which, following "full public participation" will be finalized for implementation. The blueprint is a comprehensive plan with proposed controls and regulations covering the full spectrum of waste management from generation through recycling to post-disposal environmental security.

A Provincial Environmental Council: Alberta

The Council ... shall conduct a continuing review of policies and programs of the Government ...

Environment Council of Alberta Act 1980

An earlier section contained a brief discussion of the Central Environmental Advisory Council, and reference was made to its periodic meetings with provincial environmental advisory groups. In this section, one of these is selected for examination. The choice fell to Alberta because of the range and quality of its publications: these provide a good picture of its activities and its role in environmental management in the province.

The Environment Council of Alberta (ECA) is an appointed body which reports to the Minister of the Environment. It is required by the Environment Council Act to carry out an ongoing review of government environmental policies and programs. It does this by a variety of means, including the holding of public hearings, and by research studies carried out either by its own staff or by consultants.

Public hearings, followed by the publication of a report and recommendations have been held on the environmental effects of the operation of sulphur extraction gas plants in the province; the use of pesticides and herbicides; erosion of land in northwestern Alberta; management of water resources within the Oldman River Basin; the management and disposal of hazardous waste; noise in Alberta; the agricultural land base in Alberta and so forth. Additionally there have been special reports, staff reports, conference proceedings, and reports from a number of advisory committees.

The latter constitute a network of contacts between all relevant organizations in the province. The ECA refers to them as advisors and assistants who make up an early warning system for the council and the government.

Clearly ECA is a body of substance. (Its 1983 salary bill was over $700,000; its total expenditure in that year was $1,243,000.) It is also clearly very close to the machinery of the provincial government, but it links with the public in various ways such as the advisory committees and the public hearings.

Environmental Impact Assessment

Environmental assessment law is at a crossroads in Canada

Emond 1978

New terms frequently serve the purpose of giving fresh impetus to old ideas. So it is with environmental impact assessment (EIA). Conceived in the United States and adopted in Canada, most significantly in Ontario's 1975 Environmental Assessment Act, the basic concept is that of assessing the impacts of a plan or a project. This is essentially the same idea as the "survey before plan" which is (or should be) the essential first step in any area of urban and regional planning. It differs in that it is, usually, focused on a limited matter, though this could be as minor as an access road or as major as an airport (Budden and Ernst 1973). Unlike most environmental controls it operates before rather than after the event: it seeks to prevent environmental damage rather than clear up afterwards.

Ontario was the first province to pass an Environmental Assessment Act, in 1975. Quebec followed in 1978, in an amendment to the Environment Quality Act. Saskatchewan and Newfoundland passed environmental assessment acts in 1980, and British Columbia did likewise in 1981. Other provinces have used or adapted existing legislation to produce the same results, while New Brunswick, Manitoba and the federal government have introduced environmental assessment by policy directives.

These legalistic variations are of little interest: what is of significance is, first, that all provinces by one means or another have introduced some form of environmental assessment, or environmental impact assessment, hereafter referred to as EA or EIA; and, secondly, that there are substantial differences in its use between the ten provinces, plus, in this instance, the federal government.

There is no intention to plough through the eleven separate sets of procedures. Instead a selection is made, starting, in a conventional manner, with the federal level.

Curiously, and despite its long and impressive title, *The Federal Environmental Assessment Review Process* (EARP), there is no specific federal legislation on environmental assessment. It (i.e. EARP) was introduced at the end of 1973, and amended by Cabinet decision in 1977 and 1984. Its purpose is "to ensure that the environmental consequences of all federal projects, programs and activities are assessed before final decisions are made, and to incorporate the results of these assessments into planning, decision-making and implementation." The term environment includes both the bio-physical and the social though, as we shall see, the state of the art of social impact assessment is rudimentary.

The first phase of EARP, known as the screening phase, is based on self-assessment: the federal agency screens all its undertakings for potentially significant adverse environmental effects. In so doing it is expected to arrange for public comment. If it is left unclear whether the impacts will be significant, a more searching screening study is carried out, again by the agency itself. This "initial environment evaluation" settles the issue one way or another. Only if the agency decides that there are significant effects does the next stage of EARP come into operation. This is the referring of the proposal to the Federal Environment Assessment Review Office, which has the nice acronym of FEARO: perhaps to instil some respect for the proceedings on the part of the agencies concerned?

The reference to FEARO starts the formal review phase. A panel is appointed by FEARO. Its first task is to draw up guidelines for the preparation of an environmental impact statement (EIS) specifically for the project which has been referred. These guidelines deal with the proposed content and detailed terms of reference for EIS preparation. They are subject to consultation with interested parties and arrangements are made for public input.

Once these are complete, an EIS is prepared in conformity with them by the agency concerned. This is then submitted to the panel and all interested parties, including the public. Open public meetings may be held by the panel and a variety of techniques used for obtaining public participation (as discussed in chapter 11). Oral and written briefs are received. Finally, the panel prepares its report together with recommendations. The decision is made by the minister of the agency concerned after Cabinet discussion in important cases.

A good illustration of the operation of federal procedures is provided by the case of the proposal to twin the Trans-Canada Highway through part of the Banff national park (FEARO 1982c).

It is perhaps surprising that there is any major highway through the national park. Partly it could be because environmental concerns were not so prominent when the road was built in 1960; but there was little alternative, and the national parks policy "accepts, as one of the facts of economic life, that transportation routes through the mountain parks are required in the national interest" (Ibid: 49). (The mountain parks are Banff, Jasper, Kootenay, and Yoho.)

More confusing is the maze of shared responsibility. Though the federal Ministry of Transport has responsibility for the Trans-Canada Highway, new construction is undertaken by Public Works, while maintenance and operation rests with Parks Canada. But that is not all: in the plaintive words of a

Transport   Canada spokesman at the panel hearings: " ...
there's a fundamental problem here in that there are three jurisdictions.   There's the province of Alberta, the province of
British Columbia, and the federal government; and within the
federal government, there are at least two and maybe up to five
or six jurisdictions involved." This causes problems of coordination and planning which were repeatedly raised during the panel
hearings, and on which the panel made recommendations (which
are summarized later). Formally, however, the proposal was
made by Public Works Canada for the twinning of fourteen
kilometers of the highway. An earlier review had approved the
twinning of the first thirteen kilometers from the park's east
gate: the additional twinning is an extension of this (FEARO
1979).

The panel for this review consisted of a FEARO official,
who acted as chairman, a retired director of transportation of
Public Works Canada, the Chief of Management Planning for
the western region of Parks Canada, a professor of environmental science from the University of Calgary, and an official of the
Canadian Wildlife Service. As is apparent, the panel was of
high technical competence in a variety of relevant fields.

In the spring of 1981, meetings were held with all
interested parties to discuss the review, and in August 1981 the
EIS prepared by Public Works Canada was made available. A
variety of public meetings was held both locally and in Calgary.
Senior department officials from Public Works and Parks
Canada attended throughout and made numerous presentations.
Private consultants who had contributed to the EIS gave evidence, as did Transport Canada representatives. Presentations
were made by environmental, transportation and business
groups. The total transcript of the proceedings extended to 685
pages.

Among the many issues raised, the most important of
course was the need for twinning the road. There was much
technical material on this, but also some clear differences in
attitude. A representative for the Alberta Trucking Association
referred to sixty-one deaths on the "overtaxed Trans-Canada"

and the big contribution which the twinning would make "towards reducing this type of carnage." A spokesman for the Sierra Club of Western Canada, on the other hand, argued: "at some point it must be recognized, even by DPW, that the quality of the national park must take priority over transportation needs, particularly the convenience of pleasure motorists causing traffic congestion, and numbers of tourists flocking to use the park. Transportation has reached this decision point. A four-lane freeway destroys the very values being protected by the park." There were also suggestions for alternative roads, spot improvements and a major expansion in public transport. The panel noted the potential of the latter as a long term alternative to further expansion of the highway, but concluded that "because of existing traffic congestion problems and the absence of immediately available feasible alternatives, the need for twinning" had been demonstrated (but only up to km 23: more study was required of the stretch from km 23 to km 27).

Considerable emphasis was placed, however, on the need for coordination between all the agencies involved, and on better and more comprehensive planning. There were several elements here. First there was the piecemeal approach (east gate to km 13; followed by km 13 to km 27; with future investigation of twinning beyond km 27). This was defended by Public Works on the basis of environmental concerns and the need to proceed with care. Secondly, related to the first point but on a much larger scale, was the concern for comprehensive consideration of various transportation options through the Rocky Mountains. The panel pointedly remarked that "Transport Canada has the mandate for general transportation matters." Thirdly, was the lack of concern for the cumulative effects of different development within the park. Here the panel noted that " ... cumulative demands being placed upon the park resources could eventually reach a point in certain locations, where the resources could no longer be maintained through management practices. Thus, the panel foresees that there would be advantages to considering future proposals of human activities in the project area in a broader context" (Ibid: 23). The report concludes with a long list of detailed recommendations designed to safeguard the environment or, at the least, to mitigate undesirable effects. To assist in this, stress was laid on monitoring and evaluation (to be a clear responsibility of Parks Canada).

Despite this lengthy account, there is much more in the report. Sufficient has been noted, however, to give a picture of the scope and nature of the process. Attention now turns to the Ontario scene.

Environmental Assessment in Ontario

Ontario's Environment Assessment Act is an attractive piece of paper. You can wrap gifts in it, start fires with it, and mail it to your friends. When the Legislature adopted it in 1975, there was even speculation the act could be used to safeguard the environment

Globe and Mail (Toronto)

The Ontario Environmental Assessment Act applies to all projects, statutorily termed "undertakings," of the province, municipalities and public bodies, as well as to certain major private works. Environmental assessments must be prepared for all public undertakings, unless exempted by order or regulation. For private sector undertakings, the reverse is the case: only those undertakings specifically or generally designated by regulation are covered by the act.

The process includes the submission of an environmental assessment to the Minister of the Environment; its review by relevant government departments and agencies, public inspection and comment, and possibly a hearing by the Environmental Assessment Board. Two separate decisions are involved here. First, there is the question of whether the environmental assessment document is to be accepted, with or without amendment. Secondly, there is the approval, or otherwise, of an undertaking.

An environmental assessment is acceptable if it provides an adequate basis on which to base the decisions regarding the approval of the undertaking, i.e. the second decision.

The act requires that the environmental assessment shall consist of:

(a)   a description of the purpose of the undertaking;

(b)   a description of and a statement of the rationale for the undertaking; the alternative methods of carrying out the undertaking; and the alternatives to the undertaking;

(c)   a description of the environment that will be affected or that might reasonably be expected to be affected, directly or indirectly; the effects that will be caused or that might reasonably be expected to be caused to the environment; and the actions necessary or that may reasonably be expected to be necessary to prevent, change, mitigate or remedy the effects that might reasonably be expected upon the environment, by the undertaking, the alternative methods of carrying out the undertaking and the alternatives to the undertaking; and

(d)   an evaluation of the advantages and disadvantages to the environment of the undertaking, the alternative methods of carrying out the undertaking and the alternatives to the undertaking.

The ministry's guidelines show the following steps:

(1)   identify purpose;

(2)   identify alternatives;

(3)   study environment which may be affected by alternatives;

(4)   identify effects of alternatives on the environment;

(5)   identify mitigation possibilities for alternatives;

(6)   evaluate alternatives in terms of their positive and negative effects on the environment;

(7)   decide on most acceptable alternative;

(8)   prepare EA document and submit;

(9)   if approved, implement with all practical mitigation;

(10) monitor.

In fact, a secondary process may be interjected between the eighth and ninth steps. When the review of an EA is completed, both the EA and the review are put on the public record, and a minimum of thirty days is allowed for written submissions. At this stage, the matter may be referred to the Environmental Assessment Board. Alternatively, the minister may decide to accept the EA. If he does, he has then, with Cabinet approval, also to decide whether to approve the proposed undertaking and any conditions which are to be attached. If a hearing is held, both the acceptance and approval decisions are made by the Environmental Assessment Board, though there is power for the minister to overrule the board, again subject to Cabinet approval.

Some statistics may assist in placing these various alternatives in perspective. In the year 1980-81, twenty-two reviews were completed and published on undertakings for which environmental assessments were submitted. Twelve undertakings were given approval to proceed, subject to conditions. In all of these cases, the initial assessment and review process resolved all areas of concern so that public hearings were neither requested nor required. Twenty formal submissions, six resubmissions and nine draft submissions were received on undertakings for approval under the act. Four undertakings were referred to the board for public hearings at the request of the public, and the first two hearings of the board under the Environmental Assessment Act were completed. Between 1982 and 1984 three hearings were held.

These numbers may seem small and, indeed, by U.S. standards they certainly are. The reason is that, in the light of early experience in the U.S. with the National Environment Policy Act, great care was taken to devise a screening system which would exempt insignificant developments and also provide reasonable legal certainty as to what was subject to the act and what was exempt.

Where doubts remain, proponents are encouraged to consult informally. There is also an Environmental Assessment Advisory Committee appointed, in July 1983, by the Premier, which advises on the granting of exemptions, particularly in relation to effects on public health, safety and the environment.

All guidelines, notices of completion of an EAR, notices of acceptance of an EAR, notices of approval to proceed with an undertaking, exemptions and regulations, are published in the ministry's *EA Update*.

The Ontario Environmental Assessment Board

The Ontario procedures for participation and decision-making ... include an independent board with the power to make decisions, and the public are given a full opportunity to both state their general objections and examine the technical details of the proposed project

Emond 1978

The Environmental Assessment Board is a multi-purpose body. It conducts hearings, usually of a technical nature, under the Environmental Assessment Act, the Environmental Protection Act (waste disposal sites) and the Ontario Water Resources Act (water and sewage plants). Recommendations are made to the Minister of the Environment. It also conducts hearings under the Environmental Assessment Act where it is required to determine whether an environmental assessment is adequate, and to decide whether a proposed undertaking should proceed. In contrast to the other hearings, the board's function here is a decision-making, not an advisory one. The passing of the Consolidated Hearings Act 1981 added another category of hearing. This act is aimed at streamlining the approval process by providing for a consolidated hearing where otherwise more than one hearing would be statutorily required. Finally, the board hears matters referred to it by Cabinet through orders-in-council (Ontario Environmental Assessment Board 1983).

Hearings under the Environmental Protection Act and the Ontario Water Resources Act, of which there were twenty in 1983-84, typically result in a recommendation for approval subject to conditions designed to avoid or mitigate environmental damage.

The Consolidated Hearings Act covers twelve separate pieces of legislation. It provides that, where more than one hearing is required, a consolidated hearing by a joint board can be arranged by the chairman of the Environmental Assessment Board and the Ontario Municipal Board. The joint board is made up of members of either or both of these boards. The first hearing under this act began at the end of 1981. It concerned an undertaking by Ontario Hydro to expand the Eastern Ontario Transmission System. As reported in the board's annual report for 1981-82, "the undertaking would consist of the planning of, selection of locations for, acquisition of property rights for, and the design, construction, operation and maintenance of additional bulk electricity system facilities in Eastern Ontario, including switching and transformer stations, communication and control facilities, transmission lines and related facilities." The application was made pursuant to the Environmental Assessment Act, the Planning Act, and the Expropriations Act.

Social Impact Assessment

> ... a field which must continue to evolve before widely accepted and tested analytical frameworks are possible
>
> FEARO 1982a

Environmental impact assessment systems are under constant pressure to extend their terms of reference. It is now common for social, economic and cultural issues to be dealt with. As the quotation above suggests, however, the available techniques are not well developed (Ontario Hydro 1983). Partly this is because these wider issues make conflicts explicit, and very clearly involve trade-offs. For a brief time cost-benefit analysis seemed to offer a technical solution, but this quickly fell into disrepute, partly because its limitations were not clarified. It would now be generally accepted that its role is a restricted one, and most would agree with Rapport and Friend (1979) that "from the environmental perspective, the cost-benefit approach is deemed insufficient and occasionally utterly inappropriate and irrelevant. We should note here that many very important decisions that society must make, for example in the area of human rights, would hardly be argued rationally on the basis of cost-benefit calculations. Similarly, I suggest that the integrity of ecosystems and the extinction of species are not appropriately subject to a cost-benefit calculation." The same applies, a fortiori, to social considerations.

Perhaps the most bizarre case of the indefensible use of the cost-benefit calculus is that of the Ford Motor Company's approach to improving the safety of the Pinto and Bobcat cars:

> The $11-per-vehicle cost of meeting a proposed U.S. standard for fuel tank leakage in rollover accidents was unjustified on the basis of the standard, estimated as the elimination of 180 burn deaths a year, 180 serious burn injuries, and the destruction of 2,100 cars a year in accidents. The value of a life saved was taken to be $200,000; of a serious burn injury, $67,000; and of the damage to vehicles, $700 per car. Applying these values to the estimated effects of the standard, produced a total annual benefit valuation of $49.5 million: far less than the projected annual cost of meeting the standard ($137 million) (Schrecker 1984: 45).

Nevertheless, it is easy to make heavy weather of the essentially simple question of the impact of a proposed development on the people who live in the area. That some will gain and some will lose is likely. (The unemployed of a rural village will welcome an industrial development which those who have retired to an attractive quiet rural retreat will find abhorrent.) Social and public services may be affected, and there may be problems on who is to pay for these. Indeed, much social impact assessment is concerned with either employment or services. An

illustration can be given from the community assessment part
of the EAR of the expansion of the uranium mines in the Elliot
Lake area of northern Ontario (Ontario Environmental Assessment Board 1979).

At the time of the review (1977-79) it was expected that as
a result of the expansion of the mines the population of Elliot
Lake would increase from 10,700 in 1977 to 23,700 in 1984, and
to 30,000 by 1988. The first, and eminently sensible, recommendation of the Environmental Assessment Board was that
population changes should be carefully monitored and analyzed.
The services required would be dependent on the rate and character of the growth. Much of the report, in fact, consists of a
discussion and recommendations concerning these services: housing (quantity and affordability); mobile homes; water supply
(and the danger of pollution from the mines); sewage; waste
disposal; schools; and health services. Additionally, there is a
proposal for the establishment of a social planning council, and
for an examination of the possibilities of an industrial
diversification strategy for Elliot Lake.

Of course, there are developments where the social impact
assessment has to deal with very much more difficult issues.
The Berger Commission on the Mackenzie Valley Pipeline
(1977) for instance, concluded that the construction of the pipeline should be postponed for ten years "in order to strengthen
native society, the native economy (indeed, the whole resource
sector) and to enable native land claims to be settled" (Berger
1978: 644). Indeed, in inquiries of this nature it becomes meaningless to isolate the social as if it were something distinctly
separate. As Paehlke has noted in relation to the James Bay
project, the hunting and fishing of the Cree Indians was more
than a means of earning a living. "They constitute a way of
life. Their whole culture and consciousness is bound up with a
particular place. For the Cree, environmental impacts and
social impacts are inseparable" (Paehlke 1980: 143). Many of
the federal EARs have been in areas of northern Canada where
this is the typical situation (Waddell 1981).

There is another extremity of social impact analysis which has not (as yet) arisen in Canada: this is the psychological impact doctrine, which emerged in the U.S. following the Three Mile Island accident (Kinsley 1982). Curiously, the issue related not to the Unit Two reactor which malfunctioned, but to the neighboring Unit One reactor which happened to be shut down for refueling at the time of the accident in March 1979. Except for one short period, it has remained shut ever since, awaiting approval by the Nuclear Regulatory Commission (NRC) for it to become fully operational. A group called People Against Nuclear Energy (PANE) successfully argued before the court that the reopening of the undamaged unit would create severe psychological distress and aggravate the post-traumatic neurosis which was still being suffered because of the accident at the other unit. The court ruled that NRC must make a preliminary study of PANE's psychological concerns and, if necessary, mount a full-fledged EIS covering the social concerns.

Kinsley (1982) quotes another case of a group of law students in North Carolina who filed papers to deny an operating license for a nuclear plant on the grounds that they "must study long and hard to prepare for their classes," and the thought of a nuclear plant operating nearby "will detract from their studies."

Differently minded activists have used similar arguments against environmental regulations on the grounds that their social impact is to raise costs and therefore eliminate jobs.

The nearest that Canadian experience has got to this is with the not uncommon reduction of pollution controls to safeguard employment. A notorious case was that arising from the injunction obtained by a downstream landowner near Espanola against the Kalamazoo Vegetable Parchment Company. In this so-called KVP case, the injunction restrained the discharge of pollutants into the Spanish River. The injunction was upheld by the Supreme Court of Canada. The mill was the main employer in the town, and the resulting political pressure led to a quick reaction by the Ontario government which passed a special statute dissolving the injunction and granting the mill permission   to pollute *(McKie v K.V.P. Company* [1984] O.R. 398 (H.C.) and *K.V.P. v McKie* [1949] S.C.R. 698).

New Brunswick went further along this path by enacting a blanket provision preventing "individuals from applying for injunctions which if granted, would delay or prevent the construction or operation of any manufacturing or industrial plant on the ground that the discharge from such plant is injurious to some other interest" (Emond 1975: 70).

A discussion of social impact analysis leads into the fascinating area of compensation for those affected by pollution. On this the reader is referred to Swaigen's study for the Economic Council of Canada (1981).

The Limits of Environmental Impact Assessments

The scientific community has the uncomfortable feeling that the institutional framework for environmental impact assessment is in place before the scientific base has been established

Munn 1975

It is apparent from the lengthy discussion above that the field of environmental impact assessment is a large and burgeoning one. A fuller analysis might lead to suggestions that it is getting out of hand, that it involves far too much discretion, that it involves too little follow-up monitoring and evaluation, that it obscures essentially political issues (as did cost-benefit analysis), that it represents a triumph of procedure over substance, that it is prodigious in its use of the time of professionals, developers and the public ... The list could easily be extended. Here some observations are offered on two major points: the quasi-scientific nature of EIA, and its role in the larger decision making process.

Whether EIA should be, should not be, or is not, scientific are different questions. Writings on EIA tend to implicitly assume a set of answers, typically without any acknowledgement of the underlying assumptions. Thus, the quotation at the head of this section suggests that the author, R.E. Munn, thinks that EIA should be scientific but that it is not so. Beanlands and Duinker, who quote him, are more explicit:

> Any substantial upgrading of the scientific quality of environmental impact assessment is to some degree constrained by the lack of common perspective among the participating groups. From a scientific perspective, the basic dilemma is that environmental impact assessment is the result of public pressure and political motivation; its origins cannot be traced back to either the requirements or outputs of science. Therefore, at one end of the spectrum are the government administrators who tend to see environmental assessment as the fulfillment of the required procedures or guidelines. At the other extreme are the research scientists who become involved in the development and review of impact assessment documents but often doubt whether it is an acceptable forum in which to rigorously apply the scientific method. From an industrial perspective, impact assessment is tied directly to project approval and licensing. Caught in the middle are the consultants who are expected to practice good science in a politically motivated system (1975: 2).

This is tantamount to arguing that EIA ought to be scientific but faces two obstacles: a lack of data, and the machinations of politicians. In fact, the first obstacle is likely to be permanent, if not inherent. The second is an obstacle only on the assumptions made. It ceases to be such if it is accepted that EIA is a part of the policy making and political process.

More to the point is Mitchell's question, "which actions should be required to have assessments?" He notes that "most procedures have focused upon assessments for projects, whereas many feel that policies and programs should be reviewed for their environmental consequences." He continues that "scale is another factor ... ; several small projects in isolation may create minimum environmental disturbance. When their cumulative effect is considered, their impact may be significant" (Mitchell 1980: 58).

These are substantive and much more difficult issues to address. Indeed, it seems unlikely that they can be answered in general terms. Nevertheless, it can be questioned whether an

EIA process is appropriate for the examination of policies and programs. Surely these are more appropriately considered at the parliamentary level? Unfortunately, the line between policy and administration is a fine one, and it is not easy to make distinctions between matters for local consideration within a given policy framework and matters which constitute this framework. A nice illustration is afforded by the Canadian Pacific Rail Rogers Pass review (FEARO 1982b). This development was agreed to be an urgent one, though it was also agreed that no work "which might prejudice good environmental design" should be undertaken before the panel had completed its final report. Procedures were changed to allow the panel "to identify the activities which C.P. Rail might immediately undertake without prejudicing a final recommendation as to the best way for the project to proceed."

The panel was apparently undaunted by this Solomon-like task. More significantly they accepted without demur the stated need for the project (which had been approved by the Canadian Transport Commission). In their words: "in view of the Canadian Transport Commission decision and the terms of reference provided by the minister, the panel has not examined the project rationale further." There is a clear contrast here with the Banff Highway review, where the panel was concerned to establish whether a need for the project was demonstrated. The two examples shatter any neat division between policy and administration. The real distinction is between the politically important (getting ahead with the C.P. Rogers Pass) and the politically less important (twinning the Trans-Canada Highway).

This short discussion suggests that there is a hierarchy of matters ranging from high policy (i.e. of top political importance) to minor. The procedures for debating and deciding upon them will vary, as will the degrees of scientific and political input. It is unfortunate that words are used in such an undisciplined manner and that a huge chunk of the machinery of government can be said to be subject to environmental impact assessment. When the term environment is used in its broadest sense, the mind boggles at the prospect of making any sense at all of EIA.

The matter is an important one to which we return in the next chapter. For the present, the point has been made that concepts pertaining to assessment have been stretched beyond manageable bounds. The result is widespread confusion which extends to the second point raised at the beginning of this section, namely the role of EIA in the larger decision-making process. Some critics have argued that "the fundamental weakness in existing environmental impact assessment processes is that they have been imposed as an overlay upon existing decision-making processes" (Fox 1979: 72). FEARO (1982: 42) explicitly denies this: indeed it points with obvious pride to the way in which EIA has been fully integrated into the decision-making process.

The differences are partly due to differing perspectives and simple problems of semantics. Mitchell again puts the issue clearly: how should environmental assessment be coordinated with other policies? (1980: 58). But the simplicity of the question belies its complexity. The issues are basically the same as those which arose with the attempts to devise Urban Canada policies. Their fate is recorded in chapter 2. Any attempt at fully integrated, coordinated environmental policies would undoubtedly fare similarly. There are limits to the applicability of rational models of behavior in a unitary government system: these limits are narrower in a federal state.

One final set of issues relating to EIAs require discussion here. Since they focus on impacts they inevitably raise questions of costs and benefits, in both monetary and non-monetary terms. This then leads into the question of whether environmental policies should be implemented by way of financial incentives and penalties rather than via the more usual regulatory system.

Environmental Regulation or Pricing?

Many people simply do not believe that if you raise the price of
pollution, firms will pollute less

Dewees 1980

A great deal has been written on the determination of
environmental standards (and objectives, criteria, guidelines
etc). The setting of standards is a mix of technical and socio-
political factors. It raises questions of science (cause and effect),
of quality, of enforceability, and of evaluation. Here we deal
with the debate on pricing versus regulation.

The starting point is the alleged inefficiency of regulatory
mechanisms. The allegations are typically made by economists
who point out that "pollution control is accomplished through
established standards and emission rates, negotiated between
the polluter and the regulator, often in camera. The problem
with this form of regulation, and indeed with all forms, is that
it is sometimes difficult to measure the environmental damage,
to detect the causes of pollution, and to relate them to their
sources" (Economic Council of Canada 1981: 93).

Much criticism has been directed at this bargaining process. "The public and the victims of pollution have no right to
participate in negotiations over the terms and conditions" and,
indeed, may have great difficulty in finding out what they are.
Harsh standards may be threatened and publicized, yet may be
minimal when actually applied. If the public can be kept in
ignorance there is a happy result for the politicians: the
environmentalists are pleased at the loud bark and the polluters
are satisfied with the small bite. On the other hand, positive
advantages have been claimed for bargaining. It permits flexibility in operation and can thus allow for legitimate differences
between individual polluters. A general category of this is the
harsher standards often applied to new as distinct from existing
industries or processes; but this, of course, is hardly a matter
of flexibility.

Bargaining can also act as "an interface between the technology and economics of pollution control, which until this stage have been considered in isolation." Franson et al (1982: 42) suggest that because of "the perceived need for confidentiality about financial matters, this may be the first opportunity given to the regulatory authority to consider the effects of proposed effluent standards and prospective expenditures on a particular discharger's competitive position within the Canadian economy, and, if standards for an entire industry are being set, to consider collectively that industry's position in the world market." Additionally the bargaining process can assist in plugging what Thompson has called "knowledge gaps" (1980: 37). New sources of data can be obtained by persuasion.

Finally, it can be argued that the bargaining process involves at least a crude implicit form of the balancing of costs and benefits. In other words, by negotiation, a degree of regulation is achieved which involves costs for the polluter which are reasonable in relation to the benefits accruing to the public.

These arguments have some force, but they understate the powerful position of a polluter who can argue that, beyond a point, controls can make his enterprise uneconomic. Threats of legal action might be made by the controlling agency in extreme cases, but they are infrequently used. The objective is to win over the industries concerned, not to alienate them. In any case, legal proceedings are costly, time-consuming, and of uncertain outcome.

Furthermore, it has been known for political relationships between government parties and industrialists to be such that an unfriendly stance would be unexpected.

The Organization for Economic Cooperation and Development has for long advocated the use of charges (1975). Canada, which is a member of OECD, agreed in 1974 to the implementation of the polluter-pays principle as "a fundamental principle for allocating costs of pollution prevention and control measures introduced by the public authorities." There has been little positive action following this, partly if not mainly because, as Dewees has pointed out, "there seems to be a strong consensus that the electorate will perceive simple direct regulatory action as more effective than charges or rights. That this belief may be erroneous will be of little interest to the serious politician" (Dewees 1980: 25).

Heritage Conservation

Canada, it is said, is long on geography, but short on history

Heritage conservation predates environmental impact assessment by many years, but the reviews required for EIAs, and particularly the public participation involved, has significantly enlarged active consideration for heritage. Though this specific term may not appear in the EIA legislation, there is no doubt that it is included. EIAs, of course, do not apply to all parts of government or to most private developments. There has, however, been an increasing amount of legislation on heritage conservation in recent years.

The term heritage, like environment, is an elastic one, and thus it is relatively easy for practice to evolve with changing attitudes. In British Columbia's Heritage Conservation Act, it is defined to mean "of historic, architectural, archeological, palaeontological, or scenic significance." More elaborately, Alberta's Historical Resources Act defines historic resource as "any work of nature or man, that is primarily of value for its palaeontological, archeological, prehistoric, historic, cultural, natural, scientific or aesthetic interest." By contrast, Ontario characteristically avoids definition: its Heritage Act simply provides that the Minister of Culture and Recreation "may determine policies, priorities and programs for the conservation, protection and preservation of the heritage of Ontario."

At the federal level, the Historic Sites and Monuments Act provides for the designation of sites of national significance. The federal situation, however, dramatically shows that definitions are of less interest than powers. Since property rights are the constitutionally exclusive responsibility of the provinces, federal designation has no legal effect. Thus the owner of a federally designated site is under no restrictions, other than moral ones, to keep it in good condition or even to safeguard it from demolition. (The Rideau Street Convent in Ottawa was demolished three days after it was named a national historic site: Estrin and Swaigen 1978: 384).

Provincial designations, on the other hand, normally impose legal restrictions on the future use of the property. The Applebaum-Hébert Report on Federal Cultural Policy (1982) recommended that the law be changed:

> The Department of the Environment now has the authority to prevent the destruction of Canada's natural heritage through the duly authorized environmental assessment and review process. A similar process should now be established in law to give protection to designated historic and archeological sites from unconsidered alteration or destruction ... Existing federal legislation relating to the designation of historic sites should be strengthened to compel heritage impact studies to be carried out and reviewed before any such site is sold, developed or in any way altered from its present use.

No action has been taken on this recommendation.

Before leaving the federal scene, note needs to be taken of further curiosities. The first is that federally owned lands are not subject to provincial laws. In the words of Estrin and Swaigen (1978: 385), the federal government's lack of legal responsibility "is one of Canada's greatest legal anomalies ... The situation is curious in another respect: the 1954 International Convention of the Hague obliges other countries in the world to respect the landmarks of a Canadian province, but our own federal government is under no such obligation. Strictly speaking, Bulgaria bears a greater legal duty to the Canadian heritage than does the federal government. In the United States and Australia, the governments enacted sweeping legislation to protect historic and architectural sites threatened by any federal project." Canada established a study committee: the Federal Advisory and Coordinating Committee on Heritage Preservation.

Since heritage conservation is almost entirely a provincial matter, each province operates under its own legislation. There are, of course, differences but, in this case, the differences are wide, though they may be narrowing. For instance, Nova Scotia's earlier Historic Properties Designation Act provided no controls over the demolition or alteration of designated properties. The 1980 Heritage Property Act not only prohibits unauthorized demolition or alteration of properties which have been designated, but also does likewise, for a temporary period, for a property which has been formally recommended for designation. The Saskatchewan act makes provision for heritage resource impact assessments. Alberta provides compensation in cases where designation decreases the economic value of a building. Here attention is focused on British Columbia, Ontario and Quebec.

Heritage Conservation in British Columbia

> Preservation can become business, but business always comes before preservation
>
> Holdsworth 1980

The British Columbia Heritage Act was passed in 1977. It provides for both provincial and municipal heritage conservation. In the case of a provincial heritage site, a permit is required "to destroy, desecrate, deface, move, excavate or alter ... a provincial heritage site, or a heritage object." Similar provisions relate to a burial place of historic or archeological significance; a North American Indian painting or rock carving of historic or archeological significance; and a North American Indian kitchen-midden, shell-heap, house-pit, cave or other habitation site, cairn or fortification. The parallel provisions for a municipal heritage site are much briefer: "no person shall (a) demolish a building or structure, or (b) alter the facade or exterior of a building or structure, or (c) build in land designated ... without prior approval ... of the council."

Of particular interest in this act is the specific provision for compensation where designation "decreases the economic value of the land." Such is the provision for provincial heritage designation; for municipal heritage designation, there is specific reference to "grant, loan, tax relief, or other compensation." In both cases, however, the compensation is to be "full and fair" for the loss or damage suffered by the owner.

There has not, as yet, been any review of the operation of this unusual compensation provision. The city of Vancouver, in 1978, regarded it with some concern, though it was also suggested that it "might even serve as an incentive for the owner to seek designation and encourage preservation."

The act also established the British Columbia Heritage Trust, in addition to enabling powers relating to a provincial heritage advisory board to advise the minister, and municipal heritage advisory committees "to advise the council on any matter arising ... " In addition to its broad role "to encourage and facilitate the conservation, maintenance and restoration of heritage property" the trust has the very specific and tangible task to "provide loans, grants, advice and other services to persons in the province having the aims and objectives similar to the trust." Its finance originates mainly from the British Columbia Lottery Fund.

The annual reports of the trust note that although it is "primarily a granting agency offering financial assistance to local government bodies, heritage societies and other organizations," its work ranges much wider. It publishes technical information on restoration techniques; attempts to broaden public awareness of heritage; and assists university and college students in finding employment in the field of heritage conservation. Even more eloquent than the words of its annual reports is the size of its budget, which in 1984 was $1.58 million. Whether this is considered to be paltry or impressive depends upon one's standpoint.

Heritage Conservation in Ontario

The situation is so unusual that some conservationists have concluded that the only way to grant indefinite protection to a
building is to blow it up or bury it

                                        Estrin and Swaigen 1978

Ontario's heritage legislation is curious. Under the
Archeological and Historic Sites Protection Act, the province
was enabled to designate historic sites which could not be
altered or excavated without ministerial approval. This power
was repealed by the 1974 Ontario Heritage Act which made heritage conservation a municipal responsibility. The province
remains responsible only for "ruins, burial mounds, petroglyphs
and earthworks" (Denhez 1979: 80). Ontario is now the only
province that has no provincial mechanism for protecting historic sites.

The act establishes the Ontario Heritage Foundation which
has advisory, educational and promotional functions, and can
also acquire and maintain heritage property "in trust for the
people of Ontario."

Municipal designation is at the discretion of the individual
municipalities, but the necessary bylaw cannot be passed until
the Local Architectural Conservation Advisory Committee has
been consulted, if there is one. (Municipalities are empowered
but not compelled to establish these committees: they are,
however, "strongly recommended" to do so by the Ministry of
Culture and Recreation.) The owner can object to the provincially established Conservation Review Board but, though that
board can make a recommendation to the municipal council, the
final decision rests with the council.

A designated property cannot be altered without approval
by the council, but it can be demolished after a delaying procedure has been followed. The owner makes an application to
demolish: the council then has ninety days in which to decide
whether to purchase or expropriate the property;   or

alternatively make a mutually satisfactory arrangement with the owner for the future of the property. Curiously, the council can technically refuse an application to demolish. This has the effect of delaying the demolition by 180 days. This gives further time for negotiation. At the expiry of this time the building can lawfully be demolished. Estrin and Swaigen comment that "this time limit on preservation is sometimes called the guillotine rule. The effect of the rule is that it is legally easier to demolish heritage structures than to alter them."

Timing provisions can give rise to some extraordinary maneuvers. Owners of properties slated for designation sometimes display remarkable alacrity. Early dawn demolitions have become notorious, particularly at weekends. A striking case was reported in *Municipal World* (1980: 115): "Demolition of Heritage Building without Demolition Permit and in Defiance of City's Clear Intention to Designate." In this particular case, the St Peter's Evangelical Lutheran Church in Ottawa, acting in a worldly way, started demolition "between the hours of 7 o'clock and 8.45 in the forenoon ... and had demolished more than fifty percent before being ordered to stop by the chief building official."

The powers relating to individual heritage buildings are paralleled by provisions for heritage conservation districts. This power has not been widely used. The first use was in 1980 in Pittsburgh (near Kingston). The district consists of an entire village with sixty structures housing a community of 200 people.

Another provision of the Ontario Heritage Act enables municipalities and the Ontario Heritage Foundation to enter into easements. These are protective covenants which run with the property and provide much stronger and wider protection than does designation. A heritage easement "has the happy result of keeping the heritage property in private hands while recognizing and protecting the public's interest in its preservation."

Reference also needs to be made to Ontario Hydro which, partly as a result of the Environmental Assessment Act, and partly because of increased public interest, is playing an expanding role in heritage conservation. This unique body, an organization with both public and private aspects, has extraordinary powers and, of course, large financial resources. A study commissioned by Ontario Hydro and the Ministry of Culture and Recreation envisages an even larger role in the future (Fram 1980). The report is a wide ranging one and, in fact, forms an excellent guide to heritage preservation in Ontario, and beyond.

Finally, and most recently, there is the Community Heritage Fund Program announced in 1984 by the Minister of Citizenship and Culture. The objectives of this program are to encourage local initiative in architectural conservation and to promote the conservation and stabilization of properties and areas of architectural and historical value. The program has two parts: one provides seed money to municipalities to assist them in establishing capital funds for the purpose of investing in architectural conservation; the other provides seed money for capital funds established by community based non-profit corporations.

The municipalities fund allows a municipality to make grants, loans and loan guarantees to owners of designated heritage properties. To be eligible, a municipality must have a Local Architectural Heritage Conservation Authority and it must contribute a minimum of $5,000 to the fund. The province of Ontario contributes to the establishment of this fund, to a maximum grant of $250,000. A municipality may apply for provincial funding once each year, provided that it makes a minimum $5,000 contribution for each application. This contribution may include private donations.

The non-profit corporations fund operates primarily as a revolving fund, providing finance for heritage conservation projects which have the potential of returning money to the fund and generating profits which can then be used to finance other heritage conservation projects. The non-profit corporation may buy and restore heritage properties for resale at a profit. Also, loans and loan guarantees may be made to the owners of designated heritage properties.

To be eligible, the non-profit organization must be incorporated for the purpose of heritage preservation in the province; must demonstrate its ability to effectively operate the fund; and must contribute a minimum of $5,000 to the Community Heritage Fund.

The province will contribute to the establishment of the fund, again to a maximum grant of $250,000. A non-profit corporation may apply for provincial funding once each year provided that it makes a minimum $5,000 contribution for each subsequent application. This contribution may include funds from any source except other provincial funding programs.

Heritage Conservation in Quebec

It is only in the last decade that the protection of historic buildings has become a matter of widespread popular concern

Wolfe 1985

According to Wolfe, it was not until the late sixties that the general public in Quebec became concerned about the demolition of fine old buildings though, of course, there had been small historical and preservation societies for many years. As the wrecker's hammer wrought destruction in downtown Montreal (this was the language of the time) public indignation rose and almost suddenly the Cultural Property Act was passed in 1972 (L'Heureux 1977).

An earlier (1964) Historic Monuments Act was concerned with individual buildings, and had paid little attention to ensembles of buildings, though it had been successful in designating eight precincts (Junius 1974). The 1972 act requires the minister to make an inventory of cultural property that might be recognized or classified: a long and expensive task which will not be completed for many years. The act also provides for the establishment of a commission which has responsibility for classifying cultural property: "moveables" and "immoveables."

Among the provisions of the act is a requirement that the minister, on the advice of the commission, may "declare a territory, a municipality or part of a municipality to be an historic district because of the concentration of monuments or historic sites found there. He may also, in the same manner, declare a territory, municipality or part of a municipality to be a natural district because of the aesthetic, legendary or scenic interest of its natural setting."

The concept of special districts "is also embodied in the regulations which prevent the demolition or alteration of buildings within a radius of 500 feet of a classified building in order to preserve the ambience of a given setting" (Wolfe 1985).

Though the Cultural Property Act got off to a slow start, heightened public concern resulted in significant amendments which increased its effectiveness.

> In June 1978 important modifications were made to the act. One amendment enables the commission to hold public hearings on conservation matters with a view to developing coherent forward-looking regional policies rather than reacting to punctual events. A second permits the minister, on the recommendation of the commission, to enter into agreements with municipalities to provide technical and financial aid in the preparation of plans and bylaws for the management of a classified district. The municipality then becomes responsible for the administration of the regulations, but must not change them without appropriate permission (Commission des biens culturels du Québec 1979).

The commission "is very optimistic about the broadening effect of these changes. It has ventured into new fields, undertaking studies on maritime artifacts, the agricultural and the industrial heritage, and pre-colonial archeology" (Wolfe 1985).

Chapter 11
Planning and People

It is dangerous to let the public behind the scenes. They are
easily disillusioned and then they are angry with you, for it was
the illusion they loved

Somerset Maugham 1938

Contemporary public participation is largely a product of
the activism of the sixties. This in turn came about as a result
of the disillusionment with the effects and processes of planning,
a greater understanding of its distributional aspects, a
heightened awareness of environmental and ecological values,
and sheer bafflement at the scale and complexities of contemporary life and the vast array of institutions which have been
created to cope with them.

That activism has now been institutionalized. Physical
protests against the bulldozer have given way to public hearings, commissions of inquiry, social surveys, community meetings, environment impact assessments, advisory councils, and a
multiplicity of mechanisms for appealing or objecting decisions.
Public participation is now part of the planning process. How
far true participation can survive institutionalization is an open
question. A neat illustration, which goes to the heart of the
matter, is provided by Kolankiewicz's study of pollution control
in British Columbia: "procedures for participation in setting
objectives have heavily favored the technically informed, when
the question is really one that depends at least as much on public value preferences as on technical considerations. To date,
submissions by those outside government expressing

environmental values have probably not influenced decision-making to any extent" (1981).

The particularly interesting point here is the reference to technical considerations. It might have been thought that pollution matters were essentially technical and not subject to public participation in the same way that a redevelopment scheme is. Nothing could be further from the truth, and indeed, after the quotation was written, British Columbia developed further methods of involving the public in the standard-setting process (Franson et al 1982: 101).

A comparative study of environmental standards in Alberta, Ontario, Saskatchewan and British Columbia, together with federal provisions, concluded that in fact British Columbia was the only one of these jurisdictions to hold hearings on pollution standards. More generally this is seen as a technical process involving only government and industry. The authors argue that, on the contrary, the public ought to be involved: in their view, public participation "provides direct guidance and support for public servants faced with value judgments that may involve human health or even human life trade-offs. Effective public participation is likely to enhance public understanding of risks and trade-off factors involved in establishing environmental standards" (Ibid: 9). This leads into the difficult area of enforcement where again public participation is argued to be an important, but usually absent, input. This is not just a matter of encouraging the public to report violations. It is also a matter of obtaining public confidence in, and support for, environmental control programs.

It is, in fact, "often difficult to portray an accurate picture of the enforcement process," and lack of information can easily lead to a lack of faith in the process. "It becomes easy to believe that the laws are not being enforced, that government and industry are conspiring to avoid enforcement of environmental standards" (Ibid: 196).

A positive measure taken by Ontario requires anyone responsible for severe and long standing pollution to prepare a report outlining the options available for abating the problem.

The Ministry of the Environment then evaluates the report, and both documents are made public, subject to confidentiality of any proprietary information. If the problem is a major one or if there is significant public interest, a public information session is arranged (Ontario Ministry of the Environment 1981).

There are some wider points that can be made on the issue of "technical aspects". It is worth spending some time on these.

Experts, Facts and Values

The choice of values is the heart of the planning process

Reich 1966

The more a problem can be defined or made to appear as a technical matter, the easier it is for politicians and administrators to deal with it. The difficulties which arise with "people in the way" (Wilson 1973) are avoided. Life is quieter, and it is possible to get on with the task in hand without having to justify or explain it. But the chickens may come home to roost. The transportation planning of the fifties and sixties fooled most of the people most of the time, and major political issues concerning relative provision for public and private transport were disguised as technical issues such as modal split. The desecration of urban communities which followed eventually led, via public protest against the bulldozer, to a reversal of policy and a redefinition of the problem. The situation in Canada was not as dramatic as in the U.S.A.: there was no federal highway program, except for the Trans-Canada Highway; but the issue was in essence the same, as is apparent from the Nowlans' book on the Spadina expressway (1970).

A favorite smoke screen is provided by the concept of the "public interest" being promoted by "experts". Reich describes these as a myth:

The myth begins with the assumption that there is an objective reference for the concept of what is best. The process of decision may therefore be carried on in accordance with standards or criteria ... The raw materials of decision are facts: how much will the highway cost if it follows route A or route B; how many people travel between points X and Y; what are the engineering requirements? The decision makers combine expert knowledge and professionalism with judicial bearing. The tools they use for decision are science and reason. At the core of the myth is its cardinal point: decisions are not primarily choices between values. The entire machinery of administrative law serves to deny the role of values in the planning process.

The point here is a crucial one. It is also, at one and the same time, both obvious and obscure. It is obvious in the sense that there would be general agreement that values are a matter of judgment and therefore of politics. It is obscure in the sense that the issue is so pervasive that it can be forgotten: it is not always easy to see that an argument is essentially about values (Gunton 1984).

The Public and the Professionals

> To make a reputation
> When other ways are barred,
> Take something simple,
> And make it very hard
>
> Anon

It is difficult to communicate. Sometimes this helps the planning system since the various participants can feel that they are communicating when, in fact, they are not. Alternatively one or more parties may withdraw from the process on the grounds, for instance, that participation is a sham. Either way, the machine keeps going. Indeed, it only halts when one resolute force meets another equally so; or when the communication is rendered impossible by different "languages" (Maruyama 1974: 137). The point has been made many times, and with many variations. One further example: "expert domination undermines the participation and staying power of both individuals and citizen groups. Perhaps it is this professional domination that is the telling blow that sends the once fledgling

convert   to   participatory   democracy   back   to   apathy"
(Christiansen-Ruffman and Stuart 1978: 99).

There are, however, other aspects to this. To the professional, the expert, the committed bureaucrat or politician, public participation can be seen as, at most, a means of obtaining
supplementary information about impacts and measures that
might need to be taken to alleviate problems which follow after
or during a development. At the least, public participation is
simply public relations: providing the public with information
and, possibly, reassurance. A good illustration is a revealing
comment relating to the nuclear power stations in New
Brunswick, reported in the study of public inquiries by Salter
and Slaco: both the province and the New Brunswick Power
Corporation "assumed that nuclear power plants would be
built" (1981: 61). Inquiries and studies were site-specific, choice-
specific and development-specific: they related to a particular
development in a particular location (rather than to wider questions of the need for this type of development) and were restricted to a limited range of impacts. The authors continue
that the only analysis required was a cost-benefit analysis.
Beyond that:

> The only other technical issue the Cabinet considered was
> whether New Brunswick was more earthquake prone than Pick-
> ering, the site of an Ontario nuclear power plant already in
> operation ... As watchdogs and information monitors, opponents
> of the nuclear power project operated at a severe disadvantage.
> The only resource they had for independent research was pub-
> lished literature ... At best, participants in [the Environmental
> Assessment Review Process] and in citizen meetings were con-
> sidered as a group to be satisfied during the engineering design
> process. At worst they could be easily ignored.

Even more telling is the comment on public interest groups
which "represented at the very least an element of surprise and
often a kind of mystery. The fact that they did not always
agree on certain point, and that different public interest groups
appeared to speak on behalf of the same people, made it
difficult for New Brunswick Power and government officials to

understand them. The usual response of officials was to suggest programs of public education."

This lack of communication extends into professional fields, neatly summed up in a phrase of Lax: "while the Ministry of the Environment has no medical expertise, the Ministry of Health has no environmental expertise" (1979: 67).

Each profession and discipline has its own language, its own value system, and its own structure of thinking. This is highly supportive of a political system which wants to get things done while, at the same time, providing some limited scope for public participation. The Solandt Commission (1975), for example, was established to provide an opportunity for the public to comment upon a proposed Hydro line across southern Ontario, but there was no opportunity to question whether there was a need for any line: "thus the Hydro Commission was able to sidestep the really important issue and provide less important ones for the people to discuss and argue about" (Taylor 1979: 10).

Public participation, when it is effective, plays havoc with this myopic professionalism and departmentalism. But, more usually, the conclusion is a wearisome, somewhat baffled, confusion. There is a real conflict of view between those who see the inquiry in narrow terms and those who refuse to accept predetermined battle lines.

The same issue has arisen with pre-expropriation hearing procedures. These clearly point to the basic problem. Under the federal Expropriation Act, public hearings are "realistically" simply "a conduit for complaints to the Minister of Public Works (Law Reform Commission of Canada 1978: 10). Many people ... expect the pre-expropriation hearing to be more than it ever can be ... " The reason is simple: "in many cases, the hearing is the first available public forum for people affected by a proposed project ... ; the basic problems, then, do not lie with the pre-expropriation itself ... but with the prior lack of information about and public participation in the planning process" (Loc cit).

This is the way things work out: there is no conspiracy, except in Bernard Shaw's sense that "all professions are a conspiracy against the laity." The point is worth expanding by reference to Forester's concept of planning as "communicative action" (1980: 275):

> In planning practice, communication is political. When a community organization or a developer obtains information can be as important as what information is obtained. What planners do not say can be as important as what they do say. Planners shape not only documents or information, then, but also citizens' access to information, their understanding and interpretation of such information, and their ability to participate effectively in political processes affecting their lives. The structure of the planning process reflects a systematic patterning of communication that thus influences levels of community organization, citizen participation, and autonomous, responsible citizen action.

Even more generally, all those involved in the planning process influence it in some way, whether they be planners, administrators, adjudicators, politicians or whatever.

Who Is The Expert?

> There's no greater expert than the people. They know what they want and have to fight for it
>
> Sankey 1971

Expertise is a function of time and place, as *The Admirable Crichton* amusingly showed. But the 1970s evinced a distrust of expertise and professionalism which went far wider than the readership of the books of Ivan Illich (1971 and 1977). Though this affected educationists, doctors and lawyers, and many other professions as well, it hit planners especially hard, partly because they were relative newcomers to the professional lists, and partly because the matters on which they were supposedly the experts were uniquely transparent as political in essence.

It was only a matter of time (and place) before someone hit on the idea of assisting the public, not only with finance, but also with instruction in the necessary arts of public participation. Finance is discussed in a later section; here attention is focused on a particular educational program for participators:

> A training program to enable the Saskatchewan Environmental Society to intervene effectively in the [Cluff Lake] inquiry was initiated by the Public Interest Advocacy Center. It had the following objectives:
>
> (1)   to assist a small group of sophisticated and knowledgeable non-lawyers to acquire the rudiments of the art of cross-examination;
>
> (2)   to provide a quick training in the law of civil procedure, together with some understanding of how these rules are likely to be applied in practice before a special inquiry such as the Cluff Lake Inquiry;
>
> (3)   to help to develop confidence in growing advocacy skills through actual on-the-job demonstrations as to how the work is done and direct one-to-one supervision during the hearings process;
>
> (4)   to reduce dependency on lawyers;
>
> (5)   to reduce demand for the advocacy services of the center (Roman 1979: 34).

Use was made of a guidebook on how to prepare cases for administrative tribunals. Available evidence was analyzed particularly to identify points for cross-examination: for example, internal inconsistencies, exaggerated statements and unsubstantiated assertions. Lengthy sessions were organized to debate the relevant issues, to develop avenues of questioning, to establish what additional evidence should be sought at the inquiry, and so forth. It was generally agreed that the experiment worked well.

Less happy has been the experience in Prince Edward Island. There "the biggest obstacle to the effective implementation of government-administered public participation projects appears to have been the government itself" (McNiven 1974:

35).   Public participation can easily upset the relationships between departments, and between politicians and civil servants. Moreover, in Prince Edward Island, "it was feared that if people ... were involved in the development of a plan, the expectations would be raised for immediate returns and, when these were not forthcoming, frustration would lead them to reject the plan during the phase of implementation" (Ibid: 11).

The Island does not stand alone in its failures. Indeed, failures in public participation are far more common than successes, mainly because too much is expected.

Advisory Committees

Many citizen concerns are not founded on rational argument and it would be unrealistic to assume that they can be allayed by a process that seeks to be rational

Ontario Planning Act Review Committee 1977e

Following U.S. traditions, Canadian planning was originally largely administered through ad hoc planning boards. Thus planning and politics were thought to be separated. In Ontario, the separation was made even greater by the requirement that a majority of the members of a planning board had to be citizen appointees. This was changed in 1972, following which a board could have a majority of elected politicians. The change reflected a major shift in both the nature of planning and attitudes towards it. Above all, planning was increasingly seen as a political activity which should be controlled by elected and accountable politicians. Planning boards were no longer seen "as important components in the system of checks and balances, but rather as barriers restricting the access of citizens to their elected representatives" (Ibid: 6). The trend has continued, and the 1983 act abolished planning boards completely, except in the north where there is no local government system.

Though planning may now be more democratic, the change has removed one opportunity for citizen involvement in the planning process. For this reason a number of provinces have set up planning advisory committees. (The 1983 Ontario Planning Act empowers municipalities to appoint such committees.)

There has been a number of studies of planning advisory committees (Vuchnich 1980). The one undertaken for the Comay committee, showed that they can be a mixed blessing. The advantages were seen to be fourfold. First, they enable the planning staff to call on the knowledge and resources of the community to identify concerns and to devise specific policies or plans. Secondly, they provide a means by which the public can contribute, through a few key spokesmen to the planning process. Because of the small numbers involved, good relationships are easily established between the planners and the advisors. Thirdly, they create "a pressure group through which political lobbying can be carried out effectively." Finally, they provide a mechanism for sustained public involvement in the planning process. On the other hand:

> The shortcomings of advisory committees and task forces must be weighed against their benefits. First, in several instances, the committees became non-professional planning staff for all practical purposes. This did not result in an increase in the numbers of opportunities afforded for the participation by the general public. In fact, the committees were frequently less receptive than the professional planning staff to input from the general public.
>
> Second, such committees found it difficult to work within an already established broad policy framework. They seemed to expect to establish policies exclusively for their own particular area.
>
> Third, individual committee members were sometimes open to conflicts of interests which were not always declared. Property owners, tenants, and professionals alike, as members of an advisory committee, were in a position to derive personal gain by advocating certain policies, or recommending certain land use designations. Few rules of conduct were established to regulate such situations. Fourthly, it is evident that because of their exposure to more information and different planning perspectives than the average resident, committee members can come to judge issues in a very different light than the "uninformed public" ...

Finally, there is a discernible tendency for task force members to see themselves as deciders, not advisers. When their advice is not accepted unquestioningly by staff and politicians, some committee members may become disillusioned, if not hostile and uncooperative (Ontario Planning Act Review Committee 1977e: 28).

The conclusion is that advisory committees can play a useful role, but "it seems essential that the interests of other residents must be safeguarded by providing other more conventional ways of public involvement." They must also, of course, maintain credibility with the organization they are advising (Smith 1982: 29).

Funding Public Participation

Sufficient funds must be provided to allow for the retention of a significant corps of expert witnesses, expert enough to be a match, in the eyes of the board, for the witnesses called by the other side. Failing this minimum, participation would tend to be more symbolic than real

Roman 1979

Public hearings or inquiries burgeoned in the 1970s but, with certain notable exceptions where funding had been provided, "many of the hearings are, for the public, little more than a sham." So argues David Estrin. He continues that "the proponent comes to the hearing having spent years and perhaps hundreds of thousands, if not millions, of dollars hiring experts and obtaining massive reports to convince the tribunal that its project is worthy. On the other side, persons opposed or who simply wish to participate to ensure that all the facts are before the tribunal usually have neither the resources to examine adequately and respond to such technical preparation, nor the resources to appear at the hearing through counsel" (Estrin 1979: 84).

It is the exceptions which are interesting and persuasive. For example, the Alberta Energy Resources Conservation Board noted that "local intervenors" had serious difficulties of "costs in terms of time and effort and commitment." They therefore pressed for, and obtained, authority to award costs (Plesuk 1981: 15). At the federal level, until recently, only the Canadian Radio-television and Telecommunications Commission makes "intervenor cost awards" (Fox 1979: 130).

Perhaps the best known example in Canada is the Berger Commission on the Mackenzie Valley Pipeline Inquiry (1977). Berger has argued that: "it is true that Arctic Gas carries out extensive environmental studies, which cost a great deal of money. But they had an interest: they wanted to build the pipeline. This was a perfectly legitimate interest, but not one that could necessarily be reconciled with the environmental interest. It was felt that there should be representation by a group with special interest in the northern environment, a group without any other interest that might deflect it from the presentation of that case" (1979: 5). Berger therefore arranged for a funding program, which cost nearly two million dollars, for "those groups that had an interest that ought to be represented, but whose means would not allow it." His approach was clear: "these groups are sometimes called public interest groups. They represent identifiable interests that ... should be considered. They do not represent the public interest, but it is in the public interest that they should be heard." Berger laid down five criteria which a group seeking financial assistance had to meet:

(1)   there should be a clearly ascertainable interest that ought to be represented at the inquiry;

(2)   it should be established that separate and adequate representation of that interest would make a necessary and substantial contribution to the inquiry;

(3)   those seeking funds should have an established record of concern for, and should have demonstrated their own commitment to, the interest they sought to represent;

(4)   it should be shown that those seeking funds did not have sufficient financial resources to enable them adequately to represent that interest, and that they would require funds to do so;

(5)   those seeking funds had to have a clearly delineated proposal as to the use they intended to make of the funds, and had to be sufficiently well-organized to account for the funds.

In 1981, the federal government established an experimental "intervenor funding program" to provide financial assistance to those wishing to make representations to the Environmental Assessment Panel. This fund was used in the Beaufort Sea review. Both an independent study (Graham et al 1982) and the panel (FEARO 1984: 17) concluded "that the review process was materially assisted and that intervenor funding enhanced the quality and substance of interventions from northern residents whose interests would be most directly affected if the development were to go ahead." They also recommended that intervenor funding should be made available for all future EARP reviews. At the time of writing this was under consideration.

In 1982, the federal government announced its policy for "sharing transportation costs" for participants in public consultation meetings:

In order to qualify for attendance at the headquarters and regional yearly meetings designated by the Public Consultation Policy, a public interest group or professional association must satisfy the following requirements:

(1)   be a non-profit organization with an interest in the policies and programs of Environment Canada;

(2)   indicate a financial need and be willing to make available a financial statement and budget, if requested;

(3)   indicate its reasons for wishing to attend a designated meeting for which financial assistance is being requested;

(4)   participate at the designated meeting.

In addition, to assist Environment Canada in allocating the limited funds available, the following criteria will be used as guidelines:

(1)   that there is a clearly ascertainable interest that ought to be brought to the attention of Environment Canada;

(2)   that separate and adequate representation of the interest would make a necessary and substantial contribution to the annual meetings;

(3)   that the applicant organization demonstrate or be willing to demonstrate its own commitment to, and representativeness of, the interest it seeks to represent (e.g. nature and extent of its own contribution, past involvement in similar activities, size of its constituency);

(4)   that the applicant organization not obtain funds for the same activity from other federal agencies (Environment Canada 1982a).

Such is the inevitable bureaucratization of public participation! Whether on-going reviews will simplify matters remains to be seen (FEARO 1984b).

An alternative approach is to remove responsibility for funding to a separate agency. This has been done by the Ontario Waste Management Corporation (discussed in chapter 10) which announced, in November 1984, the establishment of a $75,000 public consultation funding program. Interested groups and individuals can apply for funds to hire assistance in reviewing the lengthy technical reports of the corporation. (Sixteen of these were published in December 1984 extending to over 3000 pages.) The corporation, however, is not involved in determining who is eligible for assistance. Applications are reviewed and decided by the former Lieutenant Governor of Ontario (Hon Pauline McGibbon) and the President of the Donner Canadian Foundation (Donald Rickerd).

This is an interesting arrangement which could be adopted more widely.

Effective Public Participation

> The most important contribution to the community hearings was, I think, the insight it gave us into the true nature of native claims. No academic treatise or discussion, formal presentation of the claims by native people by the native organizations, and their leaders, could offer as compelling and vivid a picture of the goals and aspirations of native people as their own testimony
>
> Berger 1979

A great deal has been written about the desirability of public participation but there has been little analysis of its effectiveness (Burton and Wildgoose 1977; Burton 1979). Given the inherent difficulties, this is not surprising. How can the effectiveness of public participation be measured? Is the participation sufficient in itself as an essential element in the democratic process?

These are big questions which bristle with difficulties. Here attention is focused on a number of cases of public participation which, for one reason or another, appear to have some interesting and positive aspects.

The most striking is the Berger inquiry. Quotations have already been made from the Berger report, but a further one is appropriate. Given the (funded) public participation and the breadth and depth of the evidence collected, Berger clearly demonstrated that:

> A commissioner of inquiry has, or ought to have, an advantage that ministers and senior executives in the public service do not have: an opportunity to hear all the evidence, to reflect on it, to weigh it, and to make judgment on it. Ministers and their deputies, given the demands that the management of their departments impose upon them, usually have no such opportunity ...
>
> I advised the government that a pipeline corridor is feasible, from an environmental point of view, to transport gas and oil from the Mackenzie Delta along the Mackenzie Valley to the Alberta border. At the same time, however, I recommended that we should postpone the construction of the pipeline for ten

years, in order to strengthen native society, the native economy (indeed the whole renewable sector) and to enable native claims to be settled.

There is no doubt that the persuasive and powerful nature of the Berger report stemmed at least in part from the effectiveness of the public input.

A very different example is given in a paper by Deryck Holdsworth on heritage conservation (1980). He demonstrates how "increasing community involvement ... is slowly beginning to transform perspectives away from the rarity biography and establishment criteria for heritage." He also quotes the Halifax case of The Battle of Citadel Hill, where a long conflict of interests eventually ended with the safeguarding of view-corridors between the Citadel and the Harbour (Pacey 1979).

More contentious is Ontario Hydro's program for public participation (1980). The contentiousness relates partly to the definition of the issues on which public participation is encouraged and partly to the difficulties which beset any large bureaucracy, particularly when it achieves the size and power of Ontario Hydro. (Any organization of this scale inevitably has internal differences of opinion and attitude.) Further complications have arisen recently with changes in perceptions of, and policies for, the use of energy. The change from the promotion of electricity use to the conservation of electricity must have had a dramatic impact on the internal workings of Ontario Hydro, which probably will take many years to work through the system.

This is conjecture, though it provides a warning against regarding any published material as representing the up-to-date situation. The immediate point, however, is that Ontario Hydro is very much aware of the importance of its Community Relations Department; and there is nothing sinister in its battery of "public involvement techniques." The reasons for encouraging public participation are quite explicit, though undoubtedly some may experience difficulty in interpreting the statement:

Ontario Hydro encourages public involvement in the planning of new electrical facilities for the following reasons:

- to ensure the decision reflects the concerns and values of the community;

- to broaden public understanding of the need for the facilities;

- to obtain knowledge of the area, community priorities, and perceptions of possible impacts that the project may create;

- to discuss and evaluate local options during the course of the environmental assessment study;

- to establish, maintain and enhance two-way communication between Hydro and the public throughout all stages of a project (Henderson 1982: 1).

A study by Professor Risk has a less confident and joyous note, and concludes that "intelligent choices of institutions and procedures can produce better and more acceptable decisions about location, but hopes should be modest. Unhappiness and dispute cannot be avoided" (Risk 1981: 70). The truth is that, however much electricity is used, no one loves the things that go to produce it.

Much more could be written about the experience of public participation in Canada, but sufficient has been said to highlight the main issues. It is now necessary to turn to some other aspects of this amorphous subject.

Machinery for Appeals and Objections: The O.M.B.

... the OMB tries to follow government policy in making its decisions. However, in at least two types of case the OMB obviously makes policy. One type occurs when there is no clear statement of government policy. A second occurs when the board has only a generalized policy to guide it and feels obliged to make detailed policy applicable to the issues before it

Ontario Legislative Assembly 1972

Special machinery for hearing appeals against planning decisions has been established in a number of provinces. For example New Brunswick and Nova Scotia have provincial planning   appeal boards, both of which publish detailed accounts of their decisions. Other provinces have added an appellate function to an existing body, as with the Manitoba and Ontario Municipal Boards. In this section, attention is restricted to the fascinating case of the Ontario Municipal Board (OMB).

The OMB originated as the Railway and Municipal Board in 1906 but had an increasing number of functions allocated to it, including a range of planning matters. The latter make up a very wide range indeed, from appeals for amendment of zoning bylaws to approval, or otherwise, of official plans referred by the minister. The board is thus much more than an appellate body. Indeed a detailed study of its operation was entitled *Land Planning by Administrative Regulation: The Policies of the Ontario Municipal Board* (Adler 1971). It is this policy aspect of the board's work which is of particular interest.

The Ontario Municipal Board is an extraordinary gift to politicians. Though never designed for the purpose, it now has the role of deciding many of the more difficult planning issues which elected representatives are glad to shirk. In this it is abetted by the legal profession which naturally views planning as a process which is concerned with conflicts of interests which can best be resolved through an adversary process guided, and decided, by independent arbiters.

Planning, politics and law in Ontario have thus become confused. Legal concepts of impartiality and "due process" are being applied to matters of political judgment. Major issues of policy in relation to the unforeseeable future are subjected to adversary processes with the objective (if not of "proving" what the future holds or what the effects of policy will be) of judging impartially what is "right and proper."

The OMB plays a central role in this confusion. The report on the Toronto downtown plan is replete with examples. One of the three board members, W.H.J. Thompson, clearly exasperated with the lengthy and convoluted hearings, ends his dissenting opinion (which incorporates a series of character-assassinating commentaries) with the statement that the city's proposals involve "a massive change in the future direction of development of the commercial sphere of a major city and I for one, not being a planner, am reluctant to participate in the overhaul of a complicated document relating to this vital area ... I cannot endorse an implementation which, in my opinion, gambles with the economic viability of a very important segment of this country's wealth-generating mechanisms" (Ontario Municipal Board Reports 1978: 223). His colleagues in the hearing had no such reluctance. In a majority decision B.E. Smith and K.D. Bindhart concluded:

> The evidence convinced us that the two main policies of the plan, namely, the introduction of substantial amounts of housing into the central area of the city and the deconcentration of office growth, are worthy objectives and represent sound planning for Toronto. The housing policies will result in an efficient use of the transportation system and provide housing where existing services and amenities are available. It will bring vitality to an important area of the city for a much longer period of the day and will ensure the preservation of a number of valuable residential areas which presently exist in this part of the city (Ibid: 54).

Does any contemporary planner ever speak with such certainty?

Even more incredible is the quasi-legal judgment which the majority of the board pass on private enterprise. Their argument is worth reproducing at length:

> Throughout the hearing, the board was continually urged by those in opposition to the plan to allow the marketplace to determine the rate of office growth and to keep as many options open as possible by not arbitrarily restricting the intensity of development. This position is a cause of some concern to us, for equitable free enterprise can never be attained without open competition in the marketplace. We have come to the view that free enterprise is inextricably a part of the democratic system of government, and rights go hand in hand with free enterprise as well. Since these ideals are so cherished, we tend to guard zealously against their erosion, and any planning policies which appear to derogate from those ideals should be carefully scrutinized before this board gives its stamp of approval (Ibid: 25).

This political statement, which might have been taken from Hayek or Milton Friedman, is followed by a succinct lesson in political economy:

> In an ideal situation, an individual has the right to do anything he chooses until those rights interfere with the rights of others. It is in this definition of boundaries of the free market that the conflict occurs. For that reason it is necessary to introduce certain standards into our society, even though they may be somewhat arbitrary, to bring some order to the control of behavior. To some extent, all regulations represent an interference with the operation of a free market and individual rights. In a planning sense, regulations or standards take the form of official plans and zoning bylaws, but what is sought is a reasonable balance between the many forces operating in the planning area. It is in this light that the board must weigh the evidence presented.

> In maintaining the status quo which was suggested, the opportunity is lost to commence a development program for the deconcentrated land use option for the city. The time appears to be opportune to preserve stable neighborhoods and give some direction for the construction of residential dwelling units in the central areas of the city. It is therefore clear that it is impossible to maintain all options and a choice has to be made.

Given the existing system, that choice falls to the OMB. And so a judgment has to be handed down after a solemn consideration of the "evidence" (which the dissenting Mr Thompson considered to be largely worthless). Undaunted by a mountain of technical, pseudo-scientific and political papers, the two board members posed the issue in Solomon-like terms: "we therefore believe that the board should answer two questions. Firstly, whether the plan unduly interferes with the operation of a free market so that it is wrong in principle and, secondly, if there is some interference, whether that interference justifies the benefits to be derived therefrom."

Political reputations and Ph.Ds have been lost on such debates, but timidity has no place in the board's proceedings. It is required to decide, and it does so in favor of the city.

In approving the main provisions of the plan, the case of private enterprise has been judged inadequate. The planners win the trophy. But there is a consolation prize: "it is in the interest of allowing the market place to operate as freely as possible that we are modifying the plan to permit commercial densities in the high density mixed areas up to the full maximum of 4.5 times the area of the lot without the necessity of including a residential component."

These lengthy quotations from the board's report clearly indicate its role. It is an ambiguous one. It acts as if political issues can be settled impartially. The Canadian Bar Association (1977: 5) argues that the board fulfills the essential function of "a fair and impartial forum in which to resolve conflicts"; but impartiality has no place in a political decision. An impartial analysis finds no difficulty in exposing the unavoidably slender objective basis of the plan, as the dissenting Mr Thompson saw only too clearly. By their very nature, political decisions are partial to policy objectives, and typically based on unprovable contentions. The superstructure of technical studies may divert attention from this but, as the awkward Mr Thompson noted, they may constitute a tenuous basis for policy; and, in this case, he had little difficulty in demonstrating, at least to his satisfaction, that even rigorous academic analysis only proved what individual academics *believed*.

This particular OMB hearing may have been exceptional in the obviousness of its political content, but this is simply a matter of degree. The essence of a democratic system of government is that responsibility and accountability for political decisions lie with elected representatives, not with appointed boards. The complexity of modern society makes this an ideal difficult of achievement, but there can be no escape from the point that planning policies are political policies and should therefore be for elected representatives to decide upon. Some matters may, for a variety of reasons, be assigned to non-representative bodies, but it is delusion to think that their subject matter thereby becomes non-political, still less impartial.

The accidents of history which have cast the OMB in its present role are precisely that. To bring in aid of its defence arguments concerning impartiality, "protection" of citizen rights and such like simply confuse the issue. The only justification for the OMB apart from its history, is its acceptability to articulate interests.

Thus the Comay report, and its predecessors, are all correct in arguing that "the board should not be responsible for determining policy"; that it "should not be assigned nor should it have to assume a policy-making function" (Ontario Economic Council 1973: 103); that "the government should clearly state the policies it expects the OMB to follow" (Ontario Legislature 1972: 3). Similarly the Robarts report argues that the supervision of municipalities by the OMB is "a legacy from the past, when municipalities did not have sufficient political or technical sophistication to provide an adequate standard of planning without detailed checking and direction" (1977: 2:216).

When successive reports making basically the same recommendation are ignored, there is a presumption that some basic issues have been ignored or insufficiently stressed. In the case of the OMB there appear to be two such issues.

Firstly, the OMB nicely allows politicians to abrogate the responsibilities which properly fall to them. Hopefully the new commitments to provincial policy statements will change this. Secondly, it is alleged that the public has more "confidence" in the OMB than it has in its elected local government. It is difficult to establish how far this is in fact so, but the public consultation program instituted by the Ontario Planning Act Review Committee (1977b) shows that there is a wide range of opinion on this matter (a classic justification for political inaction).

The weaknesses of the OMB are easy to spell out, but it is equally easy to miss some of its strengths. Two particular points are striking. Firstly, under the chairmanship of J.A. Kennedy. the OMB became, in the late sixties, a major political force in sponsoring citizen interests (as distinct from official or developer interests). In other words, whatever theoretical limitations the board had, in practice it was instrumental in, or at the least supportive of, the promotion of the public interest as expressed by the citizenry. It was not until the 1970s that political change took place: at the provincial level with the 1971 decision to halt the construction of the Spadina Expressway; and at the local level by the 1972 Crombie election victory. Thus the OMB cannot be dismissed as a reactionary body, though some of its specific decisions and obiter dicta might suggest this.

Secondly, the OMB has had a remarkable degree of independence. While this may well be indefensible in terms of political theory it has avoided the problems posed by an alternative system. The British model is instructive here. The problem involved is that of devising a system of publicly acceptable quasi-judicial procedures for dealing with a range of planning matters, particularly at the level of the individual householder. This is not the place to embark upon a comparison of Canadian and British systems of planning. It is sufficient for present purposes to note that there is increasing pressure in Britain for a greater degree of independence for those who are appointed to consider appeals and objections. The trend towards greater independence, or at least separation from the relevant ministries, for "inspectors" leads clearly in the direction of a body such as the OMB.

The problem here is to divide issues into categories of importance or political significance. Pipelines are very different from front-yard parking. Unfortunately, it is not always easy to predict how political an issue might be. (It *could* transpire that front-yard parking could become as political an issue as expressways did with Spadina.) Nevertheless, the distinction is important, and different procedures are required in relation to major planning proposals and to the application of policy to individual cases.

Indeed, there is a real need for a classification of municipal actions, or inactions, into categories which require different types of review. Such a classification might have three major categories: policy; the application of policy; and maladministration and illegalities.

This may be oversimple, but without claiming that anything more than a preliminary review along these lines is being attempted, the following section discusses review mechanisms under these three headings. It is argued that different mechanisms are needed for each of these. Policy is a political matter requiring political review. The application of policy may involve fine matters of judgment for which an appeal procedure is appropriate. Maladministration falls within the scope of the ombudsman unless it involves legal issues which are the preserve of the courts.

Controlling the Planning Machine

There are severe limits to the reform of planning law
Kiernan 1982

(i) Policy Plans

Policy is a grand word; but the concept is a nebulous one. In the abstract it can be defined in terms of other abstractions. *Webster's Dictionary* defines it as (1)(a): prudence or wisdom in the management of affairs; (b): management or procedure based primarily on material interest; (2)(a): a definite course or method of action selected from among alternatives and in the light of given conditions to guide and determine present and future decisions; (b): a high level overall plan embracing the general goals and acceptable procedures, especially of a governmental body.

This gives us some positive clues as to what policy is. The most important, in the present context. is "to guide and determine present and future decisions." To instance the Toronto Central Area Plan (1975: Section C4-1):

It is the policy of the council that in the mutual interests of the
city and the metropolitan region, the central area should

continue to serve a primary regional role and at the same time continue to function as a major residential area of the city. It is, therefore, the policy of the council that growth in commercial offices and public institutions will continue to be accommodated in the central core of the central area consistent with the other policies of this plan respecting the encouragement of regional deconcentration and the retention of the central area low rise neighborhoods.

This highly generalized statement is a typical policy statement. It involves a number of policy objectives of a highly general nature which can be debated in broad terms. Its very generality tends to command broad acceptance or, alternatively, fundamental opposition.

Similarly, general statements about group homes or non-exclusionary zoning constitute highly generalized policies.

Policies of this nature are clearly political, and the issues they raise involve considerations of general public acceptance, and of their relationships to the policies of other organs of government. The decentralization policy of the city of Toronto must obviously harmonize with relevant provincial policies, with the general development policies of the adjacent municipalities which are intended to accept the decentralized activities, and with transportation policies, which are the responsibility of different agencies.

These are all subjects for a wide ranging planning inquiry in which the main issue is the compatibility and merits of the relevant policies of a multiplicity of agencies. Only the highest level political body can decide upon this, namely the province. The matters have nothing to do with a legal process in which an "unbiased" judge determines where justice lies.

This is not to say that an adversary style is inappropriate. Though life might be more comfortable for the governmental agencies concerned without it, an adversary style has the advantage of pointing up the weaknesses, and strengths, of the case presented by the various parties. If the comfort of governmental agencies were the prime consideration, the inquiry would be held in camera: but it goes without saying that a political process of this nature must be public. It is also a safeguard against sloppy and ill-considered policies: it positively demands a thorough review and study which is subject to public appraisal.

(ii) Policy-Application

Though ungainly, the term "policy-application" has the merit of clarity. It means precisely what it says: the application of policy to specific issues. Conceptually it is quite distinct from policy making. If the distinction were as clear in practice as it is in concept, the determination of appropriate review machinery would be simple. Policy would be a matter for political review, while policy-application would involve some type of quasi-judicial review in which the merits, or otherwise, of the application of policy to particular cases would be judged by a body at one remove from the decision making organization. It is the fact that the reality is so much more complicated which makes the problem of deciding upon appropriate review machinery so difficult. There is a world of difference between generalized policy statements and particularized actions. Policy is not applied: it is interpreted in the light of circumstances of particular cases (and in the context of time). In interpreting policy and the situation to which it relates, policy is given meaning. Indeed it has no reality other than this (Barrett and Fudge 1981).

By their nature, policies are simple statements (on which agreement is often relatively easy) which in practice relate to complex specific situations (when clashes of interest become very apparent). Moreover, the policy statements themselves frequently contain the seeds of conflict which their highly generalized articulation can mask.

This is so both within the planning field and between it and other policy areas. On the first, the previously given example of the Toronto central area plan illustrates the point nicely. Here the policy is that the central area should serve both commercial and residential functions. New office developments are to be allowed as long as they are consistent with the residential policy, as well as the deconcentration policy. But how much development of a particular kind will be allowed will inevitably depend upon future circumstances. If white collar unemployment develops, the tendency will be to increase the allowable amount of office development; if there is a housing crisis the emphasis may switch to housing development. These adjustments at the margin are seen by planners as constituting a flexible policy. In fact, of course, policy and specific actions are inseparable except in the words of the plan.

Other conflicts arise when different fields of policy lead to opposite conclusions. For instance, though all may agree with policies aimed at combatting unemployment and with policies directed to reducing pollution, what is to be done when one clashes with the other? What is the policy to be if a polluting industry can conform with environmental requirements only at the cost of closing down part of its works and making many employees redundant?

The point needs no lengthy elaboration. Policies have to be interpreted and given substance in the context of specific circumstances. It is at this stage that individual interests are most clearly affected. Thus though there may be political agreement on a "policy plan," there can be intense opposition to "policy-application". Moreover, given the fallibility of judgment, the unpredictability of the future, the impossibility of establishing the long run effect of specific decisions, and the general acceptance of the right of challenge, there is in any case a clear argument for a review of individual decisions separate from a review of policy. Perhaps the clearest illustration of this is the desirability, and the difficulty, of separating a review of transport needs and policies from a review of the location and alignment of an agreed transport route.

The British experience may be of some interest here. Currently statutory plans are of two main kinds: a structure plan, which is a broad policy plan, and a local plan, which is a detailed plan which elaborates the structure plan policies for smaller areas. Both are subject to a public inquiry undertaken by "inspectors" in England and Wales, or "reporters" in

Scotland appointed by the relevant planning minister. With a structure plan, the report on the public inquiry, or "examination in public" as it is called, is made to the planning minister, and it is he who decides whether the plan is to be approved, with or without amendment. With a local plan, however, the report is made to the local authority and they have the responsibility for "adopting" it (again with or without amendment). Proposals for development are considered by local authorities within the framework of these plans but, if it is decided to reject them, or impose conditions which the applicant finds unacceptable, there is machinery for appeal. Appeals are heard by inspectors or reporters. On minor matters (the majority), they can make the final decision: on others they may make recommendations to the planning minister who typically, but not always, accepts them. In no case does the decision rest with the municipality.

Whether or not this system is appropriate to, or acceptable in, Canada is not at issue here: all that is suggested is that there may be some attraction in the model of a hierarchy of decision making in which policy planning is subject to political review while plan-application is subject to a quasi-judicial review process.

(iii) Maladministration and Illegalities

The issues of maladministration and illegal action can be dealt with more briefly, though they are not without their difficulties.

One difficulty is simply that the OMB likes to see itself, and is often seen, as an ombudsman, protecting innocent citizens from excesses of zeal on the part of local councils. (The point is heavily made in the suggestion that OMB is a shorthand for ombudsman.) But this is to confuse functions.

In the preceding section, a distinction has been drawn between planning inquiries concerned with policy matters and planning appeals concerned with the merits of a specific planning application. In both cases, questions of maladministration and legality can arise: and such questions need to be decided by separate special machinery. For maladministration there exists the ombudsman, while for legality there is the well-established judicial system.

The powers of the provincial ombudsmen vary between the provinces, but typically they are restricted to central government administration. Only in Nova Scotia, New Brunswick and (when proclaimed) British Columbia do they extend to local government (Lundvik 1982: 88).

The Comay committee (1977) recommended that (in relation to municipal planning) these functions should be allocated to the OMB. Thus the OMB would hear grievances on allegedly "unreasonable or unfair behavior" or on the contention that "in reaching or failing to reach a decision, the council acted on incorrect or inadequate information or advice."

That there is an important, and distinct, role here is exemplified in the ombudsman's reports on those planning matters which currently fall within his jurisdiction. Nevertheless, Comay's specific wording is not as appropriate, clear or workable as the terms of reference provided in the Ombudsman Act. These refer to administration which, on his investigation:

(a) appears to have been contrary to the law;

(b) was unreasonable, oppressive, or improperly discriminatory, or was in accordance with a rule of law or a provision of any act or a practice that is or may be unreasonable, unjust, oppressive, or improperly discriminatory;

(c) was based wholly or partly on a mistake of law or fact;

(d) was wrong.

or where administrative power "has been exercised for an improper purpose or on irrelevant grounds ... " and so on.

It is also noteworthy that the ombudsman can decide not to proceed with an investigation where he considers that the complaint is trivial, frivolous, vexatious or not made in good faith, or that the complainant has not a sufficient personal interest in the subject matter of the complaint.

The issues involved here clearly extend well beyond planning; but the point being made is simply that maladministration requires treatment different from the public inquiries and appeals appropriate for the review of plans and planning applications. It is concerned with the way in which these procedures are operated.

Of course, if there is a breach of the law then the courts are the appropriate body to deal with the matter.

The Public Interest

... the system of planning now reflects the ideologies of a governing elite, of which planners in practice are a part, and serves their interests, rather than reflecting the aspirations and ideals which planners so frequently commit to paper for discussion

McAuslan 1980

The public interest is elusive, not only because there are in any typical case several publics with differing interests, but also because someone has to determine where the balance of interest lies. The issue can be usefully discussed in the terms of McAuslan's *Ideologies of Planning Law.*

Before the public health problems of the industrial revolution towns, the dominant ideology was that the law existed to protect the interests and institutions of private property. This private property interest came under strong attack as public health problems, and later planning problems, required public controls. Thus developed the public interest ideology: the ideology of law as seen by the public administrator. The movements for the "city healthy," the "city beautiful," and the "city efficient" were all illustrations of this. Private property owners might, and did, resist the increasing public interest legislation, but it could be politically unwise to do so (the fear of social unrest), it could be physically dangerous to do so (cholera was no respecter of social class), and it could be uneconomic to do so (the belief that zoning protects property values). Moreover, a great deal of the legislation was not very effective: it looked more threatening than it really was.

These two ideologies (of the private property interest and the public interest) have been paramount until relatively recently. The extent to which action in the public interest has spread is illustrated throughout this book; but the private property interest remains virile. Reference can be made to the campaign of the Canadian Real Estate Association: "a national campaign to strengthen property rights in Canada" and to have the Charter of Rights amended to incorporate "a guarantee of property rights." The Ontario Real Estate Association, in its studies of "the erosion of property rights in Ontario" has produced long catalogs of the extent to which the ideology of the public interest has prevailed over the private property interest (Oosterhoff and Rayner 1979).

The demand for the enshrinement of a property right in the Charter of Rights is an interesting one in the present context since it points to the restricted role which the courts have in limiting the power of public administrators. If an act provides for the use of a discretionary power then, assuming that all the statutory procedures have been carried out, the courts cannot override the legislation by appeal to a higher authority. If, however, the Bill of Rights were amended the courts could strike down legislation which violated the property right (Seelig, Goldberg and Horwood 1980: 110). There is little indication at present that there is any substantial political support for such a change.

In considering the operation of the public interest ideology, it has to be stressed that its essential feature is that the public interest is decided, not by the public, but by public administrators (ironically termed public servants). There is, of course, nothing sinister about this. Indeed, until recently, few would have thought of a competing ideology that law is a vehicle for the advance of public participation. This is McAuslan's third planning ideology:

It is the most recent and least developed of the ideologies both
in practice, in terms that is of legislation, circulars and cases,
and as a separate identifiable ideology backed by a separate and
clearly identifiable constituency as the private property ideology
is by the courts and the public interest ideology is by the
administrators and planners. It is none the less an ideology of
equal importance to the other two. It sees the law as the provider of rights of participation in the land use planning process
not by virtue of the ownership of property but by virtue of the
more abstract principles of democracy and justice. These in
turn come down to the argument that all who are likely to be
affected by or who have, for whatever reason, an interest or concern in a proposed development of land or change in the
environment should have the right of participation in the decision on that proposal just because they might be affected or are
interested.

Though written against a background of English planning
law and administration, McAuslan's analysis clearly has wider
relevance. The ideology of public participation was in the ascen-
dant in the 1970s, but the 1980s appear different. Public participation means the making of a public input into the decision
making process. The decision itself rests firmly with the
managers of the public interest. Put in this light some at least
of the OMB's decisions can be seen as promoting the ideology of
public participation. This was explicit in the 1966 decision
regarding the approval of a bylaw passed by the then Township
of East York: "it is the duty of this board to determine whether
or not it [the municipality's decision] will create undue hardship
on others." The decision regarding Toronto's 45 foot bylaw is
interpreted similarly by Jaffary and Makuch as indicating a concern for individual rights: in this case the rights of large real
estate companies (Jaffary and Makuch 1977: 84). It could also
be interpreted as a victory for the private property interest.
Either way, it was a defeat for the ideology of the public
interest as interpreted by the city planners.

A number of related issues arise. One is perhaps simply a
reformulation of the basic issues: what discretion is to be
allowed to planning authorities, or to their staffs? This leads
into issues of justice, to use the terminology of the legal

profession: though the underlying ideas of "fairness," "the public interest" etc are the same.   One Scottish study has noted:

> ... there are two aspects of justice in conflict: firstly, the justice created by certainty, by having fixed rules which can be relied on in all cases;   and secondly the justice arising from an independent consideration of each case in all its own particular circumstances.   The former may result in hardship and unfairness in particular cases, but all the parties involved in the given area will know the legal position and can act on that knowledge with confidence.   The latter ensures justice in the individual cases, but leaves the law, and those whose actions are guided by it, in a state of great uncertainty (Crawford and Reid 1982: 3).

The basic issue here is one which constantly arises in planning: flexibility versus certainty, or discretion versus precision, or adaptability versus stability.   The balance is drawn differently in different places and times.   This is the case not only within Canada but a fortiori between Canada and other countries.

Chapter 12
Epilogue: Some Reflections
on the Nature of Canadian Planning

Since their formal origins in the years before World War 1,
planning in Canada has never been purely British or purely
American

P.J.Smith 1986

This book is an essentially descriptive account of selected
issues of urban and regional planning in Canada. Much more
could be written, not only on the matters discussed, but also on
the many which have been omitted. The selection has been a
personal one, based on the material was collected by way of
library searches and visits to each of the ten provinces. Hopefully, it is not idiosyncratic but, for reasons of length, if nothing
else, a stop-line had to be drawn somewhere; and that place
admits of no logical determination. This follows from the pragmatic approach adopted, which stemmed basically from the
question "what is urban and regional planning in Canada, and
how does it work?"

This is an unashamedly untheoretical approach, and it
leads to difficulties which must be acknowledged. There is, for
instance, hardly any discussion of the concept of planning. The
author does not apologize for this: there are plenty of books
which deal specifically with the issue, and it was no part of his
intention to add to them. The volume is a resource upon which
more theoretically-inclined writers can draw.

Nevertheless, some attempt at generalization is required.
This is facilitated by the fortuitous geographical aspects of the
author's career. After some twenty years experience (largely,

though   not entirely, academic) of British planning, he had six years in Canada, followed by (at the time of the final revision of this text) a couple of years in the United States.

This has prompted a series of questions relating to the nature of the operation of planning in the three countries. The similarities and contrasts are fascinating, but they are also elusive. Scottish planning is different from that in England and Wales; Northern Ireland is different again. In Canada, the operation of planning in Newfoundland is very different from Ontario, while Quebec and Alberta display markedly individual characteristics. Indeed, to generalize about Canadian planning is almost inevitably a travesty of the truth. Of course, the United States is so diverse that generalization is extremely hazardous. Yet it could be argued that the internal differences are a matter of degree, not of kind, whereas there are essential differences among the countries which reflect their particular histories, cultures and values.

Comparisons of this nature have an honorable history and, indeed, some may argue that there is yet little to match the depth of analysis of the classics of Tocqueville's *Democracy in America,* Bagehot's *The English Constitution* and, later, Porter's *The Vertical Mosaic.* Lipset summed up the situation in these words:

> The United States is egalitarian and populist, Great Britain is deferential and elitist, while Canada (and Australia) fall in between (Lipset 1963a: 515).

The subject has proved to be of endless fascination, and it straddles a wide range of disciplinary fields, from sociology to marketing (Lipset 1963b; Arnold and Barnes 1979).

The object of this chapter is a modest one: it is to explore some ideas about the differences and similarities among the planning systems of three countries which share something of a common heritage, and something of a common language. The commonalities, however, begin to look less convincing when one begins to examine them. Thus, though Britain, Canada and the United States have a common heritage in democratic government, the form of the governmental systems is markedly different. The centralized British system, even with its relatively strong local government, contrasts sharply with the high degree of provincial autonomy in Canada. This, in turn, is strikingly different from the situation in the United States where the federal government has played a much more significant role in planning at the local level in such matters as, for example, environmental protection and hazardous waste disposal.

There are, of course, major differences in the size of the three countries and their populations. Canada is in area almost ten percent larger than the United States, but it has little more than a tenth of its population (most of whom are located close to the U.S. border). Great Britain has more than twice the population of Canada, but a land area about the size of Oregon or Wyoming.

Britain led the way in the industrial revolution and, as a result, produced the first large urban slums and also the first public health and planning legislation, together with a local government system increasingly well-equipped to implement some (though not all) of this. There was also a marked increase in the standard of living, but the bill for the progress made in those times is far from fully paid: as is clearly evidenced today in cities like Glasgow, Liverpool and Birmingham.

Canada, with its staples-producing economy, was very different: though this is not to suggest that urban squalor was lacking. There was little pressure for planning, though an abortive movement began in the early years of the twentieth century with a nice compound of British and American influences.

Other significant differences arose in the interwar years. The depression hit all three countries, but curiously gave rise to an unprecedented housebuilding boom in England and Wales (Richardson and Aldcroft 1968). This peaked out in 1938 at 340,000 completions; only slightly lower than the United States figure (406,000 starts). More strikingly, the figures for 1933 were 218,000 completions for England and Wales, and 93,000 starts for the United States. Over the whole interwar period,

England and Wales produced four million houses while the United States (with three times the population) produced ten million. As a result, the suburbanization of England and Wales proceeded even more rapidly than that of the United States and, given the relatively tiny size of England and Wales, its effect was even more dramatic. The embryonic planning system could not cope with the pressures; indeed, by 1937, it had reacted by zoning sufficient land to accommodate nearly 300 million people (Barlow Report 1940: 113). An important factor here was the "compensation bogey": municipalities could not prevent development without paying compensation.

The catalyst of war brought about an abrupt change in the whole climate of public opinion towards town planning and, in Britain, a system was established which dealt decisively with the compensation problem: both development rights and development values were nationalized. At the same time, local authorities were given extremely strong powers of development control.

In the United States, such provisions were inconceivable but, in any case, there was little reason for them. Land was plentiful: or, at least, appeared to be so. In Canada, the situation was different again. A mere 800,000 dwellings were added to the stock between 1921 and 1941, and little effective governmental action was taken (Saywell 1975). At the end of the second war, Canada had the worst housing shortage of the three countries. Moreover, it lacked the mechanisms for dealing with this, either through the private sector as was done in the United States, or through the public sector, as in Britain. The situation was transformed in the early postwar years with the establishment of the Central Mortgage and Housing Corporation, which provided finance and technical services and also promoted the formation of large building firms.

It would be interesting to expand this rapid review into a comprehensive analysis which, with other trends (to be touched on later), could show how differing conditions have shaped the course of planning in the three countries. That task must await another time. Here there are other differences which must be mentioned. Many of these are of an economic, political or ethnic origin. Some are more subtle than others, as revealed, for example, by the fascinating work of Goldberg, Mark and Mercer (Goldberg 1977 and 1978; Mercer 1979; Goldberg and Mercer 1980; Mercer and Goldberg 1982; Mark and Goldberg 1982).

There are also striking differences among the cities and the urban systems of the three countries. Geographers have written extensively on this but, in other directions (and with other disciplines), transatlantic comparisons have been surprisingly few. There are, of course, Alistair Cooke's "Letters from America" which, even if largely anecdotal, are insightful. But there are no letters from Britain or from Canada. Indeed, it is not too much of an exaggeration to say that Canada is a country little known outside its borders. Perhaps this is one of the reasons why Canadians are so preoccupied with "Canadian content" and "the Canadian identity." (Who was it who said that the search for the Canadian identity *is* the Canadian identity?) One history of Canada opens with the sentence, "perhaps the most striking thing about Canada is that it is not part of the United States" (Brebner 1960); but the same writer was closer to the truth when he commented that "Americans are benevolently ignorant about Canada, while Canadians are malevolently well informed about the United States" (Colombo 1976: 36).

There is an enormous number of quotations such as this, many of them superficial, some amusing, but few of any direct help in identifying the distinctive features of Canadian planning and the ways it differs from British and American. The work of Goldberg and his colleagues, though not specifically directed at this question, takes us much closer to it.

Government in Canada is complex, confused and on occasion virtually incomprehensible. Much of the reason for this lies in the federal nature of the constitution and the inevitable conflicts and compromises to which this gives rise. There is, however, another factor: one which lies much deeper in the basic character of the Canadian political system. Unlike the political systems of Britain and the United States which polarize, in rhetoric if not always in action, progressive and conservative   forces, Canadian politics is unpolarized.   In Porter's words:

> It would probably be safe to say that Canada has never had a political system with this dynamic quality. Its two major political parties do not focus to the right and the left. In the sense that both are closely linked with corporate enterprise the dominant focus has been to the right. One of the reasons why this condition has prevailed is that Canada lacks clearly articulated goals and values stemming from some charter instrument which emphasizes progress and equality. If there is a major goal of Canadian Society it can best be described as an integrative goal. The maintenance of national unity has overridden any other goals there might have been, and has prevented a polarizing, within the political system, of conservative and progressive forces ... The dialogue is between unity and discord rather than progressive and conservative forces (Porter 1965: 368).

At the provincial level some polarization has been seen, but it has typically been a short-lived swing to the left: a temporary lurch.

This distinctive characteristic of Canada is worth a little more comment since its implications are both wide and, more to the immediate point, relevant to the subject matter of this chapter. To quote further from Porter:

> Canada has no resounding charter myth proclaiming a utopia against which, periodically, progress can be measured. At the most, national goals and dominant values seem to be expressed in geographical terms such as "from sea to sea" rather than in social terms such as "all men are created equal," or "liberty, fraternity and equality." In the United States there is a utopian image which slowly over time bends intractable social patterns in the direction of equality, but a Canadian counterpart of this image is difficult to find (Porter 1965: 366).

The result has been to make Canadian governmental policies highly pragmatic and, on occasion, volatile. At the same time, the effect has been to promote certain types of political control and to restrain others. The tendency has been to give politics a low profile and certainly to "keep politics out of local government." Yet a different philosophy of "politics as business"

(Nelles 1974) has led to extensive public programs of which many a self-proclaimed socialist government could be proud.

A limited degree of politicization of local government has developed since the end of the second world war and particularly in the seventies, but the predominant view remains of a widespread distrust of politics and a hankering after the older business tradition. The tangible results are still very evident in the plethora of non-elected boards, the independence of agencies like Ontario Hydro and, in a different but perhaps more eloquent manner, in the obiter dicta of the Ontario Municipal Board. A striking illustration is to be found in the decision of the board on Toronto's 45-Foot Bylaw. In criticizing the city's chief planner for supporting this "irresponsible" method of discretionary control, the board expostulated that he was "merely attempting to satisfy the demands of the council and political expediency" (Ontario Municipal Board 1976: 238).

The equating of political control with political expediency is, of course, an old ruse for discrediting an opposing view even if, as in the case of the Ontario Municipal Board, the political philosophies are implicit and unrecognized as such by their spokesmen.

The absence of party politics at the local level is one of the striking differences between the Canadian and the British local government systems. Of course, individual council members may be elected with political party support, and their political sympathies may be common knowledge, but it is normal for voting to be on a personal basis. In fact, there is a general reluctance to associate municipal affairs with party politics: a reluctance shared by the electors and the elected.

As Feldman and Graham (1979: 101) have argued, this can be interpreted as a lack of political maturity at the municipal level:

> By and large, local politicians in Canada seek election on the basis of service rather than on the basis of an articulated platform. This feature of municipal elections is supported by the absence of parties in the majority of Canadian municipalities. Indeed, the tendency of local politicians to publicly divorce

politics (a dirty word) from municipal government perpetuates the political immaturity of the system. A second manifestation of political immaturity is the continuing perspective that municipal governments are really only a training ground for those individuals who are ambitious for elected office at a higher level. Municipal service is interpreted and used as a prelude to real politics. A final indication of the absence of political maturity is the non-existence, generally, of a rational planned policy-making process, coupled with the lack of a municipal perspective on policy. Interests tend to be articulated at the municipal level and inserted into the municipal political process in a haphazard way.

The implications for the making of urban planning policy are serious, particularly in the major urban agglomerations. Masson (1976) has argued that it is the organizational structure of the senior parties that has precluded their actively contesting local elections. This vacuum has been filled by non-partisan political organizations. As a consequence, "democracy at the local level in Canada has been undermined." Moreover:

> ... municipal political structures have not kept pace with urbanization. In the twentieth century, Canada has moved rapidly from an agricultural to an urban society ... At one time communities were smaller and had relatively homogeneous sets of values: the allocation of public goods was non-controversial. Today urban areas are heterogeneous in composition; consequently diverse socio-economic groups and neighborhoods compete for scarce public goods. Unfortunately, the political process is not designed to accommodate these increasing demands.

Some political scientists suggest that there is a growing trend towards party politics at the local level, though the evidence does not yet appear to be convincing (Masson and Anderson 1972; Masson 1976; Magnusson and Sancton 1983).

In this, as in so many aspects of governmental machinery, history is of major importance; and since local government is a provincial, not a federal, responsibility, one can expect differences among the provinces. In fact, given the widely differing histories of the ten provinces, the similarities (both in local government and in urban planning) are more striking than the dissimilarities. Certainly the early developments in Upper Canada influenced other provinces, and certain federal acts have had a standardizing effect.

Though the study of urban history is a relatively new growth in Canada (Artibise 1981 and 1984), there are accounts of the history of local government which are useful in aiding an understanding of how the machinery of planning works (Crawford 1954; Weaver 1977; Tindal and Tindal 1984). There are some salient points. As elsewhere, urbanization and its attendant problems have been major factors in the development both of local government and of urban planning. More unexpectedly in a country of the vastness of Canada, one individual played a most influential role in the introduction of planning legislation, though there was little implementation before the outbreak of the first world war. This was Thomas Adams, a British planner of international repute (Simpson 1981), who was appointed to the Commission for the Conservation of Natural Resources. (Again, unexpectedly, this was a federal body.) By 1916 only British Columbia, Prince Edward Island and Quebec did not have a planning act designed by Adams, and based on the British planning act of 1909.

Despite his British background, Adams was obliged to provide for an appointed planning board or commission. This was not only because of the widespread mistrust of elected government (Armstrong 1968: 30), but also because local government was ill-equipped for the technical work of town planning. Efficient planning required an ad hoc agency. Indeed, as P.J. Smith (1986) has noted:

> So great was the faith in the integrity and efficiency of the commission form of government that local authorities in New Brunswick and Alberta were given the option, under the planning statutes, of appointing commissions with full power to prepare and implement town planning schemes: in the North American situation, it was a logical adaptation of a planning system lifted from an altogether different administrative context.

Thus, in addition to "the city beautiful" and "the city healthy," there was a third element: "the city efficient" (Kantor 1973; Peterson 1976; Van Nus 1977; Tindal and Tindal 1984). The result was "a more complex, less accountable local government, more responsible to economy and efficiency than to the voters" (Tindal and Tindal 1984: 46). Its legacy remains with the largely non-political character of Canadian local government.

It was against this background of efficiency that zoning became so readily acceptable. Zoning is simply the restriction of land uses. It stems from the law of nuisance or, in American terminology, from police power. The popularity of zoning lies in its protective character: it purports to fix the use of land and thereby to safeguard the property values associated with the determined use. Indeed, "in the early years zoning was consciously sold to the public as a means of protection for property. This theme was central to every plea for public support for planning programs" (Ontario Economic Council 1973: 72). As we can see, the reality is different, but the power of the myth lives on.

Zoning fits in well with Canadian attitudes to orderly regulation and the limitation on the discretion to be allowed to local government. However, it is best suited for conditions of stability: with the vast changes which have taken place in the Canadian urban scene over the last quarter of a century, its substance has inevitably changed.

In comparing the Canadian planning system with that of the United States, one is struck by a fundamental difference which might be encapsulated in the suggestion that Canadian deference to authority places "peace, order and good government" above the American priority for "life, liberty and the pursuit of happiness" (Friedenberg 1980). This gives Canadian urban and regional planning a more wide-ranging and acceptable role than is the case in the United States. It stops short, however, of fully accepting the degree of discretionary controls which characterize the British planning system.

Mention has already been made of the absence of a property right from the Canadian Charter of Rights. The contrast with the United States is particularly striking when the wording of Section 7 of the Charter is compared with the Fifth Amendment to the U.S. Constitution. Section 7 states that:

> Everyone has the right to life, liberty and security of the person and the right not to be deprived thereof except in accordance with the principles of fundamental justice.

The Fifth Amendment provides:

> No person shall be ... deprived of life, liberty or property without due process of law; nor shall private property be taken without just compensation.

Thus, in place of "property" the Canadian Charter has "security of the person." Though this has precluded the vast amount of litigation on "the taking issue," it has not totally prevented it. In one case it was upheld that property rights are entrenched in the provisions of the Charter through extension of the notion of personal security (Mackenzie 1985: 13). A later case, however, refused to accept such "aggressive intellectual leaps" and concluded that no such rights existed. Mackenzie comments that the latter view is likely to prevail. Moreover:

> This being so, the existence of the Charter, while rapidly accelerating principles of fundamental fairness in other areas of Canadian law, could through the omission of property rights from the Charter severely curtail the development of principles of procedural fairness concerning property (Ibid: 15).

A further feature of the Canadian planning scene is the prime importance of the provinces. In the Confederation, the federal government has the power of the purse and considerable land holdings, but its effective strategic power is weak, and it has taken a lower profile than the federal government of the United States. The provinces are also the masters of local government both in law and generally in practice. As with Britain, they can reorganize local governments, and even create regional authorities. The big cities may be beginning to flex their muscles, but the economic conditions of the eighties are not propitious for any significant increase in their clout.

Central control of municipal and regional planning operates in both Canada and Britain, though its nature and extent   vary. Within Canada, most provinces require approval of municipal plans and zoning bylaws, though again there are differences in the character of the approval process. In Britain, which has a unitary planning code, all structure plans are subject to central approval, while secondary local plans are "adopted" by local authorities; though the central government has a reserve power to direct that a local plan "shall not have effect" until it is approved. There is no British equivalent of a zoning bylaw, but refusals by local planning authorities can be appealed to the planning ministry which can modify or overrule the local authority's decision.

There is little in the United States to compare with "central control." Plan making and implementation are essentially local issues, though the federal government has become active in highways, water and environmental matters, and a number of states have become involved in land use planning in recent years (Healy and Rosenberg 1979; DeGrove 1984). While the role in a few states may be on the increase, the general picture remains as Delafons described it in 1969:

> Planning is so intimately related to local interests that it is difficult to generalize about its objectives. So far as controlling private development is concerned, the job of the planner is largely that of anticipating the trend of private development, making adequate provision for all acceptable uses, and setting standards for new development which reflect local wishes (Delafons 1969: 36).

However, a striking feature of the planning system in the United States is the important role played by the courts: a role which may be increasing, as illustrated by the Mount Laurel cases in which the New Jersey courts set up machinery to enforce non-discrimination in the provision of housing and to over-ride the discriminatory policies and practices of certain municipalities (Burchell et al 1983; Erber 1983; Franklin 1983; Potomac Institute 1983; Mallach 1984). It could be argued that, in one sense, judicial controls in the United States take the place of the political and administrative controls of Britain and Canada.

This raises a host of interesting questions which would repay further inquiry. Unfortunately, the legal position in relation to major United States planning issues is often unclear, and the Supreme Court has frequently shied away from giving a much-needed lead. One result has been an inconsistency of decisions among the states. The same has been the case, but to a lesser extent, in Canada, though a provincial court will take account of the decisions of other provincial courts, and even those of British courts. While an aggrieved party in the United States would naturally turn to the courts for redress, in Britain he would appeal to the central planning department. On balance, Canada leans to the British model, though many of its appellate bodies are more independent than the British inspectorate.

The role of the federal government on the Canadian planning scene is an interesting if enigmatic one. Despite the constraints of the British North America Act, the federal level, after an abortive start in 1918 by Thomas Adams, the Commission of Conservation, and the Canadian Construction Association (Saywell 1975: 150), was forced by the depression to take action to provide both new housing and jobs for construction workers, with the Dominion Housing Act of 1935 and the National Housing Act of 1938 (Carver 1948). The connection with planning was none too clear: in fact, there was little enthusiasm for the legislation at all, except in relation to the hoped-for impact on employment. Nevertheless, the precedent had been set, and the federal government had proved to be effectively somewhat less hesitant than the provinces to act directly in the housing area, and indirectly in planning.

As in so many areas of social policy, it was the war which became the catalyst (Titmuss 1958); and the second National Housing Act of 1944 was a major advance in housing policy (Rose 1980) which in turn significantly affected planning policy. The overt emphasis, however, was on the creation of jobs: the act was "to promote the construction of new houses, the repair and modernization of existing houses, the improvement of housing and living conditions, and the expansion of employment in the postwar period." The establishment, in the following year, of the Central (now Canada) Mortgage and Housing Corporation was a most significant step in that it created an agency which did far more than act as a housing bank. It recruited architects and planners. It promulgated and enforced construction and layout standards. And, given its heavily British bias (Carver 1960), it played a major role in the postwar development of the suburbs (Carver 1975). Its impact, nevertheless, was less dramatic than was the case in the United States where the federal road program, tax-aided owner-occupation, and urban renewal had a major impact on the cities, sometimes of a devastating character.

This, however, is to take a narrow view of planning. On a broader front, the role of the federal government has been long established and pervasive: in transcontinental communications, in resource development and in regional planning for example. But rarely does the Canadian government act alone in these fields: typically its responsibilities are shared, often uneasily, with the provinces; and frequently the provinces have a predominant position except in terms of financial resources.

The Canadian federal role is different from that of the United States. This is most dramatically illustrated by the federal highway programs in the two countries. Canada has built only one road, the Trans-Canada Highway. Though individual provinces have financed many more, the mileage is miniscule in comparison with that of the United States. Similarly, urban renewal, during its relatively short life, involved far less federal funding in Canada (50 percent) than in the United States (95 percent) (Goldberg and Mercer 1980: 164).

This is not to imply that public sector involvement as a whole is different in the two countries. Smith (1986) has concluded that, despite some differences, "government in the United States has been just as important as government in Canada in terms of city building." He continues:

> The key distinction in terms of public sector involvement is jurisdictional. In the United States, the federal government has played the key role in urban affairs, while in Canada public sector activity stems largely from municipal and provincial

governments. This striking difference between federalism in the two countries is not quickly explained, but one view is that the belief in the "American way of life" is so pervasive "that the American character has tended to coalesce about" an almost unitary form of government; a form that "almost obviates the federal nature of the American state, since regional and/or state concerns appear to be truly overwhelmed by the sense of nationhood" (Mercer and Goldberg 1982: 16). In Canada, in contrast, one of the few unifying symbols, particularly in the western provinces, is "Ottawa bashing"; there is a perennial clash between federal and provincial governments. It can be argued, then, that the U.S. federation is far more static in the sense that the respective roles of the states and the federal government have long since been decided with the federal government in the ascendancy (the current administration notwithstanding). The Canadian confederation is far more dynamic and fluid, with power shifting among the various governments over time and space.

Nevertheless, both countries are witnessing a withdrawal of federal interest and an attempt to shift responsibilities to the provinces or states. This is partly a matter of political philosophy and partly a matter of reducing federal expenditure.

On this, there is clearly a similarity with Britain where successive public expenditure cuts have greatly affected housing and planning programs. Zero population growth has also reduced the requirements for large developments. Thus politics, economics and demographics have conspired to abolish much of the new towns program (in England and Wales), to promote the sale of public housing, to cut the highway program, to "liberalize" planning procedures, and so forth.

It used to be said that while British planning was essentially concerned with "controlling" development, the North American equivalent was overwhelmingly concerned with "promoting" development. Much of that difference has now gone; but not all of it. Indeed, perhaps the most surprising aspect of the British planning scene has been the permanence of its essential elements. The most important of these is the nationalization of development rights in land and the system of discretionary planning controls.

The contrast with zoning is marked, though more so in theory than in practice, since both Canada and the United

States have evolved new techniques of planning control which are far removed from the original rigid system of zoning.

A final point of comparison is the role of public participation in planning. The right to participation is deeply embedded in the American political system and, of course, there is always the possibility of a challenge on constitutionality (entirely foreign to Britain, but newly arrived on the Canadian scene). Public participation in both Britain and Canada has increased significantly in the last two decades, but a basic difference remains in the role played by the planning system. Put simply (and therefore exaggeratedly) the system in the United States is more concerned with determining conflicts between private interests in land, while the British system is more concerned with deciding where the public interest lies. The difference is epitomized by the absence in Britain of third party rights in most planning applications: the only parties to an application are the applicant and the local authority. Moreover, any appeal is dealt with by the central planning ministry rather than by the courts, except where there is a challenge on a point of law.

The Canadian situation is more difficult to summarize since it varies so greatly among, and sometimes within, provinces. However, one is struck by what Bregha (1977: 22) in a provocative essay, has referred to as the "cultural base of public participation." He writes:

> Public participation, however it is conceived in Canada, has many patterns and appears determined not only by education, income, and class but also by language, religion and culture. In some countries, it seems quiet, ordered, and instructive; in others, it is vocal and perpetually hangs on the brink of anarchy. In some societies, it is far more evident than in others; in still others it apparently does not exist at all. All of this suggests that public participation is much more a product of a culture than of any given political system. The latter, however, may facilitate or impede public participation: a truly totalitarian regime can make it impossible while no democracy has yet succeeded in making it as widespread and effective as political philosophers have desired.

Bregha's argument is compelling. Lotz (1979: 55) was perhaps making essentially the same point when he quipped, "in the west, there is too much geography, and too little history. In Atlantic Canada, there is too little geography, and too much history ... "

The thought is prompted that it might be the case that, in examining the various aspects of public participation, attention has been too much in certain directions (labelled "law" or "ideology") and too little in others (which might be labelled "sociology" or "political culture"). Certainly, there is a danger that Canadian planning is misleadingly interpreted either in British terms, with its highly elaborate legal apparatus of planning dominated by what McAuslan (1980) calls the public interest ideology, or in American terms where the constitutional situation is different.

This raises some large and interesting, but difficult, questions, which are worthy of further research. In Canada, at least, the developing field of urban political studies promises to provide more insights than traditional studies of law or planning have so far done (Kiernan 1982; Magnusson and Sancton 1983). But generally, the field is clearly one for interdisciplinary study.

Bibliography

(Official and institutional publishers are indicated only where the source is not apparent from the authorship or the title.)

Adler, G. M. (1971) *Land Planning by Administrative Regulation: The Policies of the Ontario Municipal Board,* University of Toronto Press

Advisory Commission on Intergovernmental Relations (1974) *A Look to the North: Canadian Regional Experience,* U. S. Government Printing Office

Advisory Commission on Reconstruction (1943) *Report,* King's Printer, Ottawa

Alberta (1984) *Environment News,* Vol. 7, No. 3, May-June 1984, (Special issue on River Basin Planning)

Alberta Institute of Law Research and Reform (1973) Report No. 12, *Expropriation,* University of Alberta

Alberta Municipal Affairs (1974) *Towards a New Planning Act for Alberta*

——————————— (1979-81) *Regional Planning System Study.* This consists of 13 working papers:

1 *Revised Terms of Reference, Regional Planning Study,* February 1979

2 *Towards a Framework for Resolving Regional Planning Issues,* April 1979

3 *A Mechanism for the Review and Approval of Regional Plans by the Alberta Government: A Proposal,* June 1979

4   *Coordination in Regional Planning: A Consultant's Report*, July 1979

5   *Guidelines for Regional Plan Review*, January 1980

6   *Plan Non-Conformity: Notes on the Shape of the Problem*, April 1980

7   *A Proposed Training Program in Planning*, April 1980

8   *Municipal Attitudes Towards Regional Planning in Alberta*, October 1980

9   *Regional Planning Experience Elsewhere: A Discussion Paper*, October 1980

10   *Public Lands and Resource Issues: A Discussion Paper*, April 1981

11   *Interim Report and Recommendations to the Alberta Planning Board*, April 1981

12   *Demands upon the System: A Consultant's Report*, May 1981

13   *A Summary of Preliminary Findings: A Discussion Paper*, September 1981

_____ (1980a) *Planning in Alberta: A Guide and Directory*, revised edition

_____ (1980b) *The New Town of Fox Creek General Municipal Plan*

_____ (1980c) *Regional Plan Review and Approval Process: Technical Review of the Edmonton Draft Regional Plan for Discussion by the Alberta Planning Board*, (prepared by the Inter-Agency Branch of Alberta Municipal Affairs)

_____ (1982) *Revised Guidelines for Regional Plan Preparation and Review*

_____ (1983a) *The Calgary Regional Plan and the Calgary Regional Planning Commission: Recommended Changes*

_____ (1983b) *A Decision Report: Calgary Regional Plan*

_____ (1984a) *The Planner as a Catalyst*

_____ (1984b) *The Historical Evolution of the Department of Municipal Affairs*

Alberta White Paper (1984) *Proposals for an Industrial and Science Strategy for Albertans 1985 to 1990*

Alexander, D. (1983) *Atlantic Canada and Confederation: Essays in Canadian Political Economy,* (compiled by E. W. Sager, L. R. Fischer and S. O. Pierson), University of Toronto Press

Alexander, E. R. (1981) "If Planning isn't Everything, Maybe it's Something," *Town Planning Review,* Vol. 52, pp. 131-42

Antoft, K. et al (1971) *Matters Related to Non-Resident Land Ownership in Nova Scotia,* Dalhousie University, Institute of Public Affairs, Discussion Paper No 71-02

Applebaum-Hébert Report (1982) *Report of the Federal Cultural Policy Review Committee*

Armour, A. (ed.) (1984) *The Not-In-My-Backyard Syndrome,* Symposium Proceedings, York University (Toronto), Faculty of Environmental Studies

Armstrong, A. H. (1968) "Thomas Adams and the Commission of Conservation," in L. O. Gertler (ed.) (1968)

Arnold, S. J. and J. G. Barnes (1979) "Canadian and American National Character as a Basis for Market Segmentation," *Research in Marketing,* Vol. 2, pp. 1-35

Artibise, A. F. J. and G. A. Stelter (1979) *The Usable Urban Past: Planning and Politics in the Modern Canadian City,* Macmillan

_____ (1981) *Canada's Urban Past: A Bibliography to 1980 and a Guide to Canadian Urban Studies,* University of British Columbia Press

_____ (1984) "Exploring the North American West: A Comparative Urban Perspective," *American Review of Canadian Studies,* Vol. 14, pp. 1-44

_____ (1986) *Power and Place: Canadian Urban Development in the North American Context,* University of British Columbia Press

Ashford, D. E. (ed.) (1980) *National Resources and Urban Policy,* Methuen

Ashworth, W. (1954) *The Genesis of Modern British Town Planning,* Routledge and Kegan Paul

Aucoin, P. and R. French (1974) *Knowledge, Power and Public Policy,* Science Council of Canada

Aucoin, P. and H. Bakvis (1984) "Organizational Differentiation and Integration: The Case of Regional Economic Development Policy in Canada," *Canadian Public Administration,* Vol. 27, No. 3, pp. 348-71

Audet, R. and A. Le Henaff (1984) *The Land Planning Framework of Canada: An Overview,* Environment Canada, Lands Directorate, Working Paper 28

Axworthy, L. (1980) "The Best Laid Plans Oft Go Astray: The Case of Winnipeg," in M. O. Dickerson, S. Drabek and J. T. Woods (eds.) (1980)

_____ and J. Cassidy (1974) *Unicity: The Transition,* University of Winnipeg, Institute of Urban Studies

Babcock, R. F. (1966) *The Zoning Game,* University of Wisconsin Press

Baker, A. (1983) "Bulldozer Mentality Dominated the First 20 Years," *Globe and Mail* (Toronto) 15 April 1983

Bankes, N. and A. R. Thompson (1981) *Monitoring for Impact Assessment and Management: An Analysis of the Legal and Administrative Framework,* University of British Columbia, Westwater Research Centre

Banting, K. G. (1982) *The Welfare State and Canadian Federalism,* McGill-Queen's University Press

Barlow Report (1940) *Report of the Royal Commission on the Distribution of the Industrial Population,* Cmd 6153, Her Majesty's Stationery Office, London

Barrett, S. and C. Fudge (eds.) (1981) *Policy and Action: Essays on the Implementation of Public Policy,* Methuen

Barrett, S. and J. Riley (eds.) (1980) *Protection of Natural Areas in Ontario,* York University (Toronto), Faculty of Environmental Studies

Baxter, D. (1974) *Speculation in Land,* University of British Columbia, Faculty of Commerce and Business Administration

_____ (1975) *Capital Taxes Pertaining to Real Property,* Real Estate Institute of British Columbia

_____ and S. W. Hamilton (1975) *A Commentary on the Ontario Land Speculation Tax Act,* University of British Columbia, Faculty of Commerce and Business Administration

Bean, W. and K. A. Graham et al (1983) *Regional Development: Constitutional Development in the Northwest Territories,* Western Constitutional Forum

Beanlands, G. E. and P. N. Duinker (1975) *An Ecological Framework for Environmental Impact Assessment in Canada,* Dalhousie University, Institute for Resource and Environmental Studies

Beaubien, C. and R. Tabacnik (1977) *People and Agricultural Land,* Science Council of Canada

Beauchamp, K. P. (1976) *Land Management in the Canadian North,* Canadian Arctic Resources Committee

_____ (1985) *Port Policy for the Canadian Arctic Coast,* Canadian Arctic Resources Committee

Bellan Report (1977) *Report and Recommendations of the Winnipeg Land Prices Inquiry Commission,* Queen's Printer, Manitoba

Bentley, C. F. (1977) "Agricultural Changes and Resource Endowments," *Agriculture and Forestry Bulletin,* University of Alberta, Faculty of Extension

Berger Commission (1977) *Report of the Mackenzie Valley Pipeline Inquiry,* Supply and Services Canada

Berger, T. R. (1978) "The Mackenzie Valley Pipeline Inquiry," *Osgoode Hall Law Journal,* Vol. 16, pp. 639-47

_____ (1979) "The Place of Impact Evaluation in Decision Making," in *Second Environmental Impact Assessment Conference,* University of British Columbia, Centre for Continuing Education

Bernard, A., J. Léveillé, and G. Lord (1974a) *Profile: Montreal 1974,* Ministry of State for Urban Affairs, Ottawa

_____ (1974b) *Profile: Ottawa-Hull 1974,* Ministry of State for Urban Affairs, Ottawa

_____ (1975) *Profile: Quebec 1975,* Ministry of State for Urban Affairs, Ottawa

Berton, P. (1982) *Why We Act Like Canadians: A Personal Explanation of Our National Character,* McClelland and Stewart

Bettison, D. D. (1975) *The Politics of Canadian Urban Development,* University of Alberta Press

Bigenwald, C. A. and N. H. Richardson (1974) *Haldimand-Norfolk: A Case Study in Planning by Provincial-Municipal Task Force,* (mimeo)

Blumenfeld, H. (1966) "The Role of the Federal Government in Urban Affairs," reprinted in H. Blumenfeld (1979a)

_____ (1979a) *Metropolis ... and Beyond,* Wiley

_____ (1979b) "Foreword" to W. T. Perks and I. M. Robinson (eds.) (1979)

_____ (1980) *On Prices of Residential Lots and Houses: A Critical Evaluation of the Data and Conclusions of the Greenspan Report,* University of Toronto, Department of Urban and Regional Planning, Papers on Planning and Design 25

_____ (1982a) *Where Did All the Metropolitanites Go?,* University of Toronto, Department of Urban and Regional Planning, Papers on Planning and Design 32

_____ (1982b) *Have the Secular Trends of Population Distribution Been Reversed?,* University of Toronto, Centre for Urban and Community Studies, Research Paper 137

Boadway, R. and F. Flatters (1982) *Equalization in a Federal State: An Economic Analysis,* Economic Council of Canada

Bocking, R. C. (1972) *Canada's Water: For Sale?* James Lewis and Samuel

Bolger, W. P. F. (1973) *Canada's Smallest Province,* Deyell (Toronto)

Bossons, J. (1978) *Reforming Planning in Ontario: Strengthening the Municipal Role,* Ontario Economic Council

Boston Gilbert Henry Associates (1980) *Waste Reduction: Criteria for Evaluating Management Options Available to Government,* Ontario Waste Management Advisory Board

Bothwell, R., I. Drummond and J. English (1981) *Canada Since 1945: Power, Politics and Provincialism,* University of Toronto Press

Bourne, L. S. (1967) *Private Redevelopment of the Central City,* University of Chicago, Department of Geography, Research Paper 112

_____ (1977) *The Housing Supply and Price Debate: Divergent Views and Policy Consequences,* University of Toronto, Centre for Urban and Community Studies, Research Paper 86

_____ and J. W. Simmons (1978) *Systems of Cities: Readings on Structure, Growth and Policy,* Oxford University Press

Bradfield, M. (1981) *Evaluation of Federal Regional Programs,* Dalhousie University, Institute of Public Affairs

Bray, C. E. (1980) "Agricultural Land Regulation in Several Canadian Provinces," *Canadian Public Policy,* Vol. 6, pp. 591-604

Brebner, J. B. (1960) *Canada: A Modern History,* University of Michigan Press

Bregha, F. J. (1978) "Further Directions for Public Participation in Canada," in B. Sadler (ed.) (1978)

Breton, R. (1982) "Regionalism in Canada," in D. M. Cameron (ed.) (1982)

Brewis, T. N. (1969) *Regional Economic Policies in Canada,* Macmillan

_____ (1976) "Regional Economic Policy: The Federal Role," in G. Schramm (ed.) (1976)

_____ and G. Paquet (1968) "Regional Development Planning in Canada: An Exploratory Essay," *Canadian Public Administration,* Vol. 11, pp. 123-62

British Columbia (1980) *The Planning Act: A Discussion Paper,* Queen's Printer, Victoria

British Columbia Court of Appeal (1981) *Hauff v Vancouver,* 28 BCLR 276 (C.A.)

British Columbia Heritage Trust *Annual Reports*

_____ (1983) *Heritage Conservation Bibliography,* compiled by J. Bradshaw (1979); updated by R. Adam (1983)

_____ (1984) *Programs and Guidelines*

British Columbia Ministry of Energy, Mines and Petroleum Resources (1984) *Land Use Policy of the Ministry of*

Energy,   Mines and Petroleum Resources: Information Paper

British Columbia Ministry of Municipal Affairs *Annual Reports*

_____ (1978) *Report of the Regional District Review Committee*

_____ (1979) *Technical Guide for the Preparation of Official Settlement Plans*

_____ (1984) *Greater Vancouver Regional District Review*

British Columbia Ombudsman (1983) *Expropriation Issues, Public Report No 3*

British Columbia Provincial Agricultural Land Commission *Annual Reports*

_____ (1982) *A Guide to the Relationship between Agricultural Land Reserves and Local Government Plans and Bylaws*

_____ (1983) *Ten Years of Agricultural Land Preservation*

British Columbia Supreme Court (1973) *North Vancouver Zoning Bylaw 4277,* [1973] 2 W.W.R. 260 (B.C.S.C.)

Britton, J. N. and J. M. Gilmour (1978) *The Weakest Link: A Technological Perspective on Canadian Industrial Underdevelopment,* Science Council of Canada

Broome Report (1969) *Political and Administrative Structure Review Committee, Report No 1,* Greater Vancouver Regional District

Brown, R. C. (1969) "The Doctrine of Usefulness: Natural Resource and National Park Policy in Canada 1887-1914" in J. G. Nelson (ed.) (1969)

Brownstone, M. and T. J. Plunkett (1983) *Metropolitan Winnipeg: Politics and Reform of Local Government,* University of California Press

Bryant, C. R. (1976) "Some New Perspectives on Agricultural Land Use in the Rural-Urban Fringe," *Ontario Geography,* Vol. 10, pp. 64-78

_____ and L. H. Russwurm (1979) "The Impact of Non-Farm Development on Agriculture: A Synthesis," *Plan Canada,* Vol. 19, pp. 122-39

Buckley, H. and E. Tihanyi (1967) *Canadian Policies for Rural Adjustment,* Economic Council of Canada

Budden, S. and J. Ernst (1973) *The Movable Airport,* Hakkert (Toronto)

Bunce, M. F. and M. J. Troughton (eds.) (1984) *The Pressure of Change in Rural Canada,* York University (Toronto), Atkinson College, Geographical Monographs 14

Burchell, R. W. and G. Sternlieb (1981) *Planning Theories in the 1980s: A Search for Future Directions,* Rutgers University, Center for Urban Policy Research

Burchell, R. W. et al (1983) *Mount Laurel II: Challenge and Delivery of Low-Cost Housing,* Rutgers University, Center for Urban Policy Research

Bureau of Municipal Research (1977a) *Food for the Cities: Disappearing Farmland and Provincial Land Policy*

_____ (1977b) *Design for Development: Where Are You?*

_____ (1981) "Do We Really Need 4000 Local Governments in Ontario?," *BMR Review,* November 1981

Burton, T. L. (1972) *Natural Resource Policy in Canada: Issues and Perspectives,* McClelland and Stewart

_____ (1979) "A Review and Analysis of Canadian Case Studies in Public Participation," *Plan Canada,* Vol. 19, pp. 13-22

_____ and A. Wildgoose (1977) *Public Participation: A General Bibliography and Annotated Review of the Canadian Experience,* Alberta Conservation Authority

Byrne Commission (1963) *Report of the New Brunswick Royal Commission on Finance and Municipal Taxation,* Queen's Printer, Fredericton

Cail, R. E. (1974) *Land, Man and the Law,* University of British Columbia Press

Cairns, A. (1979) "The Other Crisis of Canadian Federalism," *Canadian Public Administration,* Vol. 22, pp. 175-95

Calgary Regional Planning Commission (1981) *Three Hills and District Recreation Master Plan*

Callies, D. L. (1981) "Land Use Controls: An Eclectic Summary for 1980-81," *Urban Lawyer,* Vol. 13, pp. 723-63

Cambridge City (1982) *Official Plan: General City Plan 1981-2001*

Cameron, D. M. (1974) "Urban Policy" in G. B. Doern and V. S. Wilson (eds.) (1974)

_____ (1981) "Regional Economic Disparities: The Challenge to Federalism and Public Policy," *Canadian Public Policy,* 1981, pp. 500-05

_____ (ed.) (1982) *Regionalism and Supernationalism,* Institute for Research on Public Policy (Montreal) and Policy Studies Institute (London)

Cameron, K. (1984) in *PIBC News,* Vol. 25, No. 6, p. 16 (Planning Institute of British Columbia)

Campbell, M. E. and W. M. Glenn (1982) *Profit from Pollution Prevention: A Guide to Industrial Waste Reduction and Recycling,* Pollution Probe

Campbell Report (1984) *Greater Vancouver Regional District Review,* British Columbia, Ministry of Municipal Affairs

Canada (1981) *Economic Development for Canada in the 1980s,* Government of Canada

_____ (1984) Inquiry on Federal Water Policy, *Water is a Mainstream Issue,* Participation Paper

Canada Department of Forestry (1965) *The Canada Land Inventory,* Publication No 1088

Canada Department of Military Plans and Operations (1983) *An Initial Environmental Evaluation on the Proposal to Conduct Air Launched Missile Flight Tests in the Canadian Test Corridor,* National Defence Headquarters

Canada Lands Company (Mirabel) Ltd (1982) *The Future of Mirabel Peripheral Lands*

Canada Senate (1957) *Senate Special Committee on Land Use: Report*

_____ (1958) *Report of the Royal Commission on Canada's Economic Prospects*

_____ (1964) *Report of the Special Committee on Land Use in Canada*

_____ (1982) *Report of the Standing Senate Committee on National Finance: Government Policy and Regional Development*

_____ (1984) *Soil at Risk: Canada's Eroding Future,* Standing Senate Committee on Agriculture, Fisheries and Forestry

Canadian Arctic Resources Committee (1976) *Land Management in the Canadian North,* by K. P. Beauchamp

_____ (1978) *Northern Transitions: Second National Workshop on People, Resources and the Environment North of 60°,* 2 Vols.

_____ (1979) *Reflections on the Environmental Assessment and Review Process,* by W. E. Rees

_____ (1984a) "The Northern Agenda: A Memorandum to the Government of Canada," *Northern Perspectives,* Vol. 12, No. 2, November 1984

_____ (1984b) *National and Regional Interests in the North: Third National Workshop on People, Resources, and the Environment North of 60°*

Canadian Bar Association (Ontario) Municipal Law Section (1977) *Review and Critique of the Report of the Planning Act Review Committee*

Canadian Council of Resource and Environment Ministers (1977) *Environmental Impact Assessments in Canada: A Review of Current Legislation and Practice*

_____ (1979) *Forest Imperatives for Canada: A Proposal for Forest Policy in Canada*

Canadian Environmental Advisory Council (1975) *An Environmental Ethic: Its Formulation and Implications,* by N. H. Morse, Council Report 2

_____ (1977) *Towards an Environmental Ethic,* by D. A. Chant

_____ (1979) *Ecotoxicity: Responsibilities and Opportunities,* by R. H. Hall and D. A. Chant

_____ (1980) *Report of a Meeting between the Public Interest Groups and the Canadian Environmental Advisory Council,* Council Report 9

_____ (1981) *A New Approach to Pest Control in Canada,* by R. H. Hall, Council Report 10

_____ (1983) *Water Management Problems in the Third World,* by P. F. M. McLoughlin, Council Report 12

_____ (1984) *Terms of Reference of the Canadian Environmental Advisory Council,* (approved by the Minister of the Environment 16 April 1984)

_____ (1985a) *Review of Activities 1981-1982/83*

_____ (1985b) *Selected Papers from Assemblies of the Environment Councils of Canada 1975-1980*

Canadian Federation of Mayors and Municipalities (1976) *Puppets on a Shoestring,* (an excerpt is to be found in M. O. Dickerson, S. Drabek and J. T. Woods (eds.) (1980))

Canadian Institute of Planners (1980) *Task Force on Planning Acts: Interim Report*

_____ (1981) *Task Force on Planning Acts: Final Report and Recommendations*

_____ (1983) *Brief to the Federal Government Concerning Federal Policy on Land Use*

Canadian Journal of Regional Science (1982) Special issue on "Public Policy: Urban and Regional Issues," in L. Gertler (ed.), Vol. 5, No. 1, pp. 1-224

Canadian Pulp and Paper Association (1981) *Forests for the Future*

Canadian Tax Foundation (1966) *The Financing of Canadian Federation: The First Hundred Years*

Cannon. J. B. (1984) "Explaining Regional Development in Atlantic Canada: A Review Essay," *Journal of Canadian Studies,* Vol. 19, pp. 63-86

Careless, A. (1977) *Initiative and Response: The Adaptation of Canadian Federalism to Regional Economic Development,* McGill-Queen's University Press

Carr, J. and L. B. Smith (1975) "Public Land Banking and the Price of Land," *Land Economics,* Vol. 51, pp. 316-30

Carroll, J. E. (1982) *Acid Rain: An Issue in Canadian-American Relations,* "Canadian-American Committee" sponsored by C. D. Howe Institute (Canada) and National Planning Association (U.S.A.), Canadian American Committee, Washington DC, July 1982

Carver, H. (1948) *Houses for Canadians,* University of Toronto Press

_____ (1960) "Planning in Canada," *Habitat,* Vol. 3, No. 5, pp. 2-5

_____ (1962) *Cities in the Suburbs,* University of Toronto Press

_____ (1975) *Compassionate Landscape,* University of Toronto Press

Case, E. S., P. Z. R. Finkle and A. R. Lucas (1983) *Fairness in Environmental and Social Impact Assessment Processes: Proceedings of a Seminar,* University of Calgary, Faculty of Law

Central Ontario Lakeshore Urban Complex Task Force (1974) *Report,* Ontario Government Publications

Chandler, M. A. and W. M. Chandler (1980) "Politics of Resource Exploitation," in D. C. MacDonald (ed.) (1980)

Charlottetown Area Regional Development Board (1980) *The Charlottetown Plan*

Christiansen-Ruffman, L. and B. Stuart (1978) "Actors and Processes in Citizen Participation: Negative Aspects of Reliance on Professionals," in B. Sadler (ed.) (1978), pp. 77-102

Clark, A. H. (1959) *Three Centuries and the Island,* University of Toronto Press

Clarke, S.D. (1981) *Environmental Assessment in Australia and Canada,* University of British Columbia, Westwater Research Centre

Clyne Report (1964) *Report of the British Columbia Royal Commission on Expropriation 1961-63,* Queen's Printer, Victoria

Coates, W. E. and O. R. Scott (1979) *A Study of Pit and Quarry Rehabilitation in Southern Ontario,* Ontario Geological Survey, Miscellaneous Paper 83, Ministry of Natural Resources

Code, W. R. (1983) "The Strength of the Centre: Downtown Offices and Metropolitan Decentralization Policy in Ontario," *Environment and Planning A,* Vol. 15, pp. 1361-80

Colombo, J. R. (1976) *Colombo's Concise Canadian Quotations,* Hurtig

Comay Report (1977) *Report of the Ontario Planning Act Review Committee,* (see further under *Ontario Planning Act Review Committee)*

Comay, E. (1984) "Provincial Planning in Ontario: A Not-so-great Planning Fiasco," *Plan Canada,* Vol. 24, pp. 163-4

Conseil d'orientation économique du Québec (1962) *Document de base en vue de la planification*

_____ (1964) *Les exigences de la planification économique*

Corbett, J. G. (1978) "Canadian Cities: How 'American' Are They?" *Urban Affairs Quarterly,* Vol. 13, No. 3, pp. 383-94 (Book Review Essay)

Cordell, A. J. (1971) *The Multinational Firm: Foreign Direct Investment, and Canadian Social Policy,* Science Council of Canada

Corke, S. E. (1983) *Land Use Control in British Columbia: A Contribution to a Comparative Study of Canadian Planning Systems,* University of Toronto, Centre for Urban and Community Studies, Research Paper 138 (Land Policy Paper 3)

Costonis, J. J. (1974) *Space Adrift: Landmark Preservation and the Market Place,* University of Illinois Press

Cotterill, E. M. R. (1984) "The Territorial North," *Canadian Public Administration,* Vol. 27, pp. 188-96

Courchene, T. J. (1981) "A Market Perspective on Regional Disparities," *Canadian Public Policy,* Vol. 7, pp. 506-18

Cranmer, V. (1974a) *Land Use Programs in New Brunswick,* Environment Canada, Lands Directorate

_____ (1974b) *Land Use Programs in Newfoundland and Labrador,* Environment Canada, Lands Directorate

_____ (1974c) *Land Use Programs in Nova Scotia,* Environment Canada, Lands Directorate

_____ (1974d) *Land Use Programs in Prince Edward Island,* Environment Canada, Lands Directorate

Crawford, C. and C. T. Reid (1982) *Planning Officers' Advice and Undertakings: Estoppel and Personal Bar in Public Law,* Scottish Planning Law and Practice, Occasional Papers, The Planning Exchange, Glasgow

Crawford, K. G. (1954) *Canadian Municipal Government,* University of Toronto Press

Crewson, D. M. and L. G. Reeds (1982) "Loss of Farmland in South-Central Ontario From 1951 to 1971," *Canadian Geographer*, Vol. 36, pp. 355-60

Critchley, W. H., F. Abele and M. Simms (1983) *Northern Politics Review*, University of Calgary, Political Science Department

Crosbie, J. C. (1956) "Local Government in Newfoundland," *Canadian Journal of Economics and Political Science*, Vol. 22, pp. 332-46

Crowley, R. W. (1982) "The Design of Government Policy Agencies: Do We Learn from Experience?," *Canadian Journal of Regional Science*, Vol. 5, No. 1, pp. 103-23

Cullingworth, J. B. (1978) *Ontario Planning: Notes on the Comay Report on the Ontario Planning Act*, University of Toronto, Department of Urban and Regional Planning, Papers on Planning and Design 19

_____ (1979) *Environmental Planning 1939-1969, Vol. 3: New Towns Policy*, Her Majesty's Stationery Office, London

_____ (1980) *Environmental Planning 1939-1969, Vol. 4: Land Values, Compensation and Betterment*, Her Majesty's Stationery Office, London

_____ (1984a) *Canadian Planning and Public Participation*, University of Toronto, Centre for Urban and Community Studies, Research Paper 148 (Land Policy Paper 4)

_____ (1984b) "The Provincial Role in Planning and Development," *Plan Canada*, Vol. 24, pp. 142-56

_____ (1985) *Town and Country Planning in Britain*, Allen and Unwin, ninth edition

Cunningham, A. (1984) *Socio-Economic Impact Assessment, Development Theory, and Northern Native Communities*, University of British Columbia, School of Community and Regional Planning, Studies in Northern Development 4

Cutler, M. (1975) A series of articles on foreign ownership of land in *Canadian Geographical Journal*, Vol. 90, No. 1-5

Dale, L. and T. L. Burton (1984) "Regional Planning in Alberta: Performance and Prospects," *Alberta Journal of Planning Practice*, No. 3, Summer 1984, pp. 17-41

Dartmouth City (1978) *Municipal Development Plan,* City of Dartmouth, Planning and Development Department

Davis, H. C. and G. B. Hainsworth (1984) *A Critical Appraisal of the Economic Aspects of the Proposed Beaufort Sea Development,* University of British Columbia, School of Community and Regional Planning, Studies in Northern Development 2

deFayer, T. L. (1982) *Economic Development for Canadians in the 1980s,* Environment Canada, Policy Directorate, Corporate Planning Group, Background Paper

DeGrove, J. M. (1984) *Land Growth and Politics,* Planners Press

Delafons, J. (1969) *Land-Use Controls in the States,* MIT Press, second edition

Denhez, M. C. (1980) "Protecting the Built Environment of Ontario," *Queen's Law Journal,* Vol. 5, pp. 73-115

Denman, D. R. (1980) *Land in a Free Society,* Centre for Policy Studies, London

Dennis, M. and S. Fish (1972) *Programs in Search of a Policy: Low Income Housing in Canada,* Hakkert (Toronto)

Department of Indian Affairs and Northern Development (1981) *Northern Land Use Planning Discussion Paper*

———————————— (1982a) *Land Use Planning in Northern Canada*

———————————— (1982b) *Draft Discussion Paper: A Comprehensive Policy and Strategy for the Northwest Territories and Yukon*

———————————— (1982c) *The Lancaster Sound Region 1980-2000: Green Paper*

———————————— (1984a) *Northern Land Use Planning: Update, Basis of Agreement, Terms of Reference, Planning Process Framework and Related Information*

———————————— (1984b) *Report of the Task Force on Northern Conservation,* (Ministry of Indian Affairs and Northern Development, Ottawa; Ministry of Renewable Resources, Northwest Territories; Ministry of Renewable Resources, Yukon Territory)

———————————— (1984c) *The Western Arctic Claim: The Inuvialuit Final Agreement*

_____ (1984d) *The Western Arctic Claim: A Guide to the Inuvialuit Final Agreement*

Department of Regional Economic Expansion (1969) *Development Plan for Prince Edward Island*

_____ (1972) *Annual Report 1970-71*

_____ (1973a) *The New Approach*

_____ (1973b) *Assessment of the Regional Development Incentives Program*

_____ (1980) *Strategic Regional Development Overview*

_____ (1982) *Annual Report 1980-81*

Department of Regional Industrial Expansion (1985) *Annual Reports 1983-1984*

Derkowski, A. (1976) *Costs in the Land Development Process*, Housing and Urban Development Association of Canada

_____ (1977) *The Escalation of Land Prices in Winnipeg*, UDI and HUDAC of Manitoba

Design for Development: see *Ontario: Design for Development*

Dewees, D. N. (1980) *Evaluation of Policies for Regulating Environmental Pollution*, Economic Council of Canada

Dickerson, M. O., S. Drabek and J. T. Woods (eds.) (1980) *Problems of Change in Urban Government*, Wilfrid Laurier University Press

Dodge, D. A. (1975) "Impact of Tax, Transfer and Expenditure Policies of Government on the Distribution of Personal Income in Canada," *Review of Income and Wealth*, Vol. 21, pp. 1-52

Doern, G. B. (1971) "The Development of Policy Organizations in the Executive Arena," in G. B. Doern and P. Aucoin (eds.) (1971)

_____ (1982) *How Ottawa Spends Your Tax Dollars: National Policy and Economic Development 1982*, Lorimer

_____ and P. Aucoin (eds.) (1971) *The Structures of Policy-Making in Canada*, Macmillan

Doern G. B. and V. S. Wilson (eds.) (1974) *Issues in Canadian Public Policy*, Macmillan

Doerr, A. D. (1982) "Organizing for Urban Policy: Some Comments on the Ministry of State for Urban Affairs," *Canadian Journal of Regional Science*, Vol. 5, No. 1, pp. 95-101

Downey, T. J. (1982) "Ontario's Local Governments in the 1980s: A Case for Policy Initiatives," *Canadian Journal of Regional Science,* Vol. 5, No. 1, pp. 145-63

Droettboom, T. (1984) "What is Happening to Regional Planning?," *City of Vancouver Planning Department Quarterly Review,* January 1984

Dubé, Y. (1983a) *Toward A Conservation Policy for Northern Canada,* DIAND (mimeo)

———————— (1983b) *The Wonders and Pitfalls of Land Use Planning in the Northern Regions of Canada,* DIAND (mimeo)

Dwivedi, O. P. (ed.) (1980) *Resources and the Environment: Policy Perspectives for Canada,* McClelland and Stewart

Eagles, P. F. J. (1981) "Environmentally Sensitive Planning in Ontario, Canada," *Journal of the American Planning Association,* Vol. 47, pp. 313-23

Economic Council of Canada (1967) *Fourth Annual Review: The Canadian Economy from the 1960s to the 1970s*

———————— (1981) *Reforming Regulation*

Edmonton City (1980a) *Downtown Land Use Controls,* Working Paper

———————— (1980b) *General Municipal Plan: Vol. 2: Policy Reports*

———————— (1982) *Land Use Bylaw 5996*

Edmonton Metropolitan Regional Planning Commission *Annual Reports*

———————— (1984a) *An Introduction to the Role of the Edmonton Metropolitan Regional Planning Commission*

———————— (1984b) *Edmonton Metropolitan Regional Plan* (with changes adopted up to July 4, 1984)

Edmonton Regional Planning Commission (1980) *A History of Regional and Metropolitan Planning*

Eger, A. F. (1980) *Time to Approve: Land Development Risk and Regulation in Montreal 1966-1977,* Economic Council of Canada, Regulation Reference, Working Paper 10

Elkins, D. J. and R. Simeon (1980) *Small Worlds: Provinces and Parties in Canadian Political Life,* Methuen

Emanuel, A. (1973) *Issues of Regional Policies,* OECD

Emond, D. P. (1975) "A Critical Review of the Nova Scotia Environmental Protection Act," *University of New Brunswick Law Review,* Vol. 24, pp. 69-105

_____ (1982) "Environment Law at the Limits of Incremental Development," in P. Z. R. Finkle and A. R. Lucas (eds.) (1982)

_____ (1984) *Proceedings of the Symposium on Environmental Regulation,* Ontario Ministry of the Environment

Energy, Mines and Resources Canada (1981) *Mineral Policy: A Discussion Paper*

Environment Canada *Annual Reports*

_____ (1978) *Non-Resident Land Ownership: Legislation and Administration in Prince Edward Island,* Lands Directorate

_____ (1979) *Prince Edward Island Land Development Corporation: Activities and Impact 1970-1977,* Lands Directorate

_____ (1980) *Land Use in Canada: The Report of the Interdepartmental Task Force on Land Use Policy,* Lands Directorate

_____ (1981) *Federal Policy on Land Use,* Lands Directorate

_____ (1982a) *Environment Update,* Lands Directorate

_____ (1982b) *The Identification of Impacts of Federal Programs on Land Use: A Manual for Program Managers,* Lands Directorate

_____ (1982c) *Canada Water Year Book 1981-1982: Water and the Economy*

_____ (1982d) *1982 Strategic Plan*

_____ (1982e) *Environment Canada: Its Evolving Mission*

_____ (1983a) *Statement by the Hon John Roberts, Minister of the Environment 21 February 1983*

_____ (1983b) *Environment Canada and the North: Discussion Paper*

_____ (1983c) *Strategic Plan 1984-89*

_____ (1984a) *Submission to the Inquiry on Federal Water Policy*

_____ (1984b) *Water is a Mainstream Issue: Participation Paper of the Inquiry on Federal Water Policy*

_____ (1985a) *Hearing About Water: A Synthesis*, (Inquiry on Federal Water Policy)

_____ (1985b) *Currents of Change: Final Report of the Inquiry on Federal Water Policy*, (Chairman: P.H. Pearse)

_____ (1985c) *The Clean Air Act Report 1982-1984*

_____ (1985d) *Environmental Issues in Canada: A Status Report*

_____ and Ontario Ministry of the Environment (1982) *Lakefill Quality Study: Leslie Street Spit*

Environment Council of Alberta (1977-78) *Involvement and Environment: Proceedings of the Canadian Conference on Public Participation*, in B. Sadler (ed.), 2 Vols. (Vol. 1: 1977; Vol. 2: 1978)

_____ (1979) *Noise in the Human Environment*, by H. W. Jones

_____ (1982) *Environmental Standards: A Comparative Study of Canadian Standards, Standard Setting Processes and Enforcement*, by M. A. H. Franson, R. T. Franson and A. R. Lucas

_____ (1984) *Maintaining and Expanding the Agricultural Land Base in Alberta: Summary Report and Recommendations*

Erber, E. (1983) "The Road to Mount Laurel," *Planning*, (American Planning Association) Vol. 49, No. 10, pp. 4-9

Estrin, D. (1979) "The Public is Still Voiceless: Some Negative Aspects of Public Hearings," in B. Sadler (ed.) (1979)

_____ (1984) *Environmental Law*, Carswell

_____ and J. Z. Swaigen (1978) *Environment on Trial: A Handbook of Ontario Environmental Law*, Canadian Environmental Law Research Foundation and Macmillan, second edition

Faludi, A. (1973) *A Reader in Planning Theory*, Pergamon

Federal Environmental Assessment Review Office (1982a) *Environmental Assessment in Canada: 1982 Guide to Current Practice*

_____ (1982b) *CP Rogers Pass Development: Glacier National Park: Preliminary Report*

_____ (1982c) *Banff Highway Project (Km 13 to Km 27): Report of the Environmental Assessment Panel*

_____ (1982d) *An Evaluation of Funding of Public Participation in the Beaufort Sea Environmental Assessment Panel Review,* by K. A. Graham et al

_____ (1982e) *Alaska Highway Gas Pipeline, Yukon Territory: Final Report*

_____ (1983a) *CP Rail Rogers Pass Development, Alberta: Final Report*

_____ (1983b) *CN Rail Twin Tracking Program, British Columbia*

_____ (1983c) *Venture Development Project, Nova Scotia*

_____ (1984a) *Beaufort Sea Hydrocarbon Production and Transportation*

_____ (1984b) *Improvements to the Federal Environmental Assessment and Review Process: Discussion Paper*

_____ (1984c) *Port of Quebec Expansion Project*

Federal-Provincial Committee on Foreign Ownership of Land (1975) *Report to the First Ministers,* Canadian Intergovernmental Conference Secretariat, Information Canada

Federation of Canadian Municipalities (1980) *Municipal Government in a New Canadian Federal System*

_____ (1982) *Management and Planning Capabilities in Small Communities*

_____ (1985) *Municipal Infrastructure in Canada: Physical Condition and Funding Adequacy*

Feldman, E. J. and J. Milch (1980) "Options on the Metropolitan Fringe: Strategies of Airport Development," in D. E. Ashford (ed.) (1980)

_____ (1981) "Coordination or Control? The Life and Death of the Ministry of State for Urban Affairs," in L. D. Feldman (ed.) (1981)

_____ (1983) *The Politics of Canadian Airport Development,* Duke University Press

Feldman, L. D. (ed.) (1981) *Politics and Government of Urban Canada: Selected Readings,* Methuen, fourth edition

_____ and M. D. Goldrick (1976) *Politics and Government of Urban Canada: Selected Readings,* Methuen, third edition

Feldman, L. D. and K. A. Graham (1979) *Bargaining for Cities: Municipalities and Intergovernmental Relations: An Assessment,* Institute for Research on Public Policy and Butterworth

Fenge, T. et al (1979) *Land Use Programs in the Northwest Territories,* Environment Canada, Lands Directorate

_____ (1984) *Environmental Planning in Northern Canada: Musical Chairs and Other Games,* Canadian Arctic Resources Committee

Finkle, F. Z. R. and A. R. Lucas (eds.) (1982) *Environmental Law in the 1980s: A New Beginning: Proceedings of a Colloquium,* University of Calgary, Faculty of Law

Folster, D. (1981) "Dwindling Forests Pressure Province to Start Anew," *Globe and Mail* (Toronto) 25 December 1981

Forester, J. (1980) "Critical Theory and Planning Practice," *Journal of the American Planning Association,* Vol. 46, No. 3, pp. 275-86

_____ (1982) "Planning in the Face of Power," *Journal of the American Planning Association,* Vol. 48, No. 1, pp. 67-80

Forrester, J. W. (1969) *Urban Dynamics,* MIT Press

Foster, H. D. and W. R. D. Sewell (1981) *Water: The Emerging Crisis in Canada,* Canadian Institute for Economic Policy

Fowler, E. P. and R. L. Lineberry (1972) "The Comparative Analysis of Urban Policy: Canada and the United States," *Urban Affairs Annual Review,* Vol. 6, pp. 345-68

Fox, D. (1979) *Public Administration in the Administrative Process,* Law Reform Commission of Canada

Fox, I.K. (1979) "The Environmental Impact Assessment Process," in *Second Environmental Impact Assessment Conference,* University of British Columbia, Centre for Continuing Education

Fram, M. (1980) *Ontario Hydro: Ontario Heritage; A Study of Strategies for the Conservation of the Heritage of Ontario Hydro,* Ontario Ministry of Culture and Recreation

Frankena, M. W. and D. T. Scheffman (1980) *Economic Analysis of Provincial Land Use Policies in Ontario,* Ontario Economic Council

Franklin, H. M. (1983) "The Most Important Zoning Opinion Since Euclid," *Planning,* (American Planning Association) Vol. 49, No. 10, pp. 10-12

Franson, M. A. H., R. T. Franson and A. R. Lucas (1982) *Environmental Standards: A Comparative Study of Canadian Standards, Standard Setting Processes and Enforcement,* Environment Council of Alberta

Franson, R. T. and A. R. Lucas (1978) *Environmental Law Commentary and Case Digests,* Butterworths

Fredericton City (undated) *Municipal Plan,* City of Fredericton

French, R. D. (1980) *How Ottawa Decides: Planning and Industrial Policy-Making 1968-1980,* Canadian Institute for Economic Policy/Lorimer

Friedenberg, E. Z. (1980) *Deference to Authority: The Case of Canada,* M. E. Sharpe (Random House)

Friesen, G. (1984) *The Canadian Prairies: A History,* University of Toronto Press

Gayler, H. J. (1979) "Political Attitudes and Urban Expansion in the Niagara Region," *Contact: Journal of Urban and Environmental Affairs,* Vol. 11, pp. 43-60

—————————— (1982) "Conservation and Development in Urban Growth: The Preservation of Agricultural Land in the Rural-Urban Fringe of Ontario," *Town Planning Review,* Vol. 53, pp. 321-41

Gerecke, K. (1976) "The History of Canadian City Planning," *City Magazine,* Vol. 2, Nos. 3 & 4, pp. 12-13

Gerein, H. J. F. (1980) *Community Planning and Development in Canada's Northwest Territories,* Government of the Northwest Territories in cooperation with CMHC and DIAND

Gertler, L. O. (ed.) (1968) *Planning the Canadian Environment,* Harvest House

_____ (1972) *Regional Planning in Canada: A Planner's Testament,* Harvest House

_____ (1979) "The Challenge of Public Policy Research," *Canadian Journal of Regional Science,* Vol. 2, pp. 77-89

_____ (ed.) (1982) "Public Policy: Urban and Regional Issues," *Canadian Journal of Regional Science,* Vol. 5, No. 1, pp. 1-4

_____ (1982) "Introduction to Public Policy: Urban and Regional Issues," *Canadian Journal of Regional Science,* Vol. 5, No. 1, pp. 1-224

_____ (1984) "A National Planning Perspective," *Southwestern Ontario Chapter Canadian Institute of Planners Newsletter,* Vol. 6, No. 2, pp. 6-8

_____ I. Lord and A. Stewart (1975) "Canadian Planning: The Regional Perspective," *Plan Canada,* Vol. 15, p. 76

Gherson, G. (1982) "DRIE still awaits its place in the Cabinet sun," *Financial Post,* 18 September 1982

Gierman, D. M. (1976) *Rural Land Use Changes in the Ottawa-Hull Region,* Environment Canada, Lands Directorate, Occasional Paper 9

_____ (1977) *Rural to Urban Land Conversion,* Environment Canada, Lands Directorate, Occasional Paper 16

_____ (1981) *Land Use Classification for Land Use Monitoring,* Environment Canada, Lands Directorate, Working Paper 17

_____ and J. Lenning (1979) *Rural to Urban Land Conversion,* Environment Canada, Lands Directorate, Map Folio 5

Gillard, W. and T. Tooke (1975) *The Niagara Escarpment: From Tobermory to Niagara Falls,* University of Toronto Press

Giroux, L. (1981) "Le nouveau droit de l'aménagement ou l'enfer pavé de bonnes intentions ... " *Revue Générale de Droit,* Vol. 11, pp. 65-92

Glenn, J. M. (1980) "La protection du territoire agricole au Québec," *Revue Générale de Droit,* Vol. 11, pp. 209-32

Gluskin, I. (1976) *The Cadillac Fairview Corporation Limited,* Royal Commission on Corporate Concentration, Study No. 3, Supply and Services Canada

Godin, J. (1974) "Local Government Reform in the Province of Quebec" in Advisory Commission on Intergovernmental Relations (1974)

Goldberg, M. A. (1977) "Housing and Land Prices in Canada and the U.S.," in L. B. Smith and M. Walker (1977)

_____ (1978) "The BNA Act, NHA, CMHC, MSUA, Etc: 'Nymphobia' or the on-going search for an appropriate Canadian Housing and Urban Development Policy," in M. Walker (ed.) (1978)

_____ (1980) "Municipal Arrogance or Economic Rationality: The Case of High Servicing Standards," *Canadian Public Policy,* Vol. 6, pp. 78-88

_____ and J. H. Mark (1985) "The Roles of Government in Housing Policy," *Journal of the American Planning Association,* Vol. 51, pp. 34-42

Goldberg, M. A. and J. Mercer (1980) "Canadian and U.S. Cities: Basic Differences, Possible Explanations, and Their Meaning for Public Policy," *Regional Science Association Papers,* Vol. 45, pp. 159-83

Goldrick, M. (1982) "The Anatomy of Urban Reform in Toronto," in D. Roussopoulus (ed.) (1982)

Gomme, T. (1984) "Municipal Planning in Ontario," *Plan Canada,* Vol. 24, pp. 102-14

Goracz, A., I. Lithwick and L. O. Stone (1971) *The Urban Future,* "Urban Canada" Research Monograph 5, CMHC

Gordon, M. (1981) *Agricultural Land and Land Use Planning in Alberta: A Review of Planning Legislation and Practices,* Environmental Council of Alberta

_____ (1984) "There's Trouble, Here in River City: Edmonton's Annexation Fiasco," *City Magazine,* Vol. 6, No. 4, pp. 21-5

_____ and J. D. Hulchanski (1985) *The Evolution of the Land Use Planning Process in Alberta 1945-1984,* University of Toronto, Centre for Urban and Community Studies, Research Paper 156 (Land Policy Paper 5)

Graham, K. A. et al (1982) *An Evaluation of Funding of Public Participation in the Beaufort Sea Environmental Assessment Panel Review,* Federal Environmental Assessment Review Office

Graham Report (1974) *Report of the Royal Commission on Education, Public Services and Provincial-Municipal Relations,* Queen's Printer, Halifax

Greater Vancouver Regional District (1984) *Purpose and Objectives*

Greenspan Report (1978) *Federal Provincial Task Force on the Supply and Price of Serviced Residential Land,* CMHC

Grigg, D. (1965) "The Logic of Regional Systems," *Annals of the Association of American Geographers,* Vol. 55, pp. 465-91

Gunton, T. I. (1984) "The Role of the Professional Planner," *Canadian Public Administration,* Vol. 27, No. 3, pp. 399-417

Hagman, D. (1980a) "English Planning and Environmental Law and Administration: The 1970s," *Journal of the American Planning Association,* Vol. 46, pp. 162-71

_____ (1980b) *Public Planning and Control of Urban and Land Development: Cases and Materials,* West Publishing Co (St Pauls), second edition

_____ (1982) "Taking Care of One's Own Through Inclusionary Zoning: Bootstrapping Low and Moderate Income Housing by Local Government," *Urban Law and Policy,* Vol. 5, p. 169

_____ and D. Misczynski (1978) *Windfalls for Wipeouts: Land Value Capture and Compensation,* American Society of Planning Officials

Hallett, G. (1977) *Housing and Land Policies in West Germany and Britain,* Macmillan

Hamelin, L. E. (1979) *Canadian Nordicity,* Harvest House

_____ (1984) "Managing Canada's North: Challenges and Opportunities," *Canadian Public Administration,* Vol. 27, pp. 165-81

Hamilton, S. W. (1974) *Public Land Banking: Real or Illusionary Benefits?,* University of British Columbia

_____ (1975) *Public Policy and Urban Real Estate,* Ministry of State for Urban Affairs

_____ (1981) *Regulation and Other Forms of Government Intervention Regarding Real Property,* Economic Council of Canada, Regulation Reference, Technical Report 13

_____ and D. E. Baxter (1977) "Government Ownership and the Price of Land," in L. B. Smith and M.Walker (eds.) (1977)

Hausman Consulting (1979) *Attitudes Towards Post-Consumer Products in Ontario,* Ontario Waste Management Advisory Board

Healy, R. G. and J. S. Rosenberg (1979) *Land Use and the States,* Johns Hopkins University Press, second edition

Heclo, H. and A. Wildavsky (1974) *The Private Government of Public Money,* Macmillan

Hedman, R. (1977) *Stop Me Before I Plan Again,* Planners Press

Hellyer Task Force (1969) *Report of the Federal Task Force on Housing and Urban Development,* Information Canada

Henderson, R. C. (1982) *Public Involvement in Right of Way Selection Projects,* Canadian Electrical Association (mimeo)

Henley Commission (1974-6) *Commission of Enquiry, St John's Urban Region Study,* 4 Vols.

Higgins, B., F. Martin and A. Ranauld (1970) *Les orientations du développement économique régional dans la province du Québec,* Department of Regional Economic Expansion

Higgins, D. J. H. (1977) *Urban Canada: Its Government and Politics,* Gage

Hitchcock, J. R. (1985) "The Management of Urban Land: Notes Toward the Development of a Comprehensive Perspective," *Plan Canada,* Vol. 25, No. 4, pp. 129-37

_____ and J. Kjellberg (1980) *Beyond the White Paper: Planning for People in the 80s: Proceedings of a Conference,* University of Toronto, Centre for Urban and Community Studies, Major Report 17

Hodge, G. and M. A. Qadeer (1983) *Towns and Villages in Canada: The Importance of Being Unimportant,* Butterworths

Holdsworth, D. (1980) "Built Forms and Social Realities: A Review of Recent Work on Canadian Heritage Structures," *Urban History Review,* Vol. 9, pp. 123-38

Homenuck, P. and A. P. Martin (1982) "The Impact of Technology: New Pressures on Urban and Regional Planning," *Canadian Journal of Regional Science,* Vol. 5, No. 1, pp. 67-82

Hooper, D., J. W. Simmons and L. S. Bourne (1983) *The Changing Basis of Canadian Urban Growth 1971-81,* University of Toronto, Centre for Urban and Community Studies, Research Paper 139

Horton, J. T. (1977) "The Niagara Escarpment: Planning for the Multi-Purpose Development of a Recreational Resource," in R. R. Krueger and B. Mitchell (eds.) (1977)

Howard, R. (1980) *Poisons in Public: Case Studies of Environmental Pollution in Canada,* Lorimer

Hudson, S. C. (1977) *A Review of Farm Income Stabilization in British Columbia: A Report to the Minister of Agriculture*

Hulchanski, J. D. (1981) *The Origins of Urban Land Use Planning in Alberta 1900-1945,* University of Toronto, Centre for Urban and Community Studies, Research Paper 119 (Land Policy Paper 1)

_____ (1982) *The Evolution of Ontario's Early Urban Land Use Planning Regulations 1900-1920,* University of Toronto, Centre for Urban and Community Studies, Research Paper 136 (Land Policy Paper 2)

_____ (1984) *St Lawrence and False Creek: A Review of Planning and Development of Two Inner City Neighborhoods,* University of British Columbia, School of Community and Regional Planning

Illich, I. (1971) *Deschooling Society,* Harper and Row

_____ et al (1977) *Disabling Professions,* Marion Boyars

Ince, J. G. (1977) *Land Use Law: A Study of Legislation Governing Land Use in British Columbia,* University of British Columbia

_____ (1984) *Land Use Law: British Columbia Handbook 1984,* Butterworths

Insight (1984) *The New Planning Act in Action,* Insight (100 University Avenue, Toronto)

International Joint Commission (1978) *Great Lakes Water Quality Agreement of 1978*

_____ (1983) *United States-Canada Memorandum of Intent on Transboundary Air Pollution: Executive Summaries: Work Group Reports*

_____ (1984) *Second Biennial Report under the Great Lakes Water Quality Agreement of 1978*

_____ (1985) *1985 Report on Great Lakes Water Quality,* (by the Great Lakes Water Quality Board)

Jacek, H. J. (1980) "Regional Government and Development: Administrative Efficiency Versus Local Democracy," in D. C. MacDonald (ed.) (1980)

Jackson, J. N. (1976) *Land Use Planning in the Niagara Region,* Niagara Region Study Review Commission

Jaffary, K. D. and S. M. Makuch (1977) *Legal Decision-Making and Administration,* Research Report for the Royal Commission on Metropolitan Toronto

Jones, D. P. (1976) "Constitutional Law: Rights of Canadian Cities: Aliens," *Canadian Bar Review,* Vol. 54, pp. 381-91

Jones, H. W. (1979) *Noise in the Human Environment,* Environment Council of Alberta

Jones, M. V. (1971) "The Nature and Purpose of the Official Plan," *Law Society of Upper Canada Special Lectures 1971*

Junius, M. (1974) "La nouvelle politique des arrondissements historiques et naturels au Québec," *Vie des Arts,* Vol. 19, pp. 21-6

Kantor, H. A. (1973) "The City Beautiful in New York," *New York Historical Society Quarterly,* Vol. 57, No. 2, pp. 149-71

Kaplan, H. (1982) *Reform, Planning and City Politics: Montreal, Winnipeg, Toronto,* University of Toronto Press

Kasarda, J. D. (1980) "The Implications of Contemporary Redistribution Trends for National Urban Policy," *Social Science Quarterly,* Vol. 61

Kenniff, P. J. (1974) "Development Control in Canada: Evolution and Prospects," *Journal of Planning and Environment Law,* 1974, pp. 385-98

Kienholtz, E. (1980) *The Land-Use Impacts of Recent Legislation in PEI,* Environment Canada, Lands Directorate

Kierans, E. (1973) *Report on National Resources Policy in Manitoba,* Government of Manitoba

Kiernan, M.J. (1982) "The Fallacy of Planning Law Reform," *Urban Law and Policy,* Vol. 5, pp. 23-64

_____ and D. C. Walker (1983) "Winnipeg" in W. Magnusson and A. Sancton (eds.) (1983)

Kinsley, M. (1982) "Mental Cases: Meet the New Legal Doctrine of Psychological Pollution," *Harpers,* July 1982, pp. 8-9

Kipling, R. (1889) writing in 1889 about land speculation in Vancouver; quoted in Canadian Council on Social Development (1978), *Towards a Strategy for Land Reform in Canada*

Kolankiewicz, L. (1981) *Implementation of British Columbia's Pollution Control Act 1967 in the Lower Fraser River,* University of British Columbia, Master's Thesis

Krueger, R. R. (1970) "The Provincial-Municipal Government Revolution in New Brunswick," *Canadian Public Administration,* Vol. 13, pp. 51-99

_____ (1977) "The Destruction of a Unique Renewable Resource," in R. R. Krueger and B. Mitchell (eds.) (1977)

_____ (1978) "Urbanization of the Niagara Fruit Belt," *The Canadian Geographer,* Vol. 22, pp. 179-94

_____ (1982) "The Struggle to Preserve Speciality Crop Land in the Rural-Urban Fringe of the Niagara Peninsula of Ontario," *Environments: A Journal of Interdisciplinary Studies,* Vol. 14, pp. 1-10

_____ (1984) "The Urbanization of Canada's Farmlands: The Niagara Fruit Belt and the Okanagan Valley," *The Operational Geographer,* No. 4/1984, pp. 33-42

_____ and B. Mitchell (eds.) (1977) *Managing Canada's Renewable Resources,* Methuen

La Haye Commission (1968) *Rapport de la commission provinciale d'urbanisme,* Québec Ministère des Affaires Municipales

Lane, W. T. (1981) *Municipal Act: Official Regional, Community and Settlement Plans,* (mimeo)

Lang, R. and A. Armour (1982) *Planning Land to Conserve Energy: 40 Case Studies from Canada and the United States,* Environment Canada, Lands Directorate

Lang, V. (1974) *The Service State Emerges in Ontario,* Ontario Economic Council

Langford, J. S. (1982) *The Law of Your Land: A Practical Guide to the New Canadian Constitution,* Canadian Broadcasting Corporation

L'Anglais (1976) *Land Use Programs in Quebec,* Environment Canada, Lands Directorate

Lash, H. (1981) "Federal Involvement in Land Policy: Review of the Federal Policy on Land Use," *Plan Canada,* Vol. 21, pp. 64-6

Laux, F. A. (1971) "The Zoning Game, Alberta Style, Part II: Development Control," *Alberta Law Review,* Vol. 10, p. 1

_____ (1979) *The Planning Act (Alberta),* Butterworths

Law Reform Commission of British Columbia (1971) *Report on Expropriation*

Law Reform Commission of Canada (1975) *Expropriation,* Working Paper 9

_____ (1976) *Report on Expropriation*

_____ (1978) *Report on Expropriation*

Lawson, M.B.M. (1984) "The Toronto-Centred Region Plan," *Plan Canada,* Vol. 24, pp. 135-6

Lax, C. C. (1979) "The Toronto Lead-Smelter Controversy," in W. Leiss (ed.) (1979)

Leach Report (1975) *Report of the Royal Commission Inquiry into the Grand River Flood 1974,* Ontario

Leiss, W. (ed.) (1979) *Ecology Versus Politics in Canada,* University of Toronto Press

Leo, C. (1977) *The Politics of Urban Development: Canadian Urban Expressway Disputes,* Institute of Public Administration of Canada, Monographs on Canadian Urban Government 3

Leslie, P. M. (ed.) (1985) *Canada: The State of the Federation,* Queen's University, Institute of Intergovernmental Relations

Levin, E. A. (1984) *City Planning as Utopian Ideology and City Government Function,* University of Winnipeg, Institute of Urban Studies

Levitt, K. (1970) *Silent Surrender: The Multinational Corporation in Canada,* Macmillan

Lewis, J. and M. Shrimpton (1984) "Policymaking in Newfoundland during the 1940s: The Case of the St John's Housing Corporation," *Canadian Historical Review,* Vol. 65, pp. 209-39

L'Heureux, J. (1977) "La protection de l'environnement culturel canadien et québecois," *McGill Law Journal,* 1977, pp. 306-33

Lightbody, J. (1983) "Edmonton" in W. Magnusson and A. Sancton (eds.) (1983)

Lipset, S. M. (1963a) "The Value Patterns of Democracy: A Case Study in Comparative Analysis," *American Sociological Review,* Vol. 28, pp. 515-31

_____ (1963b) *The First Nation: The United States in Historical and Comparative Perspective,* Basic Books

Lithwick, N. H. (1970) *Urban Canada: Problems and Prospects,* (Lithwick Report), CMHC

_____ (1972a) "Political Intervention: A Case Study," *Plan Canada,* Vol. 12, pp. 45-56

_____ (1972b) "An Economic Interpretation of the Urban Crisis," *Journal of Canadian Studies,* Vol. 7, No. 3, pp. 36-49

_____ (1972c) "Urban Policy-Making: Shortcomings in Political Technology," *Canadian Public Administration,* Vol. 15, pp. 571-84

_____ (1978) *Regional Economic Policy: The Canadian Experience,* McGraw-Hill Ryerson

_____ (1982) "Regional Policy: The Embodiment of Contradictions," in G. B. Doern (ed.) (1982)

_____ (1983) *Human Settlement Policies in Periods of Economic Stress,* CMHC

Lorimer, J. (1978) *The Developers,* Lorimer

_____ and E. Ross (1976) *The City Book,* Lorimer

_____ (1977) *The Second City Book,* Lorimer

Lotz, J. (1977) *Understanding Canada: Regional and Community Development,* N.C. Press (Toronto)

_____ (1978) "Community Development and Public Participation," in B. Sadler (ed.) (1978)

Lundvik, V. (1982) *The Ombudsman in the Provinces of Canada,* International Ombudsman Institute, University of Alberta, Faculty of Law

Lush, P. (1981) "Buildings' History Held Key To Approval of Rights Transfer," *Globe and Mail* (Toronto) 25 December 1981

McAllister, I. (1980) "How to Re-make DREE," *Policy Options,* Vol. 1, p. 39

_____ (1982) *Regional Development and the European Community: A Canadian Perspective,* Institute for Research on Public Policy (Montreal)

McAuslan, P. (1980) *The Ideologies of Planning Law,* Pergamon

McCann, L. D. (1982) *Heartland and Hinterland: A Geography of Canada,* Prentice-Hall

McCormack, R. J. (1971) "The Canada Land Use Inventory: A Basis for Land Use Planning," *Journal of Soil and Water Conservation,* Vol. 26, pp. 141-6

McCormick, P., E. C. Manning and G. Gibson (1981) *Regional Representation: The Canadian Partnership,* Canada West Foundation (Alberta)

McCroirie, J. N. (1969) *ARDA: An Experiment in Development Planning,* Canadian Council on Rural Development

McCuaig, J. D. and E. W. Manning (1980) *The Effects on Land Use of Federal Programs in the Windermere Valley,* Environment Canada, Lands Directorate, Working Paper 8

_____ (1982) *Agricultural Land Use Change in Canada: Process and Consequences,* Environment Canada, Lands Directorate

Macdonald, D. (1984) *Alberta's Direct Control District: A Critical Examination,* University of Alberta, MCP Thesis

MacDonald, D.C. (ed.) (1980) *Government and Politics of Ontario,* Van Nostrand Reinhold, second edition

Macdonald, H. I. (1984) "A Retrospective View from the Top,"
    Plan Canada, Vol. 24, pp. 92-9

Macdonald, Sir John A. (1866) quoted in R. C. Brown, "The
    Doctrine of Usefulness: Natural Resource and National
    Parks Policy in Canada 1887-1914," in J. G. Nelson (ed.)
    (1969) *Canadian Parks in Perspective,* Harvest House, p.
    48

Macdonald, V. N. and J. Macleod (1978) *Corporate Manage-
    ment in Local Government,* Ontario Ministry of Treasury,
    Economics and Intergovernmental Affairs

McFadyen, S. (1976) "The Control of Foreign Ownership of
    Canadian Real Estate," *Canadian Public Policy,* Vol. 2,
    pp. 65-77

_____ and R. Hobart (1977) "The Economic Impli-
    cations of Foreign Ownership of Canadian Land," in L. B.
    Smith and M. Walker (1977)

McFadyen, S. and D. Johnson (1981) *Land Use Regulation in
    Edmonton,* Economic Council of Canada, Regulation Refer-
    ence, Working Paper 16

MacFarlane, C. B. and R. W. Macauley (1984) *Land Use Plan-
    ning: Practice, Procedure and Policy,* Butterworths

Mackenzie, R. M. (1978) "Land Use and Development Control
    in British Columbia," *Advocate,* Vol. 36, pp. 511-31

_____ (1985) *Canadian and U.S. Land Regulation:
    Due Process and Fundamental Fairness: Experiences in
    Canada in the Due Process,* Paper to the Planning and
    Law Division of the American Planning Association, 1985
    International Planning Conference (mimeo)

Maclennan, D. and J. B. Parr (1979) *Regional Policy: Past
    Experience and New Directions,* Martin Robertson

McNally Report (1956) *Report of the Royal Commission on the
    Metropolitan Development of Calgary and Edmonton,*
    Queen's Printer, Edmonton

McNiven, J. D. (1974) *Evaluation of the Public Participation
    Program Embodied in the Prince Edward Island Develop-
    ment Plan,* Dalhousie University, Institute of Public Affairs

McRuer Report (1968) *Royal Commission Inquiry into Civil
    Rights,* Report No. 1, Vol. 3, Ontario Government Publica-
    tions

McWhinney, E. (1979) *Quebec and the Canadian Constitution 1960-1978,* University of Toronto Press

Macenko, S. L. and V. P. Neimanis (1983) *An Overview of Crown Land Management in Canada,* Environment Canada, Lands Directorate, Working Paper 27

Magnusson, W. and A. Sancton (eds.) (1983) *City Politics in Canada,* University of Toronto Press

Makuch, S. M. (1973) "Zoning: Avenues of Reform," *Dalhousie Law Journal,* Vol. 1, pp. 294-334

_____ (1976) "Legal Authority and Land Uses in Central Toronto," *Urban Forum,* Vol. 2, pp. 23-33

_____ (1983) *Canadian Municipal and Planning Law,* Carswell

_____ (1985) "Planning or Blackmail?," *Plan Canada,* Vol. 25, pp. 8-9

Mallach, A. (1984) *Inclusionary Housing Programs: Policies and Practices,* Rutgers University, Center for Urban Policy Research

Manning, E. W. (1980) *Issues in Canadian Land Use,* Environment Canada, Lands Directorate, Working Paper 9

_____ and S. Eddy (1978) *The Agricultural Reserves of British Columbia: An Impact Analysis,* Environment Canada, Lands Directorate

Manning, E. W. and J. D. McCuaig (1977) *Agricultural Land and Urban Centres,* Environment Canada, Lands Directorate

Manning, E. W., J. D. McCuaig and E. A. Lacoste (1979) *The Changing Value of Canada's Farmland: 1961-1976,* Environment Canada, Lands Directorate

Marchak, P. (1979) *In Whose Interests?,* McClelland and Stewart

Mark, J. H. and M. A. Goldberg (1982) *Neighborhood Change: A Canadian Perspective,* University of British Columbia, Faculty of Commerce, Working Paper 24

Markusen, A. R. and D. Wilmoth (1982) "The Political Economy of National Urban Policy in the U.S.A. 1976-1981," *Canadian Journal of Regional Science,* Vol. 5, No. 1, pp. 125-44

Markusen, J. R. and D. T. Scheffman (1977) *Speculation and Monopoly in Urban Development: Analytical Foundations with Evidence for Toronto,* Ontario Economic Council

Marshall, I. B. (1982) *Mining, Land Use and the Environment: A Canadian Overview,* Environment Canada, Lands Directorate

Marshall, J. (ed.) (1984) *Citizen Participation in Library Decision-Making: The Toronto Experience,* Dalhousie University, School of Library Service and The Scarecrow Press

Martin, C. (1973) *"Dominion Lands" Policy,* in L. H. Thomas (ed.), McClelland and Stewart

Martin, L. R. G. (1975a) *Land Use Dynamics on the Toronto Urban Fringe,* Environment Canada, Lands Directorate, Map Folio 3

_____ (1975b) *National Urban Land Policy: A Review and Recommendations,* Ministry of State for Urban Affairs

Maruyama, M. (1974) "Paradigmatology and its Application to Cross-Disciplinary, Cross-Professional and Cross-Cultural Communication," *Cybernetica,* Vol. 17, pp. 135-56 and 237-81

Masson, J. K. (1976) *The Demise of "Alphabet Parties": The Rise of Responsible Party Politics in Canada,* University of Alberta, Department of Political Science, Occasional Paper 4

_____ and J. D. Anderson (1972) *Emerging Party Politics in Canada,* McClelland and Stewart

Mathias, P. (1971) *Five Studies of Government Involvement in the Development of Canada,* Lorimer

Matthews, R. (1981) "Two Alternative Explanations of the Problem of Regional Dependency in Canada," *Canadian Public Policy,* 1981, pp. 268-83

Maugham, W. S. (1938) *The Summing Up,* Doubleday

Maxwell, J. and C. Pestieau (1980) *Economic Realities of Contemporary Confederation,* C. D. Howe Research Institute

Mayo Report (1976) *Report of the Ottawa-Carleton Review Committee,* Ontario Government Publications

Melamed, A., J. Schaecter and M. Emo (1984) "The Effects of Forced Relocation in Montreal," *Habitat,* Vol. 27, No. 4, pp. 29-36

Mercer, J. (1979) "On Continentalism, Distinctiveness and Comparative Urban Geography: Canadian and American Cities," *Canadian Geographer,* Vol. 23, pp. 119-39

_____ and M. A. Goldberg (1982) *Value Differences and Their Meaning for Urban Development in Canada and the U.S.A.,* University of British Columbia, Faculty of Commerce, Working Paper 12

Metropolitan Toronto: see *Toronto Metro*

Milner, J. B. (1960) "Town and Regional Planning in Transition," *Canadian Public Administration,* Vol. 3, pp. 59-75

_____ (1963) *Community Planning: A Casebook on Law and Administration,* University of Toronto Press; quoting H. Pomeroy

_____ (1965) "An Introduction to Subdivision Control Legislation," *Canadian Bar Review,* Vol. 43, pp. 49-98

Misek, M. and M. B. Lapping (1984) "Making Land Policy: PEI's Attempts to Control Individual and Corporate Land Ownership," *Plan Canada,* Vol. 24, pp. 55-62

Mitchell, B. (1980) "The Provincial Domain in Environmental Management and Resource Development," in O. P. Dwivedi (ed.) (1980)

Montreal Urban Community (1973) *Proposals for Urban Development*

Moore, M. and G. Vanderhaden (1984) "Northern Problems or Canadian Opportunities," *Canadian Public Administration,* Vol. 27, pp. 182-209

Morley, C. G. (1972) "Legal Developments" (in Canadian Water Management), *Western Ontario Law Review,* Vol. 11, pp. 139-58

_____ (1973) "Pollution as a Crime: The Federal Response," *Manitoba Law Journal,* Vol. 5, pp. 297-311

Muller, R. A. (1978) *The Market for New Housing in the Metropolitan Toronto Area,* Ontario Economic Council

Mumford, L. (1961) *The City in History,* Harcourt Brace Javonovich

Municipal World (1980) "Demolition of Heritage Buildings without Demolition Permit and in Defiance of City's Clear Intention to Designate," *Municipal World,* Vol. 90, pp. 115-18

Munn, R. E. (1975) quoted in G. E. Beanlands and P. N. Duinker (1975)

Munro, D. (1980) "Zoning is the little guy's protection," *Financial Post,* 8 November 1980

Munroe, J. M. (1978) "Regional Economic Policies in Canada," *Canadian Journal of Regional Science,* Vol. 1, pp. 61-76

Nader, G. A. (1976) *Cities of Canada,* Macmillan, 2 Vols.

National Capital Commission *Annual Reports*

_____ (1984) *A Capital in the Making: Reflections of the Past and Visions of the Future*

_____ (undated) *The National Capital Commission: Its History, Mandate and Organization*

National Research Council (1939) *A Model Zoning Bylaw,* Ottawa

Naylor, T. (1975) *History of Canadian Business 1867-1914,* Lorimer, 2 Vols

Neimanis, V. P. (1979) *Canada's Cities and their Surrounding Land Resources,* Environment Canada, Lands Directorate, Canada Land Inventory, Report 15

_____ and R. McKechnie (1980) *Urban Growth Infrastructure and Land Capability: A Windsor Example,* Environment Canada, Lands Directorate

Nelles, H. V. (1974) *The Politics of Development: Forests, Mines and Hydro-Electric Power in Ontario 1849-1941,* Macmillan

Nelson, J. G. (ed.) (1969) *Canadian Parks in Perspective,* Harvest House

_____ (1977) "Canadian National Parks and Related Reserves: Research Needs and Management," in R. R. Krueger and B. Mitchell (eds.) (1977)

_____ et al (1979) *The Canadian National Parks: Today and Tomorrow Conference II,* University of Waterloo

_____ and S. Jessen (1981) *The Scottish and Alaskan Offshore Oil and Gas Experience and the Canadian Beaufort Sea,* CARC

_____ (1984) *An External Perspective on Parks Canada Strategies 1986-2001,* University of Waterloo and Parks Canada Liaison Committee, Occasional Paper 2

New Brunswick (1965) *White Paper on the Responsibilities of Government*

_____ (1976) *Report of the Task Force on Nonincorporated Areas in New Brunswick*

_____ (1979) *A Review of the Community Planning Act by W. E. Cooper*

_____ (1982) *New Brunswick Forest Development Strategy for the Eighties,* Department of Natural Resources

Newfoundland (1976) *St John's Urban Regional Plan,* Department of Municipal Affairs and Housing

_____ (1981) *Urban and Rural Planning Act (Town of Anytown) Land Use Zoning and Subdivision Regulations,* Ministry of Municipal Affairs

Newman, P. C. (1968) *The Distemper of Our Times: Canadian Politics in Transition 1963-1968,* McClelland and Stewart

Niagara Escarpment Commission: see *Ontario: Niagara Escarpment*

Nicholson, N. L. and Z. W. Sametz (1961) "Regions of Canada and the Regional Concept," *Resources for Tomorrow Conference: Background Papers,* Queen's Printer, Ottawa

Northern Alberta Development Council (1984) *Annual Report 1983-84*

Nova Scotia (1980a) *Interim Report of the Planning Act Review Committee*

_____ (1980b) *Rural Zoning Approaches,* Department of Municipal Affairs

_____ (1981a) *Final Report and Recommendations of the Planning Act Review Committee*

_____ (1981b) *Water Supply: A Resource in Need of Protection*

_____ (1984) *Report of the Nova Scotia Royal Commission on Forestry*

Nowlan, D. M. (1976) *Towards Home Rule for Urban Policy,* University of Toronto, Centre for Urban and Community Studies, Research Paper 83

_____ (1977) "The Land Market: How It Works," in L. B. Smith and M. Walker (eds.) (1977)

_____ (1978) *The Fundamentals of Residential Land Price Determination,* University of Toronto, Centre for Urban and Community Studies, Research Paper 101

_____ and N. Nowlan (1970) *The Bad Trip: The Untold Story of the Spadina Expressway,* New Press and House of Anansi (Toronto)

O'Brien, A. (1980a) "Father Knows Best: A Look at the Provincial-Municipal Relationship in Ontario," in M. O. Dickerson, S. Drabek and J. T. Woods (eds.) (1980)

_____ (1980b) "The Uncomfortable Partnership: A Look at Provincial-Municipal Relationships," in D. C. MacDonald (eds.) (1980)

_____ (1982) "The Ministry of State for Urban Affairs: A Municipal Perspective," *Canadian Journal of Regional Science,* Vol. 5, No. 1, pp. 83-94

Ombudsman of British Columbia (1983) *Expropriation Issues*

Ontario (1954) *The Regional Development Program of the Government of Ontario,* Ontario Department of Planning and Development

Ontario Advisory Task Force on Housing Policy (1973a) *Report*

_____ (1973b) *Recommended Guidelines for Residential Servicing in Ontario*

_____ (1973c) *Municipal Cash Imposts in Ontario: An Exploratory Study*

_____ (1973d) *Land for Housing*

Ontario Department of Municipal Affairs (1966) *Annual Report 1966*

Ontario Design for Development (1966) *Statement by the Prime Minister of the Province of Ontario on Regional Development Policy, April 5th 1966*

_____ (1968a) *Design for Development Phase 2: Statement by the Honourable John Robarts to the Legislature of Ontario, 28 November 1968*

_____ (1968b) *Design for Development Phase 2: Statement by the Honourable W. Darcy McKeough to the Legislature of Ontario, 2 December 1968*

_____ (1970a) *The Toronto-Centred Region*

_____ (1970b) *The Toronto-Centred Region White Paper*

_____ (1970c) *Northwestern Ontario Region: Phase 2, Policy Recommendations*

_____ (1970d) *Niagara (South Ontario) Region: Phase I: Analysis*

_____ (1970e) *Midwestern Ontario Region*

_____ (1971a) *Northeastern Ontario Region*

_____ (1971b) *A Policy Statement on the Northwestern Ontario Region*

_____ (1971c) *A Status Report on the Toronto-Centred Region*

_____ (1972a) *Phase Three: Statement by the Honourable William G. Davis, Premier of Ontario; and Statement by the Honourable W. Darcy McKeough, Treasurer of Ontario, June 1972*

_____ (1972b) *Prospects for the Lake Ontario Region*

_____ (1972c) *Prospects for the Georgian Bay Region*

_____ (1972d) *Prospects for the Eastern Ontario Region*

_____ (1972e) *Prospects for the St Clair Region*

_____ (1973) *Development Planning in Ontario: The Parkway Belt West*

_____ (1976a) *Ontario's Future: Trends and Options*

_____ (1976b) *Northeastern Ontario Regional Strategy*

_____ (1976c) *Toronto-Centred Region Program Statement*

_____ (1976d) *Durham Sub-Region Development Strategy*

_____ (1976e) *Renfrew County Development Strategy*

_____ (1977) *Parkway Belt West: Report of the Hearing Officers*

_____ (1978a) *Northwestern Ontario: A Strategy for Development*

_____ (1978b) *The Parkway Belt West Plan*

_____ (1979) *Northwestern Ontario: A Policy for Development*

Ontario Economic Council (1973) *Subject to Approval: A Review of Municipal Planning in Ontario*

_____ (1976) *Northern Ontario Development: Issues and Alternatives*

Ontario Environmental Assessment Board (1979) *Final Report on the Expansion of the Uranium Mines in the Elliot Lake Area*

_____ (1983) *A Guide for Hearings*

Ontario Hydro (1976) *An Approach to Classifying and Ranking Ontario's Foodlands*

_____ (1979a) *Provincial Overview of Generation Siting: The Agricultural Report*

_____ (1979b) *Towards Reconciling Ontario's Future Needs for Food and Electricity*

_____ (1980a) *Public Participation in Route and Site Planning*

_____ (1980b) *Public Participation in Project Planning*

_____ (1983) *Social Impact Evaluation Study Phase I: State of Art Review*, Report No 83187, by D. Lawrence and S. Wright of M. M. Dillon Ltd

Ontario Law Reform Commission (1967) *Report on the Basis for Compensation on Expropriation*

Ontario Legislative Assembly (1962) *Report of the Select Committee on Land Expropriation*

_____ (1972) *Report of the Select Committee on the Ontario Municipal Board*

_____ (1973) *Interim Report of the Select Committee on Economic and Cultural Nationalism: Foreign Ownership of Ontario Real Estate*

Ontario Mineral Aggregate Working Party (1977) *A Policy for Mineral Aggregate Resource Management in Ontario*

Ontario Mineral Resources Committe (1969) *Report,* Ontario Ministry of Mines

Ontario Ministry of Agriculture and Food (1976) *A Strategy for Ontario Farmland: A Statement with respect to Agricultural Development and Land Use in Ontario*

_____ (1977) *Green Paper on Planning for Agriculture: Food Land Guidelines*

_____ (1978) *Food Land Guidelines: A Policy Statement of the Government of Ontario on Planning for Agriculture*

_____ (1985) *Agricultural Land Interests Registered by Non-Residents to December 31, 1984*

Ontario Ministry of Citizenship and Culture (1984) *Community Heritage Fund Program Guidelines*

Ontario Ministry of the Environment *Annual Reports*

_____ (1981) *Policy Manual: Pollution Abatement Program: Development, Compliance and Enforcement*

_____ (1982) *General Guidelines for the Preparation of Environmental Assessments,* second edition, revised April 1982

_____ (1983) *Blueprint for Waste Management*

Ontario Ministry of Housing (1976) *Ontario Downtown Revitalization Program*

_____ (1978a) *Appointing a Committee of Adjustment: A Guideline for Municipal Councils*

_____ (1978b) *Land Use Policy Near Airports*

_____ (1979) *Survey of Thirteen Business Improvement Areas in Ontario 1979*

_____ (1980) *Minor Variances and Non-Conforming Uses: Committee of Adjustment Guidelines,* revised edition

Ontario Ministry of Municipal Affairs and Housing (1983a) *The New Planning Act: Legislative Changes*

_____ (1983b) *A Guide to the Planning Act 1983*

_____ (1983c) *Planning Advisory Committees,* (Guideline 1)

_____ (1983d) *Local Planning in Northern Ontario,* (Guideline 2)

_____ (1983e) *Delegation of Minister's Authority,* (Guideline 3)

_____ (1983f) *Community Improvement,* (Guideline 4)

_____ (1983g) *Working with the New Regulations,* (Guideline 5)

_____ (1983h) *Official Plan Policies on Public Notice,* (Guideline 6)

_____ (1983i) *Planning Application Fees,* (Guideline 7)

_____ (1983j) *Zoning and Other Land Use Controls,* (Guideline 8)

_____ (1984a) *Official Plans and the Use of Site Plan Control,* (Guideline 9)

_____ (1984b) *Official Plan Documents: Preparation, Adoption, Submission and Lodging,* (Guideline 10)

_____ (1984c) *Committees of Adjustment, Minor Variances and Non-Conforming Uses,* (Guideline 11)

_____ (1985) *A Planner's Reference to Legislation, Provincial Policies and Guidelines*

Ontario Ministry of Natural Resources *Annual Reports*

_____ (1977) *A Discussion Paper on Flood Plain Management Alternatives in Ontario*

_____ (1978) *Ontario Provincial Parks Planning and Management Policies*

_____ (1979a) *From Pits to Playgrounds: Aggregate Extraction and Pit Rehabilitation in Toronto: An Historical Review*

_____ (1979b) *Towards the 80s: A Guide to the Organization and Management System*

_____ (1981a) *Report of the Task Force on Park System Planning*

_____ (1981b) *The Forest Industry in the Economy of Ontario*

_____ (1982a) *Northeastern Ontario: Strategic Land Use Plan*

_____ (1982b) *Southern Ontario: Coordinated Program Strategy (Approved)*

_____ (1982c) *Private Land Forests: A Public Resource*

_____ (1982d) *Press Release* on provincial parks, 12 March 1982

_____ (1983a) *Mineral Aggregate Resource Planning*

_____ (1983b) *District Land Use Guidelines*

_____ (1984a) *Report of the Flood Plain Review Committee*

_____ (1984b) *Pit and Quarry Rehabilitation: The State of the Art in Ontario*

_____ (1984c) *Water Quality Resources of Ontario*

_____ and Ministry of Municipal Affairs and Housing (1982) *Flood Plain Criteria*

Ontario Municipal Board *Annual Reports*

_____ (1976) "The Ontario Municipal Board Decision on the City of Toronto's 45 Foot Bylaw," in L. D. Feldman and M. D. Goldrick (eds.) (1976)

Ontario Municipal Board Reports (1978) Vol. 8, pp. 1-248, Canada Law Book (Re Toronto Central Area Official Plan)

Ontario Niagara Escarpment (1968) *Niagara Escarpment Study: Conservation and Recreation Report,* (The Gertler Report), Ontario Department of Treasury and Economics. (The maps were published separately in 1972 in *The Fruit Belt Report.)*

_____ (1970) *Design for Development: Niagara (South Ontario) Region, Phase I: Analysis,* Department of Treasury and Economics

_____ (1972a) *The Fruit Belt Report,* Ontario Department of Treasury and Economics

_____ (1972b) *To Save the Escarpment: Report of the Niagara Escarpment Task Force,* Niagara Escarpment Interministerial Task Force

_____ (1973) *Development Planning in Ontario: The Niagara Escarpment,* Ministry of Treasury, Economics and Intergovernmental Affairs

_____ (1979) *The Proposed Plan for the Niagara Escarpment,* Niagara Escarpment Commission

_____ (1983a) *Report of the Hearing Officers,* Niagara Escarpment Proposed Plan Hearing (4 Vols.)

_____ (1983b) *Niagara Escarpment Commission's Response to the Comments Received on the Proposed Plan,* Niagara Escarpment Commission

_____ (1983c) *Response to the Hearing Officers' Report on the Niagara Escarpment Proposed Plan Hearing,* Niagara Escarpment Commission

_____ (1983d) *Niagara Escarpment Final Proposed Plan,* Niagara Escarpment Commission

_____ (1983e) *Recommendations on the Implementation of the Niagara Escarpment Plan,* Niagara Escarpment Commission

_____ (1984) *The Niagara Escarpment Plan,* Provincial Secretary for Resources, Vol. 1: *Planning and Implementation Process;* Vol. 2: *Recommended Policies of the Provincial Secretary for Resources Development;* Vol. 3: *Responses to the Hearing Officers' Report*

_____ (1985) *Niagara Escarpment Plan Modifications,* Provincial Secretariat for Resources Development

Ontario Planning Act Review Committee (1977a) *Report,* (Comay Report)

_____ (1977b) Background Paper 1, *Planning Issues: The Public Consultation Program*

_____ (1977c) Background Paper 2, *Operation of Municipal Planning*

_____ (1977d) Background Paper 3, *Municipal Planning and the Natural Environment*

_____ (1977e) Background Paper 4, *Citizen Participation in the Preparation of Municipal Plans*

_____ (1977f) Background Paper 5, *Planning for Small Communities*

Ontario White Paper (1979a) *White Paper on the Planning Act*

_____ (1979b) Background Paper 1, *Response to the Report of the Planning Act Review Committee*

_____ (1979c) Background Paper 2, *Some Legal Implications of the Report of the Planning Act Review Committee*

_____ (1979d) Background Paper 3, *Planning Act Review Committee Recommendations on Development Control*

_____ (1979e) Background Paper 4, *Amortization of Non-Conforming Uses*

_____ (1981) *Response to the White Paper on the Planning Act and the Draft Planning Act 1979*

Ontario Royal Commission on the Northern Environment (1983) *The Onakawana Project: An Example of the Environmental Assessment Process in Ontario*

Ontario Special Committee on Farm Income (1969) *The Challenge of Abundance*

Ontario Waste Management Corporation (1982a) *Annual Report 1981-82*

_____ (1982b) *Facilities Development Process: Phase 1 Report*

_____ (1983) *Facilities Development Process: Phase 2 Report*

_____ (1984a) *Facilities Development Process: Phase 3 Report*

_____ (1984b) *Annual Report 1983-84*

_____ (1985) *Facilities Development Process: Phase 4A Report*

Oosterhoff, A. H. and W. B. Rayner (1979) *Losing Ground: The Erosion of Property Rights in Ontario*, Ontario Real Estate Association

_____ and P. E. Vivian (1973) *Restrictions on the Property Right in Ontario*, Ontario Real Estate Association

Organization for Economic Cooperation and Development (1975) *The Polluter Pays Principle: Definition, Analysis, Implementation*

_____ (1980a) *Pollution Charges in Practice*

_____ (1980b) *Regional Policies in Canada*

O'Riordan, T. (1976) *The American Environment: Perceptions and Policies*, Wiley

Pacey, E. (1979) *The Battle of Citadel Hill*, Lancelot Press (Hansport, N.S.)

Paehlke, R. (1980) "James Bay Project: Environmental Assessment in the Planning of Resource Development," in O. P. Dwivedi (ed.) (1980)

Parenteau, R. (1970) "L'experience de la planification au Québec," *L'actualité économique,* Vol. 16, pp. 679-96

Parks Canada (1981) *Report of the Special Inquiry on Kouchibouguac National Park*

_____ (1982) *Parks Canada Policy*

Peacock, D. (1977) *People, Peregrines and Arctic Pipelines,* Douglas (Vancouver)

Pearse Report (1976) *Timber Rights and Forest Policy in British Columbia,* (Report of the Royal Commission on Forest Resources), Queen's Printer, Victoria, 2 Vols.

Pendergast, E.S. (1981) *Suburbanizing the Central City: An Analysis of the Shift in Transportation Policies Governing the Development of Metropolitan Toronto 1955-1978,* University of Toronto, Department of Urban and Regional Planning, Papers on Planning and Design 27

Pennance, F. G. (1967) *Housing, Town Planning and the Land Commission,* Institute of Economic Affairs (England)

Perks, W. T. and I. M. Robinson (eds.) (1979) *Urban and Regional Planning in a Federal State: The Canadian Experience,* Dowden, Hutchinson and Ross/McGraw-Hill

Perry, J. (1974) *Inventory of Regional Planning Administration in Canada,* Intergovernmental Committee on Urban and Regional Research (Toronto), Staff Paper 1

Peter, L. J. (1985) *Why Things Go Wrong, or The Peter Principle Revisited,* Morrow

Peterson, J. A. (1976) "The City Beautiful Movement: Forgotten Origins and Lost Meanings," *Journal of Urban History,* Vol. 2, pp. 415-34

Phidd, R. W. (1974) "Regional Development Policy," in G. B. Doern and V. S. Wilson (eds.) (1974)

_____ and G. B. Doern (1978) *The Politics and Management of Canadian Economic Policy,* Macmillan

Phillips, R. A. J. (1967) *Canada's North,* Macmillan

PIBC (1984) *PIBC News,* Vol. 26, No. 3, p. 5, Planning Institute of British Columbia

Pierce, J. T. (1981) "The British Columbia Agricultural Land Commission: A Review and Evaluation," *Plan Canada,* Vol. 21, pp. 48-56

Pill, J. (1979) *Planning and Politics: The Metro Toronto Transportation Plan Review,* MIT Press

Piper, J. (1976) "Saskatoon Robs The Bank," in J. Lorimer and E. Ross (eds.) (1976)

Plan Canada (1972) Special Issue "National Urban Policy," in K. D. Cameron (ed.) Vol. 12, pp. 1-128

——————————— (1984) Special Issue "Ontario Planned," in N. H. Richardson (ed.), Vol. 24, pp. 87-166

Planning Collaborative Inc and Read, Vorhees and Associates (1979) *Land Value Capture,* Ministry of State for Urban Affairs

Plesuk, B. (ed.) (1981) *The Only Game in Town: Public Involvement in Cold Lake,* Alberta Environment

Plunkett, T.J. (1965) "The Report of the Royal Commission on Finance and Municipal Taxation in New Brunswick: A Review and Commentary," *Canadian Public Administration,* Vol. 8, pp. 12-23

——————————— (1972) *The Financial Structure and the Decision-Making Process of Canadian Municipal Government,* CMHC

——————————— (1973) "Structural Reform of Local Government in Canada," *Public Administration Review,* Vol. 33, pp. 40-51

——————————— and G. M. Betts (1978) *The Management of Canadian Urban Government,* Queen's University, Institute of Local Government

Plunkett, T. J. and W. Hooson (1975) "Municipal Structure and Services," *Canadian Public Policy,* Vol. 1, p. 368

Plunkett, T. J. and J. Lightbody (1982) "Tribunals, Politics and the Public Interest: The Edmonton Annexation Case," *Canadian Public Policy,* Vol. 8, pp. 207-21

Porter, J. (1965) *The Vertical Mosaic,* University of Toronto Press

Postgate, D. and K. McRoberts (1976) *Social Change and Political Crisis,* McClelland and Stewart

Potomac Institute (1983) *Fundamental Fairness in Zoning: "Mount Laurel" Reaffirmed,* The Institute (Washington D.C.)

Pressman, N. E. (1975) *Planning New Communities in Canada,* Ministry of State for Urban Affairs

Preston, R. E. (1980) "Notes on the Development of the Canadian Urban Pattern," in R. E. Preston and L. H. Russwurm (eds.) (1980)

_____ and L. H. Russwurm (eds.) (1980) *Essays on Canadian Urban Process and Form II,* University of Waterloo, Department of Geography

Priddle, G. B. (1979) "The Parks of Ontario," in J. G. Nelson et al (1979) Vol. 1, p. 210ff

Prince Albert City (1982) *Policy Plan,* (Schedule "B" to the City of Prince Albert Municipal Plan)

Prince Edward Island (1973) *Report of the Royal Commission on Land Ownership and Land Use*

_____ (1980) *Report to Executive Council on Non-Resident and Corporate Land Ownership,* P.E.I. Land Use Commission

_____ (1982) *Report of the Select Standing Committee on Agriculture and Land Ownership,* Legislative Assemby, 29 January 1982

_____ (1983) *Annual Report of the Prince Edward Island Land Use Commission*

Protti, G. J. (1979) "Water Use by Energy Producers: Some Economic Considerations," *Canadian Water Resources Journal,* Vol. 4, pp. 23-32

Proudfoot, S. (1980) *Private Wants and Public Needs: The Regulation of Land Use in the Metropolitan Toronto Area,* Economic Council of Canada, Regulation Reference, Working Paper 12

Punter, J. V. (1974) *The Impact of Exurban Development on Land and Landscape in the Toronto-Centred Region: 1954-1971,* CMHC

Qadeer, M. (1985) *The Evolving Urban Land Tenure System in Canada,* University of Winnipeg, Institute of Urban Studies, Report 10

Québec Commission des biens culturels du Québec (1979) *Septième rapport annuel 1978-79*

Quebec Department of Municipal Affairs (1973) *Planning the Airport Region,* Information Bulletin, March 1973

Québec Ministère des Affaires Municipales (1971) *Proposition de réforme des structures municipales*

Québec Ministère de l'Agriculture (1978) *Document de consultation sur la protection du territoire agricole Québecois*

Quigley, M. (1971) *Democracy is Us: Citizen Participation in Development in the City of Toronto,* Ontario Department of Municipal Affairs

Quinn, F. (1977) "Notes for a National Water Policy," in R. R. Krueger and B. Mitchell (eds.) (1977)

Radford, K. J. and M. O. Giesen (1984) *The Analysis of Conflicts Over the Location of Airports near Major Population Centers,* University of Toronto/York University, Joint Program in Transportation Research, Report 87

Rapport, D. and A. Friend (1979) *Towards a Comprehensive Framework for Environmental Statistics: A Stress-Response Approach,* Statistics Canada

Ravis, D. (1973) *Advance Land Acquisition by Local Government: The Saskatoon Experience,* Community Planning Association of Canada

Ray, D. M. and T. N. Brewis (1976) "The Geography of Income and its Correlates," *Canadian Geographer,* Vol. 20, pp. 41-71

Rayner, W. B. (1976) *Subdivision Control in Ontario,* Canada Law Book Ltd

Reade, E. (1982) "If Planning isn't Everything ... " *Town Planning Review,* Vol. 53, pp. 65-78

_____ (1983) "If Planning is Anything, Maybe it can be Identified," *Urban Studies,* Vol. 20, pp. 159-71

Redpath, D. K. (1979) *Land Use Programs in the Yukon Territory,* Environment Canada, Lands Directorate

Reed, M. B. (1978) *Site Plan Control in Ontario,* University of Toronto, Department of Urban and Regional Planning, Papers on Planning and Design 20

Rees, W. E. (1977) *The Canada Land Inventory in Perspective,* Environment Canada, Lands Directorate, Canada Land Inventory Report 12

_____ (1979) *Reflections on the Environmental Assessment and Review Process: A Discussion Paper,* Canadian Arctic Resources Committee

_____ (1980) "EARP at the Crossroads: Environmental Assessment in Canada," *EIA Review,* Vol. 1, pp. 355-77

_____ (1982) "Planning on our Arctic Frontier: Setting the Stage," *Plan Canada,* Vol. 21, pp. 197-216

_____ (1984) *Politics, Power and Northern Land Use Planning,* University of British Columbia, School of Community and Regional Planning

Regina City (1979a) *It's our Neighbourhood: Neighbourhood Plan, Cathedral Area, Regina*

_____ (1979b) *A Neighbourhood Plan for the General Hospital Area*

_____ (1980) *The North Central Neighbourhood Plan*

Reich, C. A. (1966) "The Law of the Planned Society," *Yale Law Journal,* Vol. 75, pp. 1227-70

Reuber, G. L. (1978) "The Impact of Government Policies on the Distribution of Income in Canada: A Review," *Canadian Public Policy,* Vol. 4, pp. 505-29

Richardson, A. H. (1974) *Conservation by the People: The History of the Conservation Movement in Ontario to 1970,* University of Toronto Press

Richardson, H. W. and D. H. Aldcroft (1968) *Building in the British Economy Between the Wars,* Allen and Unwin

Richardson, N. H. (1981a) "Insubstantial Pageant: The Rise and Fall of Provincial Planning in Ontario," *Canadian Public Administration,* Vol. 24, pp. 563-86

_____ (1981b) Review of I. M. Robinson's "Canadian Urban Growth Trends" (1981) *Plan Canada,* Vol. 21, pp. 61-3

_____ (1984) *The Northern Land Use Planning Agreements: A Commentary,* Working Paper for the Beaufort Sea Environmental Assessment Panel

_____ (1985) "Macdonald and the Planners," *Plan Canada,* Vol. 25, No. 4, pp. 112-13

Richmond, D. R. (1974) *The Economic Transformation of Ontario,* Ontario Economic Council

Risk, R. C. B. (1981) "A Long Sad Story: Siting Transmission Lines in Ontario," *University of Toronto Law Journal,* Vol. 31, p. 70

Robarts Report (1977) *Report of the Royal Commission on Metropolitan Toronto,* Ontario Government Publications, 2 Vols.

Roberts, R. (1984) *Resource Town Planning: A Strategy for Policy Development,* University of British Columbia, School of Community and Regional Planning, Studies in Northern Development 1

Robin, M. (ed.) (1972) *Canadian Provincial Politics,* Prentice-Hall

Robinson, A. (1983) "Ontario Reforestation Shifts to Private Sector," *Globe and Mail* (Toronto) 28 March 1983

Robinson, I. M. (1981) *Canadian Urban Growth Trends: Implications for a National Settlement Policy,* University of British Columbia Press

_____ and D. R. Webster (1985) "Regional Planning in Canada," *Journal of the American Planning Association,* Vol. 51, pp. 23-42

Robinson, J. L. (1983) *Concepts and Themes in the Regional Geography of Canada,* Talonbooks

Robinson Report (1974) *Report on the Expropriation Act,* Ontario Ministry of the Attorney General

Rodd, R. S. (1976) "The Crisis of Agricultural Land in the Ontario Countryside," *Plan Canada,* Vol. 16, pp. 160-70

Rogers, I. M. (1984) *Canadian Law of Planning and Zoning,* Carswell (loose-leaf; cumulative supplements are issued regularly)

Rohmer, R. (1973) *The Arctic Imperative,* McClelland and Stewart

Romaine, M. J., L. F. Giovando and L. B. Solsberg (eds.) (1976) *An Environmental Impact Assessment of the Vancouver International Airport Expansion Proposals: A Summary Report,* Environment Canada

Roman, A. J. (1979) "Training for More Effective Public Participation: The Case of the Cluff Lake Hearings," in B. Sadler (ed.) (1979), pp. 29-37

Romanow, R. J., C. Ryan and R. L. Stanfield (1984) *Ottawa and the Provinces: Regional Perspectives*, Ontario Economic Council

Roots, E. F. (1977) "Mining, Environment and Control," in J. B. Stevenson (1977)

Rorke, B. (1973) *Much is Taken, Much Remains*, Duxbury Press

Rose, A. (1972) *Governing Metropolitan Toronto: A Social and Political Analysis 1953-1971*, University of California Press
_____ (1980) *Canadian Housing Policies 1935-1980*, Butterworths

Rothenberg, J. (1974) "Problems in the Modelling of Urban Development: A Review Article on Urban Dynamics," *Journal of Urban Economics*, Vol. 1, pp. 1-20

Roussopoulus, D. (ed.) (1982) *The City and Radical Social Change*, Black Rose Books (Montreal)

Rowat, D. C. (1985) *Recent Politics in Ottawa-Carleton*, Carleton University

Rowell-Sirois Commission (1940) *Report of the Royal Commission on Dominion-Provincial Relations*, King's Printer, Ottawa

Royal Commission on Local Government in England (1969) *Report 2: Memorandum of Dissent by Mr D. Senior*, Cmnd 4040-I, Her Majesty's Stationery Office, London

Rudin, J. R. (1978) *The Changing Structure of the Land Development Industry in the Toronto Area*, University of Toronto, Centre for Urban and Community Studies, Major Report 13

Rudolph, M. S. (1979) *An Assessment of Litter Abatement Programs*, Ontario Waste Management Advisory Board

Runka, G. (1978) "The British Columbia Land Commission," in *Arable Land: The Appropriate Use of a Scarce Resource*, Seminar Proceedings, University of British Columbia, Centre for Human Settlements

Russell, V. L. (1984) *Forging a Consensus: Historical Essays on Toronto*, University of Toronto Press

Rutherford, P. (ed.) (1974) *Saving the Canadian City: The First Phase 1880-1920,* University of Toronto Press

Sadler, B. (ed.) (1978) *Involvement and Environment: Proceedings of the Canadian Conference on Public Participation, Vol.1: A Review of Issues and Approaches,* Environment Council of Alberta

_____ (1979) *Involvement and Environment: Proceedings of the Canadian Conference on Public Participation, Vol.2: Working Papers and Case Studies,* Environment Council of Alberta

_____ (ed.) (1983) *Water Policy for Western Canada: The Issues of the Eighties,* University of Calgary, Banff Centre for Continuing Education

St John's (1957) *Report on the Planning, Utility Services and Metropolitan Administration of an Area Embracing the City of St John's, the Town of Mount Pearl Park-Glendale and the Surrounding Areas*

St John's City (1981) *Zoning Bylaw*

Salter, L. and D. Slaco (1981) *Public Inquiries in Canada,* Science Council of Canada, Background Study 47

Sankey, R. (1971) (community worker and resident of St Jamestown) in M. Quigley (1971)

Saskatchewan (1978) *Guide to the Saskatchewan Main Street Development Program,* Department of Industry and Commerce and Department of Municipal Affairs

_____ (1980) *Water Management in Saskatchewan*

Saskatchewan Housing Corporation *Annual Reports*

Saskatchewan Planning Act Review Committee (1982) *Planning and Development Act: Options for Change: A Policy Paper*

Saskatchewan Queen's Bench (1958) *Regina Auto Court v Regina City* (1958) WWR 167

Saskatchewan Urban Affairs (1983) *The Planning and Development Act 1983: A Summary*

_____ (1984) *Development Plans and Basic Planning Statements,* (fold-out brochure)

Saskatchewan Urban Law Review Committee (1979) *Urban Law Review: Interim Report*

_____ (1980) *Final Report*

Savoie, D. J. (1981) *Federal-Provincial Collaboration: The Canada-New Brunswick General Development Agreement,* McGill-Queen's University Press

_____ (1984) "The Toppling of DREE and Prospects for Regional Economic Development," *Canadian Public Policy,* Vol. 10, pp. 328-37

Saywell, J. T. (1975) *Housing Canadians: Essays on the History of Residential Construction in Canada,* Economic Council of Canada, Working Paper 24

Schindeler, F. F. (1969) *Responsible Government in Ontario,* University of Toronto Press

Schramm, G. (ed.) (1976) *Regional Poverty and Change,* Canadian Council on Rural Development

Schrecker, T. F. (1983) *The Conserver Society Revisited,* Science Council of Canada

_____ (1984) *Political Economy of Environmental Hazards,* Law Reform Commission of Canada

Schwartz, M. (1981) *An Examination of Quebec's Bill 90: An Act to Preserve Agricultural Land,* McGill University, School of Urban Planning

Science Council of Canada (1976) *Population, Technology and Resources,* Report 25

_____ (1977a) *People and Agricultural Land,* in C. Beaubien and R. Tabacnik (ed.)

_____ (1977b) *Canada as a Conserver Society,* Report 27

_____ (1983a) *Canada's Threatened Forests*

_____ (1983b) *The Conserver Society Revisited*

Scott, M. (1969) *American City Planning Since 1890,* University of California Press

Seelig, J. H., M. Goldberg and P. Horwood (1980) *Land Use Control Legislation in the United States: A Survey and Synthesis,* Economic Council of Canada, Regulation Reference, Working Paper 9

Sewell, J. (1977) "Where the Suburbs Came From," and "Don Mills: E. P. Taylor and Canada's First Corporate Suburb," in J. Lorimer and E. Ross (eds.) (1977)

_____ (1983) as reported in the *Globe and Mail* (Toronto) 28 January 1983

Shrimpton, M. (1981) "Housing Corporation Performed Major Role in City Development," *Evening Telegram* (St John's), 17 April 1981

Siegel, D. (1980) "Provincial-Municipal Relations in Canada: An Overview," *Canadian Public Administration,* Vol. 23, pp. 281-317

Simard, J-J. (1979) *La longue marche des technocrates,* Les editions coopératives, Albert Saint-Martin

Simeon, R. (1972) *Federal-Provincial Diplomacy: The Making of Recent Policy in Canada,* University of Toronto Press

_____ and D. J. Elkins (1974) "Regional Political Cultures in Canada," *Canadian Journal of Political Science,* Vol. 7, pp. 397-437

Simmons, J. W. (1967) "Urban Geography in Canada," *Canadian Geographer,* Vol. 11, pp. 341-56

_____ (1975) *Canada: Choices in a National Urban Strategy,* University of Toronto, Centre for Urban and Community Studies, Research Paper 70

_____ (1981) *The Impact of Government on the Canadian Federal System: Income Taxes, Transfer Payments, and Employment,* University of Toronto, Centre for Urban and Community Studies, Research Paper 126

_____ (1984) "Government and the Canadian Urban System: Income Tax, Transfer Payments, and Employment," *Canadian Geographer,* Vol. 28, pp. 18-45

_____ and L. S. Bourne (1982) "Urban/regional Systems and the State," *Progress in Human Geography,* Vol. 6, pp. 431-40

_____ (1984) *Recent Trends and Patterns in Canadian Settlement 1976-1981,* University of Toronto, Centre for Urban and Community Studies, Major Report 23

Simpson, M. (1981) "Thomas Adams 1871-1940," in G. E. Cherry, *Pioneers in British Planning,* Architectural Press

Simpson-Lewis, W. et al (1979) *Canada's Special Resource Lands,* Environment Canada, Lands Directorate, Map Folio 4

_____ (1983) *Stress on Land in Canada,* Environment Canada, Lands Directorate, Map Folio 6

Sitwell, O. F. G. and N. R. M. Seifried (1984) *The Regional Structure of the Canadian Economy,* Methuen

Smiley, D. V. (1980) *Canada in Question: Federalism in the Eighties,* McGraw-Hill Ryerson, third edition

Smit, B. (1981) *Procedures for the Long-Term Evaluation of Rural Land,* University of Guelph, School of Rural Planning and Development

Smith, L. B. (1976) "The Ontario Land Speculation Tax: An Analysis of Unearned Increment Land Tax," *Land Economics,* Vol. 52, pp. 1-12

_____ and M. Walker (eds.) (1977) *Public Property? The Habitat Debate Continued,* Fraser Institute (Vancouver)

Smith, L. G. (1982) "Alternative Mechanisms for Public Participation in Environmental Policy-Making," *Environments,* Vol. 14, pp. 21-34

Smith, P. J. (ed.) (1978) *Edmonton: The Emerging Metropolitan Pattern,* University of Victoria (Western Geographical Series 15)

_____ (1982) "Municipal Conflicts over Territory and the Effectiveness of the Regional Planning System in the Edmonton Metropolitan Area," in H. Becker (ed.) (1982) *Kulturgeographische Prozessforschung in Kanana,* Bamberger Geographische Schriften, Vol. 4, pp. 207-23

_____ (1986) "American Influences and Local Needs: Adaptations to the Alberta Planning System in 1928-1929," in A. F. J. Artibise and G. A. Stelter (eds.) (1986)

Smithies, W. R. (1974) *The Protection and Use of Natural Resources in Ontario,* Ontario Economic Council

So, F. S. et al (1979) *The Practice of Local Government Planning,* International City Management Association

Social Planning Council of Metropolitan Toronto (1976) *Regional Planning in Southern Ontario: A Resource Document*

_____ (1979) *Metro's Suburbs in Transition, Part I: Evolution and Overview*

_____ (1980) *Metro's Suburbs in Transition, Part II: Planning Agenda for the Eighties*

Soldant Commission (1975) *Report of the Solandt Commission: A Report into the Transmission of Power between Lennox and Oshawa, April 1975,* Ontario Provincial Secretary for Resources Development

Spencer, J. (1973) "The Alien Landowner in Canada," *Canadian Bar Review,* Vol. 51, pp. 389-418

Spence-Sales, H. (1949) *Planning Legislation in Canada,* CMHC

Spurr, P. (1976) *Land and Urban Development: A Preliminary Study,* Lorimer

_____ (1981) "Land Mapping Helps Solve Land Market Problems," *Habitat,* Vol. 24, pp. 17-22

Stabler, J. and M. Olfert (1980) "Gaslight Follies: The Political Economy of the Western Arctic," *Canadian Public Policy,* Vol. 6, pp. 374-88

Stachelrodt-Crook, C. (1975) *Environment and Land Use Policies and Practices of the Province of British Columbia,* University of British Columbia, Institute for Policy Analysis

Statistics Canada (1981) *Canada Year Book 1980-81*

_____ (1982) *The Municipal Structure in Canada: Problems it Creates for Users of Statistics,* Geography Staff Working Paper 1

_____ (1984) *Toronto 150: Portrait of a Changing City*

_____ (1985a) *Canada, The Provinces and The Territories: A Statistical Profile*

_____ (1985b) *Canada Year Book 1985*

Stein, S.B. (1971) "Environmental Control and Different Levels of Government," *Canadian Public Administration,* Vol. 14, pp. 129-45

Stelter, G. A. and A. F. J. Artibise (eds.) (1977) *The Canadian City: Essays in Urban History,* Macmillan

_____ (1982) *Shaping the Urban Landscape: Aspects of the Canadian City-Building Process,* Macmillan

Stephenson, J. B. (1977) *The Practical Application of Economic Incentives to the Control of Pollution,* University of British Columbia Press

Suichies, E. (1984) "Design for Development: An Insider's View," *Plan Canada,* Vol. 24, pp. 161-2

Supreme Court of Canada (1957) *Roberts and Bagwell v R*, [1957] SCR 28 75 CRTC 77 6DLR (3d) 305
_____ (1959) *Calgary Power Limited v Copithorne*, [1959] SCR 24

Sutcliffe, A. (1981) *Towards the Planned City: Germany, Britain, the United States and France 1780-1914*, Basil Blackwell

Swaigen, J. Z. (1981) *Compensation of Pollution Victims in Canada*, Economic Council of Canada
_____ and G. Bunt (1985) *Sentencing in Environmental Cases*, Law Reform Commission of Canada

Swan, H. (1978) *Federal Lands: Their Use and Management*, Environment Canada, Lands Directorate

Taraska Report (1976) *Committee of Review City of Winnipeg Act: Report and Recommendations*, Queen's Printer, Winnipeg

Tate, D. and D. Lacelle (1978) "Municipal Water Use in Canada," *Canadian Water Resources Journal*, Vol. 3, pp. 61-78

Taylor, M. E. (1979) "Ecology and Governments in Canada," in W. Leiss (ed.) (1979)

Tennant, P. and D. Zirnhelt (1973) "Metropolitan Government in Vancouver: The Strategy of Gentle Imposition," *Canadian Public Administration*, Vol. 16, pp. 124-38

Thames River Implementation Committee (1982) *Strategy for Soil and Water Management in the Thames River Basin*

Thomas, J. A. (1982) "Environmental Police in Action," *Environment Ontario Legacy*, Vol. 11, No. 1, p. 8A (July 1982)

Thomas, M. H. (1982) "Municipal Land Use Control in British Columbia," *The Urban Lawyer*, Vol. 14, pp. 847-54

Thoman, R. S. (1971) *Design for Development in Ontario*, Allister Typesetting and Graphics (Toronto)

Thompson, A. R. (1980) *Environmental Regulation in Canada: An Assessment of the Regulatory Process*, University of British Columbia, Westwater Research Centre

Thompson, P. S. (1981) *Urbanization of Agricultural Land*, Environment Council of Alberta

Thuron, C., G. Daniel and T. H. Brown (1984) *Impact of the Great Lakes on the Region's Economy,* Center for the Great Lakes

Tindal, C. R. (1977) *Structural Changes in Local Government: Government for Urban Regions,* Institute of Public Administration of Canada

_____ (1982) *You and Your Local Government,* Ontario Municipal Management Board

_____ and S. N. Tindal (1984) *Local Government in Canada,* McGraw-Hill Ryerson, second edition

Titmuss, R. M. (1958) "War and Social Policy," in his *Essays on "The Welfare State,"* Allen and Unwin

Todd, E. C. E. (1970) *The Federal Expropriation Act: A Commentary,* Carswell

_____ (1976) *The Law of Expropriation and Compensation in Canada,* Carswell

Toll, S. (1969) *Zoned American,* Grossman

Toronto City (1973) *Living Room: An Approach to Home Banking and Land Banking for City of Toronto*

_____ (1975) *Central Area Plan Review, Part I: General Plan,* City of Toronto Planning Board

_____ (1980a) *The 1976 Census: Fact or Fiction?*

_____ (1980b) *Toronto in Transition: Demographic Trends in the Toronto Region,* City of Toronto Planning and Development Department

_____ , (1981a) *Quinquennial Review,* City of Toronto Planning and Development Department

_____ (1981b) *Urban Sprawl in the Toronto Centred Region,* City of Toronto, Planning and Development Department

_____ (1982a) *A Review of City Housing Policy 1976-1981,* City of Toronto, Planning and Development Department

_____ (1982b) *Report on the Proposed Official Plan Policy to Permit Transfer of Density,* City of Toronto, Planning and Development Department

_____ (1983) *Social Change in Toronto: A Context for Human Services Planning,* City of Toronto, Planning and Development Department

_____ (1984) *Dreams of Development,* City of Toronto, Planning and Development Department

Toronto Metro (1968) *Choices for a Growing Region,* Metropolitan Toronto and Region Transportation Study

_____ (1981) *Official Plan for the Urban Structure: Metropolitan Toronto Planning Area*

Toronto Transit Commission (1979a) *Transit in Metro: Some Tough Choices*

_____ (1979b) *Final Report of the Joint Metro/TTC Transit Policy Committee*

_____ (1983) *Long Range Plan*

Trudeau, P. E. (1968) *Federalism and the French Canadians,* Macmillan

Truman, R. (1981) "Suspension of Park Plan Revives Bitter Controversy," *Globe and Mail* (Toronto) 25 November 1981

Udall, S. L. (1963) *The Quiet Crisis,* Holt Rinehart and Winston

U.K. (1979) *The United Kingdom Environment 1979: Progress of Pollution Control,* Department of the Environment, Pollution Paper 16, Her Majesty's Stationery Office, London

University of Waterloo (1982) Conference on "Ontario's Provincial Parks: Issues in the 80s: Proceedings," *Environments,* Vol. 14, No. 1

Uthwatt Report (1942) *Report of the Expert Committee on Compensation and Betterment,* Cmd 6386, Her Majesty's Stationery Office, London

Vancouver City (1974) *False Creek Official Development Plan Bylaw*

_____ (1978) *Monetary and Non-Monetary Compensation for Heritage Designation: City Manager's Report,* 3 October 1978

_____ (1979) *The Marpole Plan*

_____ (1980) *Planning Department: Annual Review 1979/80*

_____ (1981a) *Eight Years After: Case Studies under Discretionary Zoning in Vancouver*

_____ (1981b) *Planning Department: Annual Review 1980/81*

_____ (1983) "Density Transfers: An Experiment for Vancouver," *Quarterly Review*, Vancouver City Planning Department

_____ (1984a) "Eyes on Urban Design: Vancouver's Urban Design Panel," *Quarterly Review*, Vancouver City Planning Department, October 1984

_____ (1984b) *Consultant's Report on Development Permit Process*

_____ (1984c) *Transfer of Density Policy*

_____ (1985) *Planning Department: Annual Review 1984/85*

Van Loon, R. J. and M. S. Whittington (1976) *The Canadian Political System: Environment, Structure and Process*, McGraw-Hill Ryerson, second edition

Van Nus, W. (1977) "The Fate of the City Beautiful Thought in Canada 1893-1930," in G. A. Stelter and A. F. J. Artibise (eds.) (1977)

_____ (1979) "Towards the City Efficient: The Theory and Practice of Zoning 1919-1939," in A. F. J. Artibise and G. A. Stelter (eds.) (1979)

Vining, D. R. and A. Strauss (1977) "A Demonstration that the Current Deconcentration of Population in the United States is a Clean Break with the Past," *Environment and Plannin A*, Vol. 9, pp. 751-9

Vuchnich, A. C. (1980) *The Environmental Conservation Authority 1970-1977: An Assessment and Analysis*, Master of Environmental Design Thesis, University of Calgary

Waddell, I. G. (1976) "The Mackenzie Valley Pipeline Inquiry: A Personal Glimpse," *The Advocate*, Vol. 34, pp. 427-32

Waddell, K. B. (1981) *A Survey of Public Hearings in Northern Canada*, Department of Indian Affairs and Northern Development

Walker, M. (ed.) (1978) *Canadian Confederation at the Crossroads*, Fraser Institute, Vancouver

Wall, G. and J. S. Marsh (eds.) (1983) *Recreational Land Use: Perspectives on its Evolution in Canada*, Carleton University Press

Ward, E. N. (1975) *Land Use Programs in Alberta*, Environment Canada, Lands Directorate

_____ (1976a) *Land Use Programs in British Columbia,* Environment Canada, Lands Directorate

_____ (1976b) *Land Use in Manitoba,* Environment Canada, Lands Directorate

_____ (1977) *Land Use Programs in Ontario,* Environment Canada, Lands Directorate

_____ (1978) *Land Use Programs in Saskatchewan* Environment Canada, Lands Directorate

_____ (1984) *Foreign Ownership of Land and Real Estate in Canada,* Environment Canada, Lands Directorate, Working Paper 30

Warren, C. L. and P. C. Rump (1981) *The Urbanization of Rural Land in Canada 1966-1971 and 1971-1976,* Environment Canada, Lands Directorate

Watkins, M. (ed.) (1977) *Dene Nation: The Colony Within,* University of Toronto Press

Watkins, M. H. (1977) "Staple Theory Revisited," *Journal of Canadian Studies,* Vol. 12, pp. 85-95

Watson, K. F. (ed.) (1973) *Landbanking: Investment in the Future, Symposium, Vancouver,* University of British Columbia, Centre for Continuing Education

_____ (1974) *Landbanking in Red Deer,* University of British Columbia, Centre for Continuing Education

Weaver, C. and A. Cunningham (1984) *Social Impact Assessment and Northern Native Communities: A Theoretical Approach,* University of British Columbia, School of Community and Regional Planning, Studies in Northern Development 3

Weaver, C. and T. I. Gunton (1982) "From Drought Assistance to Megaprojects: Fifty Years of Regional Theory and Policy in Canada," *Canadian Journal of Regional Science,* Vol. 5, pp. 5-37

Weaver, C. and P. Richards (1985) "Planning Canada's Role in the New Global Economy," *Journal of the American Planning Association,* Vol. 51, pp. 43-52

Weaver, J. C. (1977) *Shaping the Canadian City: Essays on Urban Politics and Policy,* Institute of Public Administration of Canada

Welch, D. M. (1981) *... For Land's Sake!,* Environment Canada

Wellar, B. S. (1982) "Urban Impact Assessment in Public Policy Processes: The Canadian Record 1968-1982," *Canadian Journal of Regional Science,* Vol. 5, No. 1, pp. 39-65

Weller, G. R. (1980) "Resource Development in Northern Ontario: A Case Study in Hinterland Politics," in O. P. Dwivedi (ed.) (1980)

_____ (1981) "Local Government in the Canadian Provincial North," *Canadian Public Administration,* Vol. 24, No. 1, pp. 44-72

Whalen Report (1974) *Report of the Royal Commission on Municipal Government in Newfoundland and Labrador,* Queen's Printer, St John's

Whebell, C. F. J. (1983) "Geography and Politics in Canada: Selected Aspects," in J. H. Redekop, *Approaches to Canadian Politics,* Prentice Hall, second edition, 1983

Whittington, M. S. (1974) "Environmental Policy," in G. B. Doern and V. S. Wilson (eds.) (1974)

_____ (1984) "Territorial Bureaucracy: Trends in Public Administration in the Northwest Territories," *Canadian Public Administration,* Vol. 27, pp. 242-52

Wichern, P. H. (1983) *Local Government and Politics in Canada,* Canada Studies Foundation, Toronto

_____ (1984) *Evaluating Winnipeg's Unicity Government: Past Efforts and Present Challenges,* University of Winnipeg, Institute of Urban Studies, Research and Working Papers 9

Wiesman, B. (1980) *The British Columbia Planning Act: A Critique,* University of British Columbia, School of Community and Regional Planning, Canadian Issues 1

_____ (1982) *Bill 9 (1981): The British Columbia Land Use Act in Perspective,* University of British Columbia, School of Community and Regional Planning, Canadian Planning Issues 2

Wildavsky, A. B. (1973) "If Planning is Everything, Maybe it's Nothing," *Policy Sciences,* Vol. 4, pp. 127-53

Wilson, J. W. (1973) *People in the Way,* University of Toronto Press

_____ (1980) *The Agricultural Land Commission of British Columbia,* Simon Fraser University

_____ and J. T. Pierce (1982) "The Agricultural Land Commission of British Columbia," *Environments,* Vol. 14, pp. 11-20

Wolfe, J. M. (1985) *Planning in Quebec,* University of Toronto, Centre for Urban and Community Studies, (Land Policy Paper 6)

Wonders, W. C. (1971) *Canada's Changing North,* McClelland and Stewart

Woods Gordon (1981) *Demands Upon the System: A Consultant's Report,* Alberta Municipal Affairs

Wronski, W. and J. G. Turnbull (1984) "The Toronto-Centred Region," *Plan Canada,* Vol. 24, pp. 126-34

Young, D. (1975) "Jurisdiction Over Aliens: Does Morgan Clarify the Law?," *Osgoode Hall Law Journal,* Vol. 13, pp. 354-67

Yundt, S. E. and B. P. Messerschmidt (1979) "Legislation and Policy: Mineral Aggregates Resource Management in Ontario, Canada," *Minerals and the Environment,* Vol. 1, pp. 101-11

Yundt, S. E. and N. P. Wood (1982) *Ontario Mineral Aggregates in the 80's: Government and Industry Challenges,* Ontario Ministry of Natural Resources (mimeo)

Index

In this index the following standard abbreviations are used:

Alta	Alberta
B.C.	British Columbia
Man	Manitoba
N.B.	New Brunswick
Nfld	Newfoundland
N.S.	Nova Scotia
N.W.T.	Northwest Territories
Ont	Ontario
P.E.I.	Prince Edward Island
Que	Quebec
Sask	Saskatchewan
Y.T.	Yukon Territory